THE PSALMS OF LAMENT IN MARK'S PASSION

Stephen Ahearne-Kroll examines the literary interaction between the Gospel of Mark's passion narrative and four Psalms of individual Lament evoked in it. These four psalms depict a David who challenges God's role in his suffering, who searches for understanding of his suffering in light of his past relationship with God, and who attempts to shame God into acting on his behalf only because he is suffering. Because Mark alludes to these psalms in reference to Jesus, David's concerns become woven into the depiction of Jesus in Mark. Reading David's challenge to God as part of Jesus' going "as it is written of him" (i.e., suffering and dying according to scripture; Mark 14:21) calls into question the necessity for Jesus' death within an apocalyptic framework of meaning. Finally, the suffering king David offers a more appropriate model for Jesus' suffering in Mark than that of the servant from Deutero-Isaiah.

STEPHEN P. AHEARNE-KROLL is Assistant Professor of New Testament, Methodist Theological School in Ohio.

SOCIETY FOR NEW TESTAMENT STUDIES

MONOGRAPH SERIES   v. 142

Recent titles in the series

The Psalms of Lament in Mark's Passion

Jesus' Davidic Suffering

STEPHEN P. AHEARNE-KROLL

CAMBRIDGE UNIVERSITY PRESS
Cambridge, New York, Melbourne, Madrid, Cape Town, Singapore, São Paulo, Delhi

Cambridge University Press
The Edinburgh Building, Cambridge CB2 8RU, UK

Published in the United States of America by Cambridge University Press, New York

www.cambridge.org
Information on this title: www.cambridge.org/9780521881913

First published 2007

Printed in the United Kingdom at the University Press, Cambridge

A catalogue record for this publication is available from the British Library

Library of Congress Cataloguing in Publication data

Ahearne-Kroll, Stephen P., 1967–
The Psalms of lament in Mark's passion : Jesus' Davidic suffering / Stephen P.
Ahearne-Kroll.
    p.   cm. – (Society for New Testament studies monograph series) V, 142
Includes bibliographical references and index.
ISBN-13:   978-0-521-88191-3 (hardback)
ISBN-10:   0-521-88191-9 (hardback)
1. Bible. O. T. Psalms–Criticism, interpretation, etc.   2. Bible. N. T. Mark
XIV–XV–Criticism, interpretation, etc.   3. Bible. O. T. Psalms–Relation to Mark.
4. Bible. N. T. Mark–Relation to Psalms.   I. Title.   II. Series.
BS1430.A23   2007
226.3'06–dc22   2007014637

ISBN 978-0-521-88191-3 hardback

Much of my perspective on suffering was formed from a very early age by the suffering of my father, whose life embodied endurance in the hope of salvation.

To him I dedicate this work.

Walter J. Kroll
1919–2004

CONTENTS

ACKNOWLEDGMENTS

I wish to thank my professors and teachers over the course of my education in theology and religious studies, beginning in 1993, whose dedication and passion for the subject inspired me to continue in my work. John R. Donahue, S. J. initially inspired me to study the Gospel of Mark, and his friendship and encouragement over the years have helped me to grow in many ways. Donald Gelpi, S. J. showed great confidence in my abilities long before I had much of either, and his theological perspective continues to feed me. I would also like to thank Harold W. Attridge of Yale Divinity School for his sage advice in many areas of my academic and personal life, and for his and Jan's incredible generosity.

The members of my dissertation committee worked with care and dedication in order to sharpen my thought and clarity of presentation. I could not ask for a better team of scholars to advise me in my work. I would like to thank William Schweiker of the University of Chicago Divinity School for the many times he helped me to clarify my muddled thoughts in ways that pushed me to go to a deeper level of insight than I had realized possible. I would like to thank Hans-Josef Klauck, also of the University of Chicago Divinity School, not only for his ongoing interest in my work, but also for his professionalism and integrity in the midst of many trying situations. His support has cleared a path for me where there was none. And my thanks especially go out to Adela Yarbro Collins of Yale Divinity School, who has been an integral part of my doctoral work from its beginning. For her careful reading of my work over the years, for her openness to my ideas, and for sticking by me from beginning to end, I will be always grateful.

I would like to thank the members of the SNTS Monograph Series editorial team, most especially for John M. Court, for supporting this project and facilitating the process of this manuscript becoming a book in a very efficient manner, and Kate Brett for her professional and responsive editing oversight. I would also like to thank Allen Georgia, a student at

Methodist Theological School in Ohio, for toiling many hours to prepare the index.

I would like to pass on special thanks to my wife's parents, John and Barbara Ahearne, who have been unconditionally supportive in every way, and to my mother, Barbara Kroll, who gave me life and believed in me from the beginning.

Finally, none of this would be possible if not for the presence of my wife, Pat, whose own scholarship continues to help me grow in mine and whose integrity, sense of humor, passion, and sense of beauty makes all those around her better people. I send my thanks and love to her always.

ABBREVIATIONS

AB	Anchor Bible
ABD	*Anchor Bible Dictionary*
ANRW	*Aufstieg und Niedergang der römischen Welt: Geschichte und Kultur Roms im Spiegel der neueren Forschung.* Ed. H. Temporini and W. Haase. Berlin, 1972–
Bib	*Biblica*
CBQ	*Catholic Biblical Quarterly*
DSS	Dead Sea Scrolls
EKKNT	Evangelisch-katholischer Kommentar zum Neuen Testament
ExpTim	*Expository Times*
EvT	*Evangelische Theologie*
FoiVie	*Foi et Vie*
FOTL	Forms of Old Testament Literature
FRLANT	Forschungen zur Religion und Literatur des Alten und Neuen Testaments
Gos. Thom.	*Gospel of Thomas*
HTR	*Harvard Theological Review*
HUCA	*Hebrew Union College Annual*
HvTSt	*Hervormde teologiese studies*
Int	*Interpretation*
JQR	*Jewish Quarterly Review*
JBL	*Journal of Biblical Literature*
JR	*Journal of Religion*
JSNT	*Journal for the Study of the New Testament*
JSNTSup	Journal for the Study of the New Testament: Supplement Series
JSOT	*Journal for the Study of the Old Testament*
JSOTSup	Journal for the Study of the Old Testament: Supplement Series
JSS	*Journal of Semitic Studies*

LCL	Loeb Classical Library
LSJ	Liddell, H. G., R. Scott, H. S. Jones, *A Greek–English Lexikon*. 9th edn. with revised supplement. Oxford. 1996.
LXX	Septuagint
MT	Masoretic Text
NTS	*New Testament Studies*
NovT	*Novum Testamentum*
OTL	Old Testament Library
OTP	*Old Testament Pseudepigrapha*. Ed. J. H. Charlesworth. 2 vols. New York, 1983
PssLam	Psalms of Individual Lament
SBLDS	Society of Biblical Literature Dissertation Series
SBLSP	*Society of Biblical Literature Seminar Papers*
SBT	Studies in Biblical Theology
SUNT	Studien zur Umwelt des Neuen Testaments
VT	*Vetus Testamentum*
WBC	Word Biblical Commentary
WUNT	Wissenschaftliche Untersuchungen zum Neuen Testament
ZAW	*Zeitschrift für die alttestamentliche Wissenschaft*
ZNW	*Zeitschrift für die neutestamentliche Wissenschaft und die Kunde der älteren Kirche*

1

INTRODUCTION

In the Gospel of Mark, Jesus the Messiah dies a horribly painful and shameful death at the hands of the soldiers who serve Pontius Pilate, only after he suffers through the abandonment of his disciples, a trial before the Jewish authorities where he is mocked and beaten, and a second trial before Pilate where he is rejected by his people and mocked and beaten again by Pilate's soldiers. Yet Mark tells the story of these terrible events at the end of Jesus' days with copious references to his scriptures. Jesus goes "as it is written of him," even though he goes in such a horrific way. Upon close examination of one subset of the scripture passages evoked, namely, the Psalms of Individual Lament (hereafter, PssLam), the reader begins to question what it might mean for Jesus the Messiah to die "as it is written of him."

Although the use of scripture in the Gospel of Mark has been treated many times in the past, there have been relatively few full-length studies that exclusively deal with how Mark uses scripture in his narrative, and there have been none that have dealt solely with the PssLam in Mark. This study will examine the interaction between the Gospel of Mark's passion narrative, which I take as Mark 14:1–16:8, and the PssLam referred to in the Markan passion narrative with an eye towards exploring the question of what it might mean for Jesus the Messiah to die "as it is written of him." In this study, I will not claim to discover the hermeneutical key to Mark or make a definitive statement about Markan theology, Christology or soteriology. Scholarship over the past fifty years has shown that there is no one hermeneutical key to Mark, as well as the fact that Markan theology is not univocal or simply expressed in the narrative. My main goal in this study is to foreground the voice of the suffering David in the four PssLam evoked in Mark's passion narrative and read it through the lens of these four psalms, not as source material for the narrative but as an integral part of the multifaceted characterization of Jesus and Markan theological concerns.

This first chapter will introduce some of the important issues involved in the study. Instead of producing the traditional history of scholarship to begin the discussion,[1] I will introduce and discuss relevant scholars' work as a way of describing the major methodological issues I see as important to account for in a work such as the present one. In the course of this discussion, the reader should get a clear sense of where this study falls with respect to other studies on the use of scripture in the Gospels, in general, and in the Gospel of Mark, in particular.

At the outset, I would like to make explicit the overarching methodological assumptions that inform the entire study and that undergird its conclusions. Although I recognize and appreciate that the text of Mark as we know it has a pre-history that includes the adoption and adaptation of stories and traditions received by the author, I wish to examine the Gospel as a narrative in its final form. In this respect, I will read the narrative of Mark in light of Paul Ricoeur's narrative theory, namely, that narratives are configurations of human time, and, through the process of reading, human time and experience are re-figured or transformed. In the case of the Gospel of Mark, I will attempt to read this narrative as one that addresses the issue of the suffering and death of Jesus the Messiah.

By reading Mark's passion narrative through the lens of the PssLam, I nuance Ricoeur's general narrative theory by foregrounding these psalms in the passion narrative and giving them detailed treatment in relation to the overall plot that unfolds in the passion narrative. As we will see, attention to these PssLam in the overall plot of Mark's passion narrative makes Mark's narrative more complex in its presentation of Jesus' suffering and death and problematizes the issue in unexpected ways. Even if I do not mention Ricoeur's work again in detail, these methodological assumptions drive everything hereafter.[2] All other methodological issues that I will raise in the first and second chapters should be considered subservient to these general assumptions, in that they will act as mere tools that I will use to articulate my interpretation of Mark's emplotment of Jesus' suffering and death. This is especially the case with my detailed treatment of the interaction between the PssLam and the particular places in Mark's passion narrative where they are evoked.

---

[1] For an excellent review of scholarship on the issue of the use of scripture in the Gospel of Mark, see Thomas R. Hatina, *In Search of a Context: The Function of Scripture in Mark's Narrative* (JSNTSS 232; Sheffield: Sheffield Academic Press, 2002).

[2] See Ricoeur's *Time and Narrative* (trans. Kathleen McLaughlin and David Pellauer; Chicago: University of Chicago, 1984), I:3–87.

1 Scholarly approaches to the study of the use of scripture in the New Testament with special attention to the PssLam

In this section, I will introduce four major works on the use of scripture in the New Testament that include the PssLam as sub-topics. Doing so will allow for a brief sketch of the landscape of scholarship in the field and will also be useful for the analysis of approaches to the field that will follow in the second section.

1.1 Major works that include the PssLam

C. H. Dodd's and Barnabas Lindars' works on the use of scripture in the New Testament are foundational, in that they are well-respected attempts to reconstruct the origins and developmental history of early Christian theological speculation about Jesus with respect to the Jewish scriptures. Donald Juel's and Joel Marcus' works are more recent. Juel's work is also reconstructive of the origins of the use of scripture in the New Testament, but his focus is on the process by which certain biblical texts that are not obviously open to a messianic reading came to be read as such by early followers of Jesus. He also makes many interesting points with regard to the narrative presentation of Jesus' death as a king in Mark. Marcus' work is the most recent full-length treatment of the use of scripture in Mark that also deals with the PssLam.[3] I will give a brief summary of the relevant arguments of each scholar and then will discuss each treatment of the PssLam in particular.

C. H. Dodd's classic work *According to the Scriptures: The Substructure of New Testament Theology* attempts to discover the earliest point of the formation of the central tradition that eventually developed

---

[3] Hatina's recent study on the use of scripture in Mark is mainly a methodological study and does not address the passages in which Mark evokes the PssLam. He argues that the significance of Mark's references to scripture should not be searched for in contexts outside of Mark such as in the texts themselves, literary conventions contemporary to Mark, or in the historical context of Mark. Instead, he argues that the narrative context of Mark should be the context that determines the meaning of a particular use of scripture. See *In Search of a Context*, especially chapter 2. I agree with his basic argument that the narrative of Mark should play an important role in determining the meaning of a scriptural reference within the text. But I think there should be more of an interaction of contexts, that of Mark's narrative and that of the text evoked by Mark's narrative. Once an evocation or citation of scripture is noticed by a member of the audience, he or she is free to investigate the evocation or citation as far as possible. Each evocation should be considered on a case-by-case basis in order to determine how much of the context makes most sense for the meaning of Mark's narrative. In light of this, I think that any study of the overarching use of scripture in Mark does not account for the complexity of the narrative's evocation of scripture in particular places within the narrative.

into the New Testament. He argues for the inherent connection between this earliest *kerygma* and the Old Testament. "The Church was committed, by the very terms of its *kerygma*, to a formidable task of biblical research, primarily for the purpose of clarifying its own understanding of the momentous events out of which it had emerged, and also for the purpose of making its Gospel intelligible to the outside public."[4] In his investigation of the commonly used passages of the Old Testament in the New Testament, he concludes, "very diverse scriptures are brought together so that they interpret one another in hitherto unsuspected ways."[5]

Primary among these diverse scriptures that belong to a common stock of "testimonia" are the "psalms of the righteous sufferer," our PssLam, which, along with the servant passages of Deutero-Isaiah, offer a "plot" that is key for construing the early way in which the death and resurrection of Jesus are justified theologically by means of the scriptures. Within this schema, Dodd claims that, even though only bits and pieces of these texts are referred to in the New Testament, the whole of the "plot" of these texts was in mind for early Christian writers and thinkers. They served as a model for understanding Jesus' ministry, life, and death, almost as an abstracted mythic plot that the particular passages evoked when referred to by New Testament writers. As Donald Juel points out, Dodd's position has to be defended with evidence that a plot of typical suffering had already been worked out in Jewish tradition before the frequently cited texts were evoked in narratives. There is no such evidence, and "if there existed no mythic construct such as an apocalyptic Son of Man or a Suffering Servant or a Righteous Sufferer, but only the scriptural potential for the construction of such figures, what appear to us as coherent interpretive traditions may well be the product of our imaginations." Juel goes on to point out that the so-called plots of Psalm 22 and Isaiah 53 may not be the starting-point of theological speculation about Jesus for early Christians, but the endpoint or result of their exegetical usage of these texts.[6] In other words, the mythic plot does not precede interpretation of these texts, but rather proceeds from repeated use of these texts by early believers in Jesus.

Noteworthy in Dodd's attempt to reconstruct the pre-New Testament interpretive practices of early Christians is his willingness to consider the whole of particular biblical texts. Where he falls short is in his

---

[4]   C. H. Dodd, *According to the Scriptures: The Sub-structure of New Testament Theology* (London: Nesbet & Co., 1952), 14.

[5]   Ibid., 109.

[6]   Donald H. Juel, *Messianic Exegesis: Christological Interpretation of the Old Testament in Early Christianity* (Philadelphia: Fortress, 1988), 22.

unwillingness to allow each of these texts to offer something unique to the discussion. Instead, he groups all the texts of a particular type together in a monolithic way and assumes that all the "psalms of the righteous sufferer" function the same way and contribute the same "plot" to the understanding of Jesus.

Barnabas Lindars' *New Testament Apologetic*[7] owes much to Dodd, in that he tries to discover the doctrinal keys to early Christian thinking about Jesus by focusing on the quotations of the Old Testament found in the New Testament. He uses Dodd as a guide, but he also uses the Dead Sea Scrolls (DSS) *Habakkuk Commentary* to draw an analogy between the interpretive focus of that work and that of early Christianity: "the events of redemption are the regulative factor, and provide the key to the meaning of scripture."[8] His study proceeds with the assumption that he can get behind the writings of the New Testament to the actual origins of doctrinal formulation among early Christian thinkers through the use of certain biblical passages.

Lindars does admit that when a text is quoted, it is not always used in the same way in different places in the New Testament. His solution to this problem, based on Dodd's work, is to discount the possibility of a parallel reality of diverse understandings.[9] Instead, he arranges these interpretations in a developmental schema so as to discover stages of interpretation that correspond to the developing thought of the church.[10] The most primitive thought relates to the apologetic purposes of the early church in refuting objections to the primitive *kerygma* and in arguing for the gospel. When he arrives at the PssLam, which he calls Passion Psalms, he argues that they function similarly to Isaiah 53 in that they show that Jesus' death was not the result of divine displeasure. These psalms also answered the many questions and objections that arose in light of Jesus' death by grounding it in the prophecy of scripture – how his death is consistent with the claim that he is Messiah, why he included a traitor among his closest companions, why he suffered a criminal's death, and so forth.[11]

Like Dodd, Lindars considers the whole of each PssLam, but he is more careful to distinguish among their various functions. However, he does not attend to the New Testament narrative context of each quotation with as much care as he should have, since his purpose is more general than that. Instead, he discusses the use of the group of PssLam by referring

---

[7] Barnabas Lindars, *New Testament Apologetic: The Doctrinal Significance of the Old Testament Quotations* (London: SCM Press, 1961).
[8] Ibid., 17.   [9] Ibid., 19.   [10] Ibid., 17–19.   [11] Ibid., 88.

to any place a PsLam is evoked in the New Testament. In doing so, he can paint his developmental picture of the growth of the doctrine of early Christianity.

Donald Juel's work[12] is of a very different kind from Lindars' and Dodd's. Instead of using theological or doctrinal questions as the over-arching structure of his work, he attempts to reconstruct the actual exeget-ical ways that certain biblical texts were linked together to form the early collection of Old Testament texts commonly used by early Christians to understand Jesus' messiahship. Following his teacher, Nils Alstrup Dahl, Juel stresses the idea that early Christian exegesis centered on the attempt to *understand* the gospel. In light of this, he also argues, "the major focus of that scriptural interpretation was Jesus, the crucified and risen Mes-siah."[13] So, Jesus' messiahship was the starting-point *from which* an early Christian would turn to the scriptures, not the point *to which* an early Christian would argue starting from the scriptures, having such scrip-tural notions as a Suffering Servant, the Son of Man, the eschatological prophet, Wisdom, or the Righteous Sufferer as pre-conceived abstrac-tions already formulated for use in his or her apologetic argumentations, as Lindars argues.[14]

Furthermore, the way that early Christians dealt with scripture to try to understand Jesus' messiahship "was determined largely by the

[12] Juel, *Messianic Exegesis*.

[13] Ibid., 1. Jesus' messiahship is also the starting-point for Lindars in constructing the way early believers in Jesus may have appealed to scripture to defend the gospel to outsiders. However, the main difference between Juel and Lindars is the motivation for appealing to scripture. For Lindars, early believers appealed to scripture to convince others of the messiahship of Jesus. For Juel, early believers appealed to scripture to understand their own belief in the messiahship of Jesus.

[14] It is very difficult to argue with absolute certainty for pre-conceived notions of abstracted figures in Second Temple Judaism. John J. Collins (*Daniel: A Commentary on the Book of Daniel* [Hermeneia; Minneapolis: Fortress, 1993], 79–84) has argued that, although it is uncertain that there was a "Son of Man" concept during this time, "any-one in the late first century [B.C.E.] who spoke of one in human form riding on the clouds, appearing with an Ancient of Days, or in any terms reminiscent of Daniel 7 would evoke a figure with distinct traits that go beyond what was explicit in the text of Daniel's vision" (ibid., 84). For a more detailed examination of the issue, see John J. Collins, "The Son of Man in First Century Judaism," *NTS* 38 (1992): 448–66. Even if there was no set pre-conceived abstraction of Wisdom during this time, one could make a strong case for there being significant similarities in the various ways that personi-fied Wisdom is portrayed in Jewish literature. When early believers appealed to similar thoughts with respect to Jesus, they undoubtedly used a basic philosophical matrix to con-ceive of Christ's pre-existence, role in creation, closeness to God, and effect on humanity. However, it is not as simple as having an abstracted model into which early believers could simply insert Jesus. This is shown by the variety of literary expressions in the New Testa-ment about Christ from the perspective of Wisdom (e.g., John 1:1–18; Col 1:15–20; and Heb 1:3).

interpretive world of which the first believers were a part,"[15] namely, the interpretive traditions of early Judaism. So Juel spends a great deal of time trying to reconstruct how certain texts were grouped together in order to determine how these texts helped early Christians understand Jesus' messiahship. He weaves an exploration of exegetical methods with an exploration of the content of the texts that he brings together. The result is a disciplined and imaginative reconstruction of the origins of the use of scripture by early followers of Jesus.

The PssLam, of course, figure prominently in his investigation because they were some of the key texts that helped early Christians understand who Jesus was as Messiah. Like Dodd and Lindars before him, Juel concluded that the PssLam primarily deal with the passion of Jesus, from early believers' perspectives, and so play a key role in the construction of the story of Jesus' suffering and death. Since there is no precedent for reading PssLam messianically, he calls the logic behind the messianic use of certain PssLam (namely, Psalms 22, 31, 69) "midrashic."[16] Therefore, "precedent for reading these psalms as describing Jesus' death must . . . be sought not in traditions about righteous sufferers but in the logic of messianic exegesis."[17] He goes on to argue for midrashic links to other texts, for example Psalm 89, to show how early Christians most likely incorporated these PssLam in their speculation about Jesus as Messiah. He spends several pages on the use of the Psalms in Mark's Gospel (mainly the passion narrative), and we will have recourse to his insights later in this study. For now, I will simply mention that he resists conclusions like Dodd's that try to bring in the whole of a particular psalm to justify Jesus' death and vindication theologically. Instead, Juel argues, "the point is that words and phrases from the psalms were used to construct a framework within which to make sense of Jesus' death – and to offer testimony that his death was 'in accordance with the scriptures,'"[18] echoing Paul's statement in 1 Cor 15:3–7 and reminding his readers of the central thesis of his work.

I now turn to Joel Marcus' *The Way of the Lord* as the final work I will discuss in this section. This work is an attempt to describe the Christology of Mark by looking at the way that the text "exegetes" the Old Testament. The study has five main features, summarized well by the following statement from the introduction:

---

[15] Juel, *Messianic Exegesis*, 29.

[16] Juel does not give a definition of "midrashic," although he has a long discussion describing it as thoroughly as possible, with examples. See his chapter, "Rules of the Game," ibid., 31–58, for this discussion.

[17] Ibid., 90.   [18] Ibid., 96.

This study, then, will combine attention to the Old Testament texts themselves, a reconstruction of Mark's role in transmitting them, an examination of the way in which he expresses similar themes elsewhere in his Gospel, glances at the interpretation of the same texts elsewhere in his world, and an appraisal of the message they convey to a community living in the crisis-filled atmosphere created by the Jewish War.[19]

Unlike Dodd, Lindars, and Juel, Marcus is not primarily interested in the origins or development of the thought or the exegetical and interpretive practices in the New Testament, although these come into play throughout his study. He is more interested in performing a Christological study of Mark through the lens of the Gospel's usage of the Old Testament and the social situation of believers in Palestine during the Jewish War. Throughout the work, he consistently argues for the depiction of Mark's Jesus as a warrior king who, instead of bringing political liberation to Israel, offers a future-oriented, apocalyptic alternative to those false messiahs in Palestine who act in the image of David the warrior king for political liberation (Mark 13:21–2). Jesus as the true Messiah is the warrior king, but his victory comes through suffering and will only be fully consummated in his second coming at the end of the ages. Marcus' treatment of the Old Testament consistently bolsters this main thesis.

Much like Dodd and Lindars, Marcus argues for the use of the PssLam (which he calls Psalms of the Righteous Sufferer) in more than an atomistic way. He constructs an extensive list of allusions to the Psalms of the Righteous Sufferer and argues that certain ones be read[20] as a whole when thinking of Jesus' suffering and death; this is especially the case with Psalm 22 and, to a certain extent, with Psalm 41. He then combines his reading of these two psalms with the "trajectory" of interpretation given to these psalms in post-biblical Judaism.[21] When one does so, one can discover the eschatological model that the Psalms of the Righteous Sufferer offer for Jesus' situation. Although Jesus suffers a great deal at the end of his ministry, he dies as a warrior king on the cusp of vindication in the image of the Suffering Righteous One depicted in the Psalms,

---

[19] Joel Marcus, *The Way of the Lord: Christological Exegesis of the Old Testament in the Gospel of Mark* (Louisville, KY: Westminster/John Knox, 1992), 11.

[20] Here, Marcus seems to mean that certain psalms should be considered as a whole by the modern interpreter because Mark intended it that way.

[21] It is important for Marcus to consider all of pre-modern, post-biblical Judaism and not just the Second Temple period, because this allows him to consider later rabbinic texts in constructing trajectories of interpretation. I will discuss the problems with this approach in section 1.2.3 of this chapter.

especially as prophesied in Psalm 22, or at least in Marcus' reading of Psalm 22.[22] While I applaud Marcus' desire to include more than the specific expressions cited or evoked in Psalms 22 and 41, reading the texts as a whole is not the only exercise needed when considering an evoked text. There also needs to be a thorough rhetorical analysis of the Greek or Hebrew version of the psalm in order to understand the dynamics of the psalm in question and to understand the way that the evoked expression functions in the overall rhetoric of the psalm. This can help in discerning the possible function of the evoked text in Mark. Marcus never offers such an analysis anywhere in his treatment of the use of the PssLam in Mark. I will return to Marcus' reading of the PssLam many times later in this study, since his work is focused on the Gospel of Mark.

1.2   Ways of studying the New Testament's use of scripture

The four important studies I just discussed raise key issues for how to approach the topic of the use of scripture in the New Testament. Since no one author exclusively follows one approach, I will discuss the three most important and common issues of method (explicit and implicit in each work) and critique them in dialogue with the authors of these four works and several others.

1.2.1   *Exegesis, exegetical techniques, and biblical interpretation of Second Temple Judaism*

Some New Testament commentators have chosen to focus on the methods that writers in Second Temple Judaism used to interpret or exegete the Jewish scriptures. They do this as the sole focus of their studies or as a starting-point in order to situate a particular text within the interpretive context of Second Temple Judaism. The basic idea is to get a feel for the trends that were present in roughly the same time period of a particular writer in order to draw some conclusions about the techniques of exegesis or interpretation of that writer.[23] The techniques are usually summarized and categorized, and at times over-determined, in that the categories do not allow for overlap or innovation. The following examples will illustrate this tendency.

---

[22] "[Mark] is ... the heir of an interpretive tradition that takes these psalms as prophecies of eschatological tribulation and of the establishment of the kingdom of God, which includes the resurrection of the dead. Jesus' suffering, death, and resurrection thus become, in his interpretation, eschatological events prophesied in the scriptures" (ibid., 186).

[23] Juel does this more thoroughly than Marcus, Dodd, or Lindars.

A series of essays in a recent collection in honor of Barnabas Lindars exemplifies this type of analysis. In three of these essays, the following ancient exegetical techniques are discussed: the genre "rewritten Bible,"[24] explicit commentary on the text (the pesharim of the DSS, allegorical interpretation as exemplified by Philo of Alexandria, and the Mekilta of early rabbinic writings),[25] and the various ways of citing or referring to scripture in the midst of texts not directly commenting on scripture.[26] In the last essay, Andrew Chester also mentions several exegetical techniques used by ancient Jewish biblical interpreters in reading and interpreting biblical texts – *gezera shawa, paronomasia, notariqon, al-tiqre,* and *asmakta.*[27] Chester also discusses the thematic usage of evocations and scripture citations in many Second Temple documents such as Judith, Tobit, 1–2 Maccabees, Ben Sira, and Wisdom of Solomon.

This sort of study is helpful in understanding the scope of interpretive techniques and the imaginative diversity with which Jews and early followers of Jesus read scripture. In other words, as a descriptive exercise that helps a modern reader understand *how* ancient writers dealt with their sacred writings, this is a useful tool. It becomes problematic when the description of the interpretive techniques spills over into the description

---

[24] Philip S. Alexander, "Retelling the Old Testament," in *It is Written: Scripture Citing Scripture: Essays in Honour of Barnabas Lindars* (ed. D. A. Carson and H. G. M. Williamson; Cambridge: Cambridge University Press, 1988), 101–21. "Rewritten Bible" is the term used by Alexander.

[25] Bruce D. Chilton, "Commenting on the Old Testament (with Particular Reference to the Pesharim, Philo, and the Mekilta)," in *It is Written: Scripture Citing Scripture,* 122–40.

[26] Andrew Chester, "Citing the Old Testament," in *It is Written: Scripture Citing Scripture,* 141–69.

[27] The term *gezera shawa* means finding the meaning of a word or phrase by verbal analogy or appealing to another text to clarify the meaning of the text at hand. See Chester, "Citing the Old Testament," 143; see also Harold W. Attridge, *The Epistle to the Hebrews* (Hermeneia Series; Philadelphia: Fortress, 1989), 24; and H. L. Strack and G. Stemberger, *Introduction to the Talmud and Midrash* (Minneapolis: Fortress, 1992), 21. The term *paronomasia* means play on words or cognate roots. For example, in CD 7:9–8:2, "the proper names of Amos 5:26, *Sikkut* and *Kiyyun,* are interpreted by *sukkat* ('booth', itself taken up . . . by the 'booth of David' of Amos 9:11) and *kiyyun* ('pedestal')," Chester, "Citing the Old Testament," 143. See also Strack and Stemberger, *Introduction to the Talmud and Midrash,* 32. The term *notariqon* means the "dividing of a word and using the parts of a word as abbreviations of other words" (Chester, "Citing the Old Testament," 143); see also Strack and Stemberger, *Introduction to the Talmud and Midrash,* 33. The term *al-tiqre* refers to a text-critical method that changes the spelling of a word in the MT to make more sense in the context of the sentence. However, "the *al-tiqrî* interpretation in rabbinic literature by no means always serves textual criticism" (ibid., 259). The term *asmakta* means providing scriptural support for a particular interpretation. See Chester, "Citing the Old Testament," 145, and Strack and Stemberger, *Introduction to Talmud and Midrash,* 259. See ibid., 17–34, for an extensive discussion of rabbinical exegetical techniques where all the major terms are discussed.

of the actual interpretations that result from the techniques. For instance, it is one thing to analyze a passage in 1QS and notice that the author is using a particular method or methods of interpretation, but it is a different issue to discuss the actual content of the interpretation of a particular text in 1QS. These two issues of technique of interpretation, on the one hand, and the content of the interpretation, on the other hand, are related topics. The particular practice of exegesis draws limits around the scope of meaning an ancient writer can produce from a biblical text. However, two authors using very different exegetical techniques can arrive at similar meanings or types of meaning from the same biblical text. Techniques of interpretation are related to the meaning that is produced by the interpretive process, but they are two separate issues. Often they are not separated, and the description of exegetical techniques becomes inextricably intertwined with issues within the history of interpretation of particular biblical passages.

Richard N. Longenecker's recently revised study on interpretation of scripture in the New Testament tends toward this combination of focus on interpretive technique and history of interpretation without consideration of the necessary distinctions between these two topics. He sets out to look at extra-biblical documents (meaning documents outside the canonical Old and New Testaments) in order to discern the "hermeneutical mindset and exegetical practices" of New Testament writers.[28] After a series of chapters which divide Jewish exegetical techniques into four basic categories – literal, midrashic, pesher, and allegorical – he then moves on to try to determine any basic patterns of interpretation of scripture in the New Testament in light of his examination of extra-biblical texts. He does so without addressing the problem of whether there is any relationship between common exegetical techniques and basic patterns of interpretation of scripture. In his revised introduction, he summarizes his results by drawing the extremely general conclusion that New Testament writers used biblical materials to highlight the theme of fulfillment. Instead of directly commenting on the Old Testament and interpreting it in a way that brought it to light in their circumstances as contemporary Jews did, "[New Testament writers] began from outside the texts and used those texts principally to support their extrabiblical stance," namely their conviction that Jesus was the Messiah.[29]

One can see that for Longenecker the issues of biblical *interpretive techniques* spill over into issues of biblical *interpretations* without much

---

[28] Richard N. Longenecker, *Biblical Exegesis in the Apostolic Period* (2nd edn.; Grand Rapids, MI: Eerdmans, 1999), xx.
[29] Ibid., xxvii.

consideration of the relationship between the two. This allows him to draw very broad and general conclusions about patterns of interpretation which then allow him to read particular texts in light of the general conclusions that he makes based on his survey. However, this method is circular and does not allow for particular texts and authors to have their own voices. It is important and laudable to get a feel for the literary and cultural trends of the time during which the writings that eventually became the New Testament were written with respect to biblical interpretation in order to prevent anachronistic readings of biblical texts. But each writer and text has the potential to speak within this context in new and interesting ways. They must be allowed the opportunity to do so.

The use of the term "exegesis" to describe what happens when an author of narrative uses biblical texts to construct a story does not do justice to the complexity of the narrative. Exegesis implies direct explanation and interpretation of a biblical passage by an author. An author writing a story must draw language, images, phrases, and other literary devices from the cultural milieu – in other words, the literary symbolic matrix – in order to construct the plot, themes, characterization, and other features of the story. The result is a rich document in need of interpretation itself. Whenever an author uses biblical passages, there is a narrative interplay between two texts, both of which have their interpretive issues that must be addressed using the methodological tools appropriate to their literary forms.

The incorporation of a biblical passage into a narrative is by no means a straightforward or direct process of interpretation, and therefore "exegesis" is a misleading term. Andrew Chester, in the essay mentioned above, recognizes that there is a difference between what happens when the DSS pesharim use a biblical passage and what happens when 1 Maccabees uses a biblical passage. What one can say about the pesharim – direct commentaries on biblical texts in relation to the community's present-day circumstances – when they use a biblical passage is much more precise than what one can say about 1 Maccabees – a narrative about the uprising of the Jews under the Seleucid rule of Antiochus IV – when it uses a biblical passage. In 1 Maccabees, one must attend to plot, characterization, setting, and the rhetoric employed to tell the story of the uprising. "Exegesis" is more descriptive of the use of biblical passages in the pesharim, Philo's commentaries, or even the Epistle to the Hebrews where there is direct comment on and argument from the biblical text, but it is wholly inappropriate for the use of biblical passages in 1 Maccabees or other narratives, like the Gospel of Mark.

1.2.2   The motif of the Suffering Righteous One

Oftentimes in New Testament scholarship, scholars describe Jesus as a suffering righteous person with little argumentation or justification from the Gospels. In the early 1970s, Lothar Ruppert published two monographs on the motif, one dealing with its existence and use in the Jewish scriptures and in intertestamental literature, and the other on its application to the historical Jesus. Since then, New Testament commentators have relied on his work heavily to characterize Jesus as the Suffering Righteous One.[30] Much of the evidence for this motif comes from the PssLam, so much so that many commentators have named the PssLam the Psalms of the Righteous Sufferer in light of Ruppert's work. In the case of Mark, there is little to indicate that Jesus dies as a righteous sufferer. Therefore, the work of Ruppert must be critically reconsidered, as well as the work of those who re-name the PssLam in light of Ruppert's work and then use these psalms to characterize Jesus as a righteous sufferer in Mark.

In his first monograph,[31] Ruppert surveys the Hebrew Bible and literature of Second Temple Judaism to see whether the texts manifest the motif of the suffering of a righteous person. After detailed analysis of the data, he argues that there were three lines of development of the motif in the history of Israel. The first is the Wisdom line, which reaches its culmination in the educational, testing, and leadership theology of the Book of Wisdom. The second is the eschatological line, exemplified in the community of the Dead Sea Scrolls, especially in the person of the Teacher of Righteousness (see especially 1QH 3–8). The Teacher takes the motif of the suffering of the righteous one from the PssLam and articulates his self-understanding[32] by appealing to the image of the

---

[30] But even before Ruppert wrote, Eduard Schweizer viewed the PssLam in a similar way: "Gradually, this difference [between God's ways and human ways] was made more prominent as the church discovered the prototype of this suffering in the Psalms of the innocent sufferer. By appropriating these Psalms the church explicitly stated that God's plan of salvation was being fulfilled in this experience" (*The Good News According to Mark* [trans. Donald H. Madvig; Atlanta: John Knox, 1970], 351).

[31] *Der leidende Gerechte. Eine motivgeschichtliche Untersuchung zum Alten Testament und zwischentestamentlichen Judentum* (FzB 5; Würzburg, 1972). Ruppert summarizes the results of this work in the first two chapters of his next monograph, *Jesus als der leidende Gerechte? Der Weg Jesu im Lichte eines alt- und zwischentestamentlichen Motivs* (Stuttgart: KBW Verlag, 1972). I will cite this latter work in my discussion of the relevant points he makes in the former.

[32] Ruppert does not argue that the Teacher of Righteousness is the author of all the Qumran Hodayot, but he does say that the voice of 1QH 3–8 probably goes back to the Teacher himself. See *Jesus als der leidende Gerechte?*, 22–3. See section 3 of Chapter 3 for a discussion of the Hodayot and their use of the PssLam evoked simply in the Gospel of Mark.

suffering of Jeremiah, only from an eschatological point of view. Ruppert also argues that the community views itself as the community of the poor and interprets their afflictions as eschatological. Finally, the third is the apocalyptic line, which is the final stage of development. This line combines suffering with Isaiah 53 and views suffering as martyrdom or the suffering of a righteous person (Dan 11:33–5; 12:1–3; Wis 2:12–20; 5:1–7; *1 Enoch*; 4 Macc 18:6b–19; *4 Ezra*, and Baruch, which interpret the suffering of the righteous one in collective terms).[33] The motif of the Suffering Righteous One or ones is most fully manifest in this last stage of development, so much so that Ruppert calls the concept a "dogma."[34]

In his next monograph, Ruppert investigates the possible influence of the motif on the traditions about Jesus that gave rise to the Gospels, especially the passion traditions.[35] Since Ruppert is mainly interested in the pre-Gospel traditions and their use of the motif of the Suffering Righteous One, this study is of little relevance to the task at hand. It is enough to note at this point that Ruppert argues for a democratization of the motif of the suffering Davidic king found in the PssLam. Through this democratization, David as a character ceases to have influence on the use of the motif of the Suffering Righteous One in subsequent literature where the motif shows up.[36] So, according to Ruppert, the suffering of David as king plays no role in the way that the traditions about Jesus develop or the portrayal of Jesus in the Synoptics. I will have much to say regarding the importance of David in the characterization of Jesus in Mark later in this chapter and in Chapters 4 and 6.

Recognizing a motif in ancient literature and positing possible developmental lines and influences on other literature can sometimes be an instructive exercise. But any such exercise should proceed with a healthy dose of caution as to how certain one's conclusion can be. The literature that Ruppert uses to trace the motif and construct these developmental lines for the motif are spread over close to a thousand years. He pays no attention to the genre of each of these writings or to the social setting of their construction or reception. By collapsing these gaps in time, culture, and genre, Ruppert ignores discontinuities and thus creates a simplistic picture of the relationship between these texts and the communities that read and heard them. He takes disparate works that may or may not be related to each other literarily, abstracts an idealized figure from these texts, and then claims that the necessity of the suffering of the Righteous One rose to the level of dogma during this time period. His developmental

---

[33] See ibid., 15–28, but especially 26–8.   [34] Ibid., 28.
[35] Ibid.   [36] See especially chapter 3 of *Jesus als der leidende Gerechte?*

lines could simply reflect differing ways of interpreting a community's suffering in the face of its seemingly righteous standing before God at any given time and circumstance. The texts could have little to do with each other, and therefore grouping them together with clear developmental relationships might be too speculative. And his conclusion that the suffering of the Righteous One is a "dogma" in the Judaism of Jesus' time is far from certain.

Ruppert's study lays the groundwork for subsequent studies that rely on his work to understand Jesus and his early followers' understandings of his suffering and death. Many commentators have taken Ruppert's conclusions that the motif of the Suffering Righteous One is a "dogma" and simply applied it to the Gospels whenever a PsLam is evoked in the text. For many commentators, this has resulted in renaming the PssLam the "Psalms of the Righteous Sufferer," or the "Psalms of the Suffering Just One."

Naming the PssLam as the Psalms of the Righteous Sufferer has more to do with theological meaning than with description of content. Pre-determination of meaning based on over-generalized notions of the content of the PssLam is very common in scholarship that deals with the use of these psalms in the New Testament. Joel Marcus states, for example, "These 'Psalms of the Righteous Sufferer' correspond to H. Gunkel's form-critical category of 'laments of the individual,' but the designation 'Psalms of the Righteous Sufferer' will be retained here as more descriptive of the actual content of the psalms."[37] Many other commentators attribute a similar title or notion to these psalms.[38]

---

[37] Marcus, *The Way of the Lord*, 172.

[38] Ernest Best says of Psalm 22 in his discussion of the crucifixion, "This is a Psalm in which the sufferings of the righteous Psalmist are described." However, he goes on to say, "Nothing is said in these Psalms suggestive of any interpretation of the meaning of the Passion as redemptive, but it is worthy of note that each of them concludes in such a way as to suggest that God has delivered the Psalmist from his trials, just as God delivered Jesus in the Resurrection" (*The Temptation and the Passion: The Markan Soteriology* [2nd edn.; Cambridge: Cambridge University Press, 1990], 152). Although John R. Donahue and Daniel J. Harrington refer to these psalms as lament psalms, when discussing Mark's use of Psalm 22 in the scene of Jesus' death, they say, "Psalm 22 is a statement of confidence in God's power to act and to vindicate the suffering righteous speaker." Then they go on to describe the speaker in the psalms as "an innocent sufferer" (*The Gospel of Mark* [Sacra Pagina 2; Collegeville, MN: Liturgical Press, 2002], 451). Edward K. Broadhead says something similar: "The death of Jesus is drawn precisely into the stream of Old Testament prophecy. In particular, various lines draw upon the image of the innocent suffering one in the Psalms." He then refers to Psalms 22 and 69 as referred to in Mark 15 (*Prophet, Son, Messiah: Narrative Form and Function in Mark 14–16* [JSNTSup 97; Sheffield: Sheffield Academic Press, 1994], 204). See also Frank J. Matera, *The Kingship of Jesus: Composition and Theology in Mark 15* (SBLDS 66; Chico, CA: Scholars Press, 1982), 132, where he calls

The title "Psalms of the Righteous Sufferer" requires more explanation and argumentation than Marcus and others who use it provide. In his brief discussion he does not accurately describe the group of psalms in question ("the speaker laments the persecution that he suffers from his enemies, protests his innocence, and calls upon God to deliver him"). Ps 21:2b (LXX) speaks of the transgression of the psalmist: "Far from my salvation are the words of my transgressions" (μακρὰν ἀπὸ τῆς σωτηρίας μου οἱ λόγοι τῶν παραπτωμάτων μου).[39] Psalm 40 (LXX) does not contain an innocent or righteous sufferer, but instead the psalmist confesses his sin in verse 5. Psalm 41–2 (LXX) only implies the righteousness of the speaker when he cries out for vindication against an impious nation (42:1). In contrast, Psalm 68 (LXX) speaks not of the sinfulness of the psalmist but of his piety that caused his suffering. Certainly Psalm 68 (LXX) fits within Marcus' category, but to include all the "Psalms of Lament" in this group is not "more descriptive of the actual content of the psalms." Marcus' category "Psalms of the Righteous Sufferer" is not only an inaccurate description of two or possibly three of the four main psalms in this category used by Mark. The category determines how he and others perceive the way the psalms are used in Mark's passion narrative, thus giving a pre-determined meaning for Mark's depiction of Jesus in the passion narrative. The pre-determination of meaning of individual PssLam that occurs in much of New Testament scholarship is a direct result of following Ruppert's work uncritically.

1.2.3   Trajectories of interpretation

There is also a tendency in scholarship to look at the way a particular biblical passage is interpreted in various texts in order to determine "trajectories" of interpretation of the biblical passage. Once these trajectories are constructed, they are then brought to bear on the particular text that is being interpreted. When certain New Testament scholars attempt to examine the interpretive history of a text, there is a tendency to generalize patterns of interpretation and then claim that these patterns form a developmental trajectory of interpretation for a given passage. The idea

Ps 22:2, "the lament of the suffering just one"; and Etienne Trocmé, "Il s'agit avant tout des Psaumes 22, 69 et 109, qui ont en commun le thème du Juste persécuté" (*L'Evangile selon Saint Marc* [Commentaire du Nouveau Testament; Genève: Labor et Fides, 2000], 367). Ruppert's work on the Suffering Righteous One in Second Temple Judaism is referred to by Matera, Marcus, Donahue and Harrington, and by many others, and has certainly played a large role in perpetuating the usage of this terminology for the PssLam.

[39] Marcus, *The Way of the Lord*, 172. Translation from the Greek mine.

that one can trace the interpretive history of a text and then construct a trajectory of interpretation that determines the meaning of any given use of that text is standard practice in New Testament scholarship.

First, Marcus,[40] in his introductory remarks about his methodology, makes it explicit that the study of early Jewish and Christian interpretations of the Old Testament passages used by Mark will be one of the five foci of his study. Although he admits that it is improper to assume that Mark would have known these interpretations, he goes on to say, "we will see compelling reasons for presuming that he did and so for thinking that they provide important background to his Old Testament exegesis."[41] He also says that certain Old Testament passages were interpreted consistently, so that their interpretations were ubiquitous in the ancient world. Once these patterns are determined, "some trajectories of ancient biblical exegesis . . . explain otherwise puzzling gaps in the Markan narrative. Such exegeses . . . must be used with caution to illuminate the Markan treatments of the same texts, especially when they postdate Mark; but when so used they can be of invaluable assistance in uncovering new directions for the understanding of Mark's exegetical work."[42] This focus of his methodology continually allows Marcus to make overly general statements about how Mark is "exegeting"[43] a particular biblical passage. In other words, because Marcus does not allow the texts Mark uses, or Mark, the room for readings that do not fit into the "trajectories" of ancient biblical interpretations, he tends to impose predetermined readings of these biblical texts onto the Gospel. The result is that Marcus tends to homogenize Mark, and, by the middle of his study, his readings of particular passages become predictable and simply reinforce the patterns of interpretation that he had established at the beginning of the book.

With respect to the PssLam, Marcus marshals evidence for the eschatological interpretation of the "Psalms of the Righteous Sufferer," following Ruppert's analysis of the eschatological "transformation" of the PssLam from a prayer for this-worldly deliverance from enemies to a more eschatological hope for deliverance from enemies. Utilizing Ruppert, Marcus argues that apocalyptic sources such as Wis 2:12–20; 5:1–7; *4 Ezra*, and *2*

---

[40] I only turn to Marcus because his is the most recent study on the use of scripture in Mark that deals explicitly with the PssLam. From my findings, there is a general tendency to construct trajectories of interpretation in a way that over-determines the meaning of particular passages in the Gospels.

[41] Ibid., 10.   [42] Ibid.

[43] As I have already discussed, I do not think "exegesis" is a good term for how an ancient author of a narrative uses biblical texts. See section 1.2.1 above for a more detailed discussion.

Baruch, as well as the New Testament, "present the idea that the righteous one *must suffer on account of* his righteousness but that he will be *glorified at the eschaton*. The New Testament picture, then, reflects an apocalyptic transformation of the Righteous Sufferer motif."[44] Marcus then goes on to appeal to "post-biblical Judaism" to confirm this interpretation of the PssLam, pointing to the LXX superscript tradition which includes "εἰς τὸ τέλος" ("to" or "for the end") and the corresponding eschatological interpretation of למנצח in *b. Pesah* 117a, the tendency in the DSS to interpret the PssLam eschatologically,[45] and the places in the Targumim where certain PssLam are interpreted eschatologically, mainly Psalm 22. He concludes by saying, "It is fair to say, then, that Psalm 22 and other Psalms of the Righteous Sufferer are often interpreted in the post-biblical period as references to eschatological events, and we would present it as a working hypothesis that these psalms bring a similar eschatological context along with them in Mark."[46] What he fails to take account of is that the category of Psalms of the Righteous Sufferer is a modern construct, not an ancient grouping. If one removed the modern grouping of these psalms from the analysis, Marcus' conclusions regarding the eschatological interpretation of these psalms are actually based on very little evidence when one considers the "trajectory" of interpretation for each psalm individually.

Margaret Daly-Denton has done something similar in her recent work on the appropriation of the Psalms in the Fourth Gospel. Although she acknowledges some of the problems with using rabbinical writings as parallels in the study of the New Testament, she tries to construct trajectories of interpretation that can then be brought to bear on John's use of certain psalms. These rabbinic texts (namely, the Targum to the Psalms and the *Midrash Tehillim*):

> do . . . show the destination of trajectories which began with the inner-biblical and extra-biblical exegesis that we will explore in this chapter. Since these trajectories leave traces of their passing in the NT writings, there are many instances in which the NT confirms that later Jewish writings have preserved much earlier interpretive traditions. Our portrayal of David as psalmist,

---

[44] Ibid., 177. See Ruppert, *Jesus als der leidende Gerechte?*, 42–3. Ruppert claims that the Wisdom of Solomon passages are apocalyptic sources from Palestine that have been incorporated into the text of Wisdom of Solomon. See ibid., 23–4.

[45] Marcus does not mention the fact that the DSS interpret just about *every* biblical text that they use eschatologically.

[46] Marcus, *The Way of the Lord*, 179.

therefore, will owe much to the image which formative Judaism constructed out of the biblical and post-biblical traditions.[47]

Then she proceeds with much the same type of analysis as Marcus.[48]

The process described above with both Marcus and Daly-Denton is inherently circular, in that it involves discerning general trajectories and then applying them to particular texts. Because of the paucity of evidence in "post-biblical" Judaism, every piece of data must be used to construct accurate trajectories of interpretation, if they actually do exist. Marcus and Daly-Denton offer a good contrast. In Marcus' case, he uses everything – including the Fourth Gospel – except Mark to construct his trajectories of interpretation for a given biblical passage, and then he applies these insights to Mark. Daly-Denton uses everything – including Mark – except the Fourth Gospel in constructing her trajectories, and then she applies these insights to the Fourth Gospel. The evidence is too thin and spread over too long a period of time – at best only three or four occurrences of a given text spread over hundreds of years – for this methodology to be legitimately employed.

A good example of this is found with Psalm 41. This psalm is used in several places in ancient Jewish and Christian literature, once in 1QH 13:23–5, once in John 13:18, and once in the *Sentences of the Syriac Menander* 215–16. To draw any conclusions about the trajectory of interpretation in ancient Judaism and Christianity and then use these in interpreting the evocation of Psalm 40 (LXX) in Mark 14:18 seems tenuous, given the spread of time and genre in these three references. Yet Craig A. Evans does just this when he says, "The antithesis of sharing food and then engaging in treachery seems to have become proverbial." Then he refers to the *Sentences of Syriac Menander* and brings this insight to bear on his reading of Mark 14:17–21.[49] In the cases of other PssLam that have more references in early Judaism and Christianity, there would seem to be more of a possibility of constructing a trajectory of interpretation. This happens most frequently with Psalm 22 because of the widespread usage of the psalm in early Christianity. However, when the evidence is

---

[47] Margaret Daly-Denton, *David in the Fourth Gospel: The Johannine Reception of the Psalms* (AGJU 47; Leiden: Brill, 2000), 60.

[48] See also Douglas J. Moo, *The Old Testament in the Gospel Passion Narratives* (Sheffield: The Almond Press, 1983) 285–300, where he concludes his analysis of the use of the PssLam in the passion narrative by suggesting a typological usage of the PssLam for Jesus in part because of the way they were interpreted in "late Judaism," meaning the Judaism of the late Second Temple period.

[49] See Craig A. Evans, *Mark 8:27–16:20* (WBC 34B; Nashville: Thomas Nelson Publishers, 2001), 376.

examined, there are still too few references made to this psalm for the construction of a trajectory of interpretation within ancient Judaism.[50] Only when the evidence from Judaism is viewed in dialogue with the evidence from Christian writers can any conclusions be drawn about how Psalm 22 was interpreted in the ancient world. But this does not necessarily allow for the construction of a trajectory of interpretation for this text in the New Testament. Each place where Psalm 22 is evoked must be examined in its own particularity.

There are two further problems with constructing trajectories of interpretation. Marcus and Daly-Denton pay almost no attention to the genre of the texts that use the biblical passages. Instead, they do a brief reading of the text that refers to the biblical passage, abstract a type of interpretation, and link it to other texts that use the same passage. The result is a trajectory of interpretation. It makes no difference to these commentators that the evidence might consist of a narrative, a biblical commentary, and a poem, for example. Paul Ricoeur argued many years ago that genre and meaning are inextricably tied to each other. The way a text communicates is integral to the meaning that is communicated.[51] Lack of attention to the genre only weakens the case for a trajectory of interpretation.

Related to this is the treatment of the evoked text. Neither Marcus nor Daly-Denton base their interpretive comments about Mark's or the Fourth Gospel's use of biblical passages on any treatment of the evoked biblical text itself. Neither commentator performs any in-depth analysis on the earlier biblical text to see how the phrase or verse cited or alluded to in the Gospel functions rhetorically in the whole of the evoked text. I will say more about this below in this chapter and in Chapter 5, but I consider

---

[50] Psalm 22 is definitely referred to in the DSS in 1QH 13:31 and possibly in 12:33. In the beginning of 4QPs^f, Ps 22:15–17 is followed by quotations from Psalms 107 and 109 and then by the *Apostrophe of Zion*, an *Eschatological Hymn*, and the *Apostrophe to Judah*. Marcus argues that the suffering described in Psalm 22 is viewed as the prelude to the eschatological consummation described in the apocryphal writings that follow (*The Way of the Lord*, 179). The Targum of the Psalms and the *Midrash Tehillim* also deal with Psalm 22 interpretively. These are the only overt references to Psalm 22 in the whole of ancient Judaism. Of course, there are many places in the New Testament that refer to Psalm 22 (quotations in italics), namely, Mark 9:12; *15:24*, 29, *34*; Matt 27:29, *35*, 39, 43, *46*; Luke 18:17; *23:34*, 35; John *19:24*; 20:17; 1 Pet *5:8*; Rom 5:5; 2 Tim 4:17; Heb *2:12*; 5:7; Rev 11:15; 19:5. (These references come from Appendix IV of the 27th edition of Nestle-Aland's Greek New Testament.) Later Christian literature comments upon the Gospel's tradition of using Psalm 22 as a text that interprets or predicts Jesus' suffering. These references are too many to mention here, but Justin Martyr's *Dialogue with Trypho*, *1 Clement*, and Augustine's *Second Discourse on Psalm 21* all have extended discussions of Psalm 22 in light of Jesus' death.

[51] Paul Ricoeur, "Toward a Hermeneutic of the Idea of Revelation," in *Essays on Biblical Interpretation* (ed. Lewis S. Mudge; Philadelphia: Fortress, 1980), 73–118.

this step to be of utmost importance in discerning the way that Mark's narrative text interacts with the biblical text it evokes.

A more reasonable way to proceed is to take into account the history of interpretation as a way of understanding the cultural landscape of the time in a general way and the expectations an ancient reader or hearer may have had when encountering such a biblical text. This in no way should determine the reading of a particular text that evokes a previous biblical text. Instead of marshalling parallel interpretations for particular biblical texts, constructing trajectories of interpretation for the text, and then using the trajectory to interpret the passage in Mark that uses the text, the history of interpretation should be used as a comparative tool for discerning the way that Mark uses the passage in his narrative. One of the most useful qualities of the comparative approach is that it stimulates thought about the possibilities of interpretation of a particular text, but it does not pre-determine its meaning. The approach, if used well, provides a conversation partner that contextualizes one's investigation without drawing hard-and-fast boundaries around what can and cannot be said about a passage. Richard Hays uses the history of interpretation as one of his criteria for "hearing echoes" in Paul's writings, but he says,

> While this test is a possible restraint against arbitrariness, it is also one of the least reliable guides for interpretation . . . An investigation of the history of interpretation can extend the range of possible readings of Paul's use of Scripture, but it also can lead us to a narrowing of the hermeneutical potential of Paul's inter-textual collocations. Thus, this criterion should rarely be used as a negative test to exclude proposed echoes that commend themselves on other grounds.[52]

---

[52] Richard B. Hays, *Echoes of Scripture in the Letters of Paul* (New Haven: Yale University Press, 1989), 31. Although not explicitly stated as part of his methodology, Harold W. Attridge's study on the use of the psalms in the New Testament uses a comparative methodology when examining how particular psalms are interpreted by Hebrews. See "The Psalms in Hebrews," in *The Psalms in Community* (ed. Harold W. Attridge and Margot Fassler; Atlanta and Leiden: Society of Biblical Literature, 2003). See also Richard B. Hays and Joel B. Green, "The Use of the Old Testament by New Testament Writers," in *Hearing the New Testament: Strategies for Interpretation.* (ed. Joel B. Green; Grand Rapids, MI: Eerdmans, 1995), 31: "the NT writers' use of the OT can rarely be explained simply by discovering parallels in contemporary sources, though such parallels may provide an interesting counterpoint. This latter possibility is of special consequence if it can be seen that the NT writer is participating in an ongoing tradition of exegesis of certain OT materials." Juel walks this thin line in that he looks very carefully at the traditions and methods of interpreting various biblical texts in concert with each other in the context of Second Temple Judaism, but he

For the most part, I agree with his assessment and will follow the principles described by Hays when considering Mark's use of the PssLam. However, I will have no detailed discussion of this history of interpretation, because it would take the study too far off track. As we will see, trying to articulate how Mark uses four PssLam in the passion narrative is complex enough to occupy the many pages of this study. Discussion of the way other authors use these texts would complicate these matters beyond what is manageable for a reasonably sized monograph.

In light of Hays' comments and the shortcomings of the two approaches just discussed, it is necessary to delineate the methodology I will employ in this study. I will highlight and foreground four PssLam in the passages in which they are most likely alluded to by Mark in the passion narrative and then try to see how reading these psalms together with Mark may inform us with respect to the identity of Jesus and his relationship with God in Mark's passion narrative. So, my approach will not be a comprehensive study of Markan Christology, theology, and discipleship, but it must discuss Mark's use of the PssLam in the passion narrative in relation to these larger issues. The approach will be primarily narrative analysis, although other critical tools will be used as the need for them arises.[53] Because I wish to understand the particular way that Mark's use of the PssLam informs and forms his passion narrative, my approach will be

---

does not allow the content of previous interpretations of particular texts to over-determine his reading of texts in the New Testament that interpret comparable biblical passages. See Juel's interpretations throughout his *Messianic Exegesis*.

[53] I prefer to think of the interpretive process in the broadest of terms, methodologically. I have come to believe that approaching a text with strict, pre-determined limits on methods reverses the way the interpretive process proceeds best. Methods should be at the disposal of the interpreter to be used whenever questions that arise call for their use. By using a particular method, the interpreter addresses a text from a particular angle and answers only certain kinds of questions based upon the rubrics of that method. Imposing a certain method upon the interpretation process limits the kinds of questions the interpreter is free to ask. But if the interpreter is free to ask any question he or she wishes, then the methods can be viewed as question-answering tools available to the interpreter as the need arises. See Sandra M. Schneiders, *The Revelatory Text: Interpreting the New Testament as Sacred Scripture* (New York: HarperCollins, 1991), 111: "The approach to the text, which is itself a function of the questions that interest the researcher, ought to govern the construction of the methodology. In other words, rather than starting with a method or even an established methodology . . . the interpreter starts with the questions that he or she wants to answer." For a similar view from a sociological perspective, see Pierre Bourdieu and Loïc J. D. Wacquant, *An Invitation to Reflexive Sociology* (Chicago: University of Chicago Press, 1992), 28, where they say, "Methodology then carries over into an implicit theory of the social which makes researchers act in the manner of the late-night drunk . . . who, having lost the keys to his house, persists in searching for them under the nearest lamp post because this is where he has the most light."

based more on the narrative character of the text, the possibility that the author intended that a particular scriptural reference be recognized by the audience, and the ability of the audience to incorporate the context of the scriptural reference, namely the entirety of a given PsLam.

2 The methodology of the present study

As I stated at the outset of this chapter, the underlying hermeneutical method of this study is based upon Paul Ricoeur's narrative theory, which states that narrative configures or emplots human time in a particular way, and the process of reading a narrative reconfigures human time and experience in relation to that narrative. Simply put, the process of reading a narrative transforms the reader, because the author configures human time through narrative in such a way that the reader understands human experience differently as a result of his or her reading. I am most interested in how reading Mark's passion narrative with attention to the PssLam reconfigures human experience and allows the reader to understand Jesus' suffering and death differently as a result of the process of reading the passion narrative in this way. In order to investigate this well, I will need to develop a strategy of reading that allows me to understand and articulate this process of reconfiguration. What follows does just this.

2.1 Defining the scope

From my perspective, the issue of how Mark uses scripture is far too complex for one study. General conclusions are too difficult to defend, and there are always exceptions to overall patterns of usage of scripture that scholars claim to discover in the narrative of the Gospel. Instead, I have found it much more instructive to limit the scope of my investigation in several ways.

First, I have chosen only a subset of scripture that Mark uses, namely, the Psalms. Although this might seem to be a manageable amount of scripture to deal with, in fact it is not. The reason for this is that the collection of Psalms in the Jewish scriptures is a complex entity with a long and complicated compositional history and usage. There are discernible structures within the book itself, at least in the form that has been preserved through the years in the Jewish and Christian canons. Even if we can say something about what allows these writings to be grouped together in one collection, the genres and forms of the psalms vary significantly and must be taken into account when interpreting them or trying to determine how a secondary author interprets them.[54] This basic insight has led me to narrow the scope in a second way: I will only consider Mark's usage of a group of psalms that modern commentators have named Psalms of Individual Lament.[55] I chose to do this not just for formal reasons but also because Mark's use of the PssLam falls mainly at points in the narrative that deal with Jesus' suffering. One can safely say that Jesus' suffering as Messiah is one of the most important issues that Mark addresses for his audiences, so a full understanding of how the PssLam are incorporated in the Gospel can help deepen understanding of Jesus' suffering.

Finally, I have made two other interrelated choices to narrow the scope of this study. Because of the nature of allusions in narratives, namely the inability to prove or disprove authorial intent to evoke a previous text, I have limited my consideration to simple evocations of the PssLam in Mark. I define a simple evocation as a discernible evocation of one and only one text outside the narrative. Considering only simple evocations allows for a higher degree of certainty with regard to whether or not an author intended the evocation and, more importantly, with regard to whether or not an audience would recognize the evocation. When the references to the PssLam in Mark are limited to simple evocations, we are left with only two references outside the passion narrative in Mark. Both of these references point to Jesus' suffering in the passion narrative, and so I have decided to discuss only the passion narrative in this study.

With the scope of this study defined, let us now turn to a more detailed discussion of how I wish to proceed in the body of this work.

2.2   Author, text, and reader

When it comes to reading evocations in biblical texts, there is a constant disagreement among critics whether the author, the text, or the reader should govern the existence and meaning of an evocation. The camps of interpretation are easily discerned – strict historical critics focus on authorial intent, strict linguistic and structuralist critics focus on the text, and strict post-structuralist critics of the reader-response type focus on

---

[54] I have found that the issues of the genre and form of each psalm remain a peripheral or non-existent issue for most scholars who study their use in the New Testament. Since the form of a piece of literature affects its meaning to a certain extent – arguably a large extent – I think the form of a psalm should be considered in determining how a secondary author uses the text in a later writing.

[55] I significantly revise the traditional list of PssLam, and in Chapter 2, section 1.2 I will discuss why and how I revise the list.

the reader.[56] A much more fruitful interpretive process includes all three – author, text, and reader.

There are at least two interrelated responsibilities for the reader of ancient texts, in my view. First, the reader should respect the text as an ancient document, as a product of a cultural and historical setting other than that of the reader. Therefore, it is the responsibility of the reader to learn as much as possible about the text's cultural setting, including rhetorical and narrative devices and structures, philosophical underpinnings, and social realities, so as to minimize the chance of misunderstanding the text. This process aids the reader in understanding what the text says in all its depth and richness. The second responsibility is for the reader to be aware of his or her own cultural presuppositions, so as to prevent anachronistic readings of the ancient text as much as one can. By following through with these two responsibilities, the reader is able to engage with the text and become involved in the interpretive process in an informed way. The engagement that a reader has with the text will be as fruitful as possible, because the reader respects the conversation partner, namely the text, and is able to ask critical questions of the text as a central part of the conversation.

In the next section, I will argue for a particular type of interpretation process when reading an evocation in the Gospel of Mark.[57] The process has four steps that correspond essentially to Ziva Ben-Porat's four-step poetics of allusion.[58] Each step requires consideration of the author, text, and reader to varying degrees. The first two steps involve identifying an evocation and the evoked text. In this stage, I would argue that the text and authorial intent are most important. One can never prove an actual author's intent, especially with allusive references, nor can one completely separate out the author from the text. Demonstrating the relative probability of an evocation by appealing to the text's signals involves the author to a certain extent because the author wrote the words and constructed the text as it stands. So when one makes a claim about an evocation in the text, one is implicitly making a claim about the intention of the author, or at least about the possibility that the author intended such an evocation.[59]

---

[56] For an excellent explanation of these three foci of literary criticism, see Elizabeth Struthers Malbon, *In the Company of Jesus: Characters in Mark's Gospel* (Louisville, KY: Westminster John Knox Press, 2000), 3–21.

[57] Although I will restrict my discussion to the Gospel of Mark, my methodology could carry over to other Gospels or New Testament texts in places where less explicit forms of biblical reference are evident.

[58] Ziva Ben-Porat, "The Poetics of Literary Allusion," *PTL: A Journal for Descriptive Poetics and Theory of Literature* 1 (1979): 105–28.

[59] There is always the possibility that an author alluded to another text unconsciously, but this consideration is completely beyond verifiability.

The third and fourth steps of the poetics of allusion, reading the alluding and evoked texts[60] together both locally and more extensively, involve mainly the reader and the text. In the next section, there will be a more detailed discussion concerning reading the alluding text locally and more extensively in light of the evoked text. It is more difficult to assert with any probability that the author intended a reader to read the two texts in a certain way – either atomistically or contextually[61] – or to notice "intertextual patterns"[62] between the texts, as the reader may do in these final two steps. The insights that emerge from such a process are created by the reader and only the reader, and so the reader must take responsibility for the particular interpretation.

These last two steps are where the process of interpretation really happens, because here the reader enters into conversation with the text (and implicitly the author). If the reader has done his or her homework, he or she can enter into an informed conversation, and in the case of allusion, the reader can take the lead from the text (and implicitly the author) as to where to go when an evocation is signaled. Once the reader receives a signal concerning an evocation, it is up to the reader to determine why the evocation is there and what effect the evoked text has on the alluding text. The text seldom has clear indications that lead the reader in determining how to read the evocation. However, in a narrative text where there is no indication of a text being used as a proof text for a propositional argument or assertion, it may be fruitful for the reader to consider the evoked text as a whole in re-evaluating the alluding text. This interpretive process can fall within the limits of reading and interpreting an ancient text in a historically informed way if the reader follows the lead of the text and reads both the alluding and evoked texts in their own contexts as much as possible.

I make these assumptions explicit so that there is no misunderstanding regarding the interpretive process that I undertake below. After I argue for the existence of an evocation, I take seriously the signal from the

---

[60] The term "alluding text" will refer to the text that contains the reference. The term "evoked text" will refer to the text that is evoked by a particular reference in the alluding text. These terms are adopted from Ben-Porat.

[61] By "atomistically" I mean reading only the phrase or verse of the evoked text in conversation with the alluding text. By "contextually" I mean reading the evoked text as a whole in conversation with the alluding text.

[62] This is another term used by Ben-Porat to describe common thematic, linguistic, or other literary characteristics that are noticed by an interpreter but go beyond recognizable signals in the text that would evoke an outside text. The key here is that the intertextual patterns are discerned by the reader only after the alluding text is read in light of the evoked text.

narrative text and implicitly from the author by going to the evoked text and re-reading the alluding text in light of it. In reading the evoked text, I use all of the same rubrics that I use in reading the alluding text (i.e., study of its cultural setting, its rhetorical devices and structure, its philosophical underpinnings, and its social realities). The author of Mark most likely evoked the Greek version of the Jewish scriptures for the sake of his audiences, so the reader must respect this reality and read the Greek version as well.

When dealing with an evoked phrase or verse of the Jewish scriptures, I will read the entirety of the text from which the phrase or verse comes.[63] I do this for two reasons. First, if one wants to understand the possible meanings of a word or phrase, the word or phrase only gains particular meaning when it is placed in a context. The context of an evoked word or phrase, for our purposes, will be the entire psalm from which it comes. One can focus on the word or phrase only after it is understood how that word or phrase functions in the overall rhetorical structure of the psalm. Second, since there is no way to prove that the author of the alluding text only meant to refer to the word or phrase found in the alluding text, then there is no reason not to read the entire evoked text.[64] Not doing so risks superficiality of interpretation and perhaps oversight of something crucial for understanding the alluding text. Allusion adds depth to a text, and to shortchange that depth is to rob the alluding text of its potential richness.

Some thoughts are in order regarding who "the reader" is in this study. One of the major difficulties in dealing with the Gospel of Mark is that we know almost nothing specific about the circumstances of its creation. Although there is consensus that Mark was written within a few years of 70 CE, we can only make educated guesses at who the author was, where it was written, to whom it was written, or the makeup of its original audience.

---

[63] This is easiest with the Psalms because the "entire text" is one particular psalm. The method is more difficult when one has a larger text like Isaiah or Exodus, because the question arises as to how much of the text should be included in the reading. In cases like these, a careful analysis of the evoked text must be performed in order to determine the boundaries of the literary unit in which the evoked text is located. In the end, the reader's discretion is the ultimate judge as to how much of the evoked text to include.

[64] Again, in a narrative text where there is no indication that previous texts are referred to for proof-texting reasons, one must respect the nature of narrative in communicating what the author wants. Instead of presenting a logical, propositional argument, narratives often use images and plot dynamics to communicate with the reader, encouraging the reader to use his or her imagination in interpreting the text. This is not to say that narratives are without logic or make no "argument." But the mode of communication in narrative is so different from that of propositional argumentation that one must attend to the special features of narrative in investigating how communication happens.

With regard to Mark's original audience, or at least the readers/hearers he had in mind when he wrote the Gospel, we can know some specifics.

Following Ernest Best's careful analysis,[65] we can say that Mark's readers/hearers knew Greek, were believers in Jesus, had some basic knowledge of Jewish tradition from a literary perspective (even if Mark got some of the details wrong; cf. Mark 1:2; 2:26; 10:19), and did not know Aramaic (cf. Aramaic words or phrases translated into Greek in Mark 5:41; 7:11, 34; 14:36; 15:22, 34), some specific customs of the Pharisees (cf. Mark 7:3–4), or the Sadducees' lack of belief in the resurrection (cf. 12:18). Given these last three qualities, and the Gospel's special interest in Gentiles (cf. 7:24–30; 11:17; 13:10; 14:9; 15:39), Best argues that the majority of Mark's original intended audience were Gentile.[66] Donald Juel argues that the implied audience probably was envisioned as part of Israel because (1) they had extensive knowledge of Jewish scripture; (2) they had inside knowledge of the Jewish community (cf. the distinction between the use of the terms "Jew" and "Israel" in 14:61 and the way Jews speak of Jesus' claims about his status as compared with the way the Romans speak in 15:31); and (3) the "readers are addressed throughout the Gospel as having an investment in Israel's tradition and Scripture."[67] In addition to Juel's argument, one need not conclude that Mark's audience is Gentile if one envisions diaspora Jews far removed from the everyday workings of Palestinian Judaism and with more knowledge of the local Gentile world than the Palestinian Jewish world. Whether Jew or Gentile, the intended audience would have some detailed knowledge of Jewish scripture, either obtained through a Jewish upbringing and synagogue education or passed on through the course of communal life as a believer in Jesus as a Jewish messiah.[68]

Whatever the details of Mark's intended audience, ultimately I am the reader. But I hope to read both the PssLam and Mark's passion narrative as much as possible through the imaginative lens of an ancient believer of Jesus as Messiah who was fluent in Greek, and, therefore, who received the psalms in their Greek version as Greek documents in the voice of

---

[65] Ernest Best, "Mark's Readers: A Profile," in *The Four Gospels* (ed. F. Van Segbroeck, *et al.*; Leuven: Peeters, 1994), 839–58.

[66] Ibid., 850.

[67] Donald Juel, *A Master of Surprise: Mark Interpreted* (Minneapolis, MN: Fortress, 1994), 133–9. The quotation is from page 138.

[68] Juel argues very persuasively that Mark's audience "has a knowledge of the Scriptures." His argument points to (1) the eleven quotations introduced by formulas; (2) the extensive use of allusions to biblical passages not marked with a formula, especially in the passion narrative; and (3) the employment of scriptural interpretation used by Jesus in arguing with characters in the Gospel (cf. 7:1–13; 12:18–27 and 12:35–7). See ibid., 133–6.

David (more on this below), and who had recourse to the Greek text in his or her attempts to understand how Mark uses this psalm in telling the story of Jesus.

I do not wish to claim that I am describing a reading that an actual person in the ancient world performed either on the PssLam or on Mark's passion narrative. I am simply trying to follow the lead of the texts (and implicitly the authors of the texts) in trying to understand their literary dynamics. The author of Mark most likely evoked the Greek version of the Jewish scriptures for the sake of his earliest addressees, so I must respect this reality and read the Greek version as well. Any literary analysis of an ancient text should strive for historical accuracy, but in the end the questions that drive that analysis are those of a modern critic.[69]

2.3   The nature and identification of allusions

The poetics of allusion has garnered a considerable amount of attention in literary theory over the past thirty years.[70] All agree that an allusion, in general, is a literary device used to join a text with a referent outside that text. That outside referent can be another literary text or a cultural referent such as a current event, a person, a song, or other commonly known cultural element of a current or past time. Although theorists define allusion in slightly different ways, two general categories can be discerned regarding intentionality. Benjamin D. Sommer has synthesized the material well, characterizing two different approaches to the relationship among literary texts. "One approach is oriented toward 'influence' and 'allusion,' the other toward 'intertextuality.'"[71] The influence and

---

[69] See *1 Clem* 16:3–14, where the author quotes from Isa 53:1–12 in his attempts to understand and explain the humility of Jesus to the point that he would suffer and die on the cross. Just after this passage, the author of *1 Clement* appeals also to LXX Ps 21:7–9 to make the same point. Later, in 35:7–12, he offers a long quotation from LXX Ps 49:16–23. See also *Barn* 2:5 and 3:1–6, where he quotes from Isa 1:1–13 and Isa 58:4–10, respectively, and 11:6–7, where he quotes Ps 1:3–6 and then discusses it for the rest of the next verse. These are just a few examples where the authors of *1 Clement* and *Barnabas* appeal to large sections of scripture to make points about Christ or to exhort the audiences to a certain understanding of God's actions in Christ. Use of these texts goes beyond atomistic use of verses from unrelated texts to prove something about Jesus. It is the result of long reflection on whole sections of scripture in relation to the story of Jesus, similar to what I am doing in this study.

[70] For a good review of the scholarship, see Udo J. Hebel, "Towards a Descriptive Poetics of Allusion," in *Intertextuality* (ed. Heinrich F. Plett; Berlin: Walter de Gruyter, 1991), 135–64.

[71] Benjamin D. Sommer, *A Prophet Reads Scripture: Allusion in Isaiah 40–66* (Stanford: Stanford University Press, 1998), 6. He adopts the categories of influence and allusion, on the one hand, and intertextuality, on the other hand, from Jay Clayton and Eric Rothstein in their

allusion approach is diachronic in nature, since it tries to establish a specific text or texts to which an allusion refers and then tries to establish the influence that the evoked text has on the alluding text. As a result, there is a clear distinction between the earlier text and the later one, and the author and text are considered important to understanding the dynamic between the texts.

The intertextual approach is synchronic in nature and does not draw a strong distinction between the alluding text and the evoked text, but rather is interested in an analysis which explores the manifold ways that a given text interacts with other texts, commonplace phrases, or other cultural systems in which the text exists. "The intertextual approach relies primarily on structural linguistics and its postmodern heirs in seeing all signs, including those in a literary text, as meaningful only insofar as they stand in relation and opposition to other signs."[72] Here, the text is viewed as largely independent of its author, and so authorial intention is not a concern of such an analysis.

As I indicated in the previous section, I will use elements from both of these approaches, primarily because the author and text are only understood by a reader in a given time and place. All three are important to consider. So, the intentionality and allusion approach, which focuses on author and text, is important for this study because I wish to focus on the relationship between a given text, namely, the Gospel of Mark, and a narrowly defined set of older texts, namely, the PssLam. The Gospel of Mark is rooted in an identifiable historical and social situation[73] that a critic using the intertextual approach might overlook and that might be (and I believe is) important for understanding the interaction between the alluding and evoked texts. However, I am making a choice to read the two texts together to see whether the evoked text as a whole adds to, nuances, or affects the alluding text in any discernible and illuminating way. I will look purposefully for intertextual patterns between the two texts, and in doing so I venture into a more synchronic approach. I believe that a combination of diachronic and synchronic approaches will enable me to offer a richer interpretation of the passion narrative in the Gospel of Mark in light of the PssLam, mainly because synchronic analysis does

---

study, "Figures in the Corpus: Theories of Influence and Intertextuality," in *Influence and Intertextuality in Literary History* (ed. Jay Clayton and Eric Rothstein; Madison: University of Wisconsin Press, 1991), 3–36.

[72] Sommer, *A Prophet Reads Scripture*, 7.

[73] The specifics of this historical and social situation are difficult to determine. As a result, any historical or social context used to interpret the Gospel of Mark must remain at a fairly general level.

not constrain the interpreter to discuss only aspects of the alluding text that are demonstrably intentional with respect to the evoked text. In other words, the synchronic approach offers a bit more freedom to explore the relationship between the alluding text and the evoked text by noticing features of the texts that the author may not have consciously intended to be noticed. However, when I approach the text synchronically I will not stray from the parameters of the diachronic approach with respect to limiting my investigation to the PssLam and to reading the text as much as possible within its historical and cultural context.

Before this study proceeds further, it is necessary to define allusion and to develop and describe a method for identifying evocations with the highest degree of probability feasible. Ziva Ben-Porat defines literary allusion in the following way:

> The literary allusion is a device for the simultaneous activation of two texts. The activation is achieved through the manipulation of a special signal: a sign (simple or complex) in a given text characterized by an additional larger "referent." This referent is always an independent text. The simultaneous activation of the two texts thus connected results in the formation of intertextual patterns whose nature cannot be predetermined.[74]

According to Ben-Porat, indirectness or tacitness is the common base of all allusions, although subsequent critics have moved away from this as a necessary element of an allusion.[75] She goes on to distinguish the term "marker"[76] from "allusion" to indicate that the signal in the text should not be confused with the more complex process of allusion. Identification of the marker begins a four-stage process; the culmination of at least the third stage characterizes an allusion. The four stages are (1) recognition of the marker; (2) identification of the evoked text; (3) modification of the interpretation of the sign in the alluding text; and (4) activation of the evoked text as a whole to form connections between it and the alluding text which are not based on the markers and marked items themselves.[77] We will discuss the last two elements of the process in more detail in the next section. For now, let us concentrate on the first two elements and try to delineate a way of proceeding that will allow for some consistency in identifying the marker and the evoked text.

---

[74] Ben-Porat, "The Poetics of Literary Allusion," 107–8.
[75] See Carmella Perri, "On Alluding," *Poetics* 7 (1978): 289–307; Hebel, "Towards a Descriptive Poetics of Allusion"; and Sommer, *A Prophet Reads Scripture*, 10–17.
[76] For Ben-Porat, the terms "sign" and "marker" seem to be synonymous.
[77] Ben-Porat, "The Poetics of Literary Allusion," 110–11.

In the process of examining a text closely, stages (1) and (2) happen almost simultaneously or alternate back and forth. This happens because, if the text signals something in the mind of a reader, there is an instantaneous impulse to try to recall its origin. A marker that signals an evoked text may be simple or complex, as we mentioned above in quoting Ben-Porat. As Sommer points out, "The sign may be a poetic line or sentence or phrase, or it may consist of a motif, a rhythmic pattern, an idea, or even the form of the work or its title."[78] As a result, the process for identifying a marker is not uniform and oftentimes quite complex. Although particular words or phrases make the evocation of a previous text more certain, one must be open to other elements or complexes of elements in a given text that may act as markers to an outside text. The likelihood of the identification of a marker will depend, in part, on how persuasively a critic can argue for the marker, but in arguing one's case all elements of a given text must be examined before making a judgment. Therefore, an exhaustive list of the categories of elements to be examined cannot be created before one actually begins the analysis, but Sommer's list of elements just cited is a good basic list. An interpreter must be alert to any and all narrative, grammatical, linguistic, and rhetorical elements in a given text. The more experienced and knowledgeable readers will undoubtedly be more skilled at recognizing potential markers in a text.

Once the marker is identified tentatively, always with possible texts in mind, then one can bring in elements from outside the marked text to zero in on a possibly evoked text. For our purposes in dealing with the use of scripture in the Gospel of Mark, one should consider whether or not an allegedly evoked text is used by contemporaries of Mark.[79] If so, then the likelihood in Mark of the marker signaling that evoked text increases, and if the text is used in a similar manner by contemporary authors, then the likelihood increases even more.

All this being said, one may conclude, in the words of Richard Garner, "Poetic allusions – this is part of their power both to charm and

---

[78] Sommer, *A Prophet Reads Scripture*, 11. See also Perri, "On Alluding," 305, and James K. Chandler, "Romantic Allusiveness," *Critical Inquiry* 8 (3, 1982): 480–1. Robert Alter notes that the evoked text may be short (a line or section) or much longer (a whole work or even a corpus), *The Pleasures of Reading in an Ideological Age* (New York: Norton, 1989, 123).

[79] Because of the inability to say for sure where Mark was written, we should be fairly generous when it comes to geographical limits to the literature considered "contemporary to Mark." Since we are interested in the use of Jewish scripture, we should set a cultural limit of the investigation to those who would have considered Jewish scripture as sacred literature, namely, Jews and early Christians.

frustrate – cannot be proved or disproved."[80] The best one can hope to accomplish is to offer varying degrees of certainty with respect to intentionality. A low level of certainty with respect to intentionality need not end the discussion; it simply changes the nature of the inquiry from a diachronic to a synchronic approach and focuses more of the attention on the reader (i.e., the critic) rather than on the author and text.[81] But since this study relies on *both* diachronic and synchronic approaches, we will proceed no further if at the end of our analysis there proves to be a low degree of probability with respect to the author's intention of evoking a previous text.

2.4   Word, verse, context, or text? What to consider in an evocation

Stages (3) and (4) from Ben-Porat's process of allusion determine whether a marker acts as an allusion or not. According to Ben-Porat, unless the text to which the marker refers is identified, then the marker simply signals a vague recollection in the mind of the reader of something outside the text. This would be categorized as an echo[82] rather than an allusion. Once the evoked text is identified, stage (3) entails some modification of the interpretation of the marker in the alluding text. In other words, in most instances a reader is able to understand the marker without recourse to the evoked text, but once the evoked text is identified there is a modification of the marker in light of the evoked text.[83]

Once the marker is re-read in light of the evoked text, the reader may wish to stop there in his or her investigation, but that is not necessary. "Most literary allusions possess the potential for the fourth stage," namely the activation of the evoked text as a whole.[84] This allows the reader to draw a more complex, in-depth and wide-ranging correspondence between the alluding and evoked texts than exists at the location of the marker.[85] The process of doing so need not include the marker or

---

[80] Richard Garner, *From Homer to Tragedy: The Art of Allusion in Greek Poetry* (London: Routledge, 1990), 1.

[81] The role of the critic in a diachronic analysis is also influential in the way one analyzes the text and the conclusions one draws. However, the synchronic approach focuses more overtly on the critic's role and preferences in the analysis.

[82] The term "echo" and its distinction from allusion will be discussed in section 2.5.

[83] Ben-Porat, "The Poetics of Literary Allusion," 110–11.

[84] Ibid., 111. See also the discussion by Perri, "On Alluding," 289–95, which culminates in her working definition of allusion. The last part of the definition states, "the property(ies) evoked modifies the alluding text, and possibly activates further, larger inter- and intratextual patterns of properties with consequent further modification of the alluding text."

[85] Perri argues that allusion is distinguished from other ways of referring to outside texts by its complexity of reference. It denotes and specifies all in one sign; it denotes a concept,

the marked elements of the two texts, but can include other elements that can now be identified as intersections between the texts, unseen before the identification of the evoked text. Again, these elements can include vocabulary, thematic elements, and other narrative dynamics that can be seen as relating the alluding text to the evoked text.[86] The thinking behind this fourth stage, I believe, is that once an author evokes an earlier text, there is the understanding that the alluding text should now be read in light of the evoked text. Once the text is evoked, the reader cannot help but read the alluding text in light of it. For our purposes, the only criterion that can be relied upon when determining to what extent the two texts intersect, again, is whether the connections between the texts add anything to the reading of the alluding text.

2.5   Allusion vs. echo

In light of this description of the process of allusion, we should discuss briefly how some biblical critics think of reference to scripture in the New Testament. With respect to the distinction between "allusion" and "echo," Richard Hays' work comes to mind most quickly. Hays makes little distinction between the two phenomena, but "in general . . . *allusion* is used of obvious intertextual references, *echo* of subtler ones."[87] Sommer makes a more overt distinction between the two terms, which I think is more helpful for our purposes. Following Ben-Porat's idea of allusion not happening until there are intertextual patterns established between the alluding and evoked texts, Sommer defines echo as the phenomenon which signals a preceding text but which has little or no effect on the reading of the marker in the alluding text.[88]

---

object, or person while specifying a set of properties associated with the referent ("On Alluding," 292). I would argue that the properties associated with the referent are not fully realized without a complete reading of both the context of the sign and that of the referent.

[86] Ben-Porat, "The Poetics of Literary Allusion"; see the examples she uses to demonstrate the process on pages 113–16. Most subsequent scholars still rely on Ben-Porat's basic four-stage process in developing their own version of the process of allusion, and these critics do not stray very far from her basic process. See Beth LaNeel Tanner, *The Book of Psalms Through the Lens of Intertextuality* (Studies in Biblical Literature 26; New York: Peter Lang, 2001), 70–2, where she relies heavily on Ben-Porat for her methodology for reading the psalms intertextually. See also Sommer's *A Prophet Reads Scripture*, 10–13; and Hebel, "Towards a Descriptive Poetics of Allusion," 135–64, who modifies Ben-Porat's process, but keeps the basic core of it intact.

[87] Hays, *Echoes of Scripture*, 29.

[88] Sommer, *A Prophet Reads Scripture*, 16. Perri argues that the marker in an allusion acts both in signifying un-allusively, "within the imagined possible world of the alluding text, but through echo also denotes a source text and specifies some discrete, recoverable

Another way to think of allusion and echo is to place them on a spectrum that describes the way a New Testament author can refer to scripture (or some other outside text). Gerd Häfner has identified the following modes of reference: (1) marked quotation, (2) unmarked quotation, (3) allusion, (4) echo, and (5) biblical language.[89] If one thinks of the order of these modes of reference along a spectrum with the left being a high level of probability as to the intentionality of the author and the right being a low level of probability, then allusion falls right in the middle of the spectrum. The less certain one is about the intention of the author to evoke a certain text, the more the evocation can be considered an echo. The lines are blurred between the two, as they are between all the categories (except, perhaps, the first two), so one can understand why Hays does not distinguish between allusion and echo in any sort of systematic way. For our purposes, "allusion" will mean what Ben-Porat defines it as, namely, a process that realizes at least the first three stages of the alluding process – recognition of a marker, identification of the evoked text, and modification of the reading of the marker in the alluding text. "Echo" will mean that stages one and two are realized, but there is little or no certainty of intention and little or no effect on the alluding text.

2.6 The LXX text: translated text, translator's intention, and text reception

There are two ways to proceed when considering a text from the LXX: (1) consider the text at its inception, that is, at the moment of its translation; and (2) look at the text in its reception history. The first procedure assumes what Albert Pietersma has termed the "interlinearity" of the text. This term does not have the same meaning as other common usages of it, but, instead, it refers to the nature of the text as a translated document. At its inception, "the Greek had a dependent and subservient linguistic relationship to its Semitic parent." This interlinear way of thinking of the Greek text "recognizes that unintelligibility of the Greek text *qua Greek text* is one of its inherent characteristics."[90] So any analysis of the Greek text must take into account the Hebrew or Aramaic *Vorlage*, to whatever extent possible. If one wishes to analyze the text with regard to whether

---

property(ies) belonging to the intension [sic] of this source text" ("On Alluding," 295). Here, she blurs the distinction between echo and allusion, much as Hays does.

[89] Gerd Häfner, *"Nützlich zur Belehrung" (2 Tim 3, 16): Die Rolle der Schrift in den Pastoralbriefen im Rahmen der Paulusrezeption* (HBSt; Freiburg: Herder, 2000), 48–63.

[90] Albert Pietersma, *A New English Translation of the Septuagint: The Psalms* (New York: Oxford University Press, 2000), ix.

the translator intentionally interpreted the text for political, social, or theological purposes, then two basic ways have been proposed, still under the rubric of the point of inception of the text: (a) an analysis of the translation of individual Hebrew words or phrases with particular or strange Greek equivalents; and (b) an analysis of the whole of the text in Greek as a Greek text, rather than as a translated text. Most commentators proceed with (a) assuming the nature of the text as Pietersma understands it,[91] but Anneli Aejmelaeus[92] and Ariane Cordes[93] have argued that, although the Greek of the translated text is not "proper" Greek, theological meaning – the focus of Aejmelaeus' interest – arises only through an examination of a given text in its rhetorical whole in Greek. The very process of expressing a Hebrew or Aramaic text in Greek creates a different meaning that can only be discerned by looking at the text as a whole in Greek.

The second process by which one may proceed to analyze a LXX text is to interpret it at some point in its reception history. The extent to which one has recourse to the Hebrew or Aramaic *Vorlage* in considering the reception history depends on the makeup of the audience receiving the text. If there is reason to believe that an ancient critic or audience would have known Hebrew or Aramaic, then one can take the *Vorlage* into account when analyzing the Greek text. If there is little reason to think that the ancient critic or audience would have known Hebrew or Aramaic, then there is little reason to take the *Vorlage* into account. In

---

[91] For example, Emanuel Tov, *The Text Critical Use of the Septuagint in Biblical Research* (2nd edn.; Jerusalem: Simor Ltd, 1997), 48–9. See also Tov, "Theologically Motivated Exegesis Embedded in the Septuagint," in *Proceedings of a Conference at the Annenberg Research Institute May 15–16, 1989* (JQR Supplement; Philadelphia, 1990), 215–33. See also Staffan Olofsson, *God is My Rock: A Study of Translation Technique and Theological Exegesis in the Septuagint* (Stockholm: Almquist & Wiksell, 1990), 2, where he notes that theological exegesis usually means something similar to what Tov defines it as, namely, the introduction of "an interpretation of a phrase or a term in the Hebrew that is at variance with the literal meaning." Olofsson does not think that this definition takes into account the situation of the LXX translators and that some of the "interpretation" can be attributed to unconscious motivation based on the translator's cultural context. He deliberately restricts himself "to the study of conscious theological exegesis reflected in the choice of equivalents, i.e., cases where the translation is more influenced by the theology of the translator than by the meaning of the words in their context."

[92] Anneli Aejmelaeus, "What We Talk about When We Talk about Translation Technique," in *X Congress of the International Organization for Septuagint and Cognate Studies: Oslo 1998* (ed. Bernard A. Taylor; Atlanta: Society of Biblical Literature, 2001), 531–52; and "Translation Technique and the Intention of the Translator," in *On the Trail of the Septuagint Translators* (ed. A. Aejmelaeus; Kampen, The Netherlands: Kok Pharos Publishing House, 1993), 65–77.

[93] Ariane Cordes, "Theologische Interpretation in der Septuaginta: Beobachtungen am Beispiel von Psalm 76 LXX," in *Der Septuaginta-Psalter: Sprachliche und theologische Aspekte* (ed. Erich Zenger; HBSt 32; Freiburg: Herder, 2001), 105–21.

the latter case, the critic of the Greek should proceed to read the text in a way similar to that of the ancient critic or audience, as far as one is able to do this. Here, one can only talk about possible perceptions of the critic or audience, unless one is doing a study on an ancient commentary that deals with a specific LXX text.

The vast majority of Mark's explicit quotations come from the LXX in the form that we have it,[94] and it is most likely that most of his first-century audience would have read in Greek any LXX text referred to in his text without recourse to Hebrew. Therefore, the analysis of any text evoked from the LXX in this study will proceed with those assumptions and attempt to delineate possible perceptions of the Greek text as read by a native Greek speaker of the first century – including grammar, syntax, and rhetorical structure.[95]

3   Structure of this study and summary of the argument

Given the scope and methodological point of view described above, this study will proceed as follows. Chapter 2 will discuss some issues relevant to the study of the PssLam as a sub-genre of the Psalms, as well as the way in which David is associated with the Psalms and the ramifications of this association for the present study. Chapter 3 will examine the possible references to the PssLam in Mark's passion narrative. I will use the list of references from Nestle-Aland's 27th edition of *Novum Testamentum Graece* as a starting-point, but I will also consider references that other New Testament scholars have included in their studies. I will consider only simple evocations, as defined above.

Chapter 4 will discuss the four LXX PssLam in question, namely Psalms 21, 40, 41–2, and 68.[96] In particular, I will perform a close reading of the Greek version of each psalm in an attempt to discern the literary

---

[94] "In at least 19 of 21 cases – however the details of the readings are to be accounted for – the force of the argument or the specifics of the statements depend on the text as preserved in LXX" (Howard Clark Kee, "The Function of Scriptural Quotations in Mark 11–16," in *Jesus und Paulus: Festschrift für Werner Georg Kümmel zum 70. Geburtstag* [ed. E. Earle Ellis and Erich Gräßer; Göttingen: Vandenhoeck & Ruprecht, 1975], 172). Here, Kee is discussing direct citations of the Jewish scriptures in Mark.

[95] "Over the last few years it has been frequently demanded that the Septuagint ought to be studied as a document in its own right. Of course, this can be done . . . if you are interested in the use of the Greek Scriptures in the Christian Church" (Anneli Aejmelaeus, "What We Talk about When We Talk about Translation Technique," 533).

[96] Hereafter, all references to the PssLam in this study are to the LXX, unless otherwise specified. I say four PssLam because, as I will argue in Chapter 3, Psalms 41–2 can and should be thought of as one psalm.

structure and rhetorical dynamics of each in an effort to understand what the psalmist is trying to communicate.

Chapter 5 will discuss the depiction of Jesus in relation to David in the chapters leading up to the passion narrative in Mark, namely, Mark 10–12. As I discussed above, I will argue that Mark maintains Jesus' royal identity by appealing to Davidic imagery, but distances Jesus from David's militaristic aspects in an effort to begin portraying Jesus as a suffering royal figure.

Chapter 6 will discuss each reference to the four PssLam in the passion narrative of Mark. Using the approach developed above, I will argue that Mark's two-fold appeal to scripture in chapter 14[97] as a justification for Jesus' suffering and death is a complex phenomenon and constitutes a general appeal to scripture rather than to a specific text or texts for the reader to turn to for understanding of Jesus' suffering and death. Since these appeals to scripture are general, one must include Mark's references to the PssLam in the overall presentation of Jesus' suffering and death. The PssLam to which Mark refers in chapters 14 and 15 reveal a David who challenges God's role in his suffering, who searches for understanding of his suffering in light of his past relationship with God, and who finally attempts to shame God to act on his behalf only because he is suffering. Mark alludes to these PssLam in reference to Jesus, and therefore David's concerns become woven into the depiction of Jesus. Therefore, the general appeal to scripture to justify Jesus' suffering and death, which includes the PssLam, includes a challenge to God's role in his suffering and death.

I will also argue two additional points. First, although it is generally agreed that Mark tells his story with an underlying apocalyptic framework in mind, reading David's challenge to God as part of Jesus' going "as it is written of him" calls into question the necessity for Jesus' death within an apocalyptic framework of meaning, or at least scholarly constructs of such a framework that posit the Messiah's death as a means to an end. By the time that Jesus' death is narrated in Mark 15, the voice of the lamenting David who challenges God's decision to allow his suffering becomes loud enough to question the necessity for Jesus' death within an apocalyptic scenario where Jesus plays the role of Messiah. Second, in light of the previous point, I will argue against the notion that the Servant of Isaiah 53 offers the best model for Jesus' suffering and death in Mark. After Jesus' mocking and beatings, the only plausible evocation of Isaiah

---

[97] The first is found in Mark 14:21, "For the Son of Man goes just as it is written about him," and the second is found in 14:49, "Daily I was with you in the temple teaching and you did not arrest me; but so that the scriptures may be fulfilled."

53 in Mark 15 is in 15:27, which refers to Jesus being crucified inbetween two thieves. Most commentators think that this is a reference to Isa 53:12, which states that the Servant is numbered among transgressors. However, the evocations of the PssLam in question are numerous in Mark 14–15, with three virtual quotations from three of these psalms, and Jesus actually speaks the words of two of them. Given the strong royal overtones of the depiction of Jesus in these chapters, it makes sense to turn to the suffering David of these psalms instead of to the Suffering Servant from Isaiah 53 when trying to understand Jesus' suffering and death.

Finally, Chapter 7 will discuss some issues that I think might be affected by the main points of the study. I will first consider whether or not the characterization of Jesus as a divine warrior is justified for Mark. Here, I will examine a bit more closely Joel Marcus' *The Way of the Lord* and his argument that Jesus is a divine warrior who conquers through his death rather than through violence. Second, I will discuss the rending of the Temple veil and the centurion's statement just after Jesus' death. In particular, I will explore whether or not the rending of the veil resolves the Christology of Mark's Gospel and whether the centurion's statement should be regarded as a positive confession of faith or a negative mocking of Jesus' death. Finally, I will discuss the relationship between the resurrection and the suffering and death of Jesus in Mark. Obviously, all of these comments will have to be brief, so I will offer what I think would be worth further research.

2

ISSUES IN THE STUDY OF THE PSALMS OF INDIVIDUAL LAMENT IN RELATIONSHIP TO THE GOSPEL OF MARK

Given the fact that I will be examining the LXX version of each PsLam referred to in Mark's passion narrative, there are some important issues that need to be discussed with regard to form and content of these psalms before we can proceed with the study. In the first section, I will begin by discussing three major form critics who have formed the basis for studying the PssLam for subsequent researchers. Then I will discuss the limitations of form criticism with respect to the interests of this study. In doing so, I will also reconsider the traditional list of PssLam agreed upon by most critics and form my own list based upon what I think the fundamental characteristics of the PssLam are. Finally, I will discuss a problem that has vexed critics of the PssLam for several generations, namely, that of the relationship between the lament and praise/thanksgiving sections of many PssLam.

In the second section, I will discuss the way that, in the ancient world, David was associated with the Psalms in general and with the PssLam in particular, and then what ramifications this will have for the present study.

1   Form-critical issues in the PssLam

1.1   Form critics on the PssLam

Hermann Gunkel's work on form criticism stands at the beginning of this movement in biblical studies. It is his *Einleitung in die Psalmen* (Eng. trans. *Introduction to the Psalms*), completed by Joachim Begrich and published posthumously, that gives the most systematic formulation of his form-critical insights on the PssLam.[1] Familiar by now, Gunkel's main

---

[1]   The following discussion of Gunkel's work will be limited to chapter 6 of *Einleitung in die Psalmen: Die Gattungen der religiösen Lyrik Israels* (Eng. trans. *Introduction to the Psalms: The Genres of the Religious Lyric of Israel* [Completed by Joachim Begrich; trans. James D. Nogalski; Macon, GA: Mercer University Press, 1998]). Hereafter, only the English will be cited.

contributions to biblical studies are the recognition of the literary nature of biblical texts and the relationship between their social and cultural situation (*Sitz im Leben*) and their literary forms. With regard to the Pss-Lam, which he labels "Klagelieder des Einzelnen" (individual laments), he makes several key observations. First, they are the most common and widely attested type of psalm in the Psalter. This category is not limited to full psalms only, but includes parts of psalms of mixed form. Therefore, he asserts with confidence, "The individual complaint songs form the *basic material* of the Psalter. They stand out from other genres by their number alone."[2] Among the psalms of this type he includes Psalms 3, 5, 6, 7, 13, 17, 22, 25, 26, 27:7–14, 28, 31, 35, 38, 39, 42, 43, 51, 54, 55, 56, 57, 59, 61, 63, 64, 69, 70, 71, 86, 88, 102, 109, 120, 130, 140, 141, 142, and 143.[3] This list remains the standard list for form critics, even up to the present day.[4]

His basic methodology is comparative, with the purpose of finding generic features that allow the psalms to be categorized into groups. E. S. Gerstenberger synthesizes Gunkel's long comparative analysis well and generates the following list of basic elements:

> Invocation (appellation and initial plea or petition)
> Complaint (descriptive, reproachful, petitionary)
> Confession of sin or assertion of innocence
> Affirmation of confidence
> Plea or petition for help
> Imprecation against enemies
> Acknowledgment of divine response
> Vow or pledge
> Hymnic elements, blessings
> Anticipated thanksgiving[5]

Amidst the descriptive and comparative analysis of the content of these psalms, Gunkel demonstrates that the *Sitz im Leben* was most likely the

---

[2] Ibid., 122. Emphasis is Gunkel's.

[3] Ibid., 121. He goes on to list many other parts of psalms as well as Lamentations 3, parts of Jeremiah, Isaiah, Jonah, Ben Sira, Ezra, Job, Genesis, Deuteronomy, 1 and 2 Samuel, 1 and 2 Kings, 1 Chronicles, Tobit, Judith, and Susanna.

[4] See E. S. Gerstenberger's slightly different list on page 14 (*Psalms; Part 1: With an Introduction to Cultic Poetry* [FOTL 14; Grand Rapids, MI: Eerdmans, 1988]), which is then adopted by Adela Yarbo Collins ("The Appropriation of the Psalms of Individual Lament by Mark," in *The Scriptures in the Gospels* [ed. C. M. Tuckett; Leuven: Leuven University Press, 1997], 224).

[5] Gerstenberger, *Psalms; Part 1*, 12. Gunkel's analysis and description is found in *Introduction to the Psalms*, 152–98.

cultic life of Israel, particularly in the royal Temple in Jerusalem. "It has been clear from the beginning of this study, in other words for decades, that the genre of individual complaint songs belongs originally to certain *worship activities*."[6] He draws this conclusion from the many references to liturgical practice,[7] the mention of prayer in the Temple,[8] the time of prayer and its coordination with the time of sacrifice,[9] and the idea that the מנחה and the incense offering were already associated with the complaint songs, such as in Ps 141:2, "even though this passage contains the poem itself in place of the sacrifice."[10]

The form-critical insights concerning the general features and the cultic setting that Gunkel expressed have formed the basis of most subsequent research on the Psalms, whether in concord with Gunkel or in contrast to him. Joachim Begrich, Gunkel's student and the one who completed *Introduction to the Psalms*, certainly carried the torch passed on to him by Gunkel. Begrich's most relevant contribution to form-critical studies is associated with the *Heilsorakel* presumed in the liturgy or liturgies during which the PssLam were performed. Here, Begrich posited, the priest or liturgical official would communicate some indication of response from God to the pleas of the suppliant. The suppliant would have some experience of salvation, presumably, or at least believed that God had heard his or her cry and would come to his or her aid in a timely manner.[11]

Sigmund Mowinckel, Gunkel's younger contemporary, adopted both Gunkel's insights on the cultic setting and the insights of Begrich regarding the salvation oracle, but he put much more emphasis on the cultic setting than either Gunkel or Begrich. His interests resided in describing a general cultic setting for each psalm, reconstructing the use of the Psalms in the cult as specifically as possible.[12] Based on these interests, he viewed form criticism as insufficient for what he desired to do, so he went beyond

---

[6] Gunkel, *Introduction to the Psalms*, 123. Gunkel's emphasis.

[7] For example, "Purify me with hyssop, that I might be pure" (Ps 51:9). See ibid., 123.

[8] For example, "But I, by your great grace, may enter your house, bow down in worship before you before your holy temple" (Ps 5:8), and "'Look' when I raise my hands to your holy sanctuary" (Ps 28:2). See ibid., 124.

[9] For example, "O LORD, in the morning you hear my voice; in the morning I plead my case to you, and watch" (Ps 5:3, NRSV; ibid., 124).

[10] Ibid., 125.

[11] See Joachim Begrich, "Das priesterliche Heilsorakel," *ZAW* 52 (1934): 81–92.

[12] See Sigmund Mowinckel, *The Psalms in Israel's Worship* (trans. D. R. Ap-Thomas; Nashville: Abingdon Press, 1962), I:29ff. See also Brevard S. Childs, *Introduction to the Old Testament as Scripture* (Philadelphia: Fortress, 1979), 508–11, for an excellent discussion of the basic development of form-critical scholarship on the Book of Psalms.

it to study the Psalms from what he calls "the cult functional approach."[13] What he developed was an extremely detailed picture of what he calls the "Enthronement Festival of Yahweh," based on both internal analysis of the Psalms and the Canaanite festival of the New Year and renewal of life.[14] With regard to the PssLam, he performed a similar analysis, in that he tried to reconstruct the liturgical rites that would have given rise to these psalms. He concluded that the most likely ritual would have been one that dealt with sickness.[15] However, he did concede that this occasion might be too narrow to account for the imagery in the PssLam, so he considered other possible occasions such as personal piety, sinful confession and purification, and political or military difficulties.[16]

1.2   The limitations of form criticism of the PssLam

The influence of these three form-critical scholars remains foundational for most Psalms critics. However, there are some shortcomings that must be addressed, especially with regard to the present study. Gerstenberger's list of general characteristics reproduced above gives a clear indication of the style and bias in understanding the PssLam from a form-critical perspective. The list contains the most typical sections of the PssLam as a group, but it does little to account for the relationship among these parts. The main reason for this is that not every psalm has every basic element from the list, nor does every psalm have them in the same order, and so there is little that one can say from a form-critical perspective with regard to the *literary* function of each of these psalms as a whole. This must be left to the treatment of each individual psalm. But even Gerstenberger's form-critical analysis of an individual psalm does not address the literary question fully. Rather, there is a reliance on the liturgical setting to understand the meaning and the structure of each. In his treatment of Psalm 22, Gerstenberger makes the following comment:

> The prayer itself shows rich, if not dramatic, liturgical movement . . . Overemphasis on literary structure tends to obscure the ritual function of a psalm. Psalm 22 is a cultic prayer, the main

---

[13] Mowinckel, *The Psalms in Israel's Worship*, xxxi. Mowinckel's influence regarding the reconstruction of the exact cultic setting of each psalm continued through the rise of the "myth and ritual school," apparently adopted from similar studies in Classics research. However, most scholars now believe that such detailed reconstruction is excessively speculative, and by and large it has been abandoned. See Childs, *Introduction to the Old Testament as Scripture*, 510, for a brief discussion of this trend.

[14] Mowinckel, *The Psalms in Israel's Worship*, xxxi and I:106–92.

[15] Ibid., II:4–16.   [16] Ibid., II:17–18.

elements of which are complaint *(a)*, confidence *(b)*, petition *(c)*, and thanksgiving *(d)*, arranged in the following sequence: *a b a b c a c d*.[17]

Further on in his analysis of Psalm 22, he seeks to explain anomalies in the flow of the psalm by appealing to the hypothesis of later accretion or augmentation as a result of a long history of liturgical use. He also explains the anomalies by consistent reference to liturgical necessities and the like.[18] At one point, he addresses the abrupt scene change from verse 3 to verse 4: "This change of perspective in itself is sufficient proof that considerations of liturgy, but not of logic, psychology, or aesthetics, are preeminent in Psalm 22."[19]

The insights that Gerstenberger offers show that form criticism is primarily interested in making sense of the psalms with little regard to the literary integrity of the psalm itself. Underlying Gunkel's development of form criticism was a desire to get back to the original, pure form of each type of psalm, although there is no explicit statement of this claim in Gerstenberger's work. As accretion and augmentation happen, there is a degradation of genre and a dilution of its power, as is clear from this statement of Gunkel's:

> The complaint song of the individual begins in the confines of the cult, and lives from the material and the mood which the cult suggested. It attains size and depth when it is dissolved from the cult. However, this dissolution also becomes the core of its fall. The boundaries between it and the other genres are lost, and mixtures occur. Finally, reflection nests in the genre in place of dynamic perception and immediate contemplation, *corroding* the genre completely.[20]

For Gunkel, the PssLam, when coupled with other discernible forms, no longer have the efficacy that they once had in their pure form.

But where does this leave the PssLam for our purposes, namely, the Gospel of Mark's use of the PssLam at a time when there is no direct evidence for continued cultic use of these psalms? Do they still remain powerful and meaningful for future generations long after their original purpose has passed? They must have, or else they would not have survived as meaningful documents. And they must have made sense *literarily as individual wholes* if they were to survive their probable separation from the cultic life of Israel. To consider these possibilities, form criticism has limited value as an interpretive tool. The insights with regard to the

---

[17] Gerstenberger, *Psalms: Part 1*, 109.   [18] Ibid., 110–12.
[19] Ibid., 110.   [20] Gunkel, *Introduction to the Psalms*, 197–8. Italics are mine.

original cultic purpose of each element and the general insights about the genre as a whole cannot be the driving force for interpreting the PssLam in the late Second Temple period, not only because of the inherently speculative nature of the enterprise, but also because it is more important for our purposes to interpret these psalms in their entirety as the author of Mark and his audiences would have read or heard them. However, as a heuristic device, form-critical categories can still be useful, as are some insights from particular form critics such as Gerstenberger.

The second major critique of form criticism that is relevant for this project relates to its tendency to impose meaning on individual psalms based on the generalities it has discerned with regard to a group of psalms. More specifically, the cultic setting for the PssLam has so dominated form-critical research that other possibilities are rarely considered when interpreting an individual psalm. The most obvious example of this tendency is the salvation oracle that is presumed to have been given in the liturgical rite in which the psalm was used. The hypothesis of such an oracle goes a long way in explaining how certain sections of the psalm cohere. However, after a long discussion of the oracle in general terms, Gunkel says in a footnote, "In our texts [i.e., the PssLam], *the oracle is almost always lacking.* Only Ps 62:12ff concludes a similar poem with a revelation which the poet had just received."[21] But it is not clear that Psalm 62 is even a PsLam. It appears in Gunkel's list, but Gerstenberger does not include it. Westermann agrees with Gunkel in saying that the appeal to an oracle of salvation is "not a sufficient explanation of these Psalms."[22] However, he goes on to argue, "There is much evidence . . . in the Psalms themselves [that the oracle was received by the petitioner] . . . The one who speaks now has been transformed by God's having heard his supplication."[23] Instead of trying to argue for the existence of the oracle within or outside the psalm, Westermann looks for the effects of the oracle in the psalm, and he locates it in the way that the psalmist acknowledges God's response to his supplication. Gerstenberger concurs: "ACKNOWLEDGMENT OF DIVINE RESPONSE, on the other hand, seems to refer back to an ORACLE OF SALVATION, which, as a matter of fact, rarely occurs within the Psalter (cf. Pss 12:6; 35:3; 91:3–13) but has been recognized principally in Deutero-Isaiah."[24] But only Psalms 12 and 35 are in his PssLam list. The hypothesis of the occurrence of an oracle of salvation on the part of Gunkel, Begrich, Westermann, and Gerstenberger is unnecessary in describing the way a particular psalm functions. Perhaps the original

---

[21] Ibid., 125. Italics are mine.
[22] Westermann, *Praise and Lament in the Psalms* (Atlanta: John Knox, 1981), 65.
[23] Ibid., 70.   [24] Gerstenberger, *Psalms: Part 1*, 13.

setting of some psalms included some sort of divine oracle, but to impose this possibility on every PsLam pre-determines the meaning of at least a portion of each PsLam without consideration of the specificities of each psalm.

If the PssLam are going to live up to this form-critical label, the content of the psalms ought to reflect their name. So, the basic criterion for discerning whether a particular psalm is a PsLam should be the presence of a lament at minimum, and the lament should be the dominant element of the psalm. A lament is not just an idle complaint from a destitute person for the sake of venting one's feelings. Nor is it a simple petition for God to aid the psalmist in his difficulty. Instead, it is a literary expression of emotion with vivid descriptions of the psalmist's desperate situation primarily directed toward God in an attempt to elicit sympathy, response, and deliverance from the situation. In other words, the lament acts as an indirect but vivid and serious form of petition to God,[25] with the purpose of trying to persuade God to act on behalf of the psalmist.[26] Without this lament, the psalm should be excluded from consideration as a PsLam. As Gerstenberger asserts, the Plea or Petition is "the very heart of a complaint song."[27] Inasmuch as the lament functions as a petition, the PssLam revolve around the lament, and the other components of the psalm are conditioned by it. With this in mind, Gunkel's list should be emended to include only Psalms 6, 7, 12, 13, 17, 22, 25, 27, 28, 31, 35, 38, 39, 41, 42–3, 54–7, 59, 64, 69, 86, 88, 102, 109, 120, 140, 142, and 143.[28]

1.3   The relationship between the lament and the praise/thanksgiving in the PssLam

An element in many PssLam is an expression of praise or thanksgiving. How one should deal with this element in relation to the rest of a given PsLam has vexed commentators since the rise of form criticism. One of

---

[25] Gerstenberger says, "A COMPLAINT pictures the plight of the supplicant, sometimes in drastic words and metaphors, to remind Yahweh of his responsibilities" (ibid., 13).

[26] Tod Linafelt comes to a similar conclusion about the nature of the lament in Lamentations. See especially his treatment of the mixture of genres in chapters 1 and 2 of Lamentations on pages 49–58 of *Surviving Lamentations: Catastrophe, Lament, and Protest in the Afterlife of a Biblical Book* (Chicago: University of Chicago Press, 2000).

[27] Gerstenberger, *Psalms: Part 1*, 13.

[28] This list omits Psalms 3, 5, 11, 26, 51, 61, 63, 70, 71, 130, and 141 from Gunkel's list. It also omits these psalms plus Psalms 4, 11, 65, 66, 67, and 68 from Gerstenberger's list. It adds Psalms 12 and 41 to Gunkel's list. Psalms 70 and 71 are borderline cases, because they each include a small lament, but the lament is not dominant and therefore makes these psalms less similar to the rest of the PssLam that have laments as their driving aspect.

the most important aspects of the analysis of LXX Psalms 21, 40, 41–2, and 68 will be discerning how the praise or thanksgiving sections of the psalms fit with the lament sections of the psalms. The relationship between these sections will be determined individually for each of these psalms, but some general comments are in order with regard to this problem. Four solutions to the problem for all PssLam will now be discussed.

(1) Hermann Gunkel was the first to notice this common characteristic of the PssLam. He argued that originally the psalms of lament were a pure form, and only subsequently were the thanksgiving or praise sections added as the original form was changed or corrupted.[29] This could explain the presence of these sections, but it does not go very far to explain their function in the overall psalm once they were supposedly added to the lament form. Recall that his student Begrich developed Gunkel's thoughts on this subject and pointed to an experience of deliverance or prayer answered in the form of an oracle from God through the presiding cultic official (i.e., the *Heilsorakel*).

(2) As pointed out above, Sigmund Mowinckel took Gunkel's form-critical insights, especially his conclusions about the cultic *Sitz im Leben*, and developed a very detailed reconstruction of the use of the psalms in various liturgical situations.[30] Along with Gunkel's proposed *Sitz im Leben*, Mowinckel adopts Begrich's notion of the *Heilsorakel* as the unifying factor between the lament and the thanksgiving/praise/vow section of the PssLam.[31] Some subsequent commentators have adopted his hypothesis of a cultic *Sitz im Leben* and used it to explain the interaction of the lament and thanksgiving sections of PssLam. A classic example of this

[29] See the discussion in section 1.2 above, especially the long quotation showing Gunkel's devolutional perspective (p. 44).

[30] "We have a liturgical composition, forming (part of) the text for an organically connected series of cultic acts. Thus the psalms of lamentation with their oracles and final thanksgivings correspond to a series of ritual acts. We must suppose the psalms to be spoken by a man or by a representative of a congregation in actual or threatened distress, and to accompany the sacrifice or the rites of purification. The oracle is spoken by the cultic official on duty, the priest or the temple prophet, and it announces that Yahweh has accepted the sacrifice. And then the thanksgiving of the worshipper may follow (see Ps. 12), or the festal hymn may turn back to the oracle and build up the doxology and the expression of confidence in victory on the basis of the oracle, as in Ps. 75" (Mowinckel, *The Psalms in Israel's Worship*, 75–6).

[31] However, Mowinckel does accept Gunkel's notion of disintegration of the older, pure forms in some cases. "It cannot be denied that in the youngest psalmography we sometimes come across a mixing of the formative elements, which must be characterized as a disintegration of the old species of style, a failing of sensibility as to the original connexion between the cultic situation and the true purpose of the psalm on the one hand, and as to form and leitmotivs on the other. . . In these cases there is very often no question of a new creation in the sphere of style and poetry but simply of deficient liturgical feeling and taste" (ibid., 77).

is Peter Craigie's analysis of Psalm 22 in which he posits the following scenario: "The mixture of forms and types of language suggests strongly that the text of Psalm 22 is the basis of a liturgy, in which the worshiper moves from lament to prayer, and finally to praise and thanksgiving."[32] From this beginning-point, he assumes the liturgy in somewhat specific terms, reads the Hebrew syntax of verses 22–3 with a salvation oracle assumed, and uses the oracle as the interpretive clue to the structure of the liturgy as reflected in the psalm.

> The words come in such striking contrast to the preceding lament and prayer, that one must presuppose the declaration of an oracle . . . announcing healing and health, after the prayer (vv 20–22b), which gives rise to this sudden declaration of confidence. In the praise which follows, the individual worshiper twice makes reference to the congregation (vv 23, 26) that forms the larger context of the liturgical proceedings. The change of person and of tone in the final section (vv 28–32) indicates the congregational response and conclusion to the liturgy.[33]

He then goes on to claim that the psalm reflects the healing experience of the liturgy for the one who wrote the psalm or for the one who uses it in a similar liturgy subsequent to its composition. The explanation of the transition from lament and prayer to thanksgiving, then, is the reception of a priestly oracle "favorable to his plea."[34]

(3) Claus Westermann takes a different view of the PssLam from that of either Gunkel or Mowinckel. He follows Gunkel's cultic *Sitz im Leben*, but rejects Mowinckel's radicalization of it. Mowinckel "mistakenly placed the weight of the question totally upon the cultic events and practices underlying the Psalms."[35] He critiques Mowinckel's attribution of a number of varied psalms to a particular enthronement festival. With regard to the individual lament, "the lament is a phenomenon of

---

[32] Peter C. Craigie, *Psalms 1–50* (WBC 19; Waco, TX: Word Books, 1983) 197.

[33] Ibid., 198.

[34] Ibid. See also Gerstenberger, *Psalms: Part 1*, 13, "Likewise, Vow and ANTICIPATED THANKSGIVING are reactions to the assurance of divine help experienced during the worship ceremony." However, Gerstenberger recognizes the complexity of the Hebrew syntax and a possible corruption of the text at verse 22. He therefore nuances his interpretation of the rest of the psalm, leaving open the possibility that the psalmist only anticipates an answer, and the rest of the psalm is more of a vow of thanksgiving rather than an actual thanksgiving (112). See Chapter 4 of the present study for a more detailed discussion of the syntax of both the MT Ps 22:22 and the LXX Ps 21:22.

[35] Westermann, *Praise and Lament in the Psalms*, 165.

human existence which received its special, one may even say its peculiar character in the cult, but which nevertheless extends beyond it and which therefore must be investigated in terms of its wider occurrence as well."[36] The fundamental structure of the lament is that the lamenter is never isolated in the psalms. There is always God and there are always the "others." The relationships among these three – the lamenter, the others, and God – is not always the same, but the three elements are always present.

Westermann tries to place the lament in its proper position in the pattern of experience of God in Israel's history. He focuses less on the liturgical aspects of the lament psalms and more on the idea that lament is integral to the following pattern: Pre-history, Distress, Call for help, God listens, God saves, Praise of God. The lament expresses the distress and cry for help – and implicitly the fact that God listens and saves – within this pattern. Without the lament, the fundamental pattern of relationship between God and Israel (including the individual in the psalms) is not accurately represented and means nothing. So praise of God must have lament preceding it. On the other hand, lament is meaningless without praise:

> There is not a single psalm of lament that stops with lamentation. Lamentation has no meaning in and of itself . . . This transition [from lament to petition to praise in several combinations] in the structure of the psalm is rooted in the lament's function as an appeal . . . Understood in this way, the structure of the psalm of lament, which enables us to see the path leading to an alleviation of suffering, is one of the most powerful witnesses to the experience of God's activity in the Old Testament . . . Lamentation is turned into praise at the response to being saved (as in Psalm 22 especially).[37]

In the PssLam, "the transition is shown at the conclusion of the Psalm, which either already anticipates the saving intervention of God with a vow of praise, or in a totally different way points to a change which has taken place during the course of the Psalm itself."[38]

(4) Walter Brueggemann follows Westermann in that he rejects the need to consider the original social setting of the Psalms as the cult of Israel in order to interpret the psalms. Instead, like Westermann, he is interested in relating the genres of the Psalms to each other within wider

[36] Ibid., 168.
[37] Claus Westermann, "The Role of Lament in the Theology of the Old Testament," trans. Richard N. Soulen, *Int* 28 (1974): 26–7.
[38] Westermann, *Praise and Lament in the Psalms*, 267.

theological and existential categories. He is interested in the larger sphere of human–divine relationship as mirrored in the Psalms, which allows him to make an existential connection with the modern situation. He then uses Paul Ricoeur's three-fold notion of orientation, dis-orientation, and new orientation as the overarching categories in which each psalm can be put. The psalms of orientation are descriptive praise to celebrate the ordered world and a trustworthy God. The psalms of dis-orientation include the traditional PssLam; they describe the loss of the ordered world and call God to action. The psalms of new orientation use declarative praise to recount how God acted to overcome the distress of the person praying. He does not address individual psalms in any sort of form-critical detail, because his overall purpose is not to analyze particular psalms. Instead, he is interested in painting with broad strokes the theological picture of the Psalter as a whole, so that modern readers can make sense of it in a synthetic way.[39]

Although I have some disagreements with Westermann's position, I affirm the move that both he and Brueggemann have moved away from trying to make sense of the PssLam in terms of a cultic background. They do so for specifically theological purposes, the merits and shortcomings of which can be debated, but the idea that there are ways to make sense of each PsLam literarily as a whole is laudable. Since there is no evidence of cultic rituals of healing using the Psalms at the time the Gospel of Mark was written, there is no sense in using the insights from form criticism in this matter in order to make sense of the transition from lament to thanksgiving in these psalms.

A brief consideration of the psalms in my list of PssLam shows that there are clearly some psalms that indicate an answer by God to the pleas of the psalmist, and therefore one or more of the solutions described above can work to unite the thanksgiving or praise section to the rest of the psalm.[40] However, 26 out of 31 PssLam do not have a clear answer by God to the psalmist's pleas, and so the thanksgiving or praise in these psalms, if present, does not function in response to God's answer. Instead of the solutions described above, I propose that the factor that unites the praise or thanksgiving to the rest of the psalm is the psalmist's effort to elicit response from God. The "thanksgiving" or "praise" section is not *actual* thanksgiving or praise *after* being heard by God. Instead, it is a promise to do these things *if* God responds to the psalmist. In other words,

---

[39] See Walter Brueggemann, *The Psalms in the Life of Faith* (ed. Patrick D. Miller; Minneapolis: Fortress, 1995).

[40] These are Psalms 6, 28, 31, 54, and 56.

the praise is conditional and dependent on God's response to the pleas of the psalmist and therefore functions as a persuasive rhetorical device to convince God to act on behalf of the psalmist.[41] This position differs from those of Westermann and Gerstenberger, who consider the praise section a vow of praise, because they both assume that the psalmist has some experience of deliverance, either actual or felt. I do not assume such an experience, but instead I assume that the psalmist still perceives himself to be persecuted, oppressed, or otherwise suffering and therefore in need of God's help. This general principle must and will be tested with each PsLam considered for this study.

2   David, the PssLam and the Gospel of Mark

A key part of the argument of this study will be based upon the thesis that Jesus is depicted in Davidic terms with respect to the PssLam. I will discuss the Davidic superscripts of the Psalms in detail in Chapter 4, but for now it is enough to say that they contributed to the idea that David was the author of the book of Psalms, a belief widely held at the time of Mark's Gospel. This section will discuss the purported Davidic authorship of the Psalms, the relationship between David, the PssLam, and the Gospels, and, finally, the relationship between David and the Gospel of Mark.

2.1   Davidic authorship of the Psalms

What is clear is that as the Psalms moved away from their original usage, and the Psalter was compiled and redacted, David became an increasingly important figure with regard to the Psalms. As early as the Book of Chronicles, the Chronicler "presupposes an established corpus of psalmody associated with David."[42] The addition of Davidic superscripts in the

---

[41] Konrad Schaefer says, "Agony in the personal complaint is alleviated by cries for help and incentives for God to intervene. The psalmist pleads innocence and pledges fidelity (17:3–5; 26:1–8, 11–12) and trust (13:5; 25:1–2) to motivate God on his or her behalf. Appeals are made to God's *hesed*, the loyalty which characterizes God's covenant with Israel." However, he does not carry this idea through to the places where "the psalmist changes key." Instead, he reads the rest of these psalms as expressions of confidence or certainty that God has heard the prayer. He does admit "the reason for the change in mood remains obscure." See his *Psalms* (Berit Olam Studies in Hebrew Narrative and Poetry; Collegeville, MN: The Liturgical Press, 2001), 356.

[42] Margaret Daly-Denton, *David in the Fourth Gospel: The Johannine Reception of the Psalms* (AGJU 47; Leiden: Brill, 2000), 73. See 1 Chr 16:7, where David commands Asaph and his kindred to sing praises to God. What follows are excerpts from Psalms 105, 96, and 106. Later in chapters 23 and 25, David assigns specific groups to sacred worship duties; the singing of psalms is among the duties given to the sons of Asaph, Heman, and Jeduthun.

Hebrew *Vorlage* carried over into the Old Greek and then further on in subsequent transmissions of the original Greek translation. By the time of the Dead Sea Scrolls, David was viewed as a prolific composer of psalms. The famous passage from 11QPs[a] xxvii, 2–11 reads:

> And David, son of Jesse, was wise, and a light like the light of the sun, /and/ learned, and discerning, and perfect in all his paths before God and men. And YHWH gave him a discerning and enlightened spirit. And he wrote psalms: three thousand six hundred; and songs to be sung before the altar over the perpetual offering of every day, for all the days of the year: three hundred and sixty-four; and for the sabbath offerings: fifty-two songs; and for the offering of the first days of the months, and for all the days of the festivals, and for the <Day> of Atonement: thirty songs. And all the songs which he spoke were four hundred and forty-six. And songs to perform over the possessed: four. The total was four thousand and fifty. All these he spoke through (the spirit of) prophecy which had been given to him from before the Most High.[43]

This passage is significant for several reasons. Not only is David considered a prolific writer of psalms and songs, he also has written them for the liturgical life of Israel, healing purposes, and cultic purposes. The description of his authorship of these psalms and songs follows the description of David as wise, discerning, enlightened, learned, and perfect in his paths before God and humans. So it seems that his ability to write these psalms and songs is a direct outgrowth of his God-given qualities. Furthermore, when he spoke these psalms and songs, he did so by means of the spirit

---

[43] The Hebrew reads:

ויהי דויד בן ישי חכם ואור כאור השמש 'סופר 3 ונבון ותמים בכול דרכיו לפני אל ואנשים 2
ויתן 4 לו אלהמםוררנרתה־לפע רוח נבונה ואורה ויכתוב תהלים 5 שלושת אלפים ושש מאות
ושיר לשורר לפני המזבח על עולת 6 התמיד לכול יום ויום לכול ימי השנה ארבעה וששים
ושל וש 7 מאות ולקורבן השבתות שנים וחמשים שיר ולקורבן ראשי 8 החודשים ולכול ימי
המועדות ולייאועם הכפורים של ושים שיר 9 ויהי כול השיר אשר דבר ששה ואראעבעים וארבע
מאות ושיר 10 לנגן על הפנועים ארבעה ויהי הכול ארבעת אלפים וחמשים 11 כול אלה
דבר בנבואה אשר נתן לו מלפני העליון

The text and translation are from F. G. Martinez and E. J. C. Tigchelaar, eds., *The Dead Sea Scrolls Study Edition* (Leiden, Grand Rapids, MI: Brill and Eerdmans, 1997), II:1179. 11QPs[a] has been paleographically dated to the first half of the first century CE by James H. Charlesworth and James A. Sanders in "More Psalms of David," in *OTP* II:611–24. See Daly-Denton, *David in the Fourth Gospel*, 70, for a brief discussion of this text.

of prophecy given to him by God. These are remarkably diverse claims about one man, however special he is.[44]

Josephus also mentions that David was a prolific composer of songs. In the following passage, Josephus presents a Hellenized David "to elicit from the cultivated world respect for the much calumniated Jewish people."[45]

> David, being now free from wars and dangers, and enjoying profound peace from this time on, composed songs and hymns to God (ᾠδαὶ εἰς τὸν θεὸν καὶ ὕμνοι) in varied meters – some he made in trimeters, and others in pentameters. He also made musical instruments and instructed the Levites how to use them in praising God on the so-called Sabbath day.[46]

Although this passage does not specifically say that David composed the Psalter, or comment on the number of songs and hymns he composed, it is likely that Josephus knew the tradition of David as author of the Psalms.

Finally, Philo talks about David's musicianship, but unlike the quotations from Josephus and 11QPs above, he connects it directly with a psalm (Psalm 36), so there is a clear relationship between David's musicianship and the Psalter. Daly-Denton points out that "the memory of David's dance before the Ark (cf. 2 Sam 6:14) has clearly influenced"[47] the following passage:

> Once, after taking a sheer draught of this bright joy [of the worship and service of the Only Wise], a member indeed of Moses' fellowship, not found among the indifferent, [David] spake aloud in hymns of praise, and addressing his own mind cried, "Delight in the Lord" [Ps 36:4], moved by the utterance to an ecstasy of the love that is heavenly and Divine . . . while his whole mind is snatched up in a holy frenzy by a Divine possession, and he finds his gladness in God alone.[48]

These last two passages from Josephus and Philo corroborate the clear assertion in 11QPs that David was the author of many psalms.

---

[44] See Mark 12:36 || Matt 22:43 || Luke 20:42; Acts 1:16; 2:25, 31, 34; Rom 4:7ff for the view that David was author of the Psalms.

[45] Emil Schürer, *The History of the Jewish People in the Age of Jesus Christ* (3 vols.; Edinburgh: T & T Clark, 1973–87), I:48.

[46] Josephus, *Ant.* VII, 305. Trans. H. St. J. Thackery and Ralph Marcus, *Josephus: Jewish Antiquities* (LCL, 281, vol. V; Cambridge, MA: Harvard, 1934).

[47] Daly-Denton, *David in the Fourth Gospel*, 73.   [48] Philo, *Plant.* IX, 39.

2.2   David, the PssLam, and the Gospels

Margaret Daly-Denton has recently completed a study on the influence
of the character of David on the Fourth Gospel through its appropriation
of the Psalms. In it she traces the varied depictions and notions of David
in the time before and around the time of John's Gospel, roughly the end
of the first century. She concludes by saying,

> The material presented in this chapter indicates that the supposed
> Davidic authorship of the psalms was universally accepted by
> the time the Fourth Gospel was written. As a presupposition
> shared by its author and intended readers, it is an issue not only
> relevant but even essential to a study of Johannine reception
> of the psalms . . . In light of the reception of the historical
> superscript tradition, *it is inconceivable* that some of the psalm
> references in the Gospel would not have carried for the original
> readers resonances of David and his story. This is especially true
> of references to "laments of the individual" such as Psalm (21)
> 22 or Psalm (68) 69 which could easily be envisaged as actual
> utterances of David . . . In delineating the figure of David as
> remembered and imagined, we have sought to reconstruct an
> important feature of the horizon of expectations against which
> the psalms were received by the Johannine Community.[49]

Many of these insights hold equally well for the present study, namely,
the high likelihood that David would be evoked when a particular psalm
is referred to in Mark because of David's assumed authorship and the
tradition of linking certain psalms with events in David's life. Also, Daly-
Denton's point about the PssLam being envisaged as "actual utterances
of David" is intriguing and raises interesting questions with regard to the
words of some of these psalms being put into Jesus' mouth in Mark's
passion narrative.[50] These possibilities will be explored later in this study
when the particular PssLam are discussed in the narrative context of Mark.

   As interesting and important as Daly-Denton's study is for the reception
of the Psalms in and the Christology of the Fourth Gospel, the study lacks

---

[49] Daly-Denton, *David in the Fourth Gospel*, 110–11. Italics are mine.

[50] As I will argue in the next chapter, there are four PssLam evoked simply in Mark's
passion narrative (Psalms 21, 40, 41–2 and 68) in at least six places. Of these six evocations,
three are evocations using Jesus' direct speech (Mark 14:18; 14:34; and 15:34). The other
three evocations are used to describe actions in reference to Jesus (15:24, 29–32, and 36).
Outside of the passion narrative, there are only two simple evocations of the PssLam, as
far as I can tell. One is fairly vague and used to describe Jesus (Mark 3:21, maybe evoking
Ps 68:9), and the other is used in direct speech by Jesus (Mark 9:12, evoking Ps 21:7). I
will not discuss these two evocations in this study.

something that I consider very important for such a study of reception history and its implications, something commonly lacking in such studies. Daly-Denton discusses both overt citations of particular psalms and less overt allusions to others. However, in her discussions of these psalms nowhere does she perform any close analysis of the content or rhetoric of the Hebrew or Greek versions. Instead, she focuses mainly on the phrase or verse that is cited or alluded to by the Fourth Gospel and then argues for a particular reading of the Gospel in light of these phrases or verses. In her argumentation, she mainly uses the Psalms as a way of bringing David's story into the Fourth Gospel to explore the ways that the depiction of Jesus is affected. In my opinion, Daly-Denton misses a fundamental step toward understanding the interplay between the Psalms and the Fourth Gospel. In her effort to weave David into the Gospel, she neglects the rhetorical integrity of the psalms she deals with, and, as a result, her study misses the many ways the content of the Psalms could be working to communicate a certain picture of Jesus in the Fourth Gospel.

A different way of dealing with David in the PssLam has been suggested by Adela Yarbro Collins. In her brief treatment of the development of the Psalter and the subsequent appropriation of the final form of the PssLam, she argues that there is an analogy between the way the Teacher of Righteousness appropriated certain PssLam in the DSS Hodayot and the way David was read into the PssLam in Israel's exilic period:

> A strikingly new re-reading of the psalms of individual lament, however, is manifest in the *Thanksgiving Hymns* which have been attributed to the "Teacher of Righteousness" by Gert Jeremias. In one of these, Ps 41,10 is cited in a way that implies that the Teacher re-wrote the psalm with himself as the speaker . . . This transformation is analogous to the one posited for Psalm 22 in the exilic period, when David was written into the text as speaker. The occasion here for the move from the ordinary individual speaker or the suffering community as speaker to the special individual, the Teacher, is due to the self-understanding of the Teacher as an eschatological catalyst. This self-understanding emerges clearly in 1QH 15 (7), 12: "For Thou wilt condemn in Judgment all those who assail me, distinguishing through me between the just and the wicked." This passage suggests that the suffering of the Teacher has meaning as part of the divine eschatological plan.[51]

---

[51] Yarbro Collins, "Appropriation of the Psalms," 226–7.

She then goes on to argue that something similar happens in the case of the pre-Markan passion narrative with regard to Jesus. Here, an analogy "between the situation of the speaker in the psalm and that of the rejected and persecuted later eschatological leader was perceived and preserved."[52] Just as in the Hodayot, there is a re-reading of the older psalms in a way that predicts or pre-figures the suffering of a figure "whose destiny has universal significance."[53]

If Daly-Denton's insights are correct, namely that David must be taken into account whenever a psalm is evoked in a writing of the first century CE, then Yarbro Collins' arguments only partially describe the appropriation of the PssLam by Mark and so must be augmented. Yarbro Collins argues for an analogy between what happens in the exilic period with regard to David, on the one hand, and what occurs in the Hodayot with the Teacher of Righteousness and in the pre-Markan passion narrative (and later in Mark) with Jesus, on the other. However, there is one major difference in the Hodayot and pre-Markan passion narrative (and later Mark) as compared with the exilic re-reading of older psalms. The exilic re-reading is also a *rewriting* and *replacing* of the older sacred text with a new text that includes David in it. When the Davidic superscripts and the short descriptions that link particular psalms to situations in David's life were added, the old text was changed, and a new text was put in its place. As authoritative as the Teacher of Righteousness' Hodayot[54] and Mark's Gospel were for their communities, these authors were not intending to rewrite or replace sacred texts by their re-readings. Furthermore, the texts that the Teacher of Righteousness and Mark used already had David in them. When they re-read them, David was already the focus of these texts and, therefore, was most likely in their consciousnesses when they constructed their texts. David must be reckoned with when considering how the PssLam are appropriated by these later authors and communities.[55]

---

[52] Ibid., 232.   [53] Ibid.

[54] In section 3 of Chapter 3, I discuss several differences between the Gospel of Mark and the DSS Hodayot that should prevent scholars from drawing conclusions about the way that the author of each uses the PssLam with respect to David without paying attention to the differing genres of these works.

[55] As we will see, the Gospel of Mark evokes David several times overtly without direct reference to the PssLam both in contrast to and in concert with Jesus. Therefore, there is already a basis from which to build an argument about the aspect of Jesus' characterization in Mark with respect to David even before one begins to discuss the PssLam in Mark's passion narrative. The Hodayot, on the other hand, do not have the same overt interest in David, and one can only infer that David was important for the authors of the Hodayot based upon the fact that (1) David was generally viewed as the author of the Psalms and (2) the references to the Psalms in the Hodayot are many. The argument would not be as

2.3   David and the Gospel of Mark

Although the Davidic authorship was assumed at the time of Mark, as well as the linking of certain psalms to events in David's life, they cannot be imposed upon the text of Mark without consideration of how Mark characterizes Jesus with respect to David both in passages that use psalms and those that do not. These general assumptions about David will be considered when reflecting upon how Mark used the PssLam in his passion narrative. However, they will be conditioned by Mark's overall narrative presentation of Jesus with respect to David. To this end, in Chapter 5 I will perform a more detailed examination of the narrative progression of Mark 10–12 with respect to Davidic issues, such as kingship and messiahship. These chapters are particularly relevant because there is a series of passages that overtly use Davidic and royal imagery to present Jesus, and these chapters precede the passion narrative (chapters 14–16) where the use of PssLam is most concentrated.

Without going into detail at this point, I will anticipate that discussion here by stating that Mark 10–12 presents a progressive redefinition of messiahship with respect to David. Recently, John J. Collins has argued that when Davidic royal messianism occurs in the literature of Second Temple Judaism, it tends to be militaristic.[56] Mark 10–12 preserves the royal aspect of the messiah when portraying Jesus during his entry and ministry in Jerusalem by linking him with David and using other royal images. However, the Gospel undercuts the military associations of David so that by the end of chapter 12 the reader is left with a royal image of Jesus still associated with David, but without the political or military aspirations that might be expected of a Davidic messianic figure in Jewish contexts of the time. After chapter 12, the royalty of Jesus is ironically depicted in chapters 14–16, but the Davidic association is continued through the use of the PssLam.[57] This continuing association emphasizes the suffering aspect of David's life found in the PssLam. This is not the only well

convincing, however, because one could also say that the authors of the Hodayot were only using scriptural imagery, which was central to the way they expressed themselves as Jews, to communicate with the audience.

[56] "This concept of the Davidic messiah as the warrior king who would destroy the enemies of Israel and institute an era of unending peace constitutes the common core of Jewish messianism around the turn of the era" (John J. Collins, *The Scepter and the Star: The Messiahs of the Dead Sea Scrolls and Other Ancient Literature* [New York: Doubleday, 1995], 68).

[57] After Mark 12, the only psalms referred to by Mark are PssLam, with the exception of Psalm 110 in Mark 14:62 and the possible evocation of Psalm 51 in Mark 14:38. I will discuss the ways that Psalm 110 can be interpreted in this passage later in the study (section 2.4 in Chapter 5).

from which Mark draws to depict Jesus as a suffering messiah, but it is a clear and consistent voice which is used very carefully by Mark to align Jesus with the suffering, lamenting figure of David who cried out to God in various desperate situations. The association with the suffering, lamenting David will be important in discussing the narrative dynamics of the relationship between the passion narrative and the PssLam and the overall characterization of Jesus there.

3

THE EVOCATIONS OF THE PSALMS OF INDIVIDUAL LAMENT IN MARK'S PASSION NARRATIVE

1   Introduction

In this chapter, I will argue for several evocations of the PssLam in the passion narrative of Mark. This chapter corresponds to Ben-Porat's first two stages in her four-stage poetics of allusion which I discussed in Chapter 1.

There are several presuppositions that I wish to make clear before I begin my analysis. First, I am only looking for "simple" evocations, that is, passages in Mark's passion narrative that evoke only one PsLam. Passages in the passion narrative that evoke more than one PsLam or one PsLam along with other scriptural passages are certainly worthy of discussion. But because I wish to perform a very detailed analysis of both the particular PssLam evoked by Mark and the Markan narrative context of these evocations, my task would become too complicated if I considered anything other than simple evocations.

Second, I will follow the narrative order of Mark in examining the possible evocations. In addition, I will use the standard lists of scriptural references found in Appendix IV of Nestle-Aland's 27th edition of Novum Testamentum Graece as an initial guide to identifying the evocations of the PssLam in Mark's passion narrative. Many commentators have generated lists of evocations (usually referred to as "allusions") to the PssLam in the passion narrative of Mark and the other Gospels,[1] and I will consult them as well in determining which evocations are simple and which are complex. I will also use the list of PssLam that I delineated in the previous chapter as the only psalms to consider.

Third, part of the process of determining the likelihood of a certain PsLam being evoked by a passage in Mark will include examining the literature of the Second Temple period, especially the Jewish literature

---

[1] See Adela Yarbro Collins, "Appropriation of the Psalms," 227, n.21; Moo, *The Old Testament in the Gospel Passion Narratives*, II:1453–5; and Marcus, *The Way of the Lord*, 174–5.

written before the time of the Gospel of Mark. However, I will also examine Christian literature that is relatively literarily independent of the Gospel of Mark. I say "relatively" because the Gospel of John is one of the sources that I will turn to repeatedly to confirm my internal analysis of the possible evocations. The question of the literary independence of John from Mark or the other Synoptics has vexed commentators for many decades. For our purposes, I will assume that the literary relationship between John and Mark is significantly different from the relationship between Luke/Matthew and Mark, although there is some likelihood that the author or authors of John knew Mark in some form (written or oral). If the author of John did know Mark, he did not use Mark as a source in the sense that Matthew and Luke did. In addition, I will use Matthew and Luke as a secondary check on my initial findings. According to the Two-Source hypothesis, which is assumed in this study, Matthew and Luke used Mark in constructing their Gospels. If one or both of these Gospels shows evidence of recognizing an evocation of a PsLam in Mark, then my initial conclusion about the evocation will be strengthened.[2]

I will also begin my analysis of the possibly evoked texts with the particular verses of the evoked PssLam. If another text evokes the same verse or verses that Mark does, then the probability of evocation increases. From there, I will branch out to include evocations of other parts of the same PsLam as a way of adding to the probability of the evocation in Mark. I do this because if there are several other authors that refer to the evoked text in their writings, then it shows that the text may have been regularly used in secondary writings. If there is evidence of some sort of regularity of usage, Mark's usage of the text is less anomalous and more probable. However, I will restrict my investigation to literature of Second Temple Judaism and Christianity that is demonstrably written before Mark.[3] If I can show that others before Mark or contemporary to Mark evoked these same PssLam, then it will increase the likelihood that Mark was doing the same and that his audience might have recognized what was happening in the text.

---

[2] It would be interesting to examine later Patristic literature to see whether or not they also recognized these evocations. However, that is beyond the scope of this study.

[3] I have in mind here the inclusion of Paul's seven undisputed letters and Ephesians and Colossians (even if they were written by a follower of Paul after his death, they were most likely written soon after it and therefore right around the time of Mark). One must include the other three Gospels, because they probably used traditions that go back before the final redaction of the stories. I will exclude the rest of the documents in the New Testament, since there is little chance that they were written before Mark, or, at least, little way of demonstrating whether or not they were.

Although this study is not an investigation of the way that authors of Second Temple Jewish literature interpreted the PssLam, I will say something about the way that Mark's usage compares with other evocations of the PssLam, especially those in the Qumran Hodayot. I will leave this until the end of the chapter and restrict my comments to the specific function of these evocations for Mark and the Hodayot, rather than speculate about the interpretations of the PssLam in general.

2   Simple evocations of Psalms of Individual Lament in Mark 14–15

2.1   Joel Marcus' list of allusions to the PssLam in Mark's passion narrative

Joel Marcus has created a list of "allusions to the Psalms of the Righteous Sufferer in Mark's passion narrative."[4] In doing so, Marcus does not argue very carefully for his allusions, nor does he critically evaluate the genre of Psalms of the Righteous Sufferer. As a result, he includes in his list psalms that I have judged not to be PssLam. Among these are Psalms 10 (MT) and 37 (MT), which he asserts are alluded to in Mark 14:1 and 14:55, respectively. Since I do not judge these psalms to be PssLam, I will not include evocations of them in my analysis.

Marcus also includes some allusions that are not simple evocations, and therefore I will exclude those as well. First, Marcus asserts[5] that Pss 27:12 (MT) and 35:11 (MT) are both alluded to in Mark 14:57. For our purposes these references can be eliminated because it is a clear case of a complex allusion (the evocation of two psalms makes it not simple). Second, Marcus also includes an allusion to Ps 140:8 (MT) in Mark 14:41. However, Joachim Gnilka has called attention to usages of the phrase "the hand of the sinner" in Pss 35:11; 70:4; and 81:4, none of which are PssLam, similar to its use in Ps 140:8 (MT).[6] In addition, the use of παραδίδωμι in a way similar to Mark's usage is very common not

---

[4] Marcus, *The Way of the Lord*, 175. Marcus and most other commentators do not draw a distinction between the evocation of a text and the process of allusion that I defined in Chapter 1 (following Ben-Porat). In order to represent Marcus accurately, I will use the term "allusion" when discussing Marcus' analysis to correspond to his meaning and not to Ben Porat's.

[5] I say "assert" because Marcus offers no argumentation for his inclusion of these references. Although I may agree with the idea that Pss 27:12 and 35:11 are evoked in Mark 14:57, one ought to argue for the conclusion before asserting it.

[6] Joachim Gnilka, *Das Evangelium nach Markus: 2. Teilband. Mark 8,27–16,20* (EKKNT 2; Zurich: Benziger Verlag, 1979), 263.

only in other PssLam, but also in LXX Isaiah 53, especially verse 12. Therefore, Marcus' inclusion of the allusion to Ps 140:8 (MT) in Mark 14:41 is far from sure, certainly not simple and, therefore, excluded from my analysis.

Third, Marcus states that there is an allusion to Ps 38:11 (MT)[7] in Mark 15:40. Indeed there is lexical similarity between the two verses, namely, the phrase ἀπὸ μακρόθεν shows up in both the LXX Ps 37:12 and Mark 15:40 to describe the location of the companions to the protagonist. There is one major difference between the psalmist's situation in LXX Ps 37:12 and Jesus' situation in Mark 15:40. The psalmist's companions and friends are described as being contrary to him (ἐξ ἐναντίας), indicating an adversarial relationship when there formerly was not one. In Mark, the people who look on Jesus' situation at a distance are the four named women whom Mark describes as having followed Jesus and served him all the way from Galilee (Mark 15:41). These women are the only followers of Jesus who have not abandoned him yet, and therefore their relationship with Jesus is not adversarial like the relationship between the psalmist and his companions in LXX Ps 37:12. In addition to the allusion to Ps 38:11 (MT) noted by Marcus, Raymond Brown points to additional imagery of the psalmist being distant or alienated from companions or family in Pss 88:9 (MT) and 69:9 (MT), which is analogous to Jesus' situation in Mark 15:40.[8] There is no lexical similarity between Mark 15:40 and these two psalm verses, but the situational similarity is enough to warrant consideration. Brown's observation seems reasonable enough to make the evocation in Mark 15:40 complex and not simple. Therefore, Marcus' inclusion of the allusion to Ps 38:11 (MT) in Mark 15:40 should be eliminated from consideration due to its complex nature.[9]

Finally, Marcus includes an allusion to Ps 35:13–15 (MT) in Mark 14:61 and 15:4–5. However, Jesus' silence in these passages is much more reminiscent of LXX Isa 53:7 than Ps 35:13–15 (MT), which describes the mournful state of the psalmist and the mocking of the psalmist by his adversaries. The psalm does not explicitly mention the silence of the psalmist at all, so Marcus' inclusion of this psalm in his list of allusions is puzzling.

---

[7] Marcus uses the verse numbering of the RSV rather than the MT or LXX.

[8] Brown, *Death of the Messiah*, II:1454.

[9] Interestingly enough, although Evans usually mentions any possible parallel texts when he discusses a particular verse of Mark, he seems to follow Nestle-Aland's list in not mentioning any reference to Ps 38:12 (MT) in relation to Mark 15:40. See his *Mark 8:27–16:20* (WBC 34B; Nashville: Thomas Nelson, 2001), 510–11.

What remains of Marcus' list, then, is a series that conforms quite closely to the list found in Nestle-Aland:[10] evocations to the LXX of Ps 40:10 in Mark 14:18; Pss 41:6, 12 and 42:5 (the refrain of what was once a single psalm) in Mark 14:34; Ps 21:19 in Mark 15:24; Ps 21:8–9 in Mark 15:29–31; Ps 21:2 in Mark 15:34; and Ps 68:22 in Mark 15:36.[11] I will now look at each of these passages to determine the probability of evocation in each case.

2.2   The evocation of Ps 40:10 in Mark 14:18

Mark 14:18 reads, "And while they were reclining and eating, Jesus said, 'Amen I say to you, that one of you will hand me over, the one eating with me.'" (καὶ ἀνακειμένων αὐτῶν καὶ ἐσθιόντων ὁ Ἰησοῦς εἶπεν· ἀμὴν λέγω ὑμῖν ὅτι εἷς ἐξ ὑμῶν παραδώσει με ὁ ἐσθίων μετ᾿ ἐμοῦ.)[12] There is slight textual variation in the verse (τῶν ἐσθιόντων instead of ὁ ἐσθίων in B [Vaticanus] and 2427 co [Coptic 2427]), so there is a high degree of certainty to the reading as the 27th edition of Nestle-Aland has it. The phrase "ὁ ἐσθίων μετ᾿ ἐμοῦ" is the first possible marker we have in the pericope, mainly because of its awkwardness and redundancy.[13] This could be a case of a Markan repetition, or two-step progression, so common in Mark. The second part of a two-step progression in appositional cases tends to clarify or add precision to the first part. "Together they comprise a . . . description, in which the emphasis usually lies on the second part."[14] In this verse, ὁ ἐσθίων μετ᾿ ἐμοῦ does not clarify or specify the one handing over overtly because the only ones present are all eating with Jesus. Taken without reference to something that further clarifies the first member of the doublet, it seems redundant rather than clarifying, which is the normal function of a typical appositional doublet in Mark. But if the second part

---

[10] Nestle-Aland use the MT numbering of the Psalms.

[11] Yarbro Collins' list includes (all psalms references are to the MT) Ps 22:2 in Mark 15:34, Ps 22:8 in Mark 15:29, Ps 22:19 in Mark 15:24, Ps 41:10 in Mark 14:18, Ps 42:6, 12 and 43:5 in Mark 14:34, Ps 51:14 in Mark 14:38 (I have excluded this reference because I have excluded Psalm 51 from my list of PssLam), Ps 69:22 in Mark 15:23 and 15:36 ("Appropriation of the Psalms," 227, n.21). Brown includes all these references except that to Psalm 51 (MT) in Mark 14:38 in his list of highly probable allusions to the Psalms in the passion narratives (*Death of the Messiah*, II:1453). Both of these lists match Nestle-Aland's list precisely.

[12] All translations from the Greek in this study are mine, unless otherwise noted.

[13] Marcus, *The Way of the Lord*, 172. See also Vernon K. Robbins, "Last Meal: Preparation, Betrayal, and Absence," in *The Passion Narrative* (ed. Werner H. Kelber; Philadelphia: Fortress, 1976), 31.

[14] David Rhoads, Joanna Dewey, and Donald Michie, *Mark as Story: An Introduction to the Narrative of a Gospel* (2nd edn.; Minneapolis: Fortress, 1999), 49.

refers to something outside the immediate context, then it would function similarly to other appositional doublets in Mark, as we would expect.

As we move further along in the pericope, Jesus interprets his cryptic prediction of being handed over (παραδίδωμι) in verse 21a: ὅτι ὁ μὲν υἱὸς τοῦ ἀνθρώπου ὑπάγει καθὼς γέγραπται περὶ αὐτοῦ. Taken alone, this could be a general statement of prediction from scripture or even a general statement that indicates Mark's belief about the need to understand scripture to understand Jesus' death properly. But in combination with ὁ ἐσθίων μετ' ἐμοῦ in verse 18, this statement increases the probability that ὁ ἐσθίων μετ' ἐμοῦ is a marker and directs the reader where to look for the evoked text, namely, in scripture.[15] When one searches the scriptures for something similar to ὁ ἐσθίων μετ' ἐμοῦ, one must include lexical similarities but also motifs, themes, and other narrative dynamics in the search, as we discussed above in the section on method. The most similarities will determine the best candidates for the evoked text. The major motifs of Mark 14:17–21 are a meal with close associates and the handing over (παραδίδωμι) by a close associate.

When one searches the scriptures with these motifs, themes, and terms in mind, several possibilities arise. However, the best possible match is Psalm 40, because it has the highest number of similarities with regard to motif, theme, and terminology. It has similarities in vocabulary (ὁ ἐσθίων . . . μου in verse 10 and παραδώῃ in verse 3), as well as other similarities such as (1) some sort of treachery having occurred at the hand of a meal companion (verse 10), (2) the meal companion being a close associate of the protagonist (ὁ ἄνθρωπος τῆς εἰρήνης μου, in verse 10), and (3) being handed over into the hands of one's enemies seeming to color the entire psalm from verse 3 onward. In order to verify that this text is the evoked text, we can now bring in outside information concerning the use of Psalm 40 in other texts subsequent to its writing. Two places require attention and seem to verify that Psalm 40 has a high probability of being the evoked text of Mark 14:18.

Psalm 41:10 (MT) is used in the Hodayot in 1QHa 13:22–4 in an unmarked, modified quotation. The text reads,

> But I have been the target of sl[ander for my rivals,] cause for quarrel and argument to my neighbours, for jealousy and anger to

---

[15] Matthew retains from Mark the wording of the Son of Man going as it is written of him, but he takes out the awkward ὁ ἐσθίων μετ' ἐμοῦ (see Matt 26:21–4). Luke has neither ὁ ἐσθίων μετ' ἐμοῦ nor the statement about the Son of Man's fate being according to scripture. Instead, he has ὅτι ὁ υἱὸς μὲν τοῦ ἀνθρώπου κατὰ τὸ ὡρισμένον πορεύεται (see Luke 22:21–2).

those who have joined my covenant, for challenge and grumbling to all my followers. Ev[en those who e]at my bread have raised their heel against me; they have mocked me with an unjust tongue all those who had joined my council.

ואני הייתי על ע[ון מ]דני לריב 23 ומדנים לרעי קנאה ואף לבאי בריתי
ורגן ותלונה לכול נועדי נ[ם או]כלי לחמי 24 עלי הגדילו עקב וילינו
עלי בשפת עול כול נצמדי סודי 16

Here the speaker, presented as the leader of the community,[17] describes strife between himself and his rivals (cf. the Jewish authorities' conflicts with Jesus in Mark) and in the midst of the description uses Ps 41:10 (MT) to describe the depth of the rivalry and strife that he has caused. There is no meal scene as in Mark 14:17–21,[18] but the Teacher uses Ps 41:10 as an image to describe and lament the depth of controversy he has caused and the danger in which he found himself as a result. The usage here is not exactly the same as in Mark, but the similarities are enough to lend credibility to Psalm 40 being the evoked text in Mark 14:18.

The second passage is found in the Gospel of John, and its usage is very similar to that in the Gospel of Mark.[19] John 13:18 contains a marked quotation of Psalm 41 (MT). I use the MT numbering because it

---

[16] Text and translation from Florentino Garcia Martinez and Eiber J. C. Tigchelaar, eds., *The Dead Sea Scrolls Study Edition* (2 vols.; Leiden, Grand Rapids, MI: Brill and Eerdmans, 1997), I:172–3. All subsequent texts and translations of the Dead Sea Scrolls will be taken from Garcia Martinez and Tigchelaar.

[17] Gert Jeremias and then later Michael C. Douglas, following Jeremias, argue that the Teacher of Righteousness was the author of some, but not all, of the Hodayot. I will discuss their arguments in more detail below. Douglas calls columns 10–17 of the Hodayot "Teacher Hymns" and argues "1. that the implied author of the 'Teacher Hymns' intended the first person locutions to represent himself, and 2. that they would have been interpreted accordingly by his intended audience" ("Power and Praise in the Hodayot: A Literary Critical Study of 1QH 9:1–18:14" [Ph.D. diss., The University of Chicago, 1998], 315). He goes on to argue persuasively that the purpose of the Teacher's Book (1QH 10–17) was "to confirm the foundational status and continuing significance of the Teacher for the movement that he engendered. Another way of stating this conclusion is that throughout the Teacher's Book, the implied author is the Teacher of Righteousness" (ibid., 347). For our purposes in this section and in the subsequent references to the passages in 1QH, which all fall within columns 10–17, it is enough to say that whether or not the Teacher of Righteousness actually wrote 1QH^a 13:22–4, the voice of this particular portion of the Hodayot is that of the Teacher. Therefore, I will refer to the author of these passages of the Hodayot as the Teacher of Righteousness or the Teacher. For a complete list of the portions of 1QH that Douglas believes were written by the Teacher, see ibid., 351–2. See also Gert Jeremias, *Der Lehrer der Gerechtigkeit* (SUNT, 2; Göttingen: Vandenhoeck & Ruprecht, 1963).

[18] However, the passage probably evokes actual meals that were held in the community.

[19] This could indicate literary dependence of the later John on Mark, or it could indicate similar oral transmission of the story of the last meal of Jesus.

is disputed what exactly John was quoting.[20] However, it is clear that it is a reference to some form of Ps 41:10 (MT). John 13:18 reads, "I am not speaking of all of you; I know whom I chose; but so that the scripture may be fulfilled, 'The one eating my bread has raised up his heel against me'" (Οὐ περὶ πάντων ὑμῶν λέγω· ἐγὼ οἶδα τίνας ἐξελεξάμην· ἀλλ᾽ ἵνα ἡ γραφὴ πληρωθῇ· ὁ τρώγων μου τὸν ἄρτον ἐπῆρεν ἐπ᾽ ἐμὲ τὴν πτέρναν αὐτοῦ). The way John uses this verse is very similar to the situation in Mark 14:17–21. The setting is at the last supper, Jesus is talking of his being handed over, and he makes a prediction based on the text of Ps 41:10 (MT).

As far as I know, these are the only references to Psalm 40 in ancient Jewish and Christian literature around the time of Mark.[21] The text from the Qumran Hodayot and this text from John make it highly probable that Psalm 40 is the text evoked in Mark 14:18.

2.3   The evocation of Pss 41:6, 12; 42:5 in Mark 14:34

Mark 14:33–4 reads, "And he took Peter and James and John with him and he began to become greatly distraught and troubled[22] and he said to them, 'My soul is grieving deeply unto death;[23] remain here and stay awake'"

---

[20] See M. J. J. Menken, "The Translation of Psalm 41:10 in John 13:18," *JSNT* 40 (1990): 61–79 for an in-depth discussion of the issues.

[21] Evans points to the *Sentences of Syriac Menander*, 215–16 ("He with whom you had a meal, do not walk with him in a treacherous way") as a possible reference to Ps 41:9 (MT). However, this text was most likely written well after Mark and therefore should not be included to confirm Mark's evocation of the same psalm verse. See Evans, *Mark 8:27–16:20*, 376. For the dating of the *Sentences of Syriac Menander*, see T. Baarda, "The Sentences of Syriac Menander," ed. James H. Charlesworth, *OTP* (2 vols.; New York: Doubleday, 1985), II:584–5. Nestle-Aland lists several other references to Psalm 41 (MT): 41:10: Acts 1:16; and Ps 41:14 (MT) in Matt 15:31, Luke 1:68, and Rom 9:5. The reference to Ps 41:10 (MT) in Acts 1:16 is opaque, if there at all, since the reference is to Judas' acts as fulfilling scripture. There is no evocation of a particular part of scripture, so there is no way to tell whether Ps 41:10 (MT) is what Luke is evoking. The other three references to Ps 41:14 (MT) are also unlikely, because they are references to praise of God, something that is ubiquitous in the Jewish scriptures. None of these additional references should be considered as adding to or diminishing the likelihood that Mark is evoking Ps 40:10 in 14:18.

[22] This is Brown's translation of ἐκθαμβεῖσθαι καὶ ἀδημονεῖν. I will discuss the difficulties in the translation of these terms in Chapter 6. See *Death of the Messiah*, I:146.

[23] Many commentators argue that "unto death" (ἕως θανάτου) evokes Jonah 4:9 (see Vincent Taylor, *The Gospel According to St. Mark* [repr. 2nd edn.; Grand Rapids, MI: Baker Books, 1981], 553; C. Evans, *Mark 8:27–16:20*, 410; C. E. B. Cranfield, *The Gospel According to Saint Mark* [Cambridge: Cambridge University Press, 1966], 431; Brown, *Death of the Messiah*, I:155). Whether or not this is the case is debatable, but it does not make the passage a non-simple evocation because the text is evoked (possibly) by a different alluding phrase from the one that evokes Pss 41:6, 12 and 42:5.

(καὶ παραλαμβάνει τὸν Πέτρον καὶ [τὸν] Ἰάκωβον καὶ [τὸν] Ἰωάννην μετ᾽ αὐτοῦ καὶ ἤρξατο ἐκθαμβεῖσθαι καὶ ἀδημονεῖν καὶ λέγει αὐτοῖς· περίλυπός ἐστιν ἡ ψυχή μου ἕως θανάτου· μείνατε ὧδε καὶ γρηγορεῖτε). Within these verses, it is much easier to identify an evoked text than it was in Mark 14:18, mainly because it seems that Mark takes a recurring phrase from Pss 41:6, 12 and 42:5 and weaves it into his story by putting it on the lips of Jesus. The phrase is not marked as a quotation from scripture, and only part of it is from these psalms.[24] But there is enough lexical and syntactic overlap to make the evocation very secure. A closer look is needed to confirm this initial judgment.

As we will see in the next chapter, Psalm 41–2 can be considered one psalm. If these psalms are considered two parts of a rhetorical unity, then there is a refrain that occurs three times to form a rhythmic pattern to the whole. The refrain reads, "Why are you grieved, soul, and why do you trouble me? Hope in God for I will confess concerning him: 'My God is the salvation of my face'"[25] (ἵνα τί περίλυπος εἶ, ψυχή, καὶ ἵνα τί συνταράσσεις με; ἔλπισον ἐπὶ τὸν θεόν, ὅτι ἐξομολογήσομαι αὐτῷ· σωτήριον τοῦ προσώπου μου ὁ θεός μου). Two words from the first part of this refrain appear in Jesus' statement to Peter, James, and John in Mark 14:34, περίλυπος and ψυχή. Mark also uses εἰμί, albeit in a form different from the form used in the refrain. He also uses these words in the same order in which the refrain uses them. The only difference is the change from the interrogative of the refrain to a statement in Mark 14:34. But this is easily accounted for by the common practice of conforming the order and form of the words in an evoked text to a new narrative context.[26] Because Mark uses three out of the first five words of the first phrase of the refrain, and because he uses them in a similar order, there is a fairly high probability that he is evoking Pss 41:6, 12 and 42:5 in Mark 14:34.[27]

---

[24] Taylor says that the verse reflects usage of the language from Psalm 41–2, but he calls it an echo rather than a quotation. See *The Gospel According to St. Mark*, 552–3.

[25] I keep the translation of προσώπου fairly literal here to maintain the poetic sense of the passage. However, the term can also refer to one's personhood, or simply be translated as "person."

[26] For example, Ps 21:2 is slightly changed to fit the narrative context in Mark 15:34. See also the evocation of Isa 13:10 in Mark 13:24, and Dan 7:13 in Mark 13:26 and 14:62. These changes in the Greek texts that are evoked could also be explained by variations in the Greek version of the Jewish scriptures Mark used or by the possibility that he was evoking a Hebrew or Aramaic version of the texts and translating the texts into Greek himself.

[27] Moo states, "While these psalm verses undoubtedly constitute the source of the expression in both Mk. 14:34 = Mt. 26:38 and Jn. 12:27, it is probably not due to an intentional evocation of any one verse, but to familiarity with the language of the Psalter on the part of Jesus. . . It is probably a question here not of a direct allusion, but of a general stylistic

With respect to other ancient literature, there is a reference to Pss 41:6, 12; 42:5 in the Hodayot from Qumran. There is also a possible use of the same psalm in the Gospel of John. The Qumran reference is 1QH 16:32, which falls in the midst of the hymn's long description of suffering. The Teacher of Righteousness describes being separated from the nourishing living waters (i.e., God) that give the ability to be the powerful teaching presence for the community that the Teacher claims to be. The following is 1QH 16:29–32,[28] and the evocation of Psalms 42–3 (MT) is underlined:

> [Within me] my soul languishes day and night, without rest. And it grows like a searing fire enclosed in [my] bo[nes] whose flame consumes for days without end, devouring (my) strength by periods, and destroying (my) flesh by seasons. Breakers rush against me, and <u>my soul within me has weakened</u> right to destruction, for my vitality has left my body, my heart pours out like water . . .

> 29 ח]יי בתוכי] תתעטף נפשי יומם ולילה 30 לאין מנוח ויפרח כאש בוער
> עצור בע[צמי] עד ימימה תואכל של(ה)(בתה 31 להתם כוח לקצים
> ולכלות בשר עד מועדים ויתעופפו עלי משברים 32 <u>ונפשי עלי תשתוחחה</u>
> לכלה כי נשבת מעוזי מגויתי וינגר כמים לבי

Compare the MT of Ps 42:6a: עלי ותהמי נפשי מה־תשתוחחי. Similar to the way Mark uses LXX Ps 41:6a, 1QH 16 contains the majority of words from this line of the MT of the psalm rearranged to fit the particular literary context. In the case of 1QH 16:32, three of the five words in Ps 42:6a (MT) are used. There is also the general similarity between the contexts of Mark 14:34 and 1QH 16:32, in that both main characters are describing their suffering in the midst of a scene or expression of prayer.[29]

---

borrowing" (*The Old Testament in the Gospel Passion Narratives*, 241). Moo states this conclusion with no argumentation to support it, and so his conclusion is suspect. Francis J. Moloney does not point to a single psalm that Mark evokes in 14:34. Instead, he takes a more general approach and attributes Jesus' language to "words and expressions reflecting Israel's psalms of lament." He goes on to claim that the general pattern of the psalms of lament includes "a profound trust [that] is expressed in the ultimate victory of God over the source of evil. . . The passion has begun, and these words of lament and anxiety point forward to the horror of the events that will follow . . . However, it does not take away from [Jesus] the trust that – whatever may happen to him – God will have the last word" (*The Gospel of Mark: A Commentary* [Peabody, MA: Hendrickson, 2002], 291–2). As will be evident in Chapter 6, I think it is more helpful to consider Psalm 41–2 in particular when interpreting Gethsemane and the passion narrative, and not the speculative pattern of "Israel's psalms of lament," as Moloney asserts.

[28] Garcia Martinez and Tinchelaar, *Dead Sea Scrolls Study Edition*, I:182–3.

[29] See Brown, *Death of the Messiah*, I:154 for a brief discussion of the evocation of Psalm 41–2 in 1QH 16:32.

In the canonical Gospels, Matthew and John both have similar references to Psalm 41–2, but Matthew's is much clearer because he preserves Mark's wording from Mark 14:34. Although it would support more strongly my initial conclusion that Mark was evoking Ps 41:5, 12 and 42:6 in Mark 14:34 if Matthew slightly changed the phrasing to clarify the reference, thus indicating recognition of the reference, Matthew's preservation of Mark's wording at least does not refute my findings. In John 12:27, the evangelist arguably refers to Ps 41:7, which appears right after the first refrain of Psalm 41–2. Again, Jesus speaks the words, as he does in Mark. In John 12:27, Jesus says, "Now, my soul has been disturbed, and what should I say? 'Father, save me from this hour?' Rather, because of this I came to this hour." Raymond Brown calls this an echo of Psalm 41 and an implicit confirmation of Mark's usage of part of the refrain from Psalm 41–2.[30] While John's usage adds some validity to the hypothesis that Mark evokes Psalm 41–2, there is another possibility. Psalm 6:4 has a similar phrase, and verse 5 has language of deliverance, including σῶσόν με, which appears in John 12:27. Psalm 6:4–5 reads, "And my soul is greatly disturbed, and you, Lord, how long? Turn, Lord, rescue my soul, save me because of your mercy" (καὶ ἡ ψυχή μου ἐταράχθη σφόδρα· καὶ σύ, κύριε, ἕως πότε; ἐπίστρεψον, κύριε, ῥῦσαι τὴν ψυχήν μου, σῶσόν με ἕνεκεν τοῦ ἐλέους σου). There are more lexical similarities between Ps 6:4–5 and John 12:27 than between Ps 41:7 and John 12:27.[31] If, however, John 12:27 evokes Ps 41:7, that evocation would support the hypothesis that Mark evokes Psalm 41–2 in 14:34.

As far as I know, these are the only references to Psalm 41–2 in ancient Jewish and Christian literature.[32] Given the clear lexical and syntactic similarities between Mark 14:34 and Pss 41:6, 12 and 42:5, the use of the same phrase from the MT version of these verses in 1QH 16:32, and the possible use of Ps 41:7 in John 12:27, there is a high probability that Mark 14:34 evokes Pss 41:6, 12 and 42:5 in the Gethsemane scene.

2.4   The evocation of Ps 68:22 in Mark 15:23

Mark 15:23 reads, "And they gave him wine laced with myrrh; but he did not take it" (καὶ ἐδίδουν αὐτῷ ἐσμυρνισμένον οἶνον· ὃς δὲ οὐκ ἔλαβεν).

---

[30] Ibid., I:154–5.

[31] See Lindars, *New Testament Apologetic*, 99, n.2 for a similar analysis.

[32] Nestle-Aland lists a reference to Ps 42:3 (MT) in Rev 22:4, but as David Aune points out, the references to seeing the face of God are manifold in ancient Jewish and Christian literature. This makes the likelihood of evocation of Ps 42:3 (MT) in particular by Revelation highly unlikely. See David E. Aune, *Revelation 17–22* (WBC 52c; Nashville: Thomas Nelson Publishers, 1998), 1179–80.

Nestle-Aland's 27th edition of the Greek New Testament lists this as a possible evocation of Ps 69:22 (MT), and some commentators assert the same.[33] But as Vincent Taylor rightly points out, only Matthew is influenced by Psalm 69 (MT) and therefore changes Mark 15:23 to "they gave him to drink wine mixed with gall; and after tasting it, he did not want to drink it" (ἔδωκαν αὐτῷ πιεῖν οἶνον μετὰ χολῆς μεμιγμένον· καὶ γευσάμενος οὐκ ἠθέλησεν πιεῖν).[34] As I argued in Chapter 1, it is only proper to appeal to later Gospel parallels to confirm a possible evocation of a biblical text when there are grounds for claiming an evocation based on lexical and syntactical analysis. Appeal to uses of biblical texts by later authors can only add to the level of certainty of evocation already established by one's analysis; it cannot be the sole basis for probability, let alone certainty. Therefore, what is needed is a more thorough examination of Mark 15:23 to see if there is indeed reason to consider it an evocation of Ps 68:22.

Psalm 68:22 reads, "And they gave (me) bile for my food, and for my thirst, they gave me vinegar to drink" (καὶ ἔδωκαν εἰς τὸ βρῶμά μου χολὴν καὶ εἰς τὴν δίψαν μου ἐπότισάν με ὄξος). The only lexical similarities between this verse and Mark 15:23 are the different forms of δίδωμι and the word καί. But these are such common words that we cannot conclude that they link these two verses together.[35] One other possibility is the relationship between ὄξος in Ps 68:22 and οἶνος in Mark 15:23. The former can also mean sour wine. According to Pliny the Elder, myrrh has a bitter taste when consumed,[36] and so mixing it with wine would give the wine a bitter taste, perhaps similar to the taste of ὄξος. This would imply some relationship between wine mixed with myrrh and vinegar, and thus perhaps be a link to Ps 68:22. However, this is extremely speculative and therefore should be ruled out as a possible way in which Ps 68:22 is evoked by Mark 15:23. There are no other similarities between Mark 15:23 and Ps 68:22 from a syntactical or lexical perspective, so there is little if any chance that there is a literary relationship between these two

---

[33] See Schweizer, *The Good News According to Mark*, 344, and John Painter, *Mark's Gospel: Worlds in Conflict* (London: Routledge, 1997), 203. Brown raises the possibility of Ps 69:22 (MT) being the background for Mark 15:23, but he does not resolve the issue (*Death of the Messiah*, II:1455).

[34] Taylor, *The Gospel According to St. Mark*, 589. See also Evans, *Mark 8:27–16:20*, 501 and Brown, *Death of the Messiah*, II:942–3 for similar arguments.

[35] Brown, *Death of the Messiah*, II:942.

[36] Pliny, *Natural History* (LCL 370; trans. H. Rackham; Cambridge, MA: Harvard University Press, 1968), 12:70. Moo has a similar characterization of myrrh, but he only cites G. E. Post's article on myrrh in vol. III of the *Hastings Dictionary of the Bible* (5 vols.; Edinburgh: T&T Clark, 1898–1904). See Moo, *The Old Testament in the Gospel Passion Narratives*, 251.

verses. Therefore, Nestle-Aland's judgment regarding the reference to Ps 68:22 in Mark 15:23 should be rejected.

2.5   The evocation of Ps 21:19 in Mark 15:24

Mark 15:24 reads, "And they crucified him and they divided his clothes, casting lots for them [to determine] who would take what" (καὶ σταυροῦσιν αὐτὸν καὶ διαμερίζονται τὰ ἱμάτια αὐτοῦ βάλλοντες κλῆρον ἐπ' αὐτὰ τίς τί ἄρῃ). There is a strong possibility that Mark adapts Ps 21:19 by changing the order and form of the verse to fit his narrative context. Psalm 21:19 reads, "They divided my clothes amongst themselves and for my cloak they cast lots" (διαμερίσαντο τὰ ἱμάτιά μου ἑαυτοῖς καὶ ἐπὶ τὸν ἱματισμόν μου ἔβαλον κλῆρον). Both verbs and direct objects in Ps 21:19 also appear in Mark 15:24, some in different form – διαμερίζω, ἱμάτιον, βάλλω, and κλῆρος. In addition, the same preposition is used in association with βάλλω.[37] This high degree of lexical similarity gives a firm foundation for concluding that Mark is alluding to Ps 21:19 here. This conclusion is further supported by the similarity of context between the two verses. In Mark 15 Jesus is being crucified, and therefore he is close to death. In Psalm 21, the psalmist finds himself persecuted by his enemies, enduring the physical effects of his enemies' maltreatment of him. Verse 19 is the last verse of his description of his suffering, and the imagery could indicate that he perceives himself as being close to death.

John 19:23–4 confirms my initial findings regarding the probable evocation that occurs in Mark 15:24. John develops the episode where the Roman soldiers divide Jesus' garments after they crucify him. John explains that the soldiers divided his clothing up into four portions, but that they did not wish to destroy his tunic (χιτών). Instead, they cast lots for it. John then says that this action happened to fulfill scripture, and he quotes Ps 21:19 exactly as it appears in the LXX. So, on the one hand, we have Mark who tells the episode in one sentence and alludes to Ps 21:19 by altering it to fit into his narrative context. On the other hand, we have John who develops the episode in some detail and then contains a marked citation to this verse to explain the episode as a fulfillment of scripture. John's reading allows us safely to say that Mark 15:24 contains an evocation of Ps 21:19.

As far as I know, there are no other references to Ps 22:19 (MT) in Second Temple Jewish writings prior to the Gospel of Mark. However,

---

[37] See Brown, *Death of the Messiah*, II:953–4 for a statistical analysis of all four Gospel accounts of this episode.

there are two suggestive uses of Psalm 22 (MT) in the Qumran Hodayot that may support the hypothesis of Mark's evocation of Ps 21:19. The first is from 1QH 12:33–5a,[38] which reads,

> And I, dread and dismay have gripped me, all /my bones/ have fractured, my heart has melted like wax in front of the fire, my knees give way like water which flows down a slope, for I have remembered my guilty deeds with the unfaithfulness of my ancestors, when the wicked rose up against your covenant and the scoundrels against your word – I thought, "For my offenses, I have been barred from your covenant."

33 ואני רעד ורתת אחזוני וכול יˉרˉמ˙ ירועו וימס לבבי כדונג מ{ל}פני אש
וילכו ברכי 34 כמים מוגרים במורד כי זכרתי אשמוחי עם מעל אבוחי
בקום רשעים על בריתך 35 וחלכאים על דברכה ואני אמרתי בפשעי
נעזבתי מבריתכה

This passage has a fairly clear evocation of Mic 1:4, which has the imagery of wax melting near a fire and water pouring down a slope.[39] But the Teacher seems to combine this with Ps 22:15 (MT), which contains imagery of the psalmist being poured out like water and his heart melting like wax, similar to the description that the Teacher uses in 1QH 12: 33–4.

The second reference to Psalm 22 (MT) is in 1QH 13:31, where the Teacher again alludes to Psalm 22 (MT), but this time to verses 16 and 17. 1QH 13:31 reads: "I have dressed in black and my tongue sticks to {my} palate, because they surround me with the calamity of their heart."[40] Psalm 22:16 (MT) contains similar dry-tongue imagery: "my tongue clings to my jaws,"[41] and 22:17 contains imagery of the psalmist's enemies surrounding him: "for dogs surround me, a group of evildoers encircles me."[42] It is at least suggestive that the Teacher probably evokes the two verses before the one evoked in Mark 15:24, and that the evocation of these two verses occurs in the context of a description of the suffering that he has experienced as a result of conflict with adversaries. If nothing else, it shows that this part of Psalm 22 (MT) was used prior to Mark

---

[38] Garcia Martinez and Tigchelaar, *Dead Sea Scrolls Study Edition*, I:170–1.

[39] Mic 1:4b reads, כדונג מפני האש כחים מגרים במורד. For a discussion of 1QH 4:29–40 in light of Micah and *1 Enoch*, see George W. E. Nickelsburg, "The Qumranic Transformation of a Cosmological and Eschatological Tradition (1QH 4:29–40)," in *Madrid Qumran Congress* (Leiden: Brill, 1992), 649–60.

[40] The relevant Hebrew reads, ולשוני לח{כי} דתדבק וסבבוני בהוות לבם. See Garcia Martinez and Tigchelaar, *Dead Sea Scrolls Study Edition*, I:172–3.

[41] The MT reads ולשוני מדבק מלקוחי.

[42] The MT reads כי סבבוני כלבים עדת מרעים הקיפוני.

in a somewhat similar way, thus adding to the probability that Mark purposefully alluded to Ps 21:19 in Mark 15:24.[43]

2.6   The evocation of Ps 21:8 in Mark 15:29

Mark 15:29–30 reads, "And the passers-by reviled[44] him, shaking their heads and saying, 'Ha, the one who tears down the Temple and builds it up in three days; save yourself by coming down from the cross'" (καὶ οἱ παραπορευόμενοι ἐβλασφήμουν αὐτὸν κινοῦντες τὰς κεφαλὰς αὐτῶν καὶ λέγοντες; οὐὰ ὁ καταλύων τὸν ναὸν καὶ οἰκοδομῶν ἐν τρισὶν ἡμέραις, σῶσον σεαυτὸν καταβὰς ἀπὸ τοῦ σταυροῦ). There is a debate about whether or not this is an evocation of Ps 21:8. Taylor argues that this verse does not contain an evocation that can explain the origin of the tradition because it has more than one evoked text. Instead, it relates facts with biblical language found in Lam 2:15 or Ps 109:25 (MT), or even Wis 2:17.[45] Schweizer concurs with Taylor,[46] but Juel opts for general psalmic influence.[47] Evans points to only Psalm 22 (MT) in his discussion of the scriptural background to the mocking,[48] but Moloney adds Ps 35:21 (MT) to the possible background.[49]

The disagreement among these commentators stems from the multiple places in scripture where one can find imagery similar to that found in Mark 15:29–30. One can argue that Ps 21:8–9, Lam 2:15, Ps 109:25 (MT) and Wis 2:17 all have a legitimate claim to being the scriptural background of Mark 15:29–30, and so Taylor's assessment is the most reasonable. In other words, this is not a simple evocation, in that it does not evoke one and only one text. However, in Chapter 6, I will make the case that the evocation of Ps 21:19 in Mark 15:24 guides the audience to a particular part of scripture, and so when Mark 15:29 is heard in its narrative context, there is a high probability that Psalm 21 would be the primary text evoked by hearing Mark at this point. So, let us look more carefully at the imagery

---

[43] There is general agreement among commentators that Mark alludes to Ps 21:19 in Mark 15:24. In addition, there is always recourse to John 19:23–4 to bolster the probability of the evocation. However, there is no discussion of the use of Ps 22:16–17 in the Hodayot in any of the treatments that I have read.

[44] Here, I follow the translation of Adela Yarbro Collins, ("The Charge of Blasphemy in Mark 14:64," *JSNT* 26 (4, 2004): 379–401) who argues persuasively that βλασφημέω here is synonymous to ἐμπαίζω and ὀνειδίζω. This connotation of βλασφημέω, Yarbro Collins argues, is that of the usage commonly found in ordinary Greek of the time. See especially 396.

[45] Taylor, *The Gospel According to St. Mark*, 591.

[46] Schweizer, *The Good News According to Mark*, 348–9.

[47] Donald Juel, *Mark* (Augsburg Commentary on the New Testament; Minneapolis: Augsburg Fortress, 1990), 220.

[48] Evans, *Mark 8:27–16:20*, 505.   [49] Moloney, *The Gospel of Mark*, 322.

in Ps 21:8–9 to see if there is warrant for thinking that Mark evokes this text, at least as one among several scripture passages.

Psalm 21:8–9 reads, "All who look at me mock me, they speak with their lips, they shake their head[s], 'He hoped in the Lord, let him deliver him; let him save him because he delights in him'" (πάντες οἱ θεωροῦντές με ἐξεμυκτήρισάν με, ἐλάλησαν ἐν χείλεσιν, ἐκίνησαν κεφαλήν Ἤλπισεν ἐπὶ κύριον, ῥυσάσθω αὐτόν· σωσάτω αὐτόν, ὅτι θέλει αὐτόν). The lexical similarities between this and Mark 15:29–30 are fewer in number than between 21:19 and Mark 15:24, but there are some – κινέω, κεφαλή, and σῴζω. Aside from these lexical similarities, in both texts the main character is mocked somehow. In Mark 15:29–30, Jesus is mocked, and the author uses βλασφημέω, whereas in Ps 21:8–9, the psalmist is mocked (ἐκμυκτηρίζω) by the adversaries speaking "with lips" (ἐν χείλεσιν). In addition, both incidents of mocking have the mockers shaking their heads in derision. When Mark 15:29–30 is coupled with the more probable evocation of Psalm 21 in Mark 15:24, the possibility of Ps 21:8–9 being evoked becomes greater.[50] In this case, there are no other references to Ps 21:8–9 in Second Temple Judaism or other Christian texts independent of Mark, as far as I am aware.

2.7   The evocation of Ps 21:2 in Mark 15:34

Mark 15:34 is one of the most famous passages in all of Mark, and it is universally agreed that it is an emended quotation from Ps 21:2. There is little argumentation needed here, since the author puts the words in Jesus' mouth in transliterated Aramaic and then translates the saying into Greek. The Greek translation matches Ps 21:2a in every way except in its omission of πρόσεχες μοι and its substitution of εἰς τί for ἵνα τί. But it is so obvious that Jesus' words are from Ps 21:2a that we need not make a detailed case for its evocation.

2.8   The evocation of Ps 68:22 in Mark 15:36

The final text I wish to consider is Mark 15:36, which reads, "And someone ran and filled a sponge with sour wine, and after putting it around

---

[50] Moo thinks that the image of shaking of the head, although very common in the Hebrew Bible, probably refers to Ps 22:7 (MT) because of the frequent use of the psalm in the passion narrative. However, he argues against the connection between Mark 15:30 and Ps 22:8 (MT) based on σῴζω because in Mark, Jesus is challenged to save himself, whereas in Ps 22:8 (MT), the psalmist speaks of divine deliverance. See *The Old Testament in the Gospel Passion Narratives*, 258–9. I will discuss this point further in Chapter 6.

a reed, gave it to him to drink, saying, "Let us see if Elijah comes to take him down" (δραμὼν δέ τις [καὶ] γεμίσας σπόγγον ὄξους περιθεὶς καλάμῳ ἐπότιζεν αὐτὸν λέγων· ἄφετε ἴδωμεν εἰ ἔρχεται Ἠλίας καθελεῖν αὐτόν). The text that most commentators claim is being evoked here is Ps 68:22, which reads, "And they gave (me) bile for my food, and for my thirst they gave me vinegar to drink" (καὶ ἔδωκαν εἰς τὸ βρῶμά μου χολὴν καὶ εἰς τὴν δίψαν μου ἐπότισάν με ὄξος). As we can see, the only lexical similarities between these two verses are the uses of ποτίζω and ὄξος, but there is also the similarity of situation between the settings. In Psalm 68, the psalmist is in the middle of a vivid plea for God's mercy, one that includes a description of some of the abuse that he is receiving. In Mark 15:34, Jesus has just been mocked and has cried out for mercy to God with the words of Ps 21:2. The mockery continues in the form of giving him sour wine to drink and deriding him with a sarcastic quip: "Let's see if Elijah comes to take him down." These similarities give a certain level of probability that Ps 68:22 is being evoked in Mark 15:34.

Once again there are two other texts that confirm the initial results, one from the Gospel of John and one from the Hodayot. In John 19:28–30, John expands the possible scriptural evocation into a more detailed episode with the fulfillment of the directly cited scripture quotation, in a way similar to what happens in John 19:23–5. Just before Jesus is about to die, he says that he is thirsty. The bystanders fill a sponge with sour wine (ὄξος) and give it to him to drink. The word ὄξος is used three times in verses 29 and 30, which is the same word used in Ps 68:22. Furthermore, John says that Jesus only declares his thirst after he knew that "all things have been brought to perfection" (πάντα τετέλεσται) and "in order that scripture may be brought to perfection" (ἵνα τελειωθῇ ἡ γραφή). Therefore, John makes explicit what is implicit in Mark.

We see an evocation of Ps 69:22 (MT) in 1QH 12:11 used to describe the false teachings of the Teacher's adversaries in contrast to the drink of knowledge that he offers. The text reads, "they have denied the drink of knowledge to the thirsty, but for their thirst they have given them vinegar to drink."[51] The second half of Ps 69:22 (MT) reads ולצמאי ישקוני חמץ and is virtually quoted by the author of 1QH 12:11, although the forms have been changed slightly to fit the poetic context of the hymn.

Matthew preserves the episode from Mark but changes the wording slightly, which could indicate recognition of Mark's evocation of Ps 68:22.

---

[51] The Hebrew of 1QH 12:11 reads, ויעצורו משקה דעת מצמאים ולצמאם ישקום חומץ. See Garcia Martinez and Tigchelaar, *Dead Sea Scrolls Study Edition*, I:168–9.

Matthew polishes Mark's Greek a bit by changing δραμών δέ τις [καὶ] γεμίσας σπόγγον ὄξους περιθεὶς καλάμῳ ἐπότιζεν αὐτόν (Mark 15:36a) to καὶ εὐθέως δραμὼν εἷς ἐκ αὐτῶν καὶ λαβὼν σπόγγον πλήσας τε ὄξους καὶ περιθεὶς καλάμῳ ἐπότιζεν αὐτόν (Matt 27:48). Although Matthew changes Mark's Greek, he is careful not to obscure the lexical similarities between Mark's version and Ps 68:22. Luke does not preserve Mark's episode, because in Luke Jesus dies with no cry in the words of Ps 21:2 and therefore no mocking after his last words. However, Luke does preserve a form of Jesus being offered ὄξος in the context of an earlier mocking by the soldiers as Jesus hangs from the cross: ἐνέπαιξαν δὲ αὐτῷ καὶ οἱ στρατιῶται προσερχόμενοι, ὄξος προσφέροντες αὐτῷ (Luke 23:36). The only lexical similarity between this verse and Ps 68:22 is ὄξος, but the image is similar enough for one to be able to say that Luke may have been influenced by Mark's evocation of it sufficiently to include his own evocation in the midst of another scene.

Outside of the Gospel material, there are no other evocations of Ps 68:22 that I am aware of in literature before or contemporary with Mark. There are numerous references to other parts of Psalm 68 in the New Testament, which shows that this psalm was turned to by a variety of writers when thinking about Jesus' messiahship and his suffering. Mark 3:21 could refer to Ps 68:9 in describing Jesus' alienation from his family.[52] In Rom 15:3, Paul quotes Ps 68:10 in trying to explain that Christ did not seek his own pleasure but suffered instead. John refers to a different part of Ps 68:10 in 2:17 possibly as a way of linking Jesus' temple incident with his death.[53] Paul also has a rearranged quotation from Ps 68:23 in the midst of his argument about Israel's stumbling in the face of the gospel in Rom 11:9. And Luke has a marked quotation of Ps 68:26 in Acts 1:20 in Peter's first speech, in which he tries to explain the course of events regarding Jesus' death by appealing to the fulfillment of scripture. There are other possible evocations of Psalm 68 that could be argued, but these examples show clearly that Psalm 68 was regularly evoked by the earliest Christian writers, making Mark's evocation part of a greater pattern of appeal to this psalm.

There is no doubt that 1QH 12:11 evokes Ps 69:22 (MT), and when this evidence is combined with the evidence from John 19:29–30, confirmed with the references in Matthew and Luke, and is put in the context of

---

[52] See Yarbro Collins, "Appropriation of the Psalms," 235–6.

[53] John 15:25 also has a marked quotation: ἀλλ᾽ ἵνα πληρωθῇ ὁ λόγος ὁ ἐν τῷ νόμῳ αὐτῶν γεγραμμένος ὅτι ἐμίσησάν με δωρεάν. This phrase shows up in two PssLam, Psalms 34 and 68; therefore, it is not a simple allusion, and it is difficult to determine for which psalm John is claiming fulfillment.

the many other evocations of Psalm 68 by New Testament writers, there results a high probability that Mark 15:36 evokes Ps 68:22.[54]

3   The use of Psalms 21, 40, 41–2 and 68 in Second Temple Judaism

The study of the use of even these four PssLam in Second Temple Judaism is a very complex, if not unattainable, undertaking. In Chapter 1, I discussed in some detail the methodological difficulties of performing such a study. In short, the set of data is too small and spread over too large a time period for general statements about the use of even one psalm to represent accurately any trends that may have occurred with the interpretation of these texts. This leaves aside the question of how these psalms were used in the cultic life of Jews at the time of Jesus and Mark or in the communal gatherings of the early followers of Jesus. As interesting as the study of the cultic/liturgical use of these texts is, and as much as we would like to say something about this, unfortunately there is simply no direct evidence for the use of these particular psalms either in early Judaism or in the earliest Christian communities. The indirect evidence is found only in the text we have mentioned thus far, and it is notoriously speculative to attempt to say anything concrete and specific about the worship life of the earliest churches with only a few disparate, non-liturgical texts.

As we will see in the coming chapters, it does pay off to be detailed in allowing one author, Mark, to speak for himself about his own particular use of these psalms. Perhaps he was influenced by the way others used them in their writings, but the number of occurrences in other texts is too small, and the different genres in which evocations of these psalms occurs shape the meaning of these evocations to such an extent that the goal of constructing trajectories of interpretation or other such patterns of usage in Second Temple Judaism is fleeting at best and misguided at worst. I think a better way to proceed in most cases is to allow for a particular author to use these texts in particular ways and then note any similarities

---

[54] While most commentators think that Ps 68:22 is evoked by Mark 15:36, Ben Witherington does not mention this as a possibility (*The Gospel of Mark: A Socio-Rhetorical Commentary* [Grand Rapids, MI: Eerdmans, 2001], 399). Taylor remarks, "the contrary suggestion, that the incident drew the attention of Christians to the Psalm, which in turn influenced the vocabulary of 36a, is more probable. And, in any case, if 35f. is a fusion of two traditions, 35, 36b is not dependent upon the Psalm" (*The Gospel According to St. Mark*, 595). Whereas Taylor argues from the perspective of the history of the tradition, I argue from a narrative perspective. From this perspective, it is likely that Ps 68:22 is evoked by Mark 15:36.

or differences between that author and other texts in which there is an evocation of that text, leaving the construction of trajectories aside.

One may notice that many of the verses of the PssLam that Mark evokes in his passion narrative (in a simple way, as defined above) only appear in the Qumran Hodayot of the extant literature of Second Temple Judaism. Therefore, I would like to discuss the similarities and differences between the two works in order to compare how these four PssLam function in the Hodayot and in Mark.

Before I do this, I must point out one other occurrence of Psalm 41–2 in the literature of the time. Although the particular verses of Psalm 41–2 alluded to by Mark do not appear elsewhere, there is a reference to 41:4 and 11 in the Greek version of *3 Bar 1:2*. At this point in the story, Baruch is lamenting the fact that God let Nebuchadnezzar destroy Jerusalem. He asks God why this punishment was chosen and finishes his questioning of God with an evocation of Ps 41:4 and 11, which has the psalmist's adversaries asking, "Where is your God?" In Chapter 6, I will argue that the psalm's depiction of God's absence plays an important role in Mark's depiction of Jesus at Gethsemane. For now, it is enough to say that the author of the Greek version of 3 Baruch uses Psalm 41–2 similarly, in that he constructs a character who uses Psalm 41–2 to lament a situation of suffering that does not match his expectations of God's actions.

The Qumran Hodayot are very different in nature from both *3 Baruch* and the Gospel of Mark. In a University of Chicago dissertation submitted in 1998, Michael C. Douglas strengthens Gert Jeremias' opinion[55] in arguing convincingly that a large portion of the Hodayot (1QH 10–17) was written by the Teacher of Righteousness, who was probably the early charismatic leader of the community of the Dead Sea Scrolls. Douglas further argues that the other portions of the Hodayot were written after the death of the Teacher of Righteousness, but they were written in his voice and therefore have the same purpose and rhetorical effect as the original hymns.[56] Adela Yarbro Collins has argued recently that one of the main similarities between the use of the PssLam in the Hodayot and the Gospel of Mark is their application of the psalms to a special individual of eschatological significance. In turn, "Because of their association with the Teacher and their loyal membership in the community, the members share in his destiny, suffering to be followed by vindication."[57] In both the Hodayot and the Gospel of Mark, "a real analogy between the situation

[55] Jeremias, *Der Lehrer der Gerechtigkeit.*
[56] Douglas, "Power and Praise in the Hodayot."
[57] Yarbro Collins, "Appropriation of the Psalms," 226–7.

of the speaker in the psalm and that of the rejected and persecuted later eschatological leader was perceived and preserved. At the same time, the older psalms were re-read as predicting or at least pre-figuring the suffering of a special individual, whose destiny has universal significance."[58] Yarbro Collins is careful not to make claims that this similarity indicates a trajectory of interpretation within the Second Temple period.

While this analogy of situation between the speaker in the psalm and special individuals is similar in the Hodayot and in the Gospel of Mark, the literary function of the evocations of the four PssLam is different in each of these writings. As I mentioned in Chapter 1, I agree with Paul Ricoeur in thinking that there is an important relationship between genre and meaning.[59] As a result, the literary devices used to communicate the author's perspective and to shape the audience's understanding of the text are part of the way that the genre functions to produce meaning. In the case of the Hodayot and the Gospel of Mark, the evocations of the four PssLam may be similar in that the speaker of the psalm is associated with a later eschatological figure. But because the genres of the two texts are different, one must attend to the way the genre affects the function of these evocations.

In the Hodayot, the speaker is expressing through poetic means his own reflections on his situation of suffering, his thanksgiving to God, and his place within the community and in contrast to his adversaries. The hymns function both as prayers to God and as authoritative, or even sacred, texts that the author's community can utilize for its own communal edification. Therefore, the content, the means by which he expresses himself, and the function of the texts are very similar to those of the PssLam as they were read in the late Second Temple period in general. Since the Teacher of Righteousness and the author(s) of the texts written after his death drew upon the language along with the imagery of many biblical passages to express these authors' points of view, the evocations of the PssLam are a part of the poetics of the Hodayot that are directly related to the form and function of the texts as self-expression. In other words, the authors of the Hodayot seem to draw upon the PssLam because they are part of the authors' scriptures, which is the cultural language that can best express their own suffering and places in their community.[60]

The Gospel of Mark uses these PssLam in a narrative context rather than a poetic context. The author writes in a third person omniscient

---

[58] Ibid., 232.

[59] Ricoeur, "Toward a Hermeneutic of the Idea of Revelation," 73–118.

[60] I assume that the Teacher of Righteousness and the later authors who write in his voice share the same community.

voice as the narrator, and he puts the language of most of these psalms on the lips of Jesus[61] rather than using them for the expression of his own suffering as in the Hodayot. Because this happens in the context of a narrative rather than in self-expressive poetry, the uses of these PssLam contribute to the characterization of Jesus in a narrative sense, which is contingent upon the plot development and the narrative context rather than the self-expression of the author as in the Hodayot. I will argue in Chapter 6 that the suffering of David as depicted in these PssLam contributes significantly to the characterization of Jesus by offering a model that orients the audience and contributes to making Jesus' suffering understandable. In part, this model of Jesus as the suffering King David is conditioned by other clues in Mark's narrative that link him with David in chapters 11 and 12[62] and depict Jesus as a king in the passion narrative. By evoking images of the suffering David from the PssLam, the plot of Mark's passion narrative gains a depth of meaning that a flat reading – a reading that does not acknowledge or appreciate the evocation of these PssLam – does not offer. Mark's evocation of these PssLam goes beyond the use of biblical language as the fundamental cultural tool that the author utilizes for self-expression of suffering. It is one literary device among many that contributes to the overall presentation of Jesus as the Messiah who suffers and dies according to scripture. There is no comparable characterization in the Hodayot because the evocations of the PssLam are not embedded within a narrative framework as they are in Mark.

---

[61] This is the case in Mark 14:18 (in reference to Psalm 40), 14:34 (in reference to Psalm 41–2), and 15:34 (in reference to Psalm 21). Of the simple evocations of the PssLam in Mark's passion narrative, only Psalm 68 is not spoken by Jesus.

[62] As I will discuss in some detail in Chapter 5, David is evoked by Mark in different ways with respect to Jesus, not just as the suffering David. There are clear overtones to David's messianic status as warrior king and as chosen son, but, as I will argue, there seems to be a downplaying of the militaristic aspects of David's kingship when these images are evoked by Mark with respect to Jesus. David is a complex character in the literature of the Jewish scriptures, and his story as told by the Deuteronomist mixes positive and negative depictions of David as king. On the one hand, he is favored by God even before he becomes king, but on the other, he is shown to be morally deficient in several important ways. He dies as king of a much larger kingdom than he had when he began his rule, and so the suffering David is certainly not the last word on him, at least in the Deuteronomist's opinion. However, as the Psalter is developed through the course of Israel's history, and David becomes thought of as the author of the Psalms and the protagonist in many of them, the suffering of David is not muted. Instead, it stands right alongside that of David the son of God, the favored king, and the warrior. In fact, there are more psalms that depict the suffering of David than there are that depict his status as favored son or chosen king. The comparison between Jesus and David only goes so far, because David does not die a humiliating death the way Jesus does. But Mark clearly appeals to aspects of David's character in order to present Jesus in a particular way.

The poetics of the Hodayot and the Gospel of Mark with respect to the use each makes of the PssLam differ enough to caution against drawing too close a comparison between the two texts. There are some suggestive similarities between these texts, such as the ones that Yarbro Collins describes. But because the evocations of the four PssLam in Mark occur within a narrative, the function of these evocations must be judged in the context of the overall narrative design. Thus, the details and possible depth of meaning of the narrative, to which the evocations of these PssLam contribute, must be determined through careful narrative analysis of Mark. Any similarity of meaning or function of the evocations between the Hodayot and the Gospel of Mark must be kept primarily at the comparative level only.[63] As I mentioned in Chapter 1, the number of times that these four PssLam are evoked in pre-Markan Jewish literature is too small to make any claims regarding a trajectory of interpretation or reading conventions. One must stay within the narrative of the Gospel of Mark to understand how these evocations function within that narrative without imposing readings from outside the text.[64] Only then should comparisons be made with other uses in Second Temple Judaism and tentative, if any, conclusions be drawn regarding reading conventions in this time period.

---

[63] One of the more noteworthy similarities between the Hodayot's use of the PssLam and Mark's use of them is that both communities out of which the writings arose had an eschatological orientation. This could be an important comparison from a sociological or ideological point of view and could lead to an interesting study of how two eschatologically oriented communities interpreted the same scriptural texts to advance their own causes. In such a study, as I argue in the body of this text, issues of genre would have to be considered seriously for a full understanding of the way these communities appeal to scripture in their writings. Yarbro Collins' argument that there is an analogy of situation between the speaker of the PssLam and a special person of eschatological significance in both the Hodayot and Mark could be used as a foundation for such a study.

[64] Thomas R. Hatina makes a similar point in the second chapter of *In Search of a Context*, as I discussed in footnote 3 of Chapter 1.

4

INTERPRETATION OF THE LXX PSALMS
OF INDIVIDUAL LAMENT EVOKED IN
MARK'S PASSION NARRATIVE

The present chapter takes up the rhetorical and interpretive issues of the four PssLam[1] that are evoked in the Gospel of Mark. When I use the term "rhetorical," I do not use it in an ancient technical way to describe a certain style or technique of persuasion as used by professional Greek and Roman rhetoricians. Instead, I simply mean to investigate the way a particular psalm is constructed to communicate what the psalmist wishes to communicate. So, I look at the imagery, the grammar, the syntax, and the flow of the psalm in order to understand its literary dynamics. In my analyses of the psalms in this chapter, I delineate between describing the rhetoric and interpreting the psalm based on the rhetoric. I do this in an effort to read each psalm more carefully so that I can understand the meaning of the psalm as fully as possible. In light of these thoughts, my idea of rhetoric seems to correspond more with the modern critical notion of rhetoric, at least as described by George A. Kennedy: "The rhetoric of a poem, novel, play, or other artistic composition is thus a matter of how the text works to achieve some effect through its imagery, metaphor, figuration, irony, and narrative voices, and also of the cultural, political, and social assumptions that are inherent in the text."[2] I will examine in detail each psalm in Greek using Rahlfs' text from the 1931 Göttingen edition,[3] bringing in discussion of the MT only when it aids in understanding particular terms and only as a heuristic device that may

---

[1] LXX Psalm 41–2 will be analyzed as one psalm. See section 2.4 below for a discussion of the rationale for this.

[2] George F. Kennedy, "Historical Survey of Rhetoric," in *Handbook of Classical Rhetoric in the Hellenistic Period 330 B.C.–A.D. 400* (ed. Stanley E. Porter; Boston, Leiden: Brill Academic Publishers, Inc, 2001), 6.

[3] I recognize the recent criticism of Rahlfs' methodology in grouping manuscripts and text versions in creating his critical edition. But, to date, his is still the best (and only) critical edition available, and a reconstruction of the original Greek text is beyond the scope of this study. See Cameron Boyd-Taylor, Peter C. Austin, and Andrey Feuerverger, "The Assessment of Manuscript Affiliation with a Probabilistic Framework: A Study of Alfred Rahlfs's Core Manuscript Groupings for the Greek Psalter," in *The Old Greek Psalter: Studies in Honor of Albert Pietersma* (JSOTSup 332; ed. Robert J. V. Hiebert, Claude E. Cox,

clarify any difficulties in the grammar, syntax, or rhetorical structure of the Greek. I use the Greek versions of these PssLam because it is most likely that the author and earliest audiences of Mark would have referred to the Greek versions rather than the Hebrew versions.[4]

1   Introductory remarks about the study of the LXX Psalms

The LXX Psalms have not been studied in their own right by the vast majority of commentators on the Psalms except as a way of trying to understand the MT Psalms better. The secondary literature on the MT Psalms generally does not address the particular issues of the Greek of these psalms. Although the LXX Psalms are translations of the Hebrew Psalms, once the translation is made, the nature of each psalm changes because of the different language in which it now exists. Albert Pietersma has argued that the nature of the relationship between the Greek and the Hebrew is that there is a word-for-word, interlinear relationship between the Greek and its Hebrew *Vorlage* originally created to bring the Greek reader of the Psalms to the Hebrew version of the text.[5] This may have been the original intention of the translation, although there is no direct proof to substantiate such a claim. However, I disagree with the assessment of the translation process, because the process of translation is never simply word-for-word. The Greek verbal system and syntax are much more complex than the Hebrew verbal system and syntax. When the translator faces the prospect of translating a Hebrew imperfect, for example, there are many possibilities from which to choose when deciding how to express the clause in Greek, especially when the Hebrew imperfect is found in the context of Hebrew poetry. The choice is not simply a wooden mechanism of vocabulary equivalents, however faithful to the Hebrew the translator attempts to be. The translation is determined by the translator's interpretation of the sense that is being communicated

and Peter J. Gentry; Sheffield: Sheffield Academic Press, 2001), 98–124; Albert Pietersma, "The Present State of the Critical Text of the Greek Psalter," in *Der Septuaginta-Psalter und seine Töchterübersetzungen* (ed. A. Aejmelaeus and U. Quast; Göttingen: Vandenhoeck & Ruprecht, 2000), 12–32. Alfred Rahlfs' *Psalmi cum Odis* (Göttingen: Vandenhoeck and Ruprecht, 1931), part of the Göttingen series of critical editions of the LXX, will be used in this study. The text of the Psalter is identical to the text found in the popular two-volume version of the LXX, Alfred Rahlfs, *Septuaginta* (Stuttgart: Deutsche Bibelgesellschaft, 1979). The only difference between the versions is the more extensive critical apparatus in the 1931 edition.

[4] See Chapter 1, section 2.6 for a discussion of the use of the Greek version of these PssLam in studying the Gospel of Mark.

[5] A summary of Pietersma's theory regarding the nature of the Greek Psalter can be found in his *The Psalms*, ix.

by the Hebrew. The translator is necessarily creatively involved in the translation, and therefore the process is not a wooden mechanism but an interpretive choice. Therefore, when considering the Greek PssLam below, I will treat them as much as possible as an ancient native reader of Greek would treat them, namely, by analyzing them in their own right and not reading them through the lens of their MT counterparts, as the vast majority of commentators do. This way of reading and analyzing the LXX Psalms seems to simulate best the process of their reception by an ancient audience of Mark. In order to avoid reading the LXX Psalms through the lens of the MT, I will not rely heavily on the secondary literature on the Hebrew of these four psalms in my analyses below.

After analyzing and interpreting each psalm as a literary whole in Greek, I can determine more carefully how the psalm may contribute to the pericope in the Gospel of Mark in question or to other aspects of Mark's story of Jesus. These narrative insights will follow in Chapter 6. But before I turn to the particular psalms themselves, I must discuss in some detail their superscripts.

2   Rhetorical issues and interpretation of LXX Psalms 21, 40, 41–2, and 68

Since each psalm, with the exception of Ps 41, begins with a superscript with a reference to David and/or εἰς τὸ τέλος, I will begin with some general comments on the translation and meaning of these two characteristics of the superscripts. Then I will perform a two-stage analysis on each psalm. The first stage will address the structure of the psalm, meaning that I will indentify the major sections and subsections of the psalm in order to determine its basic flow. In order to determine the major sections and subsections, I will describe the syntax, grammar, and content of the psalms, but I will reserve discussion of the meaning of each psalm until the second stage of the analysis.

2.1   The superscripts in the Psalms

Most of the canonical psalms have superscripts of some sort, usually giving instructions for worship, descriptions of the purpose of the psalm, attributions of authorship, or associations with episodes from a biblical hero's life. Almost half of the MT psalms (71) have a superscript that associates the psalm with David. The Davidic superscript in the MT invariably contains לדוד, but whether this refers to David's authorship, an association with his life, or a dedication to him is unclear. All are legitimate ways of reading לדוד. What is agreed upon by commentators is that these superscripts, including the non-Davidic ones, were most likely not original to each psalm but added later during the process of redaction of the Psalter into its present canonical form.[6]

Alfred Rahlfs' standard text of the LXX Psalter contains thirteen additional psalms with a Davidic superscript – either τῷ Δαυιδ or τοῦ Δαυιδ – as compared to the MT versions of the Psalms.[7] Based on his particular grouping of manuscripts, Rahlfs concluded that all of these superscripts were original to the Old Greek of the Psalter.[8] Albert Pietersma has raised the question, "are these 'added' ascriptions to David part of the Old Greek text, and hence, do they reflect a Hebrew *Vorlage* different from the MT?"[9] He has convincingly argued that not all of the Davidic superscripts go back to the Old Greek and has suggested several changes to Rahlfs' *Psalmi cum Odis*.[10] None of the changes he suggested concern the psalms discussed in the present work.

One further relevant issue is another common element of the superscripts – the inclusion of εἰς τὸ τέλος. Again, the compositional history of this phrase in the Psalter is debated, but its presence in the LXX must be acknowledged and reckoned with. Joel Marcus has suggested that the translation of למנצח with the phrase εἰς τὸ τέλος "may indicate that these psalms were understood eschatologically by the Septuagint translators." The only supporting evidence that he offers is from *b. Pesah.* 117a, which interprets the phrase "eschatologically."[11] L. C. L. Brenton consistently

---

[6] There is almost universal consensus about this point. See especially Brevard S. Childs, "Psalm Titles and Midrashic Exegesis," *JSS* 16 (2, 1971): 137–50. More recently, there has been some discussion as to whether the superscripts are actually postscripts from the previous psalm in the Psalter. See Bruce K. Waltke, "Superscripts, Postscripts, or Both," *JBL* 110 (4, 1991): 583–96.

[7] LXX Psalms 32, 42, 70, 90, 92–8, 103, 136.

[8] The conventional distinction between the terms LXX and the Old Greek among scholars will not be maintained here. The Old Greek is considered to be the original Greek translation of the Hebrew *Vorlage* of any biblical writing. The LXX is, strictly speaking, only the original Greek translation of the Torah by the legendary seventy (or seventy-two) translators as described in the *Letter of Aristeas*. For present purposes, the LXX will designate the Greek version of the Hebrew Bible available to the author of Mark. At the time of the composition of Mark, there were probably several Greek translations in circulation, but modern critical scholarship has not been able to pinpoint these versions. Instead, it has reconstructed one critical version of the LXX. See Karen H. Jobes and Moises Silva, *Invitation to the Septuagint* (Grand Rapids, MI and Carlisle: Baker Academic and Paternoster, 2000), 29–104, for an excellent discussion of the state of scholarship on the development and transmission of the LXX.

[9] Albert Pietersma, "David in the Greek Psalms," *VT* 30 (1980): 213–26.

[10] See ibid., 225–6, for a list of suggested changes to Rahlfs' text.

[11] Marcus, *The Way of the Lord*, 177–8. Marcus' evidence is not reliable because of its late dating, but also because *b. Pesah.* 117a, which he cites, simply says לבא לעתיד וניגון ניצוח.

translates the εἰς τὸ τέλος as "for the end,"[12] and Pietersma translates it as "for fulfillment" (sic) without explanation in his introduction.[13]

There is no evidence from the ancient authors around the time of the Gospel of Mark or before as to how this phrase was understood in relation to the Psalms.[14] As we have seen, there is a tendency among modern scholars to interpret εἰς τὸ τέλος eschatologically, but the evidence is lacking for such an interpretation prior to the time of Mark. One would have to appeal to the general cultural matrix of the time to say that there is ample evidence of apocalyptic eschatology among Jews and early followers of Jesus, and that, therefore, it is possible that this phrase could have been understood eschatologically. But this relies on general circumstantial evidence and not on any direct evidence, rendering this interpretation speculative at best. Peter Ackroyd argues that there are no eschatological overtones in the relationship between the MT נצח and εἰς τὸ τέλος,[15] and after extensive study of τέλος and τελέω in ancient Greek literary sources, F. M. J. Waanders concludes that εἰς τὸ τέλος or ἐς τέλος has the basic adverbial meaning of "finally."[16] However, this definition does not make much sense in our present context of a liturgical poem.

If one considers the liturgical nature of the Psalms, then instead of looking at the entire phrase idiomatically, it might be illuminating to look

He does not argue that the two introductory words ניצוח וניגן have eschatological significance. Instead, he simply quotes H. D. Preuss, who says, "ניצוח and ניגן [introduce psalms] relating to the future" ("Die Psalmenüberschriften in Targum und Midrasch," *ZAW* 71 [1959]: 45–6). However, the eschatological significance of these two words is not self-evident, because not everything relating to the future is eschatological.

[12] L. C. L. Brenton, *The Septuagint with Apocrypha: Greek and English* (Grand Rapids, MI: Zondervan Publishing House, 1982; orig. 1851).

[13] Pietersma, *The Psalms.*

[14] Raymond Brown correctly points out that a later Christian messianic interpretation of Psalm 22 (MT) may have been given an eschatological overtone with the presence of εἰς τὸ τέλος, but he refrains from attributing either of these interpretations to Mark or pre-Markan Jews of the Second Temple period (*Death of the Messiah* II:1456, n.37). In addition, it is telling that in his recent study on the possible eschatological viewpoint of the Greek Psalter, Joachim Schaper never once mentions the phrase εἰς τὸ τέλος used in the superscripts as possible evidence for an eschatological interpretation of the Hebrew Psalms by the LXX Psalms translator(s). (Joachim Shaper, *Eschatology in the Greek Psalter* [Tübingen: Mohr (Siebeck), 1995]). Shaper's work has been roundly criticized for its over-reading of many eschatologically ambiguous phrases in the Psalter. See the review by Melvin K. Peters in *JBL* 116 (2, 1997): 350–2, and Claude E. Cox, "Schaper's Eschatology Meets Kraus's Theology of the Psalms," in *The Old Greek Psalter: Studies in Honour of Albert Pietersma* (ed. Robert J. V. Hiebert, Claude E. Cox, and Peter J. Gentry; JSOTSS 332; Sheffield: Sheffield Academic Press, 2001), 289–311.

[15] Peter R. Ackroyd, "נצח – εἰς τέλος," *ExpTim* 80 (1968–9): 126.

[16] F. M. J. Waanders, *The History of ΤΕΛΟΣ and ΤΕΛΕΩ in Ancient Greek* (Amsterdam, B. R. Grüner, 1983). See also, LSJ, 1773, which gives the adverbial meaning "in the end" or "in the long run" and "completely."

at some alternative meanings of τέλος and then render some possible meanings of the phrase that might correspond better with the Psalms' liturgical nature. The basic meaning of τέλος is "end," "completion," or "performance." This can take on different connotations depending on the context. For example, τέλος was used to indicate a class of people,[17] those in authority or command of a group,[18] or a station or post of duty.[19] It can also mean some task or duty that has been ordered to be completed.[20] In the literary context of these liturgical poems, τέλος could have the connotation of leader of a group or class of people as it does in many places in ancient Greek, in this case the leader of the liturgy or liturgical group performing the psalm. This would match the connotation of the Hebrew term מנצח,[21] which means "one who directs or oversees." So, the phrase εἰς τὸ τέλος would simply translate למנצח and mean "for the leader," indicating a liturgical directive similar to that of the Hebrew term and not having any eschatological overtone.

2.2   Psalm 21

Psalm 21 is the most evoked PsLam in the Gospel of Mark. It also has a long history of analysis among biblical scholars. Because it is such an

---

[17] See Dio Cassius, *Hist.*, 48.45.8, "but [he] even went farther and treated him with great honour, decorated him with gold rings, and enrolled him in the order of the knights (ἐς τὸ τῶν ὑππῶν τέλος). (Text and translation from Earnest Cary, ed. and trans., *Dio Cassius: History of Rome* (LCL; Cambridge, MA: Harvard University Press, 1914–27).

[18] See *Ajax* 1352: κλύειν τὸν ἐσθλὸν αχνδρα χρὴ τῶν ἐν τέλει ("The noble man should obey those in authority." Text and translation from Hugh Lloyd-Jones, ed. and trans., *Sophocles: Ajax, Electra, Oedipus Tyrannus* [LCL 20; Cambridge, MA: Harvard University Press, 1997]). See also *Antigone*, 67. See *Philoctetes* 95 and 385, which reads, κοὐκ αἰτιῶμαι κεῖνον ὡς τοὺς ἐν τέλει ("And I do not blame him so much as the commanders." Text and translation from Hugh Lloyd-Jones, ed. and trans., *Sophocles: Antigone, The Women of Trachis, Philoctetes, Oedipus at Colonus* [LCL 21; Cambridge, MA: Harvard University Press, 1998]). See Waanders, *The History of ΤΕΛΟΣ and ΤΕΛΕΩ*, 99–100.

[19] Herodotus uses τέλος in a sense of military categorization eleven times, four independently (7.81, 7.223, 9.42, 9.59) and seven with κατά (e.g., "It was he who first arrayed the men of Asia in companies [κατὰ τέλεα]" [1.103, cf. 7.211, 9.20, 9.22, 9.23, 9.33] and "All the rest of the riders were ranked in their several troops [κατὰ τέλεα]" [7.87]; text and translation from A. D. Godley, trans., *Herodotus, History, Books 1 and 2* (LCL 117; Cambridge, MA: Harvard University Press, 1920]). See Waanders, *The History of ΤΕΛΟΣ and ΤΕΛΕΩ*, 115–16. See also the many places in Thucydides where he has a similar usage, but see especially 1.48, where he has a similar usage except without κατά (αὐτοὶ ἐπεῖχον τρία τέλη ποιήσαντες τῶν νεῶν).

[20] See *Iliad* 11.439, where τέλος is used figuratively to refer to a sword completing its task after it is thrown. See Aeschylus, *Eumenides* 743, where τέλος denotes the judging office to which the jury is assigned. See Waanders, *The History of ΤΕΛΟΣ and ΤΕΛΕΩ* for an extensive discussion of all the nuances of τέλος.

[21] This word is the Piel participle of נצח.

important psalm for understanding the role of suffering and the characterization of Jesus and God in the Gospel of Mark, I will examine it in the most detail of the four psalms discussed in this chapter.

2.2.1   Structure

After the superscript, Psalm 21 (LXX) is a complex psalm that falls into roughly two parts: a lament and a promise of praise.[22] I will argue for the following structure:

v. 1 Superscript
vv. 2–22 Lament
    vv. 2–3 Cry to God questioning God's lack of attention
    vv. 4–6 Appeal to God's past action
    vv. 7–9 Description of situation of lamenter
    vv. 10–11 Description of relationship with God
    v. 12 Cry to God for help
    vv. 13–19 Further description of situation of lamenter
        vv. 13–14 Description of enemies
        vv. 15–16 Description of state of lamenter
        vv. 17–19 Intertwining of enemies with state of lamenter
    vv. 20–2 Cry to God for help

vv. 23–32 Vow and result of Praise
    v. 23 Vow of future praise
    vv. 24–5 Content of promised praise
    v. 26 Vow of the future praise continues
    vv. 27–32 Result of promised praise[23]

---

[22] Some early twentieth-century scholars, following late nineteenth-century scholarship, argued for Psalm 22 (MT) consisting of two separate psalms, verses 1–21 and verses 22–31. But since Begrich's work in 1934 on the *Heilsorakel*, there has been a virtual consensus that the psalm is best understood in its present form as a unity, with the shift in tone at verse 22 being the result of the supplicant receiving the word of deliverance from the worship official in a liturgical setting. See Hans-Joachim Kraus, *Psalms 1–59* (trans. Hilton C. Oswald; Minneapolis, MN: Fortress, 1993), 293, for a discussion of the relevant scholarship and for the view that the psalm is best read as a unity. See also Craigie, *Psalms 1–50*, 197, for a similar view. Frank-Lothar Hossfeld also posits that the final form of Psalm 22 underwent two redactions to the original psalm ("ein Grundpsalm"), which only included verses 1–3, 7–23. See Frank-Lothar Hossfeld and Erich Zenger, *Die Psalmen I* (Würzburg: Echter, 1993), 145.

[23] This section could be read as the result of God's actions that are requested earlier in the psalm. However, there is no clear indication in Psalm 21 that God has answered the psalmist after the lament section. In MT Ps 22:22b there is the ambiguous phrase ומקרני רמים עניתני which can either indicate a continuation of the imperative pattern from

The superscript is easily identifiable as verse 1, at least with regard to its place in the structure of the overall psalm. The next general section, verses 2–22, is distinguished both by content and syntax. Verses 2–3 and 20–2 form an inclusio of cries to God which sets off the section.[24] The content of the cries is different at each end of the section, in that verses 2–3 are a cry to God in which the psalmist implores God for an end to his being ignored in his time of need. Verses 20–2 are a cry to God for help and so more of a petition than the cry in verses 2–3. Syntactically, both ends of the section are in the second person, directly addressing God either in the imperative or the equivalent – πρόσχες in verse 2 and μὴ μακρύνῃς, πρόσχες, ῥῦσαι, and σῶσον in verses 20–2 – or in the second person indicative – ἐγκατέλιπες and εἰσακούσῃ in verses 2–3. Verses 2–3 also contain three addresses to God, with ὁ θεός functioning as vocatives, two of which have the possessive pronoun μου as part of the direct address. Verse 20 also contains the vocative κύριε as well as the emphatically expressed συ as the subject of the main imperatival subjunctive μὴ μακρύνῃς. Although there are other places between verses 2–3 and 20–2 that have direct address of God in the second person, the combination of similar syntax and content make the beginning and end of this section evident. The section's overall content differs significantly from the rest of the psalm, and a good way to describe the section is as the lament proper.

Within the lament section, there are several subsections, the identification of which makes the psalm easier to interpret. After the initial cry which questions God's present inaction, there is a shift in content to a

---

verses 21 and 22b or that God has answered the psalmist. If the latter is more likely, then the rest of the psalm is the psalmist's response of thanksgiving to God's deliverance. However, in LXX Ps 21, ומקרני רמים עניתני does not find its equivalent in verse 22b. Instead, there is καὶ ἀπὸ κεράτων μονοκερώτων τὴν ταπείνωσίν μου, which continues the imperative pattern of pattern of verses 21 and 22a. Verse 23 then begins the future-oriented speech, which I interpret as a vow of future praise that governs the rest of the psalm. See section 2.2.2.c of this chapter for a more detailed discussion of this section.

Pietersma, *The Psalms*, does not argue for a particular structure, since his task is only translation. However, he inserts breaks within the text of his translation to guide the reader of the psalm. This betrays what he thinks is the structure of Psalm 21, at least on the subsection level. His breaks do not clearly indicate what he thinks are the major sections of the psalm, but he has a structure similar to the one proposed above, with a few exceptions: (1) He does not link together verses 15 and 16 as one subsection of verses 13–19; (2) he does not provide a break between verse 23 and verses 24–5, but he does punctuate verse 23 with a colon, indicating a direct quote, as is argued above; and (3) he does not provide a break between verses 26 and 27, but does between verse 27 and verses 28–32.

[24] Verse 12 is also a cry to God for help, but it is much shorter than the cries in verses 2–3 and 20–2. The repeated cries to God in verses 2–3 and 20–2 seem more likely to set off a major section than the single cry to God in verse 12.

description of God's interaction with Israel. Verse 4 begins this description with ἐν ἁγίοις κατοικεῖς, which describes the present state of God,
followed by ὁ ἔπαινος Ισραηλ. In the next two verses, the psalmist uses
the aorist tense to reflect on Israel's past interaction with God – ἤλπισαν
three times, ἐρρύσω, ἐκέκραξαν, ἐσώθησαν, and οὐ κατῃσχύνθησαν. The
transition to the next subsection in verses 7–9 is marked by the change
in subject – third person to first person – and in content – from description of God and Israel's past intercourse with God to a description of the
lamenter and his situation.

The next subsection, verses 10–11, then begins with another change
in content and syntax. After verse 9, which contains a direct quotation of
the mocking the psalmist has received from "all who look at me" (πάντες
οἱ θεωροῦντές με), the subject changes again back to the second person
in verse 10, σὺ εἶ. The content again changes to a description of the
psalmist's relationship with God. The direct address to God continues,
culminating in an imperatival construction in verse 12. The cry to God
in verse 12 provides a good transition to the next subsection, in that it
introduces the sufferings of the psalmist described beginning in verse 13
while maintaining the direct address to God from verses 10–11.

Verses 13–19 comprise the largest subsection of the lament section.
The verbs are either in the third person plural or the first person singular in accordance with the content, which either reports the actions of
the psalmist's adversaries or depicts the misery of the psalmist himself.
The one exception can be found in verse 16c, where κατάγω appears in
the second person singular. I will discuss this in the interpretation section. The tense of the verbs is also consistently aorist, the one exception
being κεκόλληται, which is in the perfect tense. Syntactically, it is difficult to discern further divisions in this section, but the content allows
for this in that there is an alternation between description of the enemies (verses 13–14) and the state of the lamenter (verses 15–16), and
then an interlacing of the actions of these two sets of characters (verses
17–19).

Verse 20 returns to direct address to God with imperatives or imperatival constructions all the way through verse 22. The content in this
subsection is related to what went before; thus it is proper to place these
sections together in the overall lament section. In addition, the psalm
makes a sharp turn in syntax and content at the beginning of verse 23,
indicating a major division in structure. The lament has ended with a
series of exhortations to God by the lamenter for deliverance from his
miserable situation, but verse 23 begins with a verb in the future tense,

the content of which indicates a future report of God's actions on behalf of the lamenter. A new major section begins with this shift in syntax and content.

Verse 23 begins this new section, which extends to the end of the psalm. As just noted, the verbs become future indicative – διηγήσομαι and ὑμνήσω – although the addressee of the verb remains God, as indicated by the objects of the verbs – τὸ ὄνομά σου and σε, respectively. However, the verbs of verse 24 revert back to the imperative. This shift, combined with the addressees of the imperatives – οἱ φοβούμενοι κύριον, ἅπαν τὸ σπέρμα Ιακωβ, and ἅπαν τὸ σπέρμα Ισραηλ – indicate another change. Verse 25 then uses the third person singular aorist indicative to describe past actions by the LORD. The best way to explain these changes is to link these verses to the content of verse 23. In other words, the content of verses 24–5 is what the psalmist will describe in detail (διηγήσομαι) and sing a hymn about (ὑμνήσω) to his brothers (τοῖς ἀδελφοῖς μου) in the midst of the assembly (ἐν μέσῳ ἐκκλησίας).

Verse 26 signals an end to the reported, future-oriented speech of verses 24–5 as indicated by the addressee in 26a (σοῦ) and the future tense of the main verb in 26b (ἀποδώσω). If this division is correct, the verb in 26a should be provided with the tense of the main verb in 26b and therefore interpreted as implying future-oriented actions. The verse should then be translated, "From you will be my praise in the great assembly; I will give back my prayers before those who fear him."[25] Verse 27 changes back to the future tense, but the content no longer indicates a promise but, instead, indicates a future result of the praise. This future result carries through the end of verse 28, and then verses 29–30a explain why all the ends of the earth will remember and turn to the LORD and all the fathers of the nations will bow down to him. This explanation is both in the present tense (verse 29) and in the past tense (verse 30a), indicating the ongoing nature of God's relationship to the nations.

Contrary to the punctuation that Rahlfs provides in verse 30, I would argue that it makes more sense to put a period at the end of 30a instead of a comma, since the subject changes to πάντες οἱ καταβαίνοντες εἰς τὴν γῆν and the tense of the action changes to the future.[26] This would seem to indicate that the psalmist ceases his description of the nations' relationship of subservience to God and continues his description of the

---

[25] Verse 26a could also be read as a continuation of the reported, future-oriented speech from verses 24–5, but this does not account well for the change in addressee in 26a. The argument above would be more assured if the αὐτόν at the end of verse 26 were a σε.

[26] Pietersma, *The Psalms*, 19, puts a semicolon at the end of verse 30a.

effects of his praise of God, moving forward to include all mortals.[27] It would also link πάντες οἱ πίονες τῆς γῆς to the nations in verse 29, but it need not. Verse 30a could be an independent sentence whose subject is different both from the nations and from all mortals. We will discuss these possibilities further in the interpretation section below.

Verse 30c then begins another thought that brings the psalm back to the psalmist's local community. The double καί in this verse and verse 31a could signal a consecutive or subordinate relationship between the two sub-verses, "And my soul lives for him, *so* my offspring will serve him" (καὶ ἡ ψυχή μου αὐτῷ ζῇ, καὶ τὸ σπέρμα μου δουλεύσει αὐτῷ). This would fit with the next three lines if they are thought of as a continuation of the relationship expressed between God and the psalmist described in 30c. The main verbs of both verses are in the future; therefore, there is still a sense of future consequence begun back in verse 27, which is then further linked to verse 23, where the future orientation of the psalm began with the psalmist's promise of praise. Although the psalm ends with an aorist indicative verb, the tense is subordinated to the future orientation of the main verbs and therefore still stands as an indication of a future event rather than a past event. I will discuss the implications of this below.

2.2.2   Interpretation

2.2.2.a   Superscript

As is the case with most of the superscripts, the purpose of the psalm is described in general terms, and like the other Davidic psalms, the psalm is connected with David through the use of the dative construction ψαλμὸς τῷ Δαυιδ. This can be considered a dative of possession (i.e., David's psalm), agent (i.e., a psalm by David), or advantage (i.e., a psalm for David).[28] In this case, the superscript begins with the adverbial εἰς τὸ τέλος, which, as we have already seen, can be understood simply as a liturgical directive to the leader of the liturgical group.

The next part of the superscript reads ὑπὲρ τῆς ἀντιλήμψεως τῆς ἑωθινῆς, which is translated, "on behalf of (or concerning) support at dawn." Dawn is one of the times of solitude that allows reflection on one's situation in life, and, given the content of the psalm that follows, it would be an appropriate time for a reader to cry out to God in an effort

---

[27] Here, the nations and πάντες οἱ καταβαίνοντες εἰς τὴν γῆν are not synonymous. The psalmist seems to be expanding the population who will worship God from Israel to the nations to all mortals, inclusive of Israel and the nations.

[28] All of these dative uses fall under the general category of dative of interest. See Smyth §1474–94.

similar to that of the psalmist to communicate one's perceived suffering. The psalm offers a resource on which to draw and offers an important figure from Israelite history as a model for crying out to God.

2.2.2.b Lament

Verse 2 begins the lament section proper of the psalm with an expression of the relationship between the psalmist and God (Ὁ θεὸς ὁ θεός μου) and a request for attention (πρόσχες μοι). The request comes right before an indication that the psalmist feels neglected by God in his time of need. "Why did you abandon me?" (ἵνα τί ἐγκατέλιπές με;) does not just indicate a present state of being but something that has happened in the past that caused this present state. Since it is not in the present or imperfect, it does not indicate that this is a regular occurrence for the psalmist, but a one-time event. However, the psalmist is distressed enough to indicate that the feeling of abandonment has been somewhat extended. The second part of the verse perhaps gives an answer to the psalmist's question, or at least it recalls the traditional belief that the relationship between an individual and God is dependent on the actions of the individual. It describes the separation (μακράν) between what the psalmist wants and needs – τῆς σωτηρίας μου – and the psalmist's misdeeds – οἱ λόγοι τῶν παραπτωμάτων μου. Verse 2 describes the dissonance that the psalmist feels between what he expects from God based on his relationship with God – protection and presence – and what is actually happening.

Verse 3 is difficult to understand because (1) the future tense of the verbs does not easily fit with the aorist of the main verb of verse 2, and (2) the content of verse 3b (καὶ νυκτός, καὶ οὐκ εἰς ἄνοιαν ἐμοί) breaks the parallelism with verse 3a in a confusing way. First, I will discuss the issue of verse 3b. The problem arises with the phrase καὶ οὐκ εἰς ἄνοιαν ἐμοί. The most literal way to translate this phrase is, "and there is not (anything) which leads to folly for me." Pietersma translates this line, "and by night, but it will not turn into folly for me."[29] Rahlfs notes a textual emendation by J. S. Semler,[30] which changes εἰς ἄνοιαν to εἰς ἄνεσιν, presumably based on the MT of verse 3b, which reads ולילה ולא־דומיה לי.[31] J. Lust *et al.* offer a similar suggestion under the entry for ἄνοια. In citing Ps 21:3, they suggest a possible correction of the LXX by replacing εἰς

---

[29] Pietersma, *The Psalms*, 18.

[30] J. S. Semler, *Epistola ad Griesbachium de emendandis graecis V. T. interpretatibus* (1770), 13.

[31] Rahlfs, *Psalmi cum Odis*, 109. Rahlfs also refers to the *Prayer of Manesseh* 12:10 for a similar construction with ἄνεσις: καὶ οὐκ ἔστιν μοι ἄνεσις.

ἄνοιαν with εἰς ἄνεσιν in order to match up better with the MT.[32] According to the apparatus in Rahlfs, although there are no textual variations for εἰς ἄνοιαν, there are several other variations in the rest of verse 3, indicating the instability of this verse in the manuscript tradition.

Stylistically, εἰς ἄνοιαν does not fit with the rest of the verse. The parallelism common to biblical poetry is not upheld by this phrase, although violation of this stylistic rubric is not uncommon. However, the first part of the verse, καὶ νυκτός, καὶ οὐκ, begins the expected parallelism with 3a (κεκράξομαι ἡμέρας, καὶ οὐκ εἰσακούσῃ). There is no reason to expect a non-parallel structure before εἰς ἄνοιαν. The rest of the psalm confirms this stylistic expectation in that there is no verse that has a contradictory parallel structure like verse 3. Consistently throughout the psalm there is parallelism in structure or content, or both. Therefore, it seems anomalous in this context for εἰς ἄνοιαν to be the proper reading of the verse, and I would agree with Lust *et al.* as well as Semler that the text should be emended to read εἰς ἄνεσιν.

With regard to the futures, there are two options. First, the future can be taken as a normal future expressing the future actions of the psalmist and the expected response of God. Second, the future can be taken as expressing a present possibility.[33] If the futures are thought of as denoting a future time, they would be expressing strong doubt on the psalmist's part about God's willingness to listen to his cries: "My God, I will cry out to you by day, and you will not listen" (ὁ θεός μου, κεκράξομαι ἡμέραι, καὶ οὐκ εἰσακούσῃ). He is sure that God will not pay attention to his needs. Then the second part of the verse would express the adverse effects of such an action: "and [I will cry out] by night, and I do not have [anything] leading to abatement" (καὶ νυκτός, καὶ οὐκ εἰς ἄνεσιν ἐμοί). Taken this way, verse 3 is a very sharp statement indicting God for ignoring the pleas of the psalmist in his time of need.

If the futures are thought of as denoting a present possibility, then the statement still seems strongly negative against God. However, the statement is softened slightly because it only indicates a strong possibility that God will not listen. It almost becomes a conditional statement when thought of this way, because the possibility is not assured. "My God, I

---

[32] J. Lust, E. Eynikel, and K. Hauspie, *A Greek–English Lexicon of the Septuagint: Part I, A-I* (Stuttgart: Deutsche Bibelgesellschaft, 1992), 38.

[33] Smyth §1915 describes the syntax of this future in the following way: "The future may be used instead of the present of that which is possible at the moment of speaking." In 1915a, "The future may denote present intention." The second description, however, seems to be related to conditional sentences marked with εἰ, such as the future emotional (most vivid) conditional.

(could) cry out to you by day, and (but) you would not listen, and [I could cry out] by night, and I would not have [anything] leading to abatement." In a way, the psalmist is continuing his query of God started in verse 2, "Why did you abandon me?" If this is the nuance, the questions "why?" would be implied in verse 3.

Both possibilities further describe the feeling of abandonment expressed by the question in verse 2. The difference between the two is in the degree to which the psalmist expresses his consternation at being abandoned by God. The future expressing present possibility seems to fit most closely with the present situation of the psalmist as expressed by the question in verse 2. When read this way, the opening subsection of the lament would read as follows: the psalmist cries out to God, exhorts him to provide protection, and seriously questions God's involvement in his situation of as yet undescribed suffering. The imperative in verse 2a would not be present if the psalmist expressed despair. Why exhort God with an imperative if there is no hope of being answered? Therefore, the accusation of God on the psalmist's part must serve as a persuasive device to elicit action from God. We will see below how the entire psalm is unified by this effort to persuade God in different ways. Here, we see a vivid description of God's absence in the psalmist's situation. What follows in the next subsection describes the discord between the psalmist's present circumstances and his prior understanding of God's intercourse with Israel.

Verse 4 opens with an image in startling contrast (initially signaled by δέ) with what comes before it in verses 2–3. God is described emphatically in the present as "dwelling among holy ones" (σὺ δὲ ἐν ἁγίοις κατοικεῖς)[34] and as being "the praise of Israel" (ὁ ἔπαινος Ισραηλ). The psalmist views God as dwelling among the holy ones in part because that is who God is. But God as "the praise of Israel" offers a good transition to verse 5, where this epithet is elaborated in terms of the psalmist's view of God's history with the psalmist's ancestors. "Our fathers" (οἱ πατέρες ἡμῶν) placed their hopes "upon you" (ἐπὶ σοί), and they were protected by God. The verb ἐλπίζω in the aorist is repeated twice in this verse to highlight how faithful the psalmist's ancestors were to God, and in return God was also faithful in defending Israel. Verse 6a repeats the same κράζω from verse 3, here in the pluperfect, but in contrast the ancestors were saved when they cried out to God (πρὸς σέ). Again, verse 6b repeats ἐπὶ σοὶ ἤλπισαν, "they hoped in you," this time adding that the ancestors "were not put to shame"

---

[34] There is a textual variation at this point of verse 4, with ἁγίῳ instead of ἁγίοις in some manuscripts. Rahlfs chooses ἁγίοις because it is better attested.

(κατησχύνθησαν). In the course of two verses, the psalmist repeats ἐλπίζω three times, strongly reinforcing the faithfulness of the ancestors and the faithfulness of God in fulfilling their hopes. However, this repetition deeply calls into question God's present actions with regard to the psalmist. Rhetorically, the use of κράζω in verse 6 links the actions of the psalmist's ancestors with his present actions. As happened in the past with "our ancestors," the psalmist cries out to God; but unlike his ancestors, the psalmist does not receive defense, salvation, or freedom from shame. He receives abandonment and silence. The breach between what the psalmist has come to believe about God's faithfulness in times of need and what has actually happened in his particular circumstance is clearly articulated.[35]

As the appeal for God's response grows stronger, the next subsection begins describing the psalmist's lowly status among humans. The imagery begins in verse 7 with an inhuman self-description, lower than even the lowest of animals: "But I am a worm and not a person" (ἐγὼ δέ εἰμι σκώληξ καί ουχ' ἄνθρωπος). This is not just a self-designation, but a social one as well, because he goes on to say that those around him view his condition as "a disgrace of a man and a reproach of a people" (ὄνειδος ἀνθρώπου καὶ ἐξουδένημα λαοῦ). In verse 8, he tells how people reacted to him when seeing him: "All who look at me mock me, they speak with their lips, they shake their heads" (πάντες οἱ θεωροῦντές με ἐξεμυκτήρισάν με, ἐλάλησαν ἐν χείλεσιν, ἐκίνησαν κεφαλήν).

Verse 9 then describes by direct quotation a typical mocking that the psalmist received or receives: "He hoped in the LORD, let him deliver him; let him save him, for he wants him" (Ἤλπισεν ἐπί κύριον, ρυσάσθω αὐτόν· σωσάτω αὐτόν, ὅτι θέλει αὐτόν). Again, there is the repetition of the ἤλπισαν ἐπὶ αὐτόν, except this time it becomes more specific and focused on the psalmist and God, as indicated by the change in subject and the replacement of the pronoun σοί (verses 5 and 6) with the proper noun κύριον. This continues to highlight the relationship between the psalmist (the one who hopes in God) and God (the one who is supposed to fulfill those hopes). The content of the mocking takes it one step further and

---

[35] Verses 4–6 are often form-critically labeled "expression of confidence." However, this is based on the assumption that the psalmist is expressing the hope that God can act and will act on his behalf. It is also based on the desire to categorize the elements of the PssLam in a general way without attending to the particular features of each PsLam. See Johannes Heidler, "Die Verwendung von Psalm 22 in Kreuzigungsbericht des Markus: Ein Beitrag zur Frage nach der Christologie des Markus," in *Christi Leidenspsalm: Arbeiten zum 22. Psalm* (ed. Hartmut Genest; Neukirchener-Vluyn: Neukirchener, 1996), 29; Gerstenberger, *Psalms: Part 1*, 108, 110.

derides the supposed favored relation that the psalmist holds with God. The sarcasm of the mocking is thick, and when put in the mouth of the psalmist it becomes part of the expression of his shame. This shame is in sharp contrast to the psalmist's ancestors who were *not* put to shame (οὐ κατησχύνθησαν in verse 6) when they hoped in God.

In the next subsection, verses 10–12, the psalmist reverts to the past again. But unlike verses 5–6, where he reflects on the history of his ancestors, this time he reflects directly on his own personal history with God. This is not a long description of all the times he has called on God and been answered; rather it is an intimate look at the orientation of his life toward God from birth. With a series of "you are" statements directed at God, the psalmist characterizes God in relation to the psalmist: "For you are the one who drew me out from (the) womb, (you are) my hope from the breasts of my mother" (ὅτι σὺ εἶ ὁ ἐκσπάσας με ἐκ γαστρός, ἡ ἐλπίς μου ἀπὸ μαστῶν τῆς μητρός μου). Again, the hope motif comes to the fore, only this time the psalmist describes God as "my hope" and likens his present dependence on God to his dependence upon God as an infant at birth. He goes on, "Upon you I was cast from (the) womb, from the womb of my mother you are my God." (ἐπὶ σὲ ἐπερρίφην ἐκ μήτρας, ἐκ κοιλίας μητρός μου θεός μου εἶ σύ.) Verse 11a is difficult to translate, but literally it says, "Upon you I was cast from (the) womb," with the ἐπί plus accusative indicating the goal of the verb of motion.[36] Within the span of two verses, three different words for womb are used (γαστήρ, μήτρα, and κοιλία), and God is active in all three places where it is used. God is the one who acts as midwife at birth (verse 10a), the one who receives the psalmist at birth (verse 11a), and the one to whom or for whom the psalmist is born. This vivid, physically intimate imagery shows the depth of connection between the psalmist and God, at least in the psalmist's eyes; this rhetoric deepens the sense of God's absence after being so intimately present from the beginning of life and heightens the implication that God should act.

Verse 12 provides a transition from this subsection to the next with another direct plea for God's presence and action. In verse 12a the psalmist juxtaposes nearness and distance; what is distant is God, what is near is affliction. It should be the other way around, and the psalm clearly expresses a wish for these to be reversed, "Do not stand away from me, for affliction is near" (μὴ ἀποστῇς ἀπ᾽ ἐμοῦ, ὅτι θλῖψις ἐγγύς). Finally, the subsection ends: "Because there is no helper" (ὅτι οὐκ ἔστιν ὁ βοηθῶν).

---

[36] See Smyth §1689.3.a.

When read together the two lines of verse 12 seem to culminate in blaming the affliction of the psalmist on the absence of God – affliction is near because there is no helper (ὅτι οὐκ ἔστιν ὁ βοηθῶν). This is a bold move that makes a transition to a further description of the state of affairs of the psalmist and the evildoers who are making him miserable.

Verses 13–19 have an interesting and dynamic rhetorical feature, which heightens the urgency of the psalmist's expression of his dire situation. As I argued above when discussing the structure of the psalm, verses 13–14 describe the enemies of the psalmist, verses 15–16 describe the state of the lamenter, and verses 17–19 bring these two together in a graphic description of the psalmist's interaction with his enemies, presumably in the past, since the verbs are in the aorist. Animal imagery, used in verse 7, is used once again in verse 13, but here the enemies are described as "many young bulls" (μόσχοι πολλοί) and fat bulls (ταῦροι πίονες). The power differential cannot be greater than between a worm and young, fat bulls. These powerful enemies were not just present, they encircled and surrounded the psalmist – an image that indicates their readiness to attack and the lack of escape available to him. Verse 14 develops this notion further by using lion imagery to describe their stance toward the psalmist. "They opened their mouth(s) at me, like a lion who ravishes and roars" (ἤνοιξαν ἐπ' ἐμὲ τὸ στόμα αὐτῶν ὡς λέων ὁ ἁρπάζων καὶ ὠρυόμενος). Clearly, the imagery is meant to incite fear and describe the imminent doom of the psalmist.

Verse 15 turns back toward the psalmist. He was "poured out like water" (ὡς ὕδωρ ἐξεχύθην), his bones were scattered (καὶ διεσκορπίσθη πάντα τὰ ὀστᾶ μου), his "heart became like wax melting in the midst of" his inward parts (ἐγενήθη ἡ καρδία μου ὡσεὶ κηρὸς τηκόμενος ἐν μέσῳ τῆς κοιλίας μου). All of these images describe a vivid but understandable response to enemies who appear as powerful bulls and ravaging, roaring lions. Verse 16 continues the imagery: "My strength was dried up like clay, and my tongue has been been glued to my throat" (ἐξηράνθη ὡς ὄστρακον ἡ ἰσχύς μου, καὶ ἡ γλῶσσά μου κεκόλληται τῷ λάρυγγί μου). But then the verse takes a curious and important turn. It finishes with the statement, "And *you* sent me down into (the) dust of death" (καὶ εἰς χοῦν θανάτου κατήγαγές με). Who is the "you"? It is either the enemies or God, and since κατήγαγές is in the singular, it would seem to be referring to God. Slipped into the description of the enemies and the psalmist is a direct statement implicating God in his dire suffering. This goes beyond lamenting as self-expression and deepens the implied accusation in verse 12 that God caused the psalmist's suffering because there was no helper for him.

Verse 17 returns to a similar description of the enemies, this time calling them dogs (κύνες) and a gathering of evildoers (συναγωγὴ πονηρευομένων). Undomesticated dogs lived as scavengers both on the outskirts of cities and within them, feeding off of dead animals and other refuse from garbage or discarded food.[37] As used here in verse 17 (and again in verse 21) this image is clearly an ominous sign of death. Dogs would surround someone if the person was near death and there was a chance for food. The image brings the description of the situation to its most critical point. Verse 17c, "they dug through my hands and feet" (ὤρυξαν χεῖράς μου καὶ πόδας), is the first indication of physical harm that is done to the psalmist, thus consummating the interaction between the psalmist and his enemies.[38] The subject is the unexpressed evildoers, but when coupled with the dog imagery the strophe portrays a type of violence that would take place after death as the dogs begin to vie with one another in dragging the body away for food.

Verses 18 and 19 continue with the death imagery: "I counted all my bones, but they gazed and looked upon me. They divided my clothes among them and for my clothing they cast lots" (ἐξηρίθμησα πάντα τὰ ὀστᾶ μου, αὐτοὶ δὲ κατενόησαν καὶ ἐπεῖδόν με. διεμερίσαντο τὰ ἱμάτια μου ἑαυτοῖς καὶ ἐπὶ τὸν ἱματισμόν μου ἔβαλον κλῆρον). Much more clearly than the dog imagery, these verses make it apparent that the enemies of the psalmist consider him as good as dead. Indeed, the psalmist

---

[37] Edwin Firmage, "Zoology" (*ABD*, ed. David Noel Freedman; New York: Doubleday, 1992), VI:1143.

[38] The MT of verse 17c reads, כארי ידי ורגלי. Literally translated, this reads: "Like a lion are my hands and feet." There has been a long debate about what this actually means. See J. J. M. Roberts, "A New Root for an Old Crux, Ps. XXII 17c," *VT* 23 (1973): 247–52; Gregory Vall, "Psalm 22:17b: 'The Old Guess,'" *JBL* 116 (1997): 45–56; John Kaltner, "Psalm 22:17b: Second Guessing 'The Old Guess,'" *JBL* 117 (1998): 503–6; Brent A. Strawn, "Psalm 22:17b: More Guessing," *JBL* 119 (3, 2000), 439–51, for good summaries of the debate. The usual argument involves emendation of the text somehow to make more sense of the verse, given the difficulty in determining what "like a lion are my hands and feet" could mean. In the latest attempt to shed light on this topic, Strawn attempts to maintain the textual integrity of the verse by drawing upon iconographic images of lions in the Ancient Near East. He argues for the possibility that there was a verb that dropped out of the manuscript tradition after כארי, perhaps something that would indicate ripping or tearing, e.g., טרף. He argues for this based on iconographical and zoological evidence that points toward lions devouring their prey by dismemberment and leaving certain body parts of its prey, like the hooves, undevoured. Although the evidence is not conclusive, in Strawn's opinion it offers the best explanation with minimal emendation of the text.

The LXX apparently read the MT כארי as a form of the verb כרה "to dig" as in Ps 7:16 and translated it with ὀρύσσω. However, this was most likely not a Christianization of the Hebrew, since Jerome preserves a reading of the Hebrew כארו "to bind." Aquila and Symmachus understood the Hebrew this way as well. See Robert G. Bratcher and William D. Reyburn, *A Handbook on Psalms* (New York: United Bible Societies, 1991), 221.

sees himself that way as well. The subsection ends with stark and vivid imagery of extreme persecution and defeat.[39]

Verse 20, as well as the fact that the psalm was even written, is witness to the hyperbolic nature of the imagery used in the psalm thus far. Obviously, the psalmist survived to write this psalm, but he uses this imagery to drive home the seriousness of his situation to elicit God's response all the more. Verse 20 reverts to pleading for salvation and protection, forming an inclusio with verses 2–3 with respect to syntax and content and setting off this section from the rest of the psalm. The emphatic σύ begins verse 20, and four imperative constructions follow in the next six lines – μὴ μακρύνῃς, πρόσχες, ῥῦσαι, and σῶσον. The πρόσχες recalls verse 2a, the opening cry for help to God, and βοήθειάν μου recalls verse 12b. Both of these terms were used in ways that seriously challenged the actions of God, and when read here with verse 20 the implication is even more of a challenge: "If you have not attended to me up to now, nor have you been my help, even to the extent that this brought on more suffering and shame, do so now!" To reinforce the dire circumstances, more imagery is brought in and old imagery is repeated amidst the imperatives to remind God from what the psalmist needs saving – "from the sword" (ἀπὸ ῥομφαίας), "from the hand of the dog" (ἐκ χειρὸς κυνός), "from the mouth of the lion" (ἐκ στόματος λέοντος), and "from the horns of the unicorns" (ἀπὸ κεράτων μονοκερώτων). Along with these repeated and new images of danger, the psalm adds three different expressions to describe the psalmist – "my life" (τὴν ψυχήν μου), "my only begotten life" (τὴν μονογενῆ μου), and "my lowliness" (τὴν ταπείνωσίν μου) – which describe the psalmist's condition in a progressively precarious way. Rhetorically, the Greek communicates both the danger that exists and the insecurity of the psalmist.

By the end of this section, the force of the cry to God is intense, and the psalmist's pathos is palpable. The three cries to God punctuate the lament portion of the psalm, moving it along and keeping the descriptions of the situation directly tied to God. Interwoven among the descriptions of the

---

[39] What the actual situation of the psalmist is remains irrelevant. The imagery is not present to describe what actually happened but to communicate the perception of suffering from the psalmist's point of view. Whatever actually happened to elicit the writing of this psalm – sickness, persecution for difference of lifestyle or belief, attack on one's life – is not only undescribed in the psalm but is not important for the function of the psalm for either the psalmist or the reader. Joachim Gnilka attributes the psalmist's "emaciated body" (*abgemagerten Körper*) to serious sickness (*schwerer Krankheit*). The suffering of the psalmist is that of Jesus on the cross, but then he generalizes Jesus' suffering to address all of humanity by bringing in the suffering of the "righteous one," who supposedly stands for every righteous person (*Das Evangelium nach Markus*, II: 316–17). In section 1.2.2 of Chapter 1 of this study, I argued against the idea of the Righteous Sufferer, and so any argument based upon this concept raises suspicions for me.

situation of the lamenter are two appeals to the psalmist's understanding of his relationship with God, both his communal history and his personal history. These literary dynamics work together to create a powerfully sympathetic effect by drawing in the reader to the psalmist's predicament and raising questions about where God is and why God is not acting. With each cry these questions become more urgent and profound, and the dissonance between the way things ought to be for the psalmist and the way things actually are (in his view) becomes intensely pronounced. Since the addressee of the psalm is not primarily the reader but God, the attempt to elicit sympathy, and therefore response, from God becomes strikingly clear.

2.2.2.c Promise and result of praise

At first glance, the next section seems to be a non sequitur from the previous section. The tone of the language switches from dark and dire to upbeat and hopeful. The tenses of the main verbs change from mostly secondary (mainly aorist) to mostly primary (mainly future). The voice of the psalmist changes from exhortation to praise. I have addressed in detail several classic positions on the literary problem of the transition from lament to praise in the psalms of lament in Chapter 2, section 1.3. In short, Gunkel and Mowinckel argue for an outside experience of the psalmist, namely the reception of an oracle from the priest or God, indicating that God has answered and indeed saved the psalmist from his predicament. The psalmist's praise is a result of experiencing salvation. Westermann takes a different tack, in that he sees praise as the last element, following lament, of a pattern of experience of God on Israel's part. Praise, in fact, gives meaning to lament, something that would be meaningless without it. I disagree with all of these scholars, because I see the praise section as part of the overall effort on the part of the psalmist to elicit a response from God. The praise is real praise, but it is conditional, future-oriented praise that the psalmist vows to give God in return for deliverance.

As mentioned above, verse 23 begins a change in syntax. The first word is the main verb of the sentence and sets the tone for the entire section. The verb is διηγήσομαι – a first person singular, future, active, indicative – and likewise in the second strophe the main verb is ὑμνήσω. There is no clear indication that the psalmist has been heard by God, only a future-oriented pledge to tell about God's name to the psalmist's brothers and "hymn you" (ὑμνήσω σε) in the midst of the assembly. This pledge could be read as a response to the feeling of being heard, but this reading relies on clarifying the ambiguity by bringing in hypothetical reconstructions of a salvation oracle.[40] An assumption of response by God is certainly possible, especially if one takes the direct quotation of the future praise as an indication of the response of God to the psalmist's pleas. In addition, verse 32 could be taken as reporting that God has indeed acted. However, there are other ways to read these verbs in Greek, as I will argue next.[41]

A better way of understanding verses 24–5 and verse 32 is to try to make sense of them in accordance with the lament section of the psalm. As we have seen, the entire lament builds a strongly persuasive case that God should respond to the psalmist's pleas. Verses 23–32 could be read as a continuation of these pleas, only here the psalmist is offering a "deal" with God, a promise of praise before the congregation in return for response and deliverance by God. This argument has been put forth convincingly by Tony W. Cartledge, but his argument is based on the MT and, in part, on the conventions of Hebrew poetry.[42] The Greek does not have the structure of a conditional sentence according to the rules of Greek syntax, so we must argue from content rather than syntax.[43]

According to Cartledge, the traditional form-critical "outline" is inadequate because it assumes an amalgam of various forms as well as a liturgical *Sitz im Leben*. Once he identifies the literary form that signals the vow in Hebrew, he argues that the whole of the psalm is generally structured in a way to point "toward the end of making a vow to praise God when the prayer is answered."[44] By looking at the psalms of lament in

---

[40] See Chapter 2, section 1.1 for a discussion of the *Heilsorakel* as proposed by Begrich and Mowinkel.

[41] In the MT, the syntax of verse 22 is debated because of the form עֲנִיתָנִי. In contrast, the Greek of this verse is quite straightforward, perhaps reflecting a smoothing-out of the problems raised by עֲנִיתָנִי by reading it as a nominal form. This verse has vexed commentators, and there tend to be as many solutions as there are commentators. However, it is possible to make sense of this verse as it stands. Because analysis of the Hebrew of this verse is beyond the scope of the present study, I will not argue for the solution to the syntactical problems in the verse here.

[42] Tony W. Cartledge, "Conditional Vows in the Psalms of Lament: A New Approach to an Old Problem," in *The Listening Heart: Essays in Wisdom and the Psalms in Honor of Roland E. Murphy* (ed. Kenneth G. Hoglund JSOTSup 58; Sheffield: JSOT Press, 1987), 77–94.

[43] The LXX translates the second part of volitive sequences, such as the one present in verse 23, with various purpose clause constructions (usually ἵνα with the subjunctive), so it is impossible to tell the sense of the Greek solely by syntax.

[44] Cartledge, "Conditional Vows," 88. See Gerstenberger, *Psalms; Part 1*, 112, where he states without argument, "The thanksgiving song in vv. 23–27 features all the necessary elements of a ceremony in commemoration of a salvation experience . . . except the narration of past affliction . . . This song is therefore not an independent thanksgiving prayer but an anticipatory psalm that belongs to the preceding complaint and apparently was recited together with it in the hour of petition."

this way, he highlights the idea that the vow is the last and most powerful way of entreating God to act:

> Finally, perhaps because it is the strongest motivation, the psalmist may also appeal to God's desire for public praise through his vow. Again, it is not by chance that he may follow this with a comment regarding the pleasure which God takes in offerings of praise and thanksgiving, or with a statement of confidence that the prayer will be answered.[45]

The Greek lacks the literary structure of a conditional sentence or a purpose clause, but an argument from the content and sense of Psalm 21 (LXX) leads to the same conclusion that this last section begins with a vow of praise. Once this is granted, the rest of the psalm becomes much easier to interpret. This will become clearer as we progress through the interpretation of the psalm.[46]

After the initial vow is made in verse 23, verses 24–5 contain the content of the promised praise, which is a call to fear and glorify the LORD in verse 24, as signaled by the three aorist imperatives αἰνέσατε, δοξάσατε, and φοβηθήτωσαν, and a retelling of what God did for the psalmist in verse 25, "Because he did not despise, nor was he angry at the prayer of the poor, nor did he turn his face away from me, and when I cried out to him he listened to me" (ὅτι οὐκ ἐξουδένωσεν οὐδὲ προσώχθισεν τῇ δεήσει τοῦ πτωχοῦ οὐδὲ ἀπέστρεψεν τὸ πρόσωπον αὐτοῦ ἀπ᾽ ἐμοῦ καὶ ἐν τῷ κεκραγέναι με πρὸς αὐτὸν εἰσήκουσέν μου). This ends the direct quotation of the promised praise, since in verse 26 the subject of the main verb switches back to a first person singular (ἀποδώσω) and the object is God (παρὰ σοῦ).

Verse 26 forms an inclusio of content with verse 23, in that they surround the direct quotation of the promised praise. Both verses contain future verbs promising that the psalmist will praise God in the assembly (ἐν μέσῳ ἐκκλησίας in verse 23b and ἐν ἐκκλησίᾳ μεγάλῃ in verse 26a). This promise of praise in the great assembly can function as a powerfully persuasive device for convincing God, because the worship and devotion

---

[45] Cartledge, "Conditional Vows," 89.

[46] Cartledge correctly points out the reluctance of most commentators to see the vow for what it is, namely, a way of trying to persuade God to act. "These comments [i.e., those of Westermann, Begrich, A. A. Anderson, and de Vaux] show that scholars are clearly reluctant to ascribe conditional vows or 'bargains' to the psalmists. But would the psalmists have walked such an ethically 'higher plane' [a reference to Anderson's comments] than others who had experienced similar distress? . . . Why should the psalmist not feel the same inner urge [as Absalom and Hannah] to motivate divine action by the promise of an offering?" (ibid., 84).

of God's people is something that becomes increasingly important to God in the psalmic material of the Jewish scriptures.[47] In this case, the promise is directed at those who fear God (οἱ φοβούμενοι κύριον in verse 24a and φοβηθήτωσαν αὐτόν in 24b) and made before those who fear God (ἐνώπιον τῶν φοβουμένων αὐτόν in verse 26). The word ἀποδίδωμι can have the connotation of repaying what one owes or promised, and therefore in this context it can be thought of as a promise to fulfill the vowed prayers of praise that the psalmist makes in this section. The effect of this vow and the carrying-out of this vow will not only raise up in praise those devoted to God, but it could have the effect of inspiring and deepening the fear of those community members who have slipped in their devotion to God. The implication is that the psalmist's praise will be so powerful that he will inspire the entire congregation by reporting the great deed of God, if God acts. In addition, the psalmist also claims that the mere act of praise will come from God as a result of God's response to the psalmist's cry of help (παρά σοῦ ὁ ἔπαινός μου in 26a). Not only will the psalmist sing the praises of God for answering, but also he will honor God as the originator of the act of praise.

As I argued above, the rest of the psalm reports the future results of the promised praise mixed with declarations of God's kingship (verse 29a) and the fact that the Lord acted (verse 32). However, both of these statements are still couched within the future orientation of the section. God's kingship is the reason why "all the ends of the earth will remember, and they will turn to the Lord, and all the families of the nations will bow down," which in turn is a result of the answer to his cries from God for which the psalmist hopes. And if the Lord acts, then the result will be that future generations will announce God's righteousness. The effect of the praise in the remaining verses of the psalm spans temporal, spatial, and societal spectra as it builds out from the psalmist's congregation to the nations and humanity in general and then returns to the psalmist's local kin. It spans time both back to God's past relationship with the nations and into the indefinite future of the psalmist's offspring. Finally, it reaches

---

[47] Cartledge argues that early vows usually promised a sacrifice in return for whatever was asked for ([MT] 2 Sam 15:8; 1 Sam 1:11; Lev 7:16; 22:18–23, 38; Num 15:3, 8; 29:39; Deut 12:6, 11, 17, 26; 23:18–23; Jonah 2:10; Mal 1:14). However, the Psalms began to substitute vows of praise for vows of sacrifice, insisting that God is more pleased with praise than with animal sacrifice ([MT] Psalms 40:7, 50:12–15, 51:17–19, 69:31–2, etc.) (ibid., 85). See also A. Weiser, *The Psalms* (OTL; Philadelphia: Westminster, 1962), 21; Sigmund Mowinckel, *The Psalms in Israel's Worship*, II:19–22, 40. Westermann, however, argues that one should not think of the vow as a spiritualizing of the animal sacrifice: "Praising is not a substitute for sacrifice, but had its own original meaning alongside of sacrifice" (*Praise and Lament in the Psalms* [Atlanta: John Knox, 1981], 77).

from the lowliest member of humanity to the loftiest in stature. The effect of his praise is widespread, even universal, and promises much honor for God if his cries are answered and he is delivered from his misery.

After the discussion of the promised actions among the psalmist's community members, verse 27a begins to move to the lower levels of status in the community by referring to the poor and their most basic need, food. "The poor will eat and be filled up" (φάγονται πένητες καὶ ἐμπλησθή-σονται), and then 27b moves outward from the immediate community to promise the praise of "those who seek him [God]" (οἱ ἐκζητοῦντες αὐτόν). It is not clear who is being referred to here. It could be those beyond the psalmist's immediate community but still within Israel, or it could be moving beyond Israel to include the nations. The ambiguity provides a good transition to verse 28, but before verse 28 there is one more line in which the temporal dimension begins to become prominent, namely, with the appositional phrase in 27c, "Their hearts shall live forever" (ζήσονται αἱ καρδίαι αὐτῶν εἰς αἰῶνα αἰῶνος). The phrase is used in parallel with "those who seek him"; this is an indication that "their hearts" is a poetic way of saying "they."

Verse 28 clarifies the ambiguity of the subject of verse 27 in that it clearly moves beyond the Israelite community to include the whole world, expressed in poetic language: "All the ends of the earth will remember, and they will turn to the LORD" (μνησθήσονται καὶ ἐπιστραφήσονται πρὸς κύριον πάντα τὰ πέρατα τῆς γῆς). It continues in parallelism to include "all the families of the nations" (πᾶσαι πατριαὶ τῶν ἐθνῶν), but in both portions of the verse the psalmist makes remarkable claims. First, because of the psalmist's praise of God in return for God's response, the ends of the earth will remember and turn themselves to God. It is unclear what they will remember, but presumably it will be the actions of God on behalf of the psalmist. Furthermore, they will turn themselves to God, and then they will "bow down before you" (προσκυνήσουσιν ἐνώπιόν σου). The direct address to God appears again (σου), and the psalmist, in his attempt to convince God to act, claims that God's response and the psalmist's subsequent praise will effect the conversion of all the nations so much that the nations worship the God of Israel. There is not much more honor that can come to God through the actions of the psalmist than to have the entire world pay homage to the God of Israel. This is nothing less than universal unity of divine worship.

Verse 29 continues the powerful, hyperbolic language by affirming the rightness of the worship the psalmist describes in verse 28. It is right that all the nations will worship God because "dominion is the LORD'S, and he rules over the nations" (ὅτι τοῦ κυρίου ἡ βασιλεία, καὶ αὐτὸς δεσπόζει τῶν ἐθνῶν). In other words, the correct order of the world is that God has dominion over all the nations, and therefore it is right that all the world worships God. The psalmist is claiming that his praise after God's saving response to his pleas will put the world in right order. As a result of his praise, the nations will rightly and justly worship the God of Israel, who has dominion over them anyway. This would elevate the honor of God to a remarkable, but proper, level.

The talk about the nations is concluded in verse 30a, forming a nice inclusio with verse 27a. Here the other end of the social spectrum is reached as the psalmist goes from the poor in verse 27a to the rich (lit., "all the fat ones of the earth," πάντες οἱ πίονες τῆς γῆς). Verse 30a further justifies the rightness of the worship of the nations, even the most well-off of their members. The aorist verbs here are difficult to reconcile with the rest of this section, in that they are the only non-primary tense verbs that lie outside of the direct quotation in verses 24–5, with the exception of ἐποίησεν in verse 32b, which I will discuss below. Given the context of verse 30a, the psalmist's explanation of what will result from his praise of God's response, coming right after a general statement of truth about God's dominion over all the nations, it would seem best to think of these aorists as resultative aorists, a type of aorist which "denotes the result, end, or effect of an action."[48] If this is the case, the discussion about the nations concludes nicely and allows for a change in Rahlfs' punctuation to a period rather than a comma at the end of verse 30a.

The next line of the verse extends beyond just the nations to include all humanity throughout all times: "All those who go down into the earth shall fall before him" (ἐνώπιον αὐτοῦ προπεσοῦνται πάντες οἱ καταβαίνοντες εἰς τὴν γῆν). Many commentators think of this verse as an eschatological anticipation of God's reign,[49] but there is no reason to go that far. The word καταβαίνοντες is a present active participle, so it does not connote

---

[48] Smyth, §1926.

[49] Konrad Schaefer, *Psalms*, 56: "The poet, who feels about as low as one can get, a worm, who has been laid 'in the dust of death,' envisions a beatific future for all those 'who go down to the dust'; (verses 15, 29). This part connects the fate of the afflicted with the future of God's reign." Kraus, *Psalms 1–59*, 300: "Even the dead are included in the great homage . . . The dead have no connection to Yahweh, and they do not praise him . . . שאול is a place far removed from cultus. But now the barrier is broken down. Also those who sleep in the earth (Dan 12:2) are drawn into the homage to Yahweh." Volkmar Hirth, "Psalm 22 als zeitumspannendes Gebet," in *Christi Leidenspsalm: Arbeiten zum 22. Psalm* (ed., Hartmut Genest; Vluyn: Neukirchener, 1996), 23, adds this eschatological dimension to God's rule based on (1) the poor's reversal of fortune, (2) the fact that God rules over all peoples, and (3) all generations will worship God into the indefinite future. See also Hubert Irsigler, "Psalm 22: Endgestalt, Bedeuten und Funktion," in *Beiträge zur Psalmenforschung: Psalm 2 und 22* (ed. Josef Schreiner; Würzburg: Echter Verlag, 1988), 196.

all those who have died, rather all those who do die, that is, all humans. This is simply a continuation of the social and temporal expansion begun at the start of this section. Now it is not just the local community of the psalmist, nor just Israel, nor just the nations, nor just the poor, nor just the rich, but "all who go down into the earth" who will worship. It is a summary statement of all that was said leading up to the verse, a statement of the universal effect of the psalmist's promised praise if God responds by saving him.

Verse 30c shifts back to an individual level, back to the situation of the psalmist with a statement of the piety asserted by the psalmist himself: "And my soul lives for him" (καὶ ἡ ψυχή μου αὐτῷ ζῇ). As argued above, the καί in verse 31a could signal a subordinate relationship to 30c. If so, then what follows causatively, resultatively, or consecutively from the psalmist's dedication to God is that the psalmist's offspring shall serve God (καὶ τὸ σπέρμα μου δουλεύσει αὐτῷ). Again, the temporal and social realms are stretched into the future and include the offspring of the psalmist. This continues in the next three lines, in that the future gener-ation will proclaim (ἀναγγελοῦσιν) the righteousness (δικαιοσύνην) of God and that he acted (ὅτι ἐποίησεν ὁ κύριος). Not only does the psalmist promise his praise if God acts, but, because of his praise, he becomes the father of a tradition of proclamation to a people who will be born (λαῷ τῷ τεχθησομένῳ) that will retell God's righteousness as evidenced by God's actions.

2.2.2.d   Summary

From the foregoing analysis and interpretation, it is clear that the lament portion of Psalm 21 dominates the entire psalm. In it, the psalmist tries to elicit a response from God in a number of ways: by accusing God of absence in his time of need; by appealing to God's interaction with Israel's ancestors and pointing out that God is not acting consistently with him; by vividly describing the suffering and shame that he has endured because of God's absence – in contrast to the ancestors' salvation from shame; by describing the intimate connection with God that the psalmist has experienced from birth, which deepens the sense of God's absence in the present; by implicating God in the psalmist's suffering because of his absence during the description of the persecution he receives from his enemies; and by describing his state as progressively precarious to the point of being taken for dead. The whole of the lament is punctuated by three cries to God that embody all the suffering and betrayal, all the feelings of abandonment and silence that the psalmist describes in the previous twenty-one verses. Throughout, the psalmist intimately ties

God to himself in the sense that he sees God as the source of his suffering because God is absent and not attending to his cries for help. The psalmist attempts to elicit a response from God in the hope of saving action, and he does so with vivid and sometimes shocking rhetoric.

The vow of praise section is very different in tone, but its purpose is the same as the lament – to elicit a response from God. The vow of praise is a conditional vow, and the descriptions have hyperbolic imagery and rhetoric equal in magnitude to those of the lament. In this case, however, the vow of praise appeals to the glorifying effect that responding favorably to the psalmist's cries will have on God. All the world will praise the one who saves the psalmist, because the psalmist will remain faithful to his promise to spread the news of God's saving response. But everything hinges on God's action or inaction in response to the psalmist's situation of suffering.

In the eyes of the psalmist, there is much riding on God's pending response. God's relationship with the psalmist, God's credibility as a consistent adherent to the covenantal relationship made with Israel, God's very ways of dealing with humanity, God's exaltation in Israel, and the possibility of universal adherence to the God of Israel are all hanging in the balance, in the eyes of the psalmist. Although these are exaggerated claims, they are needed to shake an absent and silent God from perceived complacency in the face of the psalmist's desperate situation.

I will wait to contemplate the effect of reading the psalm with David as the imagined author of the psalm or voice of the psalmist until Chapter 6. For now it is enough to say that the persuasive power of the vivid language and imagery of the lament section of Psalm 21 is strengthened because the person speaking is not just an ordinary member of the community of Israel. Instead, God's chosen king is speaking this way to God. The words carry more persuasive weight, on the one hand, but they also lend a higher degree of legitimacy to demanding God's action in the face of suffering. In other words, if David is justified in calling God to act in such direct and challenging ways, then (1) he can act as a model that legitimizes such interaction with God for all members of Israel, or (2) as chosen representative of Israel, he can perform such laments to God on behalf of the whole community, if need be.

In the previous section, I said "the psalmist makes remarkable claims" when he claims that all the nations of the earth will come to God as a result of his praises. These claims become slightly less remarkable when they are thought of as coming from David. As king of Israel, he was the only one who could draw nations to God because of his power as the king and leader of Israel, divinely chosen as such. David's power to draw nations to God can also be thought of as a reflection of God's power, since God is the one who gave him the power to act as king.

Similar reasoning can be employed with the PssLam discussed below, all attributed to David by the time Mark was written. But I postpone such reasoning until Chapter 6, when I discuss the complex interaction of these PssLam with Mark's passion narrative.

2.3   Psalm 40

2.3.1   Structure

As I discussed in the opening paragraphs of this chapter, the standard commentaries and articles on the Psalms do not offer detailed analyses of the structure of Psalm 40 in Greek because they all comment on the structure of the Hebrew Psalm 41.[50] The few articles that deal exclusively with Psalm 41 take the same approach.[51] The structure of the Hebrew and Greek versions of the psalm may be similar, but because the structure of the psalm is determined by its syntax and content, which in turn are determined by the language in which the text is analyzed, it is important to determine the structure of the Greek version on its own terms.

I will argue for the following structure:

v. 1 Superscript
v. 2 Beatitude
v. 3–4 Petition/wish for one named in Beatitude
v. 5 Plea for mercy and healing
v. 6–10 Lament: description of situation
v. 11 Plea for mercy, elevation, and revenge
v. 12–13 Expression of confidence
v. 14 Praise of God.

[50] There seems to be a consensus that Psalm 41 is of mixed form, containing elements of lament and wisdom with a thanksgiving/doxology at the end. The doxology (41:14) is also viewed as the closing doxology of the first book of the Psalter. By the time this psalm was appropriated by early Christian writers like Mark, it was in its Greek form(s) as a unity. If one is interested in studying the interplay between the psalm's Greek form and a Gospel narrative, then the analysis should be performed on the Greek Psalm 40. For analyses of the Hebrew Psalm 41 as a mixed wisdom, lament, and thanksgiving psalm, see Kraus, *Psalms 1–59*; Peter C. Craigie, *Psalms 1–50*; Manfred Oeming, *Das Buch der Psalmen: Psalm 1–41* (Neuer Stuttgarter Kommentar: Altes Testament 13/1; Stuttgart: Verlag Katholisches Bibelwerk GmbH, 2000); and Hossfeld and Zenger, *Die Psalmen I*.

[51] Loren R. Fisher, "Betrayed by Friends: An Expository Study of Psalm 22," *Int* 18 (1, 1964): 20–38; P. Auffret, "'O bonheurs de l'homme attentif au faible!' Etude structurelle du Psaume 41," *Bijdragen* 50 (1989): 2–23.

The superscript is self-evident in form, as is the beatitude. As the psalm moves to verse 3, we notice that the verbs are aorist optatives in 3a (διαφυλάξαι, ζήσαι, μακαρίσαι) indicating either a wish or an imperatival construction. Verse 3b follows with μὴ παραδώῃ which is a negation of an aorist subjunctive in the third person. Given the parallelism that usually occurs in poetry of this sort, we can take this as a prohibitive subjunctive, which has much the same force as the optatives of verse 3a, if they are taken imperatively.[52] The next verse begins with another aorist optative (βοηθήσαι) in 4a, following the same pattern as in verse 3a, but then it contains a second person singular aorist active indicative in 4b (ἔστρεψας), breaking the pattern of third person singular exhortation found in verse 3 and 4a. Instead of relying on grammatical structure, we must look at the content of these verses to see how they are functioning structurally. I will address this issue below in the interpretive section. Since there is such a clear change in subject, content, and grammar between verses 4 and 5, let us agree that structurally there is a break after verse 4.

The next section, verses 5–11, begins and ends with a cry for mercy that frames a lament over the psalmist's situation. The section is very easily distinguishable and in need of little discussion. Verse 12, however, is not so straightforward. The key to determining the structural function of verse 12 lies in the phrase ἐν τούτῳ, which often signals a causative or instrumental relationship with what immediately precedes it.[53] However, ἐν τούτῳ in the LXX often introduces a vow, a conditional statement, or a statement of fact.[54] Therefore, it is most likely that ἐν τούτῳ refers to verse 13,[55] with the two ὅτι constructions of verse 12 resulting from indirect

---

[52] Therefore, we can translate verse 3, "Let the Lord guard him, and let him live and bless him in the land; and let him (the Lord) not hand him over into the hand of his enemy." In English, in the third person it is difficult to distinguish between optative of wish and the imperatival optative. I have chosen to use "let" as the more imperatival sense, with "may" as the wish sense. In my view the imperatival optative is not as strong as the imperative. Instead, the imperatival optative corresponds more closely to the hortatory subjunctive (or in this case, the subjunctive of prohibition), rather than to the imperative.

[53] Smyth does not discuss the construction ἐν τούτῳ explicitly, but he draws a distinction between οὗτος and ὅδε, saying that the former refers to what precedes and the latter to what follows. He does note that sometimes the reverse is true, especially with the neuter, which is present in verse 12. See the discussion in §1238–56. Blass, Debrunner, and Funk §219 (2) give a translation of "for that reason" for ἐν τούτῳ and cite Acts 24:16 and John 16:30 as two clear examples of this phrase referring to what precedes.

[54] Of the thirteen places where ἐν τούτῳ is used causatively or demonstratively, eleven point to what follows the phrase. See Gen 34:15, 22; 42:15, 33; Ex 7:17; Num 16:28; Josh 3:10–11; 1 Sam 2:10 (quinquies); Wis 16:8; *Ps. Sol.* 5:17; Jer 9:23. See Gen 24:14, 44 for examples of ἐν τούτῳ referring to what precedes it.

[55] ἐν τούτῳ translates בזאת, but this gives us no guidance, since בזאת can be used for reference backward or forward. See Bruce K. Waltke and Michael O'Connor, *An Introduction to Biblical Hebrew Syntax* (Winona Lake, IN: Eisenbrauns, 1990), 309.

discourse created with ἔγνων.[56] So the verse would read: "By this I know that you have favored me, (and) that my enemy will certainly not rejoice because of me," followed in verse 13 by the content of what the psalmist knows, namely that in the past God has helped him and established him forever, creating an unresolved tension between the present state of the psalmist and the fact that in the past God has established him forever.

Verse 14 then follows and completes the structure of the psalm by offering a benediction, which declares God blessed and thus praises him, as opposed to describing the blessed state of the person who pays attention to the poor in verse 2.[57] Form-critically, one can see a mixture of forms in the psalm, even in the Greek. However, as a unit, it seems to function most like a PsLam. We will see this more clearly below, because I will argue that the whole psalm is directed toward God as a way to persuade God to act on behalf of the suffering psalmist. The lament is at the heart of the psalm as the major element used to appeal to God for help.[58]

2.3.2 Interpretation

After the superscript, which attributes the psalm to David or implies that it was written for David (ψαλμὸς τῷ Δαυιδ), the psalm begins with a beatitude for the one who considers the poor and needy and an assurance of his deliverance by the Lord on the day of evil. This statement seems to be a general didactic saying that describes the order of social relations favored by God, since care for the poor is a primary criterion of a just order in Israel's sacred literature.[59] Verses 3 and 4 continue in this vein,

---

[56] The MT of 41:12 reads: בּוֹאת יָדַעְתִּי כִּי־חָפַצְתָּ בִּי כִּי לֹא־יָרִיעַ אֹיְבִי עָלָי. The double כי can be interpreted similarly to the Greek, but the second כי could also be read as a causal particle. A third possibility is that the second כי could be an emphatic particle. Given the parallelism in the verse, it is most likely that the verb יָדַעְתִּי is assumed in the second part of the verse leading to a reading similar to the one I propose for the Greek.

[57] See Joseph A. Fitzmyer, *The Gospel According to Luke I–IX* (AB 28; New York: Doubleday, 1981), 633, who describes the distinction between the terms μακάριος and εὐλογητός. The distinction rests in who the object of blessing is. With μακάριος, the human is the object of God's blessing and "the beatitude/macarism admits that the happy condition results from God's blessing, but emphasizes the concrete manifestation of the blessing." On the other hand, εὐλογητός is only used to describe God's blessedness as a way of praising him. The beatitude-form is not used of God but only of humans to describe "the person's resultant happy, prosperous, or fortunate condition."

[58] "Most of all it should be plain from our structural analysis that PLEA or PETITION for help . . . forms the very heart of a complaint song. There is hardly one pertinent psalm (only Psalm 88 comes close) that omits this central element. In fact, all the other elements can be interpreted as preparing and supporting the petition . . . Complaints always try to change a situation of injustice and misery for the better," Gerstenberger, *Psalms; Part 1*, 13.

[59] For example, Psalm 82; Jeremiah 22; Deuteronomy 10, 16, 24, 27; much of Amos; Isaiah 1, 58; Job 31; Zechariah 7 are among the many passages that describe this criterion.

but instead of asserting confidence in God's protection of the one who considers the poor, as the MT may,[60] the verbs are all in the form of an exhortation to God for protection, life, blessing, and aid during sickness, positively, and not being handed over to enemies, negatively, with regard to such a person. Following the beatitude of verse 2, verse 3 can be read as an exhortation for the continuation of the just social order as determined by God. If one considers the poor, then advocating that person's well-being is to wish for the same thing that God has willed. The psalmist presents God's fundamental concerns for humanity by means of a general and impersonal statement about how anyone with concerns for the poor should act. By making this general statement, the psalmist indirectly establishes his piety by expressing assent to God's ways and thereby taking the side of God with respect to social relations. In other words, the psalmist says, "This is the way humans should act in light of God's ways, I assent to it, and blessed is the one who does so." This sets up the rest of the psalm, which is a personal appeal to God by the psalmist, by aligning the particular person of the psalmist with anyone who considers the poor, that is, the righteous person in the eyes of God. The fact that the psalmist confesses his sin in verse 5 can be viewed as repentance of actions that take him away from this righteous way.

Verse 4 continues the urging begun in verse 3, but it becomes more specific. The psalmist's desire is for the person who considers the poor to be helped during sickness, and he closely associates with this help the general qualities that should result from a person's just action. Verse 4b becomes even more specific, appealing to a past action of God with an aorist verb and appealing directly to God in the second person of the aorist. And it is not just general help during sickness that the psalmist recalls, but it is care during sickness – "his whole bed you turned over during his sickness" (ὅλην τὴν κοίτην αὐτοῦ ἔστρεψας ἐν τῇ ἀρρωστίᾳ αὐτοῦ). Although this phrase is difficult to understand in a precise way, as it is in the MT,[61] the tense and person of the verb and the description of some caring action on the part of the subject, God,[62] make the verse intelligible

---

[60] All of the verbs from verses 3a and 4a are in the imperfect; 3b has the construction אל + perfect, indicating a negative imperative. These imperfect verbs could be read as jussives, but the common future translation is also possible. Therefore, in the MT verses 3 and 4 could continue the beatitude of verse 2. The Greek is much more clearly some form of wish or exhortation, since the verbs are not in the indicative.

[61] The MT reads, כל־משכבו הפכת בחליו.

[62] Craigie, *Psalms 1–50*, 320, reads this half of the verse as a metaphor portraying God as a nurse who provides the sick person with some comfort and consolation. Hossfeld, in *Die Psalmen I*, 262, reads this verse as God reversing the sickness, turning it into health for the sick person. Both of these commentators recognize the grammatical difficulty of the Hebrew in the verse and the somewhat ambiguous nature of the image. But both also affirm the overall intelligibility of the verse, in that it indicates help by God during sickness.

enough to show the psalmist's intention of positively describing God's past action during illness.

The psalmist quickly takes the psalm from the most general statement of justice in verse 2, which expresses his understanding of God's ways, to general exhortations to give the fruits of justice in verse 3, which express his alignment with God's will, to a more specific extrapolation of God's blessing of a just person in verse 4a, namely help during sickness, to a specific instance of past action that resulted in care during sickness in verse 4b. This progression sets up the description of the psalmist's particular case of suffering in the next section. Verses 2–4 are at once an affirmation of God's justice and a preparation for challenging that justice in relation to the psalmist's specific situation of suffering. The juxtaposition of verses 2–4 with the next section raises the question of where his desperate situation fits into this scheme of justice.

Verse 5 begins with the statement "ἐγὼ εἶπα," which puts the following verses in the context of reported speech. The question is where the reported speech ends. The words that follow are in the second person, so we should see where the second person verbal subjects end in order to determine where the reported speech ends. It is possible to read verse 6 as the end of the reported speech, but verses 11–13 pick up the second person address to God again. Grammatically, it makes sense to include verses 6–13 in the reported speech, and possibly even verse 14, if one considers the blessing spoken to God in the third person. Below, I will discuss the implications of the conclusion that all these sections are reported speech.

The cry for mercy in verse 5 comes just after the psalmist's recollection of God's past actions and wish for more of the same. The cry for healing in verse 5b is coupled with the reason that healing is needed – namely, the psalmist's sin against God. This sin goes undescribed; the acknowledgment is perhaps a general statement of the psalmist's lowly condition in comparison with God. It could also be an act of repentance or a plea for mercy. If so, then the plea for mercy leads nicely into the next verse in which the psalmist begins to describe the way that his enemies have treated him, namely with abusive speech. Twice in this section, in this verse and in verse 9, the psalmist reports in direct speech the ridicule he receives from his perceived enemies. In verse 6b, they anticipate his death so that his name may perish, which is a double death – his actual death and the forgetting of his name after death.[63]

---

[63] See, for example, Sir 15:6; 37:26; 40:12; 41:10–13; 44:8; Qoh 7:1; Prov 10:7; Job 18:17. See John J. Collins, *Jewish Wisdom in the Hellenistic Age* (Louisville, KY: Westminster/John Knox Press, 1997), 79.

Verse 7 is confusing because of the unexpressed subject of the verbs[64] and the content of the verse. If we take verse 7 as continuing the directly quoted speech begun in verse 6b, then the subject of the verbs is the psalmist, and the speakers are the enemies. Taken together with verse 6b, verse 7 continues the content of the evil that the enemies have spoken against the psalmist. The verse is a simple past condition: "And if he came in to see, he spoke foolishly; his heart gathered lawlessness to himself, he went out and spoke." The verse is cryptic with regard to the accusation being leveled against the psalmist by his enemies. All that can be said for certain is that the enemies are accusing him of being lawless in some way and then going out and spreading it about verbally in a customary way, as indicated by the imperfect tense[65] of the last two verbs.[66] Even if we cannot say with any specificity what the content of verses 6b–7 means, the psalmist gives the clear sense that his enemies view him as someone who has continually caused trouble in the past to the extent that they wish him dead and forgotten forever.

Verses 8 and 9 continue with the description of more abusive speech against the psalmist. In verse 8, all the psalmist's enemies whisper against him together and devise evil things for him. In verse 9, they utter a word of lawlessness, "The dead man will never rise again, will he?" In verse 10, even the one closest to the psalmist has joined in: "For even the man of my peace, in whom I hoped, the man eating my bread, magnified treachery against me" (καὶ γὰρ ὁ ἄνθρωπος τῆς εἰρήνης μου, ἐφ᾽ ὃν ἤλπισα, ὁ ἐσθίων ἄρτους μου, ἐμεγάλυνεν ἐπ᾽ ἐμὲ πτερνισμόν). The psalmist ends his lament here with the worst possible scenario – his closest friend has failed to respond to his need and has acted duplicitously against him, even though it is not specified what exactly the friend did.[67] This is in sharp contrast to the way things ought to be, as described in verses 2–4.

---

[64] The same issue is in the MT: ואם־בא לראות שוא ידבר לבו יקבץ־און לו יצא לחוץ ידבר.

[65] The syntax of verse 7 in the MT is that of a real condition introduced with אם and a perfect in the protasis and a series of imperfects in the apodosis. This construction connotes more of a present-future orientation of the conditional rather than the simple past condition of the Greek construction, although the distinction is not as clear in Hebrew as it is in Greek.

[66] Although λαλέω used at the end of verse 7 is a common word for speaking, it can have the nuance of chatter or speech that is not very useful or important. The translator or translators of the Psalter use this word in a variety of ways, so there is no discernible tendency to use λαλέω in a negative way.

[67] The phrase, "ἐμεγάλυνεν ἐπ᾽ ἐμὲ πτερνισμόν" is somewhat ambiguous in its content, but it clearly communicates an antagonistic response to the psalmist. The noun appears twice in the LXX, here and 4 Kdms 10:19, and in other Greek literature it only occurs in reference to Psalm 40. In 4 Kingdoms, it is clearer that the noun means cunning, since Jehu lures the worshippers into the temple of Baal. There he offers the burnt offering to Baal to make the gathering seem authentic, and then he orders the worshippers to be slaughtered and the temple of Baal to be destroyed. It is not so clear in Psalm 40 how the psalmist's

The psalm then moves to another cry for mercy in verse 11, framing the lament, but this time the psalmist cries, "Raise me up and I will pay them back" (καὶ ἀνάστησόν με, καὶ ἀνταποδώσω αὐτοῖς).[68]

As I argued above, ἐν τούτῳ in verse 12 refers to what follows it, and the two ὅτι clauses in the same verse signal indirect discourse supplementing ἔγνων. Therefore, the content referred to with ἐν τούτῳ actually begins in verse 13. Much like verses 2–4, verse 13 describes past events to remind God of what he has done in the past, but this time it is not for a general just person, but for the psalmist: "So, *me*, because of (my) guilelessness, you helped, and you established me before you forever" (ἐμοῦ δὲ διὰ τὴν ἀκακίαν ἀντελάβου, καὶ ἐβεβαίωσάς με ἐνώπιόν σου εἰς τὸν αἰῶνα). The emphatic ἐμοῦ, both in its form and placement, emphasizes the relationship of which the psalmist reminds God in this verse: (paraphrasing) "It is *I* here for whom you have done these things in the past; what about now?" The διὰ τὴν ἀκακίαν is an additional key to understanding this verse. In the past, God has helped the psalmist and established him because of his innocence. This is in sharp contrast to verse 5, in which the psalmist asks for mercy and healing *because of his sin*. In the past, the psalmist reminds God, help and establishment came because of the psalmist's blamelessness; but what about now, when sin is present? Together verses 12 and 13 function to express confidence in God's ability to act on behalf of the psalmist,[69] but at the same time they challenge God to act as he has in the past. The psalmist's confession of his sin displays his lack of arrogance before God, but it does not diminish his direct call for God to act. The psalmist acts as a human should, repentant and humble before God, and now he is challenging God to act as God should, responsive to his suffering. In other words, the psalmist is challenging God to live up to his side of the relationship assumed by the psalmist by acting on behalf of the psalmist.[70] Verse 14 then rounds

---

friend acts cunningly. The verb πτερίζω in this sense is a metaphorical extension of the idea of biting or striking at the heel. πτερνισμός translates עקב, which is a standard word for heel, which makes the image easier to translate, but not necessarily easier to understand, since this is an image that seems to have no direct analog in English. Perhaps one way to think of it is that one who strikes at the heel is not noticed until the injury occurs. This insinuates cunning to be able to sneak up to the victim without being seen.

[68] Cries for revenge are common in psalms of lament or complaint psalms, as Gunkel and Gerstenberger (and others) refer to them. See Gerstenberger, *Psalms: Part 1*, 12.

[69] The expression of confidence is also a common trait of the psalms of lament or complaint. Ibid.

[70] Cartledge, "Conditional Vows," 81. See also Walter Brueggemann, "The Psalms as Prayer," in *The Psalms in the Life of Faith*, 55, where he assumes a covenantal relationship between God and the psalmists and then builds an argument that explores the obligations on both sides of that relationship.

out the psalm with an unconditional praise of the God of Israel. Knowing that God delights in praise, it is performed in anticipation of God's definitive act as a persuasive device to elicit God's response to the psalmist's desperate situation.[71]

2.3.3   Summary

As the psalm ends, the psalmist has tried every way he can to entreat God. He has appealed to the past actions of God and to the just way that God would prefer things to be socially; he has aligned himself with God's will; he has cried out for mercy, healing, and forgiveness; he has described his desperate situation; he has expressed his confidence in God's ability to respond while at the same time issuing a challenge to God to act as he has in the past to show that the psalmist is pleasing to God; and finally, he has praised God in advance of an answer. But there is no answer, and this is highlighted by the fact that the whole of the psalm from verse 5 onward is placed in a context of reported speech, with the psalmist reporting his travails to God. By the end of the psalm, the reader expects a quotation recording God's answer. The psalm ends without God's response, and thus an ambiguity arises in the mind of the reader as to where God is in the midst of this psalmist's isolation and suffering. It is clear that the psalmist stands with God, because his entire appeal is directed toward God. But where does God stand? By raising this question, the psalm leaves the reader to reflect more deeply on the nature of the relationship between God and humans. There is no answer in the psalm, and in fact the psalm is not about finding answers. Rather it is about asking questions, expressing the reality of human suffering and the abandonment felt in the

---

[71] Cartledge, "Conditional Vows," 81; 86. This reading is contrary to the most commonly held view developed by Claus Westermann originally in *The Praise of God in the Psalms* (trans. Keith Crim; Richmond: John Knox Press, 1965), 15–35, and his, "The Role of Lament," 20–38, later reprinted in *Praise and Lament in the Psalms* (Atlanta: John Knox Press, 1981). This view essentially says that the point of praise in the PssLam is to indicate that God has heard the complaint and petition and that there has been a change in the situation of the psalmist. In "The Role of Lament," 26–7, Westermann states, "There is not a single psalm of lament that stops with lamentation. Lamentation has no meaning in and of itself . . . This transition [from lament to petition to praise in several combinations] in the structure of the psalm is rooted in the lament's function as an appeal . . . Understood in this way, the structure of the psalm of lament, which enables us to see the path leading to an alleviation of suffering, is one of the most powerful witnesses to the experience of God's activity in the Old Testament . . . Lamentation is turned into praise at the response to being saved (as in Psalm 22 especially)." While the lament may not be an end in itself, I think that the praise elements of these psalms are better interpreted as a persuasive device in certain psalms, rather than as a response to being saved.

midst of it, and probing more deeply into the mystery of God's interaction with humanity.

2.4 Psalm 41–2

The vast majority of commentators think that Psalms 42 and 43 (MT) were originally one psalm, mainly because many manuscripts have them together as one psalm. In addition, the repetition of the same three lines in 42:6, 12 and 43:5 lend a balance to the whole of the two psalms, if considered together, and the repetition of the content of 42:10b in 43:2b strengthens the link between them.[72] There is also no title at the beginning of Psalm 43, which is unusual in this part of the Psalter.[73] However, the LXX does give the second psalm a Davidic title – ψαλμὸς τῷ Δαυιδ – which creates a degree of separation between the two psalms. In spite of this separation, I will treat them as a unity. The reason is mostly convenience, since the alluding text (Mark 14:34) refers to an evoked phrase that occurs in both of these psalms (LXX Ps 41:6, 12 and 42:5). Because there is evidence of a unity of these two psalms, and since the reader would look at both of these psalms if he or she understood the allusion in Mark 14:34, it is best to consider the two psalms together, with Psalm 42 acting as a continuation of the structure and rhetoric of Psalm 41.

2.4.1 Structure

The structure is very easily discernible in these psalms because it is based not upon syntactical constructions but repetition of content. Therefore, there is no need to argue in detail for its structure as I did with the previous two psalms. I will only briefly discuss the structure outlined as follows:

> 41:1 Superscript
> 41:2–6 Strophe 1
>> v. 2–3 Expression of psalmist's state before God
>> v. 4 Description of suffering
>> v. 5 Description of past and future action of psalmist
>> v. 6 Refrain
> 41:7–12 Strophe 2

---

[72] See Kraus, *Psalms 1–59*, 437; Craigie, *Psalms 1–50*, 325; Bratcher and Reyburn, *A Handbook on Psalms*, 398; Hossfeld and Zenger, *Die Psalmen I*, 265; Gunkel, *Introduction to the Psalms*, 312, 327.
[73] Craigie, *Psalms 1–50*, 325.

    v. 7 Statement of psalmist's state and resulting vow of action
    v. 8 Description of God's qualities
    v. 9 Description of psalmist's piety
    v. 10–11 Cry to God
    v. 12 Refrain
   [42:1a Superscript]
   42:1b–5 Strophe 3
    v. 1b–3 Cry to God
    v. 4 Vow of praise
    v. 5 Refrain

  The structure of these two psalms treated as a unit is very different from the other PssLam discussed in this chapter. It is more rhythmic and hymnic than any of the others, and it does not contain easily discernible components common to many PssLam.[74] The most striking difference is that there is not a proportionately long lament section that dominates the unit as in Psalms 21, 40, and 68. What characterizes this as a PsLam is its rhythmic pattern of description of the psalmist's situation (within and outside the direct cries to God) and a refrain expressing confidence in God, rather than a dominant component of lament.

2.4.2 *Interpretation*

2.4.2.a *Superscript*

The superscript begins with the familiar εἰς τὸ τέλος, discussed above in section 2.1 of this chapter, and it continues with the phrase εἰς σύνεσιν τοῖς υἱοῖς Κορε. The reference to the sons of Korah probably means that the psalm originated with a group of psalmists known as the Korahites.[75] This group is described in 2 Chr 20:19 as leading the Israelites in praise, and in Num 26:58 they are listed as one of the five major levitical families. Over time, the family appears to have lost its influence in the cultic life of Israel,[76] and it is unlikely that the family was known at all in the Hellenistic or Roman periods. Even if the Korahites were unfamiliar to first-century readers,[77] the fact that the psalm is offered for understanding governs the meaning of the psalm by associating it with wisdom. Perhaps

---

[74] See Gerstenberger, *Psalms; Part 1*, 178–9.
[75] Bratcher and Reyburn, *A Handbook on Psalms*, 398.
[76] Rodney R. Hutton, "Korah, 2," *ABD* IV:100–1.
[77] The unfamiliarity with the Korahites during the first century probably strengthened the widespread opinion that David was the author of all the psalms.

this psalm is offered to give insight into the psalmist's struggle to make sense of his suffering, since the content of the psalm depicts the psalmist oscillating between, on the one hand, description of his suffering and pained cries to God, and repeated self-assurance, on the other hand.

2.4.2.b Strophe 1

The first strophe begins with a poetic and beautiful image in verse 2, which communicates the depth of dependence on God the psalmist has, or at least sees himself as having. A deer does not just prefer drinking from springs of water to other activities, but it utterly depends upon such springs for survival in the wilderness. If the deer does not get water, it will die. The verb ἐπιποθέω communicates this depth-dimension very well, in that it is a desire that cuts to the core of being; "yearn" or "long for" are good English equivalents. In addition, the image of a deer drinking from a spring of water in the wilderness is an arrestingly peaceful and beautiful image. All that one can do is behold the beauty when a scene such as this one is observed. The image communicates for the psalmist how right it is for his "soul" to be with God. As we move to the next verse, we learn about the desperation that can come in the face of God's absence from the psalmist's life.

Verse 3 continues the drinking image of verse 2: "My soul has thirsted for the living God" (ἐδίψησεν ἡ ψυχή μου πρὸς τὸν θεὸν τὸν ζῶντα). This sets up the next line, which asks in a longing way, "When will I come and appear to the face of God?" (πότε ἥξω καὶ ὀφθήσομαι τῷ προσώπῳ τοῦ θεοῦ;). This question is never answered in the psalm, even in the seemingly reassuring refrain that is repeated three times. The psalmist's desire to see God is rooted in his belief that (1) God is not present to him, (2) if he were present, then their union would be as beautiful as the deer at the spring, and (3) he would be saved as a result of God's presence.

Verse 4 is the first description of the psalmist's suffering. It is not very specific or concrete, but it is clear that he is in some sort of predicament that elicits a response from some onlookers. His description in verse 4a vividly depicts the result of his suffering: "My tears have become bread for me day and night" (ἐγενήθη μοι τὰ δάκρυά μου ἄρτος ἡμέρας καὶ νυκτός). So far, there no indication of what might be causing the psalmist's suffering – sickness, physical affliction, or persecution by enemies – other than God's absence, and the next line amplifies this sense: "while it is said to me each day, 'Where is your God?'" (ἐν τῷ λέγεσθαί μοι καθ' ἑκάστην ἡμέραν Ποῦ ἐστιν ὁ θεός σου;). There is an indication here that the psalmist sees the real problem as the interrelated issues of the suffering he endures and the absence of God that allows his suffering. As we will see in the next section, Psalm 68 deals with a similar issue, only much more forcefully.

Verse 5 opens with ταῦτα ἐμνήσθην (I remembered these things). It is not clear to what "ταῦτα" refers; presumably it means the questions that are asked of him regarding God's absence amidst his suffering. That would be enough to elicit a pouring-out of the psalmist's soul to himself to which he refers in the rest of the first line of verse 5. The remaining two lines of verse 5 are difficult to understand for two interrelated reasons. The presence of the ὅτι and of the future tense of the verb that follows makes it difficult to understand the ὅτι clause as a causative construction. Another way to understand the ὅτι clause is as a clause dependent on ἐμνήσθην. If this is the case, then ταῦτα refers forward to the content of the dependent clause, namely, that the psalmist will go to the Temple and confess God with rejoicing. Remembering this also causes the psalmist to pour out his soul to himself in self-encouragement that deliverance from his suffering is still a possibility if he can go to the Temple to confess God. The hope expressed in this verse does not erase the suffering caused by God's absence, but it does make it more tolerable.

The first strophe finishes with the first of the refrains: "Why are you grieved, soul, and why do you trouble me? Hope in God, for I shall confess concerning him: 'My God is the salvation of my face[78]'" (ἵνα τί περίλυπος εἶ, ψυχή, καὶ ἵνα τί συνταράσσεις με; ἔλπισον ἐπὶ τὸν θεόν, ὅτι ἐξομολογήσομαι αὐτῷ· σωτήριον τοῦ προσώπου μου ὁ θεός μου). In this first strophe, the refrain seems to act as a way of self-encouragement. The psalmist is trying to steel himself by expressing his intention to seek God's help in the Temple. He seems to be saying that perhaps his confession of his belief in God's ability to deliver him will result in God's saving presence. This is not a statement of confidence in the form-critical sense of the term, but a statement of hope that his continued pious actions before God and community will result in rectifying the situation that gives occasion to the psalm itself – the troubling absence of God causing his suffering.

2.4.2.c   Strophe 2

The second strophe starts out in verse 7 with a brief description of the psalmist's state: "My soul is troubled[79] in itself" (πρὸς ἐμαυτὸν ἡ ψυχή

---

[78] I choose to preserve the literal image of πρόσωπον by translating it "face." The word can also mean "person" or "life." The sense is that the psalmist is confessing his belief that God can save him from the suffering he is enduring.

[79] The aorist passive here (lit. "my soul was caused to be troubled") makes most sense as "my soul is now in a state of being troubled" or "my soul is troubled."

μου ἐταράχθη). The verse then continues to describe what the troubled state of the psalmist causes – memory of God's greatness. The future tense of the verb in verse 7b does not suggest a future vow; rather, it refers to an act in the more immediate future, namely the description of God in verses 8–9. These verses praise the overwhelming nature of God, whose presence causes even the depths to cry out at his awesome powers. The psalmist shares this sense of being overwhelmed by the greatness of God when he says, "all your waves and your billows have come over me" (πάντες οἱ μετεωρισμοί σου καὶ τὰ κύματά σου ἐπ᾽ ἐμὲ διῆλθον). In verse 9, the psalmist again weaves his own life into God's qualities, in a sense making himself part of God's world again: "By day the Lord will command his mercy, and by night a song is with me, a prayer to the God of my life" (ἡμέρας ἐντελεῖται κύριος τὸ ἔλεος αὐτοῦ, καὶ νυκτὸς ᾠδὴ παρ᾽ ἐμοί, προσευχὴ τῷ θεῷ τῆς ζωῆς μου). In a masterful way, the psalmist joins together the action of God (commanding his mercy) with his own actions (having a song and prayer to God, his life), which communicates the concord with God that the psalmist tries to live by; but at the same time he conveys the impression of the separation from God (God acts during the day, and he acts at night) that plagues him.

Verses 10–11 express this incongruity in the form of a cry to God: "I will say[80] to God, 'You are my protector; why did you forget me? Why do I go around looking angry while my enemy afflicts (me)? While crushing my bones, those who afflict me insult me while they say to me each day, "Where is your God?"'" (ἐρῶ τῷ θεῷ Ἀντιλήμπτωρ μου εἶ· διὰ τί μου ἐπελάθου; ἵνα τί σκυθρωπάζων πορεύομαι ἐν τῷ ἐκθλίβειν τὸν ἐχθρόν μου; ἐν τῷ καταθλάσαι τὰ ὀστᾶ μου ὠνείδισάν με οἱ θλίβοντές με ἐν τῷ λέγειν αὐτούς μοι καθ᾽ ἑκάστην ἡμέραν Ποῦ ἐστιν ὁ θεός σου;). This cry to God emphasizes the effect that the absence of God has on the psalmist, because it was just in the last verse (as well as woven in throughout the psalm) that he has recognized the awesome and merciful qualities of God, and, therefore, God's ability to save him. In other words, through his cry, he describes his suffering, acknowledges the greatness of God, and challenges God to act on his behalf. This is a pattern we have already seen in Psalms 21 and 40, and we will see it again in Psalm 68.

The second repetition of the refrain ends the strophe. In this case, because of what precedes it the refrain functions less as hopeful self-assurance and more as a challenge to God, in keeping with the tone of this particular strophe.

---

[80] Again, the future form of the verb has a more immediate sense rather than a vow of action at some point in the foreseeable future.

2.4.2.d   Strophe 3

Verse 1 begins with a typical Davidic superscript, which I have already discussed in section 2.1 of this chapter. The verse escalates the demanding tone of the second strophe with a direct challenge to God: "Judge me, God, and decide my case [brought] from a nation[81] not pious" (κρῖνόν με, ὁ θεός, καὶ δίκασον τὴν δίκην μου ἐξ ἔθνους οὐχ ὁσίου). Implicit in this imperative is the idea that the psalmist is acting in a holy way, and therefore God should see this and act. The psalmist follows with another direct plea for rescue, this time "from an unjust and deceitful person" (ἀπὸ ἀνθρώπου ἀδίκου καὶ δολίου ῥῦσαί με).

Verse 2 follows with a modified form of verse 10 in strophe 2, only here, instead of "protector" (ἀντιλήμπτωρ), God is "my strength" (κραταίωμά μου), and instead of "forgetting" the psalmist (μου ἐπελάθου), God "rejects" him (ἀπώσω με). The rest of the verse repeats verse 10b from the second strophe. Along with the wording, this verse repeats the dissonance between God's character and his lack of action on behalf of the psalmist. The rhetorical questions heighten the effect and communicate clearly that there is something wrong with this situation in the psalmist's eyes. How can God be his protector and strength and still cause his suffering by abandoning him? This is the underlying complaint of the psalm.

Verse 3 carries on with another imperative that cries to God for help. Again, the psalmist appeals to the wondrous qualities of God (τὸ φῶς σου καὶ τὴν ἀλήθειάν σου) as having the ability to sustain the psalmist so much, so that the result is communion with God. If God sends these representatives of his presence, then the psalmist will be guided toward God in the place where he is really present – the Temple, as indicated by the progressively specific imagery of "your holy mountain" and "your dwelling places" (ὄρος ἅγιόν σου and τὰ σκηνώματά σου). Once there, the psalmist vows in verse 4 to approach the altar of God. In God's presence, he vows to confess (in a thankful way: ἐξομολογήσομαι) with music, a fitting "sacrifice" at the altar of God. This vow has the same overtone as the conditional vows of Psalms 21 and 40, in that the psalmist is saying, "If you send your light and truth, which guide me to your house, I will approach the altar and offer a sacrifice of praise."

---

[81] I understand ἐξ as indicating origin. The idea of a case being brought against the psalmist by an impious nation is not clear, although it becomes more thinkable if the voice of the psalmist is viewed as David. The impious nation could be viewed as Israel at one of the times David perceived himself as isolated from the people (e.g., 2 Sam 15:3 "The hearts of the Israelites have gone after Absalom"). If David thought he was on God's side, then God's judgment would favor him over and against the impious Israelites.

The strophe ends with the third repetition of the refrain. Given the content of this strophe, the refrain still functions for the psalmist as a self-encouraging reminder of the hope he has that his piety will result in God's presence and, therefore, the psalmist's rescue. However, this strophe has the most direct challenge to God of any of the three. The psalmist challenges God's role as the psalmist's strength and protector by challenging God's abandonment of the psalmist. In addition, this strophe contains a conditional vow, which, as we have seen in Psalms 21 and 40, can function as persuasive rhetoric that urges God to act on behalf of the psalmist. Therefore, in the context of this strophe, the refrain gains a new dimension, one that goes beyond self-encouragement and includes a persuasive overtone that attempts to entice God to act based on God's salvific abilities.

2.4.2.e   Summary

The repetition of the refrain, then, functions in various ways throughout the psalm, depending upon the content of the strophe. The psalm builds in its exhortation to God so that by the time the third refrain comes, the psalmist looks for an answer to the question, "Why did you reject me?" The self-encouragement expressed in the refrain is present throughout, but by the end of the psalm, because of the direct challenge to God and the conditional vow expressed in the third strophe, the refrain also functions as a key part in the overall rhetoric of the psalm in attempting to persuade God to act on behalf of the psalmist. Therefore, ultimately, these two psalms try to use this rhythmic repetition as a persuasive device before God. There is no answer from God, but the psalmist has tried to make his case.

2.5   Psalm 68

Like Psalm 21, Psalm 68 has a long history of use in the story of Jesus' suffering and death. However, it has not commanded the sort of attention in the secondary literature that Psalm 21 has, perhaps because none of the words of the psalm found their way onto Jesus' lips in the canonical Gospels.

2.5.1   Structure

The structure of Psalm 68 is not easily delineated into sections, mainly because the sections tend to overlap at their borders. This makes for a flowing psalm with only one sharp break in tone between sections, which happens at verse 31. Nevertheless a structure is discernible as follows:

v.1 Superscript
vv. 2–22 Lament
    vv. 2–5 Description of situation, beginning with a plea to God
    vv. 6–7 Repentant plea to God to overlook sins
    vv. 8–13 Description of suffering as a result of piety
    vv. 14–19 Appeal to God for deliverance (overlapping with next subsection)
    vv. 20–2 Shaming of God

vv. 23–30 Wish for destruction of enemy (overlapping with previous subsection)
    vv. 23–9 Extended appeal to God to destroy enemy
    v. 30 Appeal to God for salvation

vv. 31–7 Vow of praise coupled with reasons for vow

Once again, the superscript is structurally self-evident, beginning with the common εἰς τὸ τέλος and ending with the typical Davidic element τῷ Δαυιδ. The next verse starts the longest of the three major sections of the psalm. The lament proper dominates the psalm, as it does in Psalms 21 and 40. It begins with a simple plea, Σῶσόν με, ὁ θεός. The aorist imperative that begins the body of the psalm has an important role syntactically, in that it governs the nuance of the verbs in the first part of the section through verse 5, after which there is a continuation of the aorist aspect in different forms, all with an imperatival sense. The aorist imperative at the head of the section allows one to think of the subsequent aorist indicative forms in verses 2–5 as having a perfective quality to them.[82] Therefore, the rest of verse 2 should be translated (literally) "because the waters have come in (εἰσήλθοσαν) as far as [threatening] my life,"[83] and verse 3a should be translated "I have been stuck (ἐνεπάγην) in the muck of the deep (and am still stuck there), and there is no support," and so on.

Verse 6 begins the next subsection with an acknowledgment of sin against God, followed by two pleas to God in verse 7 that ask for protection of those around the psalmist who may be affected by his foolishness

---

[82] See Smyth, §1940, for a discussion of the perfective nuance of the aorist aspect. The examples he cites are all from direct speech, which is comparable to this psalm since the psalmist is speaking directly to God.

[83] Literally, "waters came in as far as my soul," but the sense of the image is to convey being overwhelmed with his suffering just as much as if his life were threatened by a flood of water.

(ἀφροσύνη) and his transgressions (πλημμέλειαι). The content marks a shift, but the form of the verbs is still aorist. In verse 6a there is a gnomic aorist (ἔγνως), expressing a general truth or ongoing situation, and the aorist in verse 6b (ἐκρύβησαν) can be thought of in a perfective sense because it is direct speech and follows the gnomic aorist in 6a.

Verse 8 flows from verses 6 and 7 in terms of syntax with the causative ὅτι that begins the verse, but the content and tone shift from repentance to a somewhat accusatory description of the psalmist's suffering that results from his piety and commitment to God. Again, the aorists have a perfective sense, so there remains a strong element of syntactical continuity with the previous subsections, which lends a feeling of urgency and immediacy to the expression of the psalmist's suffering. The content of verse 14 flows smoothly from the descriptions of the suffering resulting from piety, in that there are two parallel, elliptical sentences in 14a and b in which the psalmist describes his ongoing piety. Following the syntax of the previous verses, the nuance of the supplied copulative verbs should be in continuity with the perfective sense of the aorists in verses 8–12.[84] Verse 14c makes the transition to the next section complete with a plea in the aorist imperative for God to listen to the psalmist – the first in a long series of pleas that overlaps with the next section.

When we come to verse 18 there is an overlap with the next section at verse 18c, in that the reason given by the psalmist for God to attend to his need is that he is afflicted (θλίβομαι). The tone seems to match the tone of shame that pervades verses 20–2, where the psalmist continually appeals to the fact that he is afflicted and that God knows it plainly. By pointing out the affliction and then saying point blank to God that he also knows these things, the psalmist heaps a strong element of shame upon God, especially if God does not act. The aorists of verse 21 again should be read in a perfective sense. This section leads into the next at verse 22 as the psalmist introduces an unspecified "they" as the subject (ἔδωκαν and ἐπότισαν). We have a sense of who "they" are from previous verses, especially verse 5 (οἱ μισοῦντές με δωρεάν, and οἱ ἐχθροί μου οἱ ἐκδιώκοντές με ἀδίκως) and verse 15 (οἱ μισοῦντές με), but the psalmist never specifically reveals who they are in this section. The section ends with a final direct appeal for God's saving presence in verse 30.

The psalm shifts in tone and syntax in verse 31, in that the tense of the verbs shifts from a present/perfective sense to a future sense, and

---

[84] There are two imperfects in verse 13 (ἠδολέσχουν and ἔψαλλον) that can be understood as describing past actions that have not been completed, giving a sense of ongoing action.

the tone shifts from one of desperation to one of praise.[85] Here begins the vow of praise common to many PssLam and present also in Psalms 21 and 40 as discussed above. In the midst of the vow, verse 33 shifts from a future indicative to a third person plural aorist active imperative and then to a second person plural aorist active imperative. But it need not be asserted that this shift indicates an actual address to a congregation, in this case the poor (πτωχοί). It could be a device that makes the vow that much more real and effective rhetorically by giving the content of what the vow will entail when the psalmist actually does perform it, if God responds to save him. Verse 34 follows the imperatives in verse 33 with two aorists (εἰσήκουσεν and ἐξουδένωσεν), so, just as previously in the psalm, the aorists can be understood in a perfective sense expressing reasons why the psalmist should praise God in the future.[86] The aorist could also be describing past actions of God as a way to remind God of those actions. Verse 35 repeats the imperatival structure of verse 33, only this time the reasons for the psalmist's exhortation to praise are given in the future tense in verses 36–7, rounding out the future orientation of the vow begun in verse 31.

2.5.2   Interpretation

One of the most prominent features of Psalm 68 is the repeated use of the causative ὅτι. It occurs in verses 2, 8, 10, 18, 27, 34, and 36, and spans all three sections of the psalm. I will attend to each in due time, but it is important to point out this feature of the psalm because it plays an important part in its rhetoric. In each place the psalmist uses it to offer reasons for God to act. In concert with the images used by the psalmist, it provides an effective way of trying to persuade God.

2.5.2.a   Superscript

The superscript has the common εἰς τὸ τέλος and τῷ Δαυιδ which I have discussed above, so only ὑπὲρ τῶν ἀλλοιωθησομένων remains to be discussed. There is no immediate literary context for this statement, since it is separated from the rest of the psalm by being in the superscript. This makes it difficult to narrow down the possibilities for how to construe

---

[85] The first verb in verse 31, αἰνέσω, is either the first person singular future active indicative or the first person singular aorist active subjunctive, but given the parallel line that follows in verse 31b, it should be read as a future.

[86] One could also think of the aorists here as gnomic aorists, expressing general truths. Either the gnomic or perfective aorists would yield a similar rhetorical effect of trying to persuade God to act.

the phrase. The basic meaning of ἀλλοιόω in the passive is "to be changed or altered." When coupled with the phrase εἰς τὸ τέλος it is tempting to think of this in an eschatological way, but the connotation in many of the usages is negative. For example, Dio Cassius uses this word with the connotation of being estranged.[87] Xenophon and Euphro both use it with the connotation of being changed for the worse, as does the LXX Book of Lamentations.[88] Given the content of the rest of the psalm, with its description of the protagonist becoming estranged from his family and community as a result of his pious loyalty to God, ἀλλοιωθησομένων makes most sense as a term that describes those whose future may hold something that changes them for the worse. When put in a prepositional phrase with ὑπέρ, the term can act as a title that describes the audience who would find the psalm most useful.

2.5.2.b *Lament (verses 2–22)*

The main body of the psalm begins with an imperative crying for God's salvation. As argued above, this imperative governs not only the subsequent syntax of the first part of the psalm, but, when coupled with the ὅτι that follows it, it also governs the subsequent content. "Save me, God, because . . ." is a direct request, and what follows is a vivid metaphorical description of the desperate state of the psalmist. For the first few verses, the psalmist describes in metaphorical and hyperbolic terms how he feels – swamped, overwhelmed by the oncoming storm of rejection, and in danger of being swallowed up by it. It is not until verse 4 that God is implicated in the suffering. Although there is no direct blame of God yet, part of the suffering results from the fact that the psalmist has been unanswered by God for so long in the midst of his suffering. The language is vivid – he has grown tired from crying out (ἐκοπίασα κράζων), his throat has become hoarse (ἐβραγχίασεν ὁ λάρυγξ μου), and his eyes have grown weary from hoping in God (ἐξέλιπον οἱ ὀφθαλμοί μου ἀπὸ τοῦ ἐλπίζειν ἐπὶ τὸν θεόν μου). The last verse of this subsection (verse 5) contains a more concrete description in that the psalmist names those who play a large role in his suffering – οἱ μισοῦντές με δωρεάν and οἱ εχθροί μου οἱ εκδιώκοντές με ἀδίκως.

What is most striking is the personal nature of his address to God (τὸν θεόν μου), which heightens the effect of the abandonment the psalmist expresses, as well as the culpability of God. Unlike the rhetoric of Psalm 40, where the psalmist carefully and subtly communicates that he has

---

[87] *History of Rome* 37, 11. See LSJ, 70.
[88] Xenophon, *Cyropaedia* 3.3.9; Euphron Comicus 10; LXX Lam 4:1. See LSJ, 70.

taken the side of God and expects that God will reciprocate, Psalm 68 is much bolder in communicating a similar idea. Here, he states flatly that he has cried out constantly to God, and all that he has received in return is a hoarse throat, weary eyes, and more enemies than he can count. His enemies are the immediate cause of his suffering, but the real reason the psalmist cries out in this psalm is because of the lack of response by his God. This comes right up front in the beginning of the psalm and thus colors the rest of it.

Verses 6–7 contain the repentant plea of the psalmist, with verse 7 forming a transition in content to the long description of the psalmist's suffering in verses 8–13. Verse 6 expresses another dimension of the relationship that the psalmist understands himself to have with God. It is one where the psalmist's foolishness (ἡ ἀφροσύνη) and transgressions (αἱ πλημμελείαι) are clear before God, communicating the psalmist's vulnerability. On the other hand, the verse juxtaposes God's omniscience with God's abandonment of the psalmist already conveyed in verse 4. The psalmist makes this clearer and more directly implicates God later in verse 20. Verse 7 continues to characterize God as a powerful force in that the psalmist calls God, "Lord, Lord of powers," (κύριε κύριε τῶν δυνάμεων) and "God of Israel" (ὁ θεὸς τοῦ Ἰσραηλ). The transition to verses 8–13 comes in the form of two parallel wishes that other pious people not be put to shame because of the psalmist (ἐπ' ἐμοί). Then verse 8 begins with another ὅτι, which causatively connects the ἐπ' ἐμοί with what follows: "Because on account of you I have borne insult, humiliation has covered my face" (ὅτι ἕνεκα σοῦ ὑπήνεγκα ὀνειδισμόν, ἐκάλυψεν ἐντροπὴ τὸ πρόσωπόν μου).

Verse 9 explicates the insults and the shame – becoming alienated from his family – and is followed by another ὅτι at the beginning of verse 10 giving the causes for his alienation. It is clear here that the psalmist is implicating God because it is on account of the psalmist's piety that he suffers at the hands of his kinfolk. His zeal for the house of God threatens to consume him (κατέφαγέν με) just as the storm from verse 3 threatens to swallow him up (κατεπόντισέν με). He even goes so far as to see himself as the scapegoat for God, as the one who receives the insults meant for God. Only because God is absent and the psalmist is visibly pious does he receive these insults. He becomes a substitute for God because God is absent, so not only is God not responding to the psalmist's desperate situation, the fact that God is absent means that he receives even more insults from those who hate him. Verses 11–13 compound this charge made by the psalmist: when he fasts, it becomes an insult for him; when he publicly repents, he becomes "a parable[89] to them" (ἐγενόμην αὐτοῖς εἰς παραβολήν); he even becomes the subject of gossip for those hanging around the gates and a subject of drinking songs for the town drunkards. He received all this in return for his piety and faithfulness to God.[90]

Verse 14 begins a long subsection pleading with God to rectify the psalmist's situation by delivering him from the suffering. The way he appeals is respectful and knowledgeable about the ability of God to save him in God's own time and goodness. Verse 15 mixes the literal description of his adversaries (τῶν μισούντων) with figurative language reminiscent of the early parts of the psalm (σῶσόν με ἀπὸ πηλοῦ, ἵνα μὴ ἐμπαγῶ· ῥυσθείην . . . ἐκ του βάθους τῶν ὑδάτων ["save me from the mud, so that I may not be stuck; may I be delivered . . . from the depth of the waters"]), and verse 16 continues this metaphorical water imagery that communicates impending danger and the personification of this danger.

Verses 17–19 repeat the respectful pleas to God for deliverance, with two important ὅτι clauses, one at the beginning and one at the end of the verses. The first one in verse 17 gives God the reason for responding to the psalmist – "because your mercy is good" (ὅτι χρηστὸν τὸ ἔλεός σου). When coupled with the first part of the second line of verse 17 (κατὰ τὸ πλῆθος τῶν οἰκτιρμῶν ["according to the abundance of your compassion"]), it forms a double appeal to God's mercy as the reason for God to answer the psalmist in his distress. The pleas in verse 17 have the double effect of crying out to God for help and communicating that the psalmist understands and acknowledges the merciful characteristics of God. The ὅτι clause in verse 18 has a similar double effect, but the appeal to mercy is less about reminding God of the psalmist's proper understanding of the divine nature and more about reminding God regarding the commitment entailed in the relationship, at least from the psalmist's perspective. The content of the ὅτι clause is simple – θλίβομαι, I am afflicted. When coupled with the ἕνεκα clause of verse 19 (ἕνεκα τῶν ἐχθρῶν μου ῥῦσαί με), the psalmist appeals to God based solely on his suffering – because the psalmist is afflicted, God must attend to him. There is no appeal to the justice of God or to the righteousness of the psalmist, only to the psalmist's suffering. That should be enough for God to respond, in the psalmist's eyes.

---

[89] παραβολή can simply mean an illustration, comparison, or analogy. The present context certainly gives it an overtone of mocking. So, putting on sackcloth has become an illustration of foolish piety.

[90] If this argument is correct, then verse 10b may have originally read "and the insults of those who insult you have fallen on me."

The close of this subsection sets up the next, where the claim made on God turns into a full-blown attempt to shame God into action. Verse 20 begins with the emphatic σὺ γὰρ γινώσκεις τὸν ὀνειδισμόν μου καὶ τὴν αἰσχύνην μου καὶ τὴν ἐντροπήν μου ("For you know my insult and my shame and my humiliation"), and continues with ἐναντίον σου πάντες οἱ θλίβοντές με ("before you are all those who afflict me"). It has become so bad that the psalmist's insult and misery have become expected for him, even an everyday occurrence (ὀνειδισμὸν προσεδόκησεν ἡ ψυχή μου καὶ ταλαιπωρίαν). But there is no deliverance for him, because the sympathizer he waits for and the comforter he seeks (i.e., God) are nowhere to be found (verse 21). As a result, "they" (i.e., the psalmist's enemies) make even the basics of food and drink a source of misery for the psalmist, giving him bile (χολήν) and vinegar (ὄξος) instead of food and drink that would sustain him (verse 22). Just as in verses 4 and 9–13, the psalmist communicates that God's absence causes and compounds his suffering.

This subsection reflects the main purpose of the whole first section, in that it clearly tries to elicit a response from God by not only pointing out the psalmist's suffering but also by calling God to account for the fact that the suffering is clear to God and yet God does nothing about it. God does not respond. There is no appeal to the psalmist's righteousness, only an appeal to the mercy of God and the presupposition that God should answer someone whose suffering is so blatant before an all-knowing deity.

2.5.2.c   Desire for the destruction of the enemy (verses 23–30)

After the psalmist has laid bare his suffering before God, he begins his tirade against his enemies, a common motif in PssLam.[91] In this case, as in so many of the subsections from the lament section, there is an overlap in content with what precedes it. Here verse 22 reintroduces the enemies after only brief mentions of them in verses 15, 19, and 20. Verse 23 begins a series of seven verses in which the psalmist appeals to God for the destruction of his enemies. In direct contrast to the "food" that his enemies give him in verse 22, the psalmist now wishes for the enemies' table to be a source of trouble for them. The next verse continues this parallel with the psalmist's situation, in that he wishes for their eyes to grow dark so that they cannot see – paralleling the weariness of the psalmist's eyes in verse 4 – and he wishes that "their backs bend constantly" (τὸν νῶτον αὐτῶν διὰ παντὸς σύγκαμψον) – paralleling the voluntary "bending"

---

[91] See Chapter 2, section 1 for a discussion of the form-critical analysis of the PssLam and the references there.

(συνέκαμψα) he performs in his fasting as described in verse 11. Whereas his weariness of eyes and bending down happen as a result of his piety and devotion to God, not to mention the fact that this same piety and devotion result in public insult and derision, the psalmist points out that the enemies are not receiving these same afflictions, even though they are acting in ways that are impious and unjust to the psalmist. The psalmist is attempting to convince God to thrust the affliction he is receiving for his piety onto his enemies, whom the psalmist sees as much more deserving of affliction than he is.

Verse 25 furthers the invective against the enemies, only this time it comes in direct address to God rather than in the indirect, third person imperatives of verses 23–4: "Pour out your anger upon them, and may the heat of your anger overtake them" (ἔκχεον ἐπ᾽ αὐτοὺς τὴν ὀργήν σου, καὶ ὁ θυμὸς τῆς ὀργῆς σου καταλάβοι αὐτούς). The psalmist seems to be trying to redirect the wrath he thinks God is directing at him. Verse 26 begins an effort on the psalmist's part to go beyond redirecting the personal suffering he has been undergoing. Instead, by wishing for their villages and dwelling places to be uninhabited, he wishes for the entire social unit of the enemies to be decimated. Verses 28b–9 continue this social theme, but instead of the barrenness of their places of habitation, the psalmist wishes for their ultimate destruction: "And let them not come into your righteousness; let them be wiped out of the book of the living and let them not be written with the righteous ones" (καὶ μὴ εἰσελθέτωσαν ἐν δικαιοσύνῃ σου· ἐξαλειφθήτωσαν ἐκ βίβλου ζώντων καὶ μετὰ δικαίων μὴ γραφήτωσαν).[92] He wishes for the enemies to be completely excluded from the human community that finds favor with God, but at the same time he subtly reminds God that he belongs to this community. He indirectly sets himself off from his enemies socially by making a claim that he knows about this righteous community and thinks of himself as being within its boundaries. Wishing for the exclusion of his enemies from this group not only heightens the invective against them but also serves to put him on God's side and alert God to his assumed place with "the righteous ones."

---

[92] It is unclear whether the notions of these verses, especially the phrase ἐξαλειφθήτωσαν ἐκ βίβλου ζώντων, were intended to be read in eschatological terms by the translator of this psalm. However, it certainly could be understood this way by a native Greek speaker around Mark's time. But given the immediacy of the psalm as a whole, I do not think that too much weight should be put on the possible eschatological overtones of these verses. The psalm seems most interested in expressing the need for immediate action on God's part to relieve the psalmist from his misery and affliction at the hands of his enemies. These verses simply form part of the invective against the enemies, expressing the immediacy of his affliction.

Sandwiched in between these wishes for social exclusion of the enemy is another ὅτι clause in verse 27. Again, a reason for God to respond to the psalmist's requests is given through this construction. Although the content of the clauses ultimately finds fault with the enemies, the way that the psalmist constructs the accusation against them also implicates God. The enemies pursue the psalmist, but he describes himself as "the one whom you struck" (ὅν σὺ ἐπάταξας) and as one of "your wounded ones" (τῶν τραυματιῶν σου).[93] Persecuting the psalmist and adding to his pain certainly make the invective directed toward the enemy understandable, although ethically questionable, but by identifying himself as stricken and wounded by God the psalmist makes a striking statement about God. God not only is the one to whom the psalmist appeals for help and deliverance, God is the one who strikes and causes the wounds of the psalmist. Furthermore, by saying that his enemies should be made to pay for worsening his stricken and wounded state, the psalmist indirectly implicates God for causing it in the first place. In other words, by the logic of the verse, the enemies and God are performing the same actions against the psalmist,[94] and by crying for the punishment of his enemies, the psalmist also implicates God as the source of his suffering.

The verbally violent section ends with one final implicit appeal to the mercy of God based on the sad state of the psalmist: "I am poor and in pain, the salvation of your face, O God, has taken hold of me" (πτωχὸς καὶ ἀλγῶν εἰμι ἐγώ, καὶ ἡ σωτηρία τοῦ προσώπου σου, ὁ θεός, ἀντελάβετό μου). Again, we can take the aorist in a perfective sense because it follows an imperative in the previous verse. Therefore, the implication of the verse is: "I am poor and in pain, therefore, since your salvation has taken hold of me before, let it do so again."

2.5.2.d Vow of praise

Finally, we come to the vow of praise beginning in verse 31, an element common to all the psalms discussed in this chapter. Much as in Psalms 21

---

[93] The plural here is curious. There is a suggested emendation to the text that upholds the parallelism of the verse but does not accurately represent the MT. According to Rahlfs, the manuscripts have "τραυματῶν μου" rather than "τραυματιῶν σου" as suggested by Grabe. But given the individual nature of the psalm thus far, it is difficult to understand why the psalm switches to the plural when describing suffering, unless this indicates that the psalmist refers to himself and his family or allies who suffer as he does.

[94] This fits with the ancient notion that God is responsible for the good and the bad that happens to humans. Because of belief in God's sovereignty within this cultural context, God can act in whatever way God chooses. By constructing the psalm as he does, the psalmist seems to raise the theological question of why this is the case when suffering is so painfully detrimental to the psalmist.

and 40, the vow here functions as a conditional vow to praise God in return for God's action on behalf of the psalmist. Since the syntactical structure is especially similar to Psalm 21, in that the whole section is governed by the future tense (αἰνέσω and μεγαλυνῶ in verse 31) and the content of the vow (arguably) is governed by the initial future promise of the vow, there is no need to argue extensively for the possibility of this interpretation as I did for Psalm 21. I will simply point out certain unique features of the content of Psalm 68's vow and how they function rhetorically in the whole of the psalm.

Unlike Psalm 21, the vow in Psalm 68 has a sacrificial image that communicates the importance and possible power of the effect of the praise that the psalmist promises. Verse 32 reads, "(for) it [the praise] will be more pleasing to God than a young bull bearing horns and hooves" (καὶ ἀρέσει τῷ θεῷ ὑπὲρ μόσχον νέον κέρατα ἐκφέροντα καὶ ὁπλάς). Young bulls were valuable animals in Israelite cultic sacrificial practice,[95] and the young bull was even more valuable because of its youth, signifying the low possibility of blemish and the potential for helping populate and sustain the future of the herd. To say that his praises will be more pleasing to God than the sacrifice of a young bull is a strong statement about the persuasive power of the vow he has made to praise God.

Verses 33–7 can be read as the content of the praise that the psalmist vows to make. In this case, the praise is in the form of exhortation to the community gathered before him, especially directed to "the poor" (πτωχοί in verse 33 and οἱ πένητες in verse 34) and "his [God's] bound ones" (οἱ πεπεδήμενοι αὐτοῦ in verse 34). The praise reports the saving actions of God in the past as the reason for the praise and rejoicing of the poor (with a characteristic ὅτι clause), but given the conditional nature of the vow, this should be read as not having happened yet. In other words, the psalmist is saying, "If you answer my cry for deliverance, God, I will report it to the congregation and exhort those who are in situations similar to the one I was in to turn to you for help and not to lose hope." The promised praise continues in verse 35 with an exhortation to all of creation to join in the praise, followed in verse 36 by the final ὅτι clause of the psalm, which extends all the way to the end of the psalm. Much like the other ὅτι clauses, this one offers the reason for the action that

---

[95] From biblical data alone, the average ratio of sheep to cattle was about 8:1. Judging on the basis of more widespread Ancient Near Eastern economic and other data, the relative value of cattle would be ten times greater than sheep. See Firmage, "Zoology," 1119–20.

precedes it or follows it. In this case, it gives the motivation for all of creation to praise God: God will save Zion and fill the cities of Judah with occupants who will inherit the land and serve God and love God's name.

The two final ὅτι clauses of the psalm have different temporal frames of reference, but both are constructed to generate the hope of those who will listen to the vowed praise. The one in verse 34 generates hope based on the past actions of God, if he indeed acts, and the one in verses 36–7 generates hope by painting a vision of the future long hoped-for in Israel's history – inheritance of the land and occupation of it by God-serving and God-loving people. The promised vow is constructed in such a way that the entire community will be lifted up by the hope it communicates. This is very persuasive for the psalmist's case before God because it places the hopes of the entire community on whether or not God responds to the cries of the psalmist.

2.5.2.e   Summary

What is most striking about Psalm 68 is the direct and indirect ways in which the psalmist implicates God in his suffering. From the beginning of the psalm, the psalmist personally addresses God. Throughout the description of his suffering, the biggest complaint of the psalmist is not the insults and afflictions he experiences at the hands of his enemies. Rather, the psalmist implicates God as the reason that he is suffering so much. His faithful piety has resulted in insult and affliction, and furthermore the insults that he has received were meant for God. The only reason the psalmist has received them is because God is absent. The suffering gets so bad for the psalmist that he expects it on a regular basis, but even this is not the source of the betrayal he expresses. It is the fact that God has not acted. Perhaps the most insightful part of the lament is the reason the psalmist eventually gives God to act – because he is afflicted and God knows about it. There is no appeal to the psalmist's righteousness or blamelessness or to justice in general. There is only appeal to the bare fact that the psalmist is suffering and in need of God's help, a fact that raises the question of the propriety of the portrayal of God as one who causes suffering for those who sin.

The psalmist's invective against his enemies functions to express the fury he feels about his situation, but it also cleverly and subtly reminds God of the fact that God has a responsibility to act on his part. He separates himself from the enemy, thus taking the side of God. At the same time, he alerts God to this fact and reveals God simultaneously as the one to whom he appeals for help and the one from whom his affliction comes. Further on in the vow of praise, the psalmist pins the hope of the entire community on whether God acts on his behalf or not. By the end of the psalm, the psalmist has attempted to persuade God to act by heaping a great deal of shame on God. It is almost as if he is trying to shock God into action with his direct and biting implication of God in the misery that he is experiencing, while at the same time appealing to the mercy and saving ability of God.

3   Conclusion

We have seen the literary power of four PssLam in this chapter. All four psalms attempt to persuade God in various ways to act on behalf of the psalmist as he experiences suffering. Although one can notice patterns in the literary forms that each psalm contains – lament, vow of praise, and wish for the destruction of the enemy – it is important to balance these common rhetorical features with attention to the details that each individual psalm presents. The details and rhetorical structure of each psalm are vital for gaining an adequate understanding of the way each psalmist attempts to succeed in persuading God to act on the psalmist's behalf. Only then can one appropriately bring these psalms into conversation with later texts that use them for differing reasons.

When reading these psalms in Greek, it is also important to read them as honestly as possible, without trying to have every psalm turn out to have a happy ending. Yes, there are positive images in each psalm, but the overwhelmingly dominant aspect of these psalms is the fact that the psalmist is suffering and cries out to God as a result of his perceived abandonment by God, which compounds the suffering of the psalmist. Even the positive aspects of these psalms do not communicate the result of God's saving action. Instead, they attempt to persuade God to act, just as the lament portions do. Everything in each of these psalms deals with this central problem of the abandonment, the silence, and the absence of God for a long enough period of time that it becomes a life-altering, and perhaps a life-threatening, situation. The open-ended nature of these psalms raises serious questions about the nature of the divine–human relationship and forces individuals and community members to enter into an ongoing search for answers to these questions. Perhaps this is the point of such texts. If one rushes towards answers in an effort to make everything turn out neat and tidy, then there is a serious danger of missing important dimensions of life that need to be addressed. Later, we will see how Mark does not shy away from such questions. Instead, he continues the tradition of asking the difficult questions taken up in these psalms, only this time the search for insight into human suffering focuses on the suffering of the Messiah, with implications that reach to the cosmic level.

5

JESUS AND DAVID IN MARK 10–12

1   Introduction

David is a complex figure with a long history in ancient literature. Just a few of the images of David that could be discussed in a detailed way are "king," "shepherd," "poet," "musician," "warrior," "sage," "father of a dynasty," "founder of the Temple and its cult," "messiah," "persecuted and pursued," "pious one," "prophet," and "judge." I have already discussed the issue of David as psalmist in section 2.1 of Chapter 2, which showed how prolific and inspired a composer of sacred song he was thought to be.[1] Although the paradigms of the messiah in the Second Temple period were varied, as well as the images of David, one aspect of the ideology of Davidic kingship in this period contained a strong element of violent, earthly, militaristic leadership associated with an eschatological war.[2]

We should not think of messianism as a monolithic, abstract concept, but the image of the Davidic messiah as an earthly warrior king

---

[1] The bibliography on David is large, as one would expect, but a good recent treatment of David in relation to the Psalms with a good bibliography on David is Daly-Denton, *David in the Fourth Gospel*, especially 59–114. See also Collins, *The Scepter and the Star*, 20–73, for a discussion of Davidic messianism in the Hebrew Bible and Second Temple Judaism. For other good treatments, see Jouette M. Bassler, "A Man for All Seasons: David in Rabbinic and New Testament Literature," *Int* 40 (2, 1986): 156–69, and Louis H. Feldman, "Josephus' Portrait of David," *HUCA* 60 (2001): 129–50.

[2] A detailed study of David in Second Temple Judaism and his place in the messianic expectations is beyond the scope of this chapter. The literature from the period that witnesses to the warrior king messiah includes *Ps. Sol.* 17:21–5 (which in turn fashions its imagery by using Isa 11:2–4 and Ps 2:9, two passages that have royal imagery associated with David); 4Q285 (which is fragmentary, but calls the Prince of the Congregation the bud of David, and he leads Israel into battle); 1QSb (where the Prince of the Congregation has a military and judicial role); CDa (where Balaam's oracle is interpreted to refer to the Prince of the Congregation [most likely a Davidic king], stressing his military role); and 4Q246 (the debated "Son of God" text, which, if it is a messianic text, clearly describes the "Son of God" as having a military role). See Collins, *The Scepter and the Star*, 49–73 and 154–72; and his *Apocalypticism in the Dead Sea Scrolls* (London: Routledge, 1997), 80–5 for discussions of these texts and their messianic overtones.

is important to keep in mind when reading Mark 10:46–52; 11:1–25; 12:1–12; and 12:35–7, because there is a striking lack of application of this type of messianic image to Jesus when he is linked with David in these passages. Other images of David should play a part in understanding these passages fully, but the goal of this chapter does not reside in performing a thorough exegesis and interpretation of these four passages. Instead, I wish to argue that Mark portrays Jesus in relation to David as a way of downplaying the militaristic aspects of Davidic messiahship, while at the same time upholding the association with David. I will argue that the association between Jesus and David in the Gospel is a preparation for the use of the PssLam in the passion narrative, where these Davidic psalms are used to portray and express the depth and pathos of Jesus' suffering. This chapter will focus on the four passages listed above, and the next chapter will focus on the passion narrative.

2   David and the Son of David in Mark 10–12

2.1   Blind Bartimaeus (Mark 10:46–52)

The story of Bartimaeus' healing in Mark 10:46–52 is not just a miracle story.[3] As with other miracle stories, Mark takes the episode and imbues it with meaning that goes beyond the reporting of an event that shows the power of Jesus.[4] As we will see, Bartimaeus is portrayed as a character that embodies understanding of who Jesus is and the proper response of a would-be follower of Jesus.[5] This makes him a character whose opinion

---

[3] Donahue and Harrington, *The Gospel of Mark*, 319; Amos N. Wilder, *Early Christian Rhetoric: The Language of the Gospel* (Cambridge, MA: Harvard University Press, 1964), 65. Robert H. Gundry argues that, although there are other motifs in the passage (mainly faith), they all are subjugated to or amplify the miraculous healing of Bartimaeus (*Mark: A Commentary on His Apology for the Cross* [Grand Rapids, MI: Eerdmans, 1993], 596–7).

[4] See, e.g., Mark 3:1–6, where Mark uses traditional material about the healing of a withered hand to reveal the hard-heartedness of his opponents and to set up the confrontation between the Jewish authorities and Jesus, which eventually culminates in Jesus' death in Jerusalem. See also Mark 6:30–42, where Mark tells the feeding of the five thousand in a way that highlights the connection with important wilderness experiences in Israel's history (see Marcus, *The Way of the Lord*, 23–4, who follows U. Mauser, *Christ in the Wilderness: The Wilderness Theme in the Second Gospel and Its Basis in the Biblical Tradition* [SBT 39; Naperville, IL: Alec R. Allenson, 1963]) and in a way that foreshadows the last supper in 14:22–5.

[5] I do not use the term "disciple" here because in Mark the term usually is limited to those who are in Jesus' inner circle. Jack Dean Kingsbury denies that Bartimaeus becomes a disciple of Jesus, but argues that he simply follows Jesus along the way to Jerusalem as part of the crowd accompanying him to the city. In other words, he reads ἠκολούθει αὐτῷ ἐν τῇ ὁδῷ literally. Technically, he is correct, pointing out that Jesus does not call Bartimaeus, and therefore the pattern of previous call stories in Mark, which do result

the reader can trust, encouraging him or her to assent to the declaration that Jesus is "Son of David."

For the first and only time in the Gospel of Mark, "Son of David" is used as a title for Jesus in 10:46–52. There are other places where Jesus is associated with David before and after this passage (e.g., 2:23–7; the three other passages to be discussed below; and all throughout the passion narrative), but the specific title "Son of David" is used only here. The passage stands as a narrative transition from the previous section (8:22–10:45) to the next section (11:1–12:44),[6] in that it concludes the "journey narrative" (8:22–10:52), acting as a bookend with the first healing of a blind man in 8:22–6, and introduces the next section, Jesus' triumphal entry into and ministry in the Temple (11:1–12:44).[7]

With regard to Bartimaeus naming Jesus as the "son of David," there are several things to consider, for our purposes. On the surface level, it

in disciples, is not repeated here. In fact, as Kingsbury points out, Jesus does not call Bartimaeus, and he dismisses him with the command ὕπαγε, which, Kingsbury argues, following Gerd Theissen, is a quasi-technical term that Jesus uses to dismiss the formerly afflicted person after he performs a healing. These points are well-taken, but even Kingsbury admits that Bartimaeus is held up as a "model of faith." For Kingsbury, "faith" in this context means trust in Jesus' ability to heal him. See his *The Christology of Mark's Gospel* (Philadelphia: Fortress, 1983), 104–5, n.159. Gundry also concludes that Bartimaeus is not a disciple: "The road and the following carry only mundane meanings, not the connotation of discipleship on the way to the Cross" (*Mark*, 595). Kingsbury's and Gundry's notions of discipleship seem to be in line with the understanding of μαθητής as a technical term. In this sense, Bartimaeus is not a disciple of Jesus. But it is not only the ones who are individually called by Jesus that should be considered followers of Jesus in Mark, and therefore part of Jesus' circle of adherents, part of his "family" (Mark 3:33–4), if not of his inner-most circle. There are also those who are called to repent and believe in the good news (1:15) in general who can be thought of as part of this group. In this sense, Bartimaeus responds properly to Jesus as a would-be follower should, and certainly provides a counterpart to the negative characterization of many of the disciples who are individually called by Jesus. Members of this more widely defined group may embody some of the qualities of the ideal disciple without actually being a disciple in the technical sense. See my "'Who Are My Mother and My Brothers?' Family Relations and Family Language in the Gospel of Mark," *JR* 81 (2001): 9. John Painter calls καὶ ἠκολούθει αὐτῷ ἐν τῇ ὁδῷ "pregnant with the Markan understanding of discipleship." He goes on to say, "Bartimaeus, rather than the twelve, has become the image of the true disciple" (*Mark's Gospel*, 153). See also Schweizer, *The Good News According to Mark*, 224–5, and Leslie Houlden, "Why Were the Disciples Ever Called Disciples?" *Theology* 105 (Nov/Dec, 2002): 411–17.

[6] See Vernon K. Robbins, "The Healing of the Blind Bartimaeus in Markan Theology," *JBL* 92 (1973): 224–43; Stephen H. Smith, "The Literary Structure of Mark 11:1–12:40," *NOVT* 31 (April 1989): 104–24; contra Craig A. Evans, *Mark 8:27–16:20* (WBC 34B; Nashville: Thomas Nelson Publishers, 2001), 126, who includes this passage in the next section ("Jesus Confronts Jerusalem" 10:46–13:37). The sections in Mark tend to blend into each other; therefore, precisely delineating the boundaries of distinct sections is oftentimes very difficult.

[7] See Donahue and Harrington, *The Gospel of Mark*, 257 and 319–20. Contra Gundry, *Mark*, 597.

is plausible to think that Jesus' reputation had built to such a level that some biographical information about him might have been known by those who had heard of "Jesus of Nazareth" (Ἰησοῦς ὁ Ναζαρηνός). The fact that he was reported to be a descendant of David could have been part of this information.[8] But this seems beside the point, especially when "Son of David" is such a loaded term in the time of the Gospel of Mark. Upon closer examination, the use of the term in the passage certainly goes beyond the question of whether or not Jesus was actually a descendant of David.

As Jesus and his companions come out from Jericho, the blind beggar, Bartimaeus, sits on the side of the road and cries out for mercy, "Son of David, Jesus, have mercy on me!" (υἱὲ Δαυὶδ Ἰησοῦ, ἐλέησόν με). When the crowd tries to silence him, he cries out even louder, "Son of David, have mercy on me!" (υἱὲ Δαυίδ, ἐλέησόν με). The second time he cries out he drops the name of Jesus completely in his cries for mercy, amplifying the title "Son of David." This captures Jesus' attention, and his response to Bartimaeus is not one of rebuke, like the responses of others who heard Bartimaeus (10:48). He does not express consternation at the name given to him by Bartimaeus, nor does he ignore Bartimaeus. He simply asks that Bartimaeus be called to him.[9] When Bartimaeus learns that Jesus wants to talk to him, he drops his cloak and comes over to Jesus. The cloak is an interesting detail in the story. For a poor beggar like Bartimaeus, the cloak would be his most important possession, because it would be the only defense against the elements both at night and during the day. His casting it aside to come to Jesus for healing shows the confidence

---

[8] See Evans, *Mark 8:27–16:20*, 129–30, for a discussion of the historicity of Jesus' Davidic lineage.

[9] As Gundry correctly points out, the verb that is used here to call Bartimaeus is φωνέω. Gundry states, "The verb for calling is not the καλέω of call-stories, but φωνέω. Jesus does not call Bartimaeus directly as in call-stories. The call has the purpose of inquiring what Bartimaeus wants, not of commanding that he follow" (*Mark*, 596). Although the story is certainly different in several ways compared with "call-stories" from a form-critical point of view, the basic flow of the story shows it to have similarities to the typical call story. However, in this case, Jesus calls Bartimaeus in response to Bartimaeus' insistence on attention from Jesus. See Hans Dieter Betz, "The Early Christian Miracle Story: Some Observations on the Form Critical Problem," *Semeia* 11 (1978): 74, where he says, "In vv. 49–50, the miracle story 'flips over' into another literary genre, the 'call story'." He argues that this is the case because of the way that Jesus summons Bartimaeus to him. From Bartimaeus' perspective, he goes from the outermost limits of society – that of beggar on the side of the road – to face-to-face contact with Jesus and eventually to follower of Jesus. Therefore, it may go too far to limit the characterization of this story based on the absence of καλέω. If this were the sole, or most important, criterion for characterizing a call story as such, then Mark 1:16–20, the first call story in Mark, would have to be excluded, along with the calling of Levi in Mark 2:14. These two are both clearly call stories.

he must have in Jesus' ability to heal him and reinforces the foregoing presentation of Jesus as a powerful healer and exorcist.[10]

Once the topic of healing comes into the foreground in this passage, it reminds the reader of the consistent presentation of Jesus up to this point in Mark as a healer and exorcist. The convergence of the healing motif with "Son of David" as the designation for Jesus limits the possibilities of meaning evoked by the title alone. As D. C. Duling notes, "The address 'Son of David' could be a link between the magical tradition about Solomon and the activity of Jesus as exorcist and healer."[11] Bruce Chilton has convincingly argued that the overtones of the Solomonic tradition of healing and exorcism associated with "the Son of David" in the *Testament of Solomon* arise when reading this story in Mark.[12] In the *Testament of Solomon*, the title "Son of David" is used at the outset to describe Solomon. As is well known from the story, Solomon has great powers over demons and evil spirits, much as Jesus does in the Gospel of Mark, and Evans claims that the *Testament of Solomon* testifies to "the widespread fame of David's son."[13] However, the *Testament of Solomon* is considerably later in date than Mark's Gospel, which makes our reliance on the testament's tradition of Solomon's abilities of exorcism tenuous as a basis for any claims we make about Mark's convergence of the title "Son of David" and the healing powers of Solomon. But there is earlier evidence of the association of Solomon with exorcism, healing, and magic[14] that may attest to this as a common association at the time of Mark. In the Dead Sea Scrolls, 11Q11 2:2–3 reads: "[. . .] Solomon, and he will invo[ke . . .] [. . . the spir]its and the demons, [. . .]".[15] Josephus also makes the association between Solomon and healing when he

---

[10] R. Alan Culpepper goes further than this: "The garment, therefore, represents that which the disciple leaves behind to follow Jesus" ("Mark 10:50: Why Mention the Garment?" *JBL* 101 [1982]: 131–2). For Painter, Bartimaeus' casting aside of his cloak "is not simply an action which expresses the overcoming of the obstacle to his quest for sight. The action of leaving his beggar's cloak . . . signified his leaving of his possessions. In due course Mark makes clear that, unlike the rich man of 10:17–22, but like the fishermen (10:28), Bartimaeus left all to follow Jesus" (*Mark's Gospel*, 152).

[11] Dennis C. Duling, "Testament of Solomon: A New Translation and Introduction," in *OTP*, I:960, 1985. See also Dennis C. Duling, "Solomon, Exorcism, and the Son of David," *HTR* 68 (1975): 235–52.

[12] See Bruce Chilton, "Jesus *ben David*: Reflections on the *Davidssohnfrage*," *JSNT* 14 (1982): 88–112.

[13] Evans, *Mark 8:27–16:20*, 132.

[14] The grouping together of exorcism, healing, and magic need not be troubling, since in the ancient world the boundaries between these three practices were blurry.

[15] [. . .] הרו[חות והשדים . . .] [. . . א]ה שלומה ויקר[א . . .]. Text and translation from Garcia Martinez and Tigchelaar, *Dead Sea Scrolls Study Edition*, II:1201. For a discussion of this text see Pablo A. Torijano, *Solomon the Esoteric King* (Leiden: Brill, 2002), 43–53.

says that Solomon composed incantations by which illnesses are cured. Josephus also credited Solomon with leaving behind powerful forms of exorcisms.[16] So, when Mark brings together the title "Son of David" and the motif of healing, there is a high likelihood that he was trying to focus the meaning of the title on the Solomonic associations of healing.[17]

The question remains whether Bartimaeus is a reliable character or not. In other words, is the fact that Bartimaeus calls Jesus "Son of David" a positive or negative thing for Mark? Werner H. Kelber thinks putting "Son of David" on the lips of Bartimaeus signifies that the title is not used positively. He reasons backwards narratively from the fact that Jesus dies abandoned and alone. When Bartimaeus joins those with Jesus "on the way" to Jerusalem, this is an indication that he joins those who eventually abandon Jesus.[18] We must look at the story in its narrative context to see whether Kelber accurately interprets Bartimaeus' title for Jesus.

When Jesus grants his request "to see again" (ἀναβλέπω) by saying, "Your faith has saved you" (ἡ πίστις σου σέσωκέν σε), Bartimaeus "immediately saw again and followed him on the way" (εὐθὺς ἀνέβλεψεν καὶ ἠκολούθει αὐτῷ ἐν τῇ ὁδῷ). In the Gospel of Mark, Jesus' healing does not necessarily elicit a response of following after him.[19] For example, the healing of the paralytic in 2:12,[20] the healing of the woman with a flow of blood in 5:34,[21] and the healing of the blind man in 8:26[22] all have a miracle as a central narrative element, but there is no response by the beneficiary that involves following Jesus. So it is significant that

---

[16] *Ant* VIII.45–6. The first sentence of section 45 is especially relevant, "God also granted him [Solomon] [the ability] to learn the skill against demons [i.e., exorcism] for the benefit and healing of people" (παρέσχε δ' αὐτῷ μαθεῖν ὁ θεὸς καὶ τὴν κατὰ τῶν διαμόνων τέχνην εἰς ὠφέλειαν καὶ θεραπείαν τοῖς ἀνθρώποις). Translation mine. Text from H. St. J. Thackeray, "Josephus," *LCL* 281 (Cambridge, MA: Harvard University Press, 1950). See Philip S. Alexander, "Incantations and Books of Magic," in Emil Schürer *et al.*, *The History of the Jewish People in the Age of Jesus Christ* (Edinburgh: T&T Clark, 1995), III:367; and Torijano, *Solomon the Esoteric King*, 95–105, for a discussion of this passage.

[17] Donahue and Harrington concur (see *The Gospel of Mark*, 317), but Gundry does not (see *Mark*, 600–1).

[18] Werner H. Kelber, *The Kingdom in Mark* (Philadelphia: Fortress, 1974), 94–5.

[19] See Whitney Taylor Shiner, *Follow Me! Discipleship in Markan Rhetoric* (SBLDS 145; Atlanta: Scholars Press, 1995), 79.

[20] Here, at Jesus' command to take his mat and go home, the paralytic follows Jesus' orders.

[21] Here, Jesus tells the woman to "go in peace, and be healed of your disease" (ὕπαγε εἰς εἰρήνην καὶ ἴσθι ὑγιὴς ἀπὸ τῆς μάστιγός σου), and then the episode ends there. The reader is not told what the woman does. Obviously, this is not important to Mark, or else he would have narrated some action to give closure to the passage.

[22] Here, Jesus sends the man away to his home ordering him not to go into the village before he goes home. There is no response by the healed blind man, and Mark does not narrate what the man did in response to Jesus' command.

this response by Bartimaeus to being healed by Jesus is included, and Jesus does not correct or respond negatively to Bartimaeus' actions.[23] How should we understand Bartimaeus' response?

The section that this passage closes is very concerned with discipleship and what the proper response to Jesus' actions and identity is.[24] The section begins with Peter's correct confession of Jesus as Messiah (8:27–30), but the reader quickly learns that proper confession is not enough. Peter does not respond properly to Jesus once he confirms Peter's confession and describes his inevitable suffering at the hands of the Jerusalem authorities. In 8:31–3 Jesus quickly rebukes him and explains that the proper response to Jesus' identity as Messiah is to follow after him by taking up one's cross (8:34). There is further detailed instruction in this section about what it means to be a proper disciple. Jesus explains what it means to be the greatest (one must be the "servant of all" [πάντων διάκονος] [9:35]); Jesus tells the rich man who wishes to inherit eternal life to sell all he has, give to the poor and then "come follow me" (δεῦρο ἀκολούθει μοι) (10:21); and at the request of James and John to be seated at Jesus' left and right hand in his glory, Jesus offers instruction about how to exercise authority properly. If one is to have authority, one must exercise it in the same way that Jesus does, in self-sacrificial service to others (10:42–5). So, Bartimaeus' response to being healed by Jesus – to follow Jesus on the way, after leaving his cloak – certainly fits within this rubric of how a disciple should act in light of Jesus' presence and actions.[25]

Because of Bartimaeus' response of following Jesus on the way, the reader has every confidence that Bartimaeus is a reliable character, and so his identification of Jesus as "Son of David" should be taken seriously. Mark presents Jesus in this story as "Son of David," but in doing so, he

---

[23] Contrast Mark 5:18–19, where the healed demoniac begs (παρακαλέω) Jesus "in order that he might be with him" (ἵνα μετ' αὐτοῦ ᾖ). Jesus refuses and tells him to go into his village and tell what the Lord had done for him. In addition, after Jesus heals the leper in 1:41, he commands the leper to remain silent and to give the proper Mosaic offering for his healing. However, the leper ignores Jesus and instead proclaims the matter freely, so that Jesus can no longer move about openly in that area. He must now remain in the deserted places (ἔξω ἐπ' ἐρήμοις τόποις ἦν) (1:45).

[24] Donahue and Harrington, *The Gospel of Mark*, 320.

[25] Without explanation, Donahue and Harrington come to the same conclusion, "Bartimaeus emerges as an exemplar of faith in Jesus" (ibid., 319). However, Evans interprets the story with a focus on Jesus rather than Bartimaeus. He claims it is further demonstration of Jesus' mission, as anointed by the Spirit of God, "to proclaim good news to the poor and to open the eyes of the blind." For Evans, Bartimaeus is just a minor character that introduces another dimension to Mark's Christology, namely, Jesus as son of David (see *Mark 8:27–16:20*, 134–5).

associates this title with healing. This episode begins a series of passages that portrays Jesus as a Davidic figure, but here the first impulse by Mark is not to stress David's royal, earthly, militaristic, or political qualities. Instead, by constructing the story of the healing of the blind Bartimaeus in such a way as to combine the title "Son of David" with the healing of a reliable character, he stresses the tradition of healing that is associated with Solomon as the son of David.[26]

2.2   The triumphal entry (Mark 11:1–25)

Following the clear association between Jesus and the Son of David in 10:46–52, the next passage intensifies Jesus' association with David through the story of Jesus' entry into Jerusalem.[27] Overt royal imagery in this passage abounds, and as we will see, this imagery aligns Jesus squarely with David as king this time, not as Son of David the healer and exorcist. However, in a similar way Mark limits the range of meaning evoked by the term "David." Mark also constructs this portion of his narrative in such a way as to align Jesus with David as king and simultaneously to undercut the association of Jesus with the earthly, militaristic, and political aspects of David's royalty. Because this part of Mark's narrative is very complex, being laced with many important issues for the characterization of Jesus and his relationship with the Temple, I will limit my analysis to how Jesus is portrayed in relation to David. This will help focus my inquiry and lay the groundwork for further conclusions about how Mark uses David's association with the PssLam in his characterization of Jesus.

[26] In contrast to the *Psalms of Solomon* 17, which characterizes the Son of David as a warrior king, "Here . . . Jesus wields his Davidic authority in order to have mercy on one who is afflicted (1:47–8, 52), to heal and in this fashion to 'save' (10:52)" (Kingsbury, *Christology*, 106–7).

[27] Against Gundry, who says, "the interconnections of 11:1–10 with 10:46–52 lack depth and significance" (*Mark*, 634). But the details that he points out (no "son of David" in 11:1–10; Bartimaeus throws away his garments as useless, whereas the crowds place them in front of Jesus to pave his way; Jesus' pronouncement of "salvation by faith" [10:52] and his coming in the name of the Lord [11:9] do not match) may not provide lexical similarities deep enough for Gundry, but the thematic similarities are undeniable (Jesus' connection with David and the fact that the crowds shout "Hosanna!" to Jesus, pointing to the desire for salvation similar to Jesus' announcement of it to Bartimaeus). It makes sense narratively that these passages are connected in the sequence that Mark puts them. Frank J. Matera argues that the whole of chapters 11–12 should be read under the rubric of the Son of David question, because Mark places references to David at the beginning and end of the section. He goes on to say, "Thus, as Jesus enters Jerusalem the acclamation of 11:10 anticipates the coming Kingdom of David and recalls the cries of Bartimaeus (10:47–48)" (*Kingship*, 68). See also Kingsbury, who says, "Publicly identified by Bartimaeus as the Son of David, Jesus approaches Jerusalem under the auspices of this title" (*Christology*, 107).

After Jesus instructs two of his disciples to commandeer a colt "upon which no one had sat yet" (ἐφ᾽ ὅν οὐδεὶς οὔπω ἀνθρώπων ἐκάθισεν; Mark 11:2), they spread their cloaks upon the animal, and Jesus sits upon it and rides up to Jerusalem toward the Temple. Most scholars at least entertain the hypothesis that there are similarities between this opening scene in the four-part story in Mark[28] and the ninth chapter of Zechariah, especially verse 9.[29] The first fifteen verses of Zechariah 9 contain a prophetic oracle. First, it tells of the destruction of foreign territories (presumably hostile to Israel) by God (Zech 9:1–8), followed by the hope of the coming of a king:[30] "righteous and saving is he, gentle and riding on an ass, even a new colt" (δίκαιος καὶ σῴζων αὐτός, πραῢς καὶ ἐπιβεβηκὼς ἐπὶ ὑποζύγιον καὶ πῶλον νέον) (LXX Zech 9:9).[31] After the king comes, he[32] will command peace, gain a widespread

---

[28] Here, I follow Paul Brooks Duff in seeing the entirety of verses 1–25 as one story. See "The March of the Divine Warrior and the Advent of the Greco-Roman King: Mark's Account of Jesus' Entry into Jerusalem," *JBL* 111 (1992): 55–71.

[29] Matera, *Kingship*, 70, 71; Evans, *Mark 8:27–16:20*, 140. Although Mark does not explicitly quote Zech 9:9 here, both Matt 21:4–5 and John 12:14–15 do, which raises the likelihood that the imagery would have been recognizable to first-century followers of Jesus. Gundry claims, "Mark is interested in Jesus' dignity, not in his meekness, in Jesus' divine sonship, not in his kingship; so he does not quote Zech 9:9" (*Mark*, 626). This argument seems rather unlikely, given Mark's penchant for allusion rather than quotation of scripture (see Matera, *Kingship*, 71, who agrees with this assessment), not to mention the overwhelmingly royal presentation of Jesus both in this passage and in the passion narrative. He goes on to argue that the lack of quotation of Zech 9:9 by Mark is evidence for the historicity of the procession as it is told, "for the derivation of the story from Zech 9:9 would probably have left quoted phrases, perhaps quoted statements as well. But we find none" (ibid., 632). Schweizer shies away from too close an association with Zech 9:9, given that it is not quoted and, in his opinion, not clearly alluded to. Instead, he opts for intentionality on the part of Jesus to model the entry after Zech 9:9 to counter the general expectations of the Davidic Messiah who would drive out the Romans by force (*The Good News According to Mark*, 227). Kelber points to the role of the Mount of Olives, the centrality of the Temple, the unused colt, the strewing of branches, the shouts of Hosanna, and the acclamation of Hallel Psalm 118:26 to claim, "all these features appear to produce the scenario of a messianic entrance in the vein of Zech. 9:9–10." He also footnotes six other scholars in agreement with this position (*The Kingdom in Mark*, 92).

[30] It is debated as to whether this king is human or divine, and most scholars think that he is human. However, drawing on the possible allusions to Zeph 3:14–15, where the king is Yᴀᴡᴇʜ and not a Davidide king, David L. Petersen states, "By connotation through allusion, the author indicated that the arrival of this king should be celebrated in much the same way that Yahweh's presence as king deserves accolade. Moreover, the logic of the poems in Zechariah 9 suggests that the presence of the king depends on the prior presence of the deity in Jerusalem (Zech. 9:8)" (*Zechariah 9–14 and Malachi, A Commentary* [OTL; Louisville, KY: Westminster John Knox Press, 1995], 57–8).

[31] I quote the LXX here for the same reasons that the LXX of the PssLam is used, namely, that Mark most likely read and referred to the Greek version of the scriptures when composing his narrative.

[32] The LXX here has a third person singular subject and the Hebrew has the first person singular subject.

dominion, free prisoners, strengthen Israel, and "wield" them "like a warrior's sword" against Greece (9:10–13). Finally, the oracle describes the march of God as a warrior who protects Israel in battle, ultimately causing victory for Israel (9:14–15). The oracle is decidedly violent and depicts God as a warrior for Israel, over which no nation can claim victory because of God's protection. The king is closely associated with God in this oracle in his actions and, consequently, in his warrior-like overtones.

The scene in Zech 9:9 of a warrior king riding a beast of burden into Jerusalem is reminiscent of Solomon's ride into Jerusalem in 3 Kgds 1:38–48.[33] In this passage, David's closest advisors have Solomon ride David's mule (ἡμίονος) and lead him to Gihon, a spring near the Kidron Valley. There, Zadok anoints Solomon with oil, after which a trumpet is blown and the people shout, "Let King Solomon live!" (ζήτω ὁ βασιλεὺς Σαλωμων; 3 Kgds 1:39). After this, there is a procession, Solomon leading the people as they rejoice and play music so loudly that "the earth shook at their sound" (ἐρράγη ἡ γῆ ἐν τῇ φωνῇ αὐτῶν; 1:40). This coronation of Solomon occurs during the time after the oldest son of David, Adonijah, had illegitimately co-opted his throne and claimed kingship in Jerusalem. When Adonijah hears the celebration and learns of Solomon's coronation, his rule as king comes to an end. David appoints Solomon king as a way of re-establishing his rule just before he dies. With Solomon in place, the Davidic kingship can continue. Genesis 49:10–11 also associates a donkey with royalty, as well as 2 Sam 16:2. According to David L. Petersen and Carol L. and Eric M. Meyers, it was also common for kings in the ancient Near East to ride on donkeys.[34] This background may explain the convention of a king riding on a beast of burden in procession but not the description of him as "gentle" (πραΰς).[35] We will come back to this point below, but, with these points in mind, let us return to the Gospel of Mark.

Just after Jesus begins to ride the animal, many of those who go ahead of him spread their garments on the ground in front of him as he processes up to the city. This detail adds to the royal flavor of the incident, in that it recalls 2 Kgs 9:13, where the bystanders took off their cloaks and spread them on the stairs for King Jehu as he processed up the steps just after his anointing as king over Israel. This action by those with Jesus, along

---

[33] Evans, *Mark 8:27–16:20*, 142; Matera, *Kingship*, 70.

[34] Petersen, *Zechariah 9–14*, 58. Carol L. Meyers and Eric M. Meyers, *Zechariah 9–14* (AB 28C; New York: Doubleday, 1993), 129.

[35] "The sole exception to this pervasively royal imagery is the term 'humble,' which is used here to redefine the character of the divine king" (Petersen, *Zechariah 9–14*, 58).

with the spreading of a bed of leafy branches (στιβάς), prepares a royal way for him as he goes up to the city.[36]

Clearly, from the very beginning of Jesus' procession, royalty is a strong connotation of the account. Jesus' actions are indeed modeled after the king's triumphal entry in Zech 9:9, and the connection with David is quickly made explicit by Mark with the exultation by those surrounding Jesus in the procession. Mark does this by having those in the procession exclaim something that closely resembles a combination of Pss 118:25–6 and 148:1: "Hosanna! Blessed is the one who comes in the name of the Lord . . . Hosanna in the highest places!"[37] Neither of these is a "Davidic" psalm, that is, neither has a Davidic superscript. But as we have seen, in the first century CE David was most likely considered to be the author of the Psalter, and Psalm 118 can certainly be read as a royal psalm with David as its subject, at least in this part of the psalm.[38]

If the association with David is not clear enough by the exclamation using two psalms, then Mark makes it explicit by interjecting between the two "Hosanna" exclamations the phrase, "Blessed is the coming kingdom of our father, David!" (εὐλογημένη ἡ ἐρχομένη βασιλεία τοῦ πατρὸς ἡμῶν Δαυίδ; Mark 11:10). The coming kingdom of David is certainly an eschatological image in the sense that it evokes the future, hoped-for end of Gentile rule and the restoration of freedom and self-rule that was realized during David's reign, but also to a certain extent during the Hasmonean dynasty. The eschatological coming of a Davidic messiah to restore Jewish independence was part of the cultural landscape at the time of Mark, and so the imagery could also be understood messianically.[39] And in the *Ps. Sol.* and the Dead Sea Scrolls mentioned above[40] it was an earthly, militaristic image, in that the Davidic messiah would re-establish

---

[36] Kingsbury, *Christology*, 107.

[37] Here, Mark retains a Greek transliteration of a Hebrew term from each of these psalms rather than a quotation of the LXX psalms, perhaps adding realism to his story. Some see this as an indication of the historical authenticity of the report (see Evans, *Mark 8:27–16:20*, 144–5).

[38] "Originally, Ps 118:26a may have welcomed an ordinary pilgrim, but the shift from the third person singular in v 26a to the second person plural in v 26b favors a welcome of the Davidic king in v 26a (quoted in Mark 11:9) and of his people or troops in v 26b (unquoted in Mark 11:9–10)" (Gundry, *Mark*, 630).

[39] Gundry argues that the phrase itself is not messianic, but the context into which the phrase is put in Mark gives it a messianic quality. See *Mark*, 630. Matera thinks that the setting of the episode being on the Mount of Olives also lends a messianic character to the story. He cites Josephus' mention of the false prophet "the Egyptian" launching his messianic entry into Jerusalem from the Mount of Olives (*Ant.*, XX, 8, 6; *J. W.* II, 13, 5); and Acts 1:6, where the apostles ask Jesus on the Mount of Olives if he will establish the Kingdom of Israel at that time (*Kingship*, 69).

[40] See footnote 2.

Jewish independence on earth by violently overthrowing the Gentile hege-mony over Israel. One further point is that the kingdom is described as ἡ ἐρχομένη βασιλεία, which seems to indicate that the crowds think this hoped-for kingdom is in the process of coming to fruition with Jesus' Zechariah 9-inspired procession into Jerusalem.[41] Just as in the Barti-maeus story that precedes this one, Jesus in no way responds negatively to the association with David.

The picture in Jesus' procession is one of a powerful king processing up to his city.[42] Paul Brooks Duff has convincingly argued for clear similar-ities between Jesus' procession and Greco-Roman entrance processions, at least as described in literary sources of the time. Duff examines many accounts of ancient entrance processions – either of kings coming into newly conquered cities or generals returning to their home cities after a victory – and concludes that these processions have some common characteristics that would create certain expectations for a first-century reader. According to Duff, the minimal processional structure has two components: (1) the entering ruler/conqueror is met at the gates of the city by the citizens and escorted into the city with hymns and acclamations; and (2) the goal of the procession is the local temple, where a ritual of appropriation takes place, usually a sacrifice, whereby the entering ruler appropriates the newly won territory. There is a similar structure for pro-cessing generals, the main difference being that the general processes into his own city.[43]

---

[41] Evans thinks that the historicity of the procession is without question and that the action was originally intended to be messianic. The report was embellished by later redactors to look even more messianic (*Mark 8:27–16:20*, 140).

[42] Kelber argues that Mark's version of Jesus' procession is actually not an entrance scene because it happens outside the city. He argues that the leafy branches that Jesus' companions cut "from the fields" (ἐκ τῶν ἀγρῶν, 11:8b) point to a rural setting, and then he states, "It is only after Jesus has been hailed that he enters the city and temple, by himself (11:11a . . .), unobserved and unapplauded. Thus the acclamation incident is kept out of the reach of Jerusalem, so that strictly speaking Mark does not portray an entrance scene" (*The Kingdom in Mark*, 93). Although Kelber may be correct in his details, the insinuation in the flow of the story is that the procession began outside the city and continued until Jesus entered the city. Just because the scene begins in a rural setting and Jesus enters the Temple area apparently alone does not mean that the scene does not include a procession. The fact that Jesus rides a beast of burden and those around him went ahead and followed (οἱ προάγοντες καὶ οἱ ἀκολουθοῦντες) clearly indicates a procession.

[43] Duff, "The March of the Divine Warrior," 58–62. D. R. Catchpole performs a similar analysis by looking at twelve examples of celebrated entries. He comes to the following conclusion about the elements that make up the pattern of these entries: "(a) A victory already achieved and a status already recognised for the central person. (b) A formal and ceremonial entry. (c) Greetings and/or acclamations together with invocations of God. (d) Entry to the city climaxed by entry to the Temple, if the city in question has one. (e) Cultic activity, either positive (e.g., offering of sacrifice), or negative (e.g., expulsion of objectionable persons and

Duff goes on to conclude: "One thing that emerges from the ... entrance processions is a pattern whereby a ruler/general symbolically appropriates a city by way of ritual, whether that city be foreign or his own. The appropriation of the city is echoed both in the elements of the procession but, more important, by a ritual ceremony at the end. Without this final act, the entrance ceremony is incomplete."[44] These processions set up an expectation for something similar to happen when a first-century reader comes to the narration of Jesus' procession into Jerusalem. According to Duff, Mark enhances this expectation further by alluding to the divine procession in Zechariah 14.

Following Robert M. Grant's suggestion that there is a clear connection between Zechariah 14 and Mark 11:16, especially at the point where Jesus does not allow any vessels to be carried through the Temple,[45] Duff explores the connection between Zechariah 14 and Mark 11:1–25. He finds several points of comparison that link the two passages together: (1) Mark 11:1 situates the scene near the Mount of Olives (cf. Zech 14:4); (2) the procession of Jesus and his companions is like that of YHWH the divine warrior coming into Jerusalem in Zechariah 14; and (3) Mark 11:16 mentions the vessels in the Temple, which recalls the reference to vessels in the Temple in Zech 14:20–1. A closer examination of Zechariah 14 is needed to evaluate Duff's conclusions.

The advent of God in Zechariah 14 is clearly eschatological, mainly because of the future time frame and the "Day of the Lord" language. The Lord will come to Jerusalem after the nations have made battle against

---

the cleansing away of uncleanness)." See "The 'Triumphal' Entry," in *Jesus and the Politics of His Day* (ed. E. Bammel and C. F. D. Moule; Cambridge: Cambridge University Press, 1984), 321. There are several aspects of Catchpole's analysis that make me prefer Duff's. First, the range of primary data that Catchpole uses to draw up the elements of the pattern of celebrated procession is too narrow. He restricts his analysis to 1 and 2 Maccabees and Josephus, instead of casting a wider net into Greco-Roman literature as a whole. Second, his elements are not synthesized properly, in that he simply lists just about every element, whether it is contained in every story or not. For example, his fifth element, negative cultic activity (i.e., expulsion of objectionable persons and cleansing away of uncleanness), only occurs in one of the processions he examines. And finally, the elements of his pattern look too much like Mark's rendition of Jesus' entry not to raise suspicions that his understanding of the "Triumphal Entry" colored his analysis of the primary sources he examined. In fact, he even says, "Mark 11 contains all of these major and recurrent features" (ibid., 321).

[44] Duff, "The March of the Divine Warrior," 64.

[45] See Schweizer, *The Good News According to Mark*, 231, for a similar assertion. Bruce Chilton focuses on the statement in Zech 14:20–1 that talks about there not being traders in the Temple (*The Temple of Jesus: His Sacrificial Program within a Cultural History of Sacrifice* [University Park, PA: Pennsylvania State University Press, 1992], 135–6). But the term is actually "Canaanite" in both the MT (כנעני) and the LXX (Χαναναῖος). It is not until the Targum that the term is understood to mean "trader" or "merchant," according to Evans (*Mark 8:27–16:20*, 173).

the city and have subdued it. God will set things right using might and power over creation, "and the Lord will become king over all the earth; in that day, the Lord will be one and his name will be one" (καὶ ἔσται κύριος εἰς βασιλέα ἐπὶ πᾶσαν τὴν γῆν· ἐν τῇ ἡμέρᾳ ἐκείνῃ ἔσται κύριος εἷς καὶ τὸ ὄνομα αὐτοῦ ἕν, Zech 14:9). The kingship that God institutes will be a kingship over all the nations, with appropriate punishments for those nations who war against Jerusalem or do not go up to Jerusalem to offer the proper sacrifice and worship during the festivals (14:10–19). Finally, all of the vessels in Jerusalem will be sanctified to the Lord and therefore be usable in the Temple (14:20–1a), and "no longer will there be a 'Canaanite' in the house of the Lord almighty on that day" (οὐκ ἔσται Χαναναῖος οὐκέτι ἐν τῷ οἴκῳ κυρίου παντοκράτορος ἐν τῇ ἡμέρᾳ ἐκείνῃ, 14:21b). So, with the advent and procession of the divine king in Jerusalem, the city will become holy, free of Gentile rule, and protected by God. Proper worship in the Temple will be instituted, and the city will be the religious center of God's creation.

The similarities between Mark 11 and Zechariah 14 are certainly there, as Duff argues.[46] The only clarification I would add to Duff's argument is that although Zechariah 14 recalls the divine warrior image, it is not the *procession* of the divine warrior that brings it into contact with Mark 11. It is primarily the *content* of Zechariah 14 that is relevant for Mark, rather than the form of the *procession* of the divine warrior. Although Duff does not say this very clearly, he would most likely agree that it is a combination of the form of the Greco-Roman entrance procession and the image of the divine warrior taking his place in Jerusalem to rule the world that creates a certain expectation for the reader of Mark. When read together with the procession of Jesus in Mark 11:7–10 and Jesus' action in the Temple in 11:15–17, Zechariah 14 clearly puts his actions in line with the image of the divine warrior king and gives Jesus' procession an eschatological overtone.

Let me summarize the imagery and the readers' possible expectations built by Mark's story of Jesus' procession thus far. First, the procession of Jesus – introduced by the story of Jesus' prescience,[47] lending a high level of authority to what follows – is modeled after the procession of an Israelite king. Second, the allusion to Zech 9:9, combined with the allusions to Zechariah 14, gives the procession an eschatological overtone,

---

[46] However, Gundry dismisses the connection between Zechariah 14 and Mark 11:1–10. He deals with the passage in a different way, not seeing 11:1–25 as one connected story, but nonetheless denies any connection with Zechariah 14. See *Mark*, 633.

[47] This incident could also simply reflect a prior arrangement that Jesus made with the owner of the beast of burden. However, in the story there is no clear indication of this, so it lends an aura of prescience and authority to Jesus.

in that the procession connotes the advent of divine rule in Jerusalem over the entire world. Zechariah 14 tells of God's desire to establish his final rule over the nations from Jerusalem, and Zech 9:9 tells of his royal agent that will help him do this.[48] Furthermore, the rule will be established militarily and violently (Zech 14:3–4, 12–15). Third, the royal portrayal is colored by the inclusion of Davidic imagery in the exultation of Mark 11:9–10. This Davidic imagery adds a messianic overtone to the procession and enhances the earthly militaristic aspect of the advent of the king in Jerusalem. Finally, as Duff has argued, Jesus' procession begins in a way similar to many literary descriptions of Greco-Roman entrance processions. These processions consistently have the feature of the king or military ruler consummating his procession with a ritual of appropriation, usually a sacrificial rite in the local temple.

Several aspects of Mark 11:1–25 undercut this imagery and these expectations. First, although earthly, militaristic, Davidic imagery is evoked by Jesus' actions, one aspect of the story looms large which raises questions about how Jesus is pictured. The imagery that Mark specifically evokes from the militaristic, violent, warrior king oracle in Zechariah 9 is not violent. Zechariah 9:9 has the curious image of the king as gentle (πραΰς). Carol and Eric Meyers say that the imagery of the humble king riding on an ass has the effect of "reversing the power imagery associated with a king's rule." They even think that Matt 21:5 and John 12:15 use this imagery in a way that "remains faithful to the original intent of Zechariah."[49] The Gospels of Matthew and John make explicit what Mark's Gospel expresses through allusion. Deirdre J. Good has argued that the term πραΰς in Hellenistic Greek has the nuance of "disciplined calmness," rather than that of someone who is gentle in a submissive way. The term is often used to describe educated leaders (e.g., kings) who exhibit proper discipline of emotions in exercising their leadership well by showing compassion for their subjects.[50] So, the expectations Mark builds by his rendition of the procession of Jesus on a beast of

---

[48] The image of God establishing his rule through the use of an agent can be thought of as analogous to the imagery in Daniel 7, where there is a similar relationship between the Ancient of Days and the one like a son of man as agent of the Ancient of Days. Donahue and Harrington say the allusions to Zech 9:9 and 14:4 give the passage a messianic focus (*Mark*, 324). See J. Collins, *The Scepter and the Star*, 31–4, for a discussion of Zech 9:9 in the context of messianism in Second Temple Judaism. Carol L. and Eric M. Meyers characterize Zech 9:9 as "unmistakably eschatological," but only as foreshadowing "the emergence of messianic language in intertestamental literature and the New Testament" (*Zechariah 9–14*, 127). Zechariah 14 talks exclusively about God's activity in claiming the city and instituting divine rule in Jerusalem.

[49] Meyers and Meyers, *Zechariah 9–14*, 129.

[50] Deirdre J. Good, *Jesus the Meek King* (Harrisburg, PA: Trinity Press International, 1999), 4–6 and 82–7.

burden up to Jerusalem, accompanied by all the Davidic, messianic, and earthly, militaristic overtones that the exultation in Mark 11:9–10 contains, are reshaped by the idea that the king, that is, Jesus, is calm and exercises his leadership in ways that show compassion for his subjects in the image of the king in Zech 9:9. In other words, Jesus is exhibiting the power of a king here, but he is doing so with disciplined calmness rather than in a violent way.

Second, the structure that Mark gives to his story of Jesus' procession is such that it interrupts the readers' expectations about what should happen at the end of the procession. Duff argues that two straightforward narratives, that of the entrance into/"cleansing" of the Temple and that of the fig-tree incident, are each broken up and arranged in an interlocking pattern of *abab*.[51] The effect of this is to delay Jesus' action in the Temple and to color what he does by the cursing of the fig tree and its subsequent interpretation. For our purposes, the focus will remain primarily on the Temple action. The delay, however, is key in disrupting expectations.

First, imagine a procession by a king into a newly acquired city, such as the procession of Alexander the Great into Jerusalem described by Josephus (*Ant.* XI.332–7). In this account, the king arrives and is greeted by the citizens, in this case the high priest and "all the Jews," outside the city gates. The citizens run beside the king, Alexander, as he enters the city, a massive crowd excitedly ushering him into Jerusalem. The first thing that Josephus says that the king did when he entered the city was to go to the Temple and offer sacrifice. He also offered due honor to the priests and high priest, and then the priests showed him the sacred writings of Israel, in this case the prophecy in the Book of Daniel declaring that one of the Greeks would destroy the Persian empire, which Alexander promptly agreed was referring to him. The pattern of Alexander's procession is typical: greeting outside the gate, celebratory accompaniment by the citizens of the city as the king processes into the city, and entrance into the

---

[51] Duff, "The March of the Divine Warrior," 67. Evans also argues for rearrangement of pre-Markan material, but he argues that the fig-tree episode is split and used to frame the story of Jesus' action in the Temple. See *Mark 8:27–16:20*, 160. See Schweizer, *The Good News According to Mark*, 230, for a similar argument. Matera sees the entry in Mark 11:1–11 as a separate story, with verses 1 and 11 as Markan redactional framing (*Kingship*, 70). Donahue and Harrington comment upon and interpret Mark 11:12–25 as one story (*The Gospel of Mark*, 326–33). William R. Telford's interest lies in the fig-tree episodes; he sees them as purposely put where they are by the redactor for particular theological reasons having to do with the Temple. Although he does not clearly posit a structure like Duff's, it is very close to his implied structure with regard to the purposeful arrangement of these episodes (*The Barren Temple and the Withered Tree: A Redaction-Critical Analysis of the Cursing of the Fig-Tree Pericope in Mark's Gospel and Its Relation to the Cleansing of the Temple Tradition* [JSNTSup 1; Sheffield: Sheffield Academic Press, 1980], 39–49).

Temple in order to offer sacrifice. The reader expects this basic pattern, and Josephus delivers. So, second, if the typical procession through the city had the king stop short of consummating through sacrifice the newly formed relationship with the city's residents, this would be contrary to the reader's expectations of the literary description of such a procession. Instead, the reader might raise questions about the king's authority and about whether the citizens should trust that the king would be an effective ruler for them, especially if the excuse was the late hour, as it was in Jesus' case. It would certainly not endear the king to the readers. Because Jesus does not follow through with what is expected of him when he reaches the Temple in Mark's story, his authority as a divinely appointed king is suspect. This portrayal of Jesus certainly does not embody the picture of strength that a Davidic messianic ruler would have under customary circumstances.

Third, and closely related to the second, is the action that Jesus takes in the Temple. As we discussed in the first point above, the expectation of the procession is for Jesus to consummate his action by some ritual of appropriation, such as sacrifice in the Temple, especially when read along with Zechariah 14, which describes the eschatological event where God, the divine warrior, takes his place in Jerusalem and establishes a universal kingship. But what happens is quite anti-climactic. First, after the acclamation in Mark 11:9–10, Jesus "entered into Jerusalem into the temple, and after looking around at everything, he went out to Bethany with the twelve because it was already late" (εἰσῆλθεν εἰς Ἱεροσόλυμα εἰς τὸ ἱερὸν καὶ περιβλεψάμενος πάντα, ὀψίας ἤδη οὔσης τῆς ὥρας, ἐξῆλθεν εἰς Βηθανίαν μετὰ τῶν δώδεκα; Mark 11:11). The end of Jesus' procession does not end like the typical procession.[52] There is no ritual of appropriation. Instead, Jesus simply enters the Temple and does nothing

---

[52] Evans recognizes the strange conclusion to Jesus' procession, but he does not put the story within the context of other contemporary processions. In discussing the form of the story, he says, "Had the early church invented the story of the entrance, or thoroughly revised a more or less ordinary story of entrance, we should have expected a more pronounced Christological element and surely a more impressive conclusion . . . It seems more probable that what we have here is a fragment of an authentic story, which the tradents and eventually the evangelist himself passed on but without being in full possession of the facts" (*Mark 8:27–16:20*, 138). He then goes on to discuss the possible role of Psalm 118 in Jesus' lack of action when he does enter the Temple precincts. On the basis of the Targum paraphrase of Psalm 118, he claims that Jesus may have expected a priestly greeting when entering the Temple, but he did not receive one. "This is admittedly speculative, but it could explain the awkward, anticlimactic ending of the entrance narrative" (ibid., 146). He goes on to say that because Jesus did not receive this welcome in the Temple, "all that he could do was look over the precincts and then retire to Bethany with his disciples" (ibid., 147). The problem of the lateness of the Targum of Psalm 118 raises serious questions about Evans' attempt to make sense of the ending of the procession by appealing to this Aramaic source. Matera

but look around and leave. There is no consummation of power or appropriation of the city. When Jesus finally does take action in the Temple the
next day, one could argue that he tries to appropriate the temple mount,
or at least uphold its sanctity, but he does it in a strange way. Instead of
reclaiming his city like the divine warrior king of Zechariah 14, he tries
to disrupt the workings of the temple mount because "he did not allow
anyone to carry a vessel through the temple mount" (οὐκ ἤφιεν ἵνα τις
διενέγκῃ σκεῦος διὰ τοῦ ἱεροῦ, Mark 11:16).[53] Zech 14:21 insinuates that
all the inhabitants of Jerusalem will be able to use their cooking vessels
as holy vessels because the whole city is holy. Jesus' actions imply that
vessels being carried through the temple mount are from the outside and
therefore are not holy enough to be carried through the sancified area.
Instead of rejecting the Temple, as some commentators suggest,[54] Jesus
may be declaring the profanation of the temple mount under its current
administration and attempting to re-sanctify it by ceasing unholy activity within it. In other words, Jesus is declaring that the temple mount is
holy but not being treated as holy, and therefore normal activity within it
should cease in order to prevent its further profanation. So, although the
content of Zech 14:20–1 provides a lens through which to interpret Jesus'
actions in the Temple, they are in contrast with Zech 14:20–1 rather than
in continuity with it.

After looking at this story in some detail, it is clear that at the same
time that Mark builds expectations for Jesus to be a Davidic warrior
king who takes possession of his holy city by an entrance procession
with eschatological and messianic overtones, the evangelist also strongly
conditions them by evoking the image of the king as gentle and making
Jesus' procession end in an anticlimactic way. His eventual action in the
Temple, interrupted by the fig-tree cursing, adds to the undercutting of the
expectations swirling around the story, in that he still does not perform
a symbolic appropriation. Instead, he performs an action that calls into
question the workings of the Temple and those who are charged with
its administration. Although his actions are not exactly gentle, in that he
clearly asserts his power by overturning the tables and preventing vessels
from being carried through the Temple, he does not act as a conquering

---

says that the anticlimactic ending to the entry is purposeful, because the Davidic promises
cannot yet be publicly proclaimed: "The reason is that the redactor has carefully reserved
the title 'King' for Chapter 15 when it will be impossible to misunderstand the character of
Jesus' kingship" (*Kingship*, 73).

[53] Duff, "The March of the Divine Warrior," 68.

[54] Etienne Trocmé goes too far in saying that Mark, through his narration of Jesus' actions
here, proclaims the end of the Temple, depriving it of all legitimacy, "even as a simple place
of prayer" ("même comme simple lieu de prière," *L'Evangile selon Saint Marc*, 290).

king or general. The story ends with the interpretation of the fig-tree incident, which, when read with the Temple incident, seems to refocus the location of authentic leadership in piety away from the Temple and toward Jesus and those instructed by Jesus.

Through this careful construction of 11:1–25, Mark challenges the reader to reform his or her expectations about who Jesus is and what he is doing. He is a royal figure, an eschatological figure, and a messianic figure. But his connection with David is not what one would expect. He does not act like the processing king triumphantly taking possession of his conquered city. He does not act with military violence to establish his kingship but acts in a way that defies expectation. In the story of the healing of Bartimaeus, Mark evokes the Son of David when characterizing Jesus while at the same time limiting that evocation to the healing powers associated with Solomon as son of David. In 11:1–25, Mark does something similar; he evokes David to describe Jesus, aligning him with the royal Davidic messiah,[55] but at the same time, he downplays the earthly, militaristic, and violent aspects of his messianic action one might expect with such an evocation.[56]

---

[55] After a negative reading of the Bartimaeus story and the Son of David question in Mark 12:35–7, Kelber argues that 11:1–10 does not align Jesus with the messianic kingdom of David, but does just the opposite. He proposes that the acclamation in 11:9–10 is very "un-Markan" and so actually functions to put the wrong confession onto the lips of the crowds. As a result, "A wedge is driven between the Kingdom of God and the kingdom of David, and Jesus is on his way to the former, rejecting the latter" (*The Kingdom in Mark*, 92–7). However, neither in the Bartimaeus story (see section 2.1) nor in the procession to Jerusalem does Jesus rebuke those who associate him with David. Mark carefully defines the relationship between Jesus and David, but he does not make a complete break with it, as Kelber argues.

[56] Marcus interprets Mark's apparent interplay with Zechariah 14 as an interplay with all of Zechariah 9–14. He offers a reading that portrays Mark, through Jesus' actions, offering an alternative to the Jewish revolutionaries contemporary with the writing of his Gospel. The alternative would not downplay the warrior Messiah they were expecting; rather, it would uphold the military imagery but interpret it apocalyptically. In other words, Mark promotes the militaristic Davidic Messiah image, but the way that the conquering happens is changed. Jesus as the Messiah conquers through his death on the cross, and God takes on the role of the militant force behind the apocalyptic holy war that the Messiah Jesus is fighting through his suffering. However, Marcus bases his reading of Mark's alternative interpretation of Zechariah 9–14 on scanty evidence and tenuous argumentation with respect to the revolutionaries' way of interpreting Zechariah 9–14. For example, he states "The allusions to Zech 9–14 in Mark 14:22–28 [which he bases in large part on the allusions to Zech 9:9–13 in Mark 11:1–11], then, may well be read by Mark and his audience in such a way that they provide a contrast to the interpretation of those passages circulating in Jewish revolutionary circles known to them" (*The Way of the Lord*, 160). However, his entire argument rests on the one reference to one revolutionary, "the Egyptian," mentioned by Josephus, and the beginning of his march on Jerusalem from the Mount of Olives. Although Josephus never mentions Zechariah 9, Marcus surmises a connection with it and

2.3   The rejected Davidic Son of God (Mark 12:1–12)

The parable of the vineyard in Mark 12:1–12 must be discussed briefly, since Psalm 118 is commonly used in early Christian reflection on Jesus, as it is in the passage just considered,[57] and Davidic overtones come to the fore with its usage here in Mark. I will not perform an extensive analysis of the passage; instead, I will focus attention on the Davidic overtones possibly present in the passage, putting aside the Isaian background and the issue of the relationship between the Temple and the Jewish authorities.

As Frank J. Matera has pointed out, regardless of modern scholars' reluctance to attribute allegorical speech to Jesus, the passage in its present form is an allegory,[58] or at least an allegorical parable.[59] Although there is no explicit allegorical interpretation given after the story, as in Mark 4:13–20, there is enough of a hint that Mark presents this as an allegory by the statement in 12:12, "They sought to arrest him, and they were afraid of the crowd, for they knew that he had spoken the parable against them" (καὶ ἐζήτουν αὐτὸν κρατῆσαι, καὶ ἐφοβήθησαν τὸν ὄχλον, ἔγνωσαν γὰρ ὅτι πρὸς αὐτοὺς τὴν παραβολὴν εἶπεν). In light of this allegorical feature, Psalm 118 must lend a certain kind of overtone to the passage

advances the idea that "Jewish revolutionar*ies*" were interpreting this passage in such a way as to inspire and interpret their actions as messianic. See *The Way of the Lord*, 154–64.

[57] See Matt 11:3; 21:9, 42; 23:39; Luke 13:35; 19:38; 20:17; Heb 13:6; 1 Pet 2:4, 7 for New Testament quotations from Psalm 118.

[58] Matera, *Kingship*, 75. Schweizer says, "It is the only parable in the Synoptics which strongly resembles an allegory (cf. 4:1–9)." He then goes on to argue, under clear influence of Jülicher, that such allegorical interpretation is characteristic of the early church. See *The Good News According to Mark*, 239. Kingsbury calls this story a parable, but says that "a number of the parable's traits assume allegorical significance," *Christology*, 115. Joachim Jeremias does not hesitate to call it an allegory from the very beginning of his treatment of the passage (*The Parables of Jesus* [2nd rev. edn.; trans. S. H. Hooke; New York: Charles Scribner's Son, 1972], 70); but then by the end of his examination of the social setting of the story, he says "Mark 12:1ff. is not an allegory, but a parable drawing upon a definite situation" (ibid., 76). He opts for the story originally being a parable which has been allegorized by Mark and Matthew, but less so by Luke. His argument depends in part on the non-allegorical form of the story in the Gospel of Thomas (he follows C. H. Dodd's analysis here). However, he does not entertain the possibility that Thomas (and Luke, to a certain extent) de-allegorized the story and presented it in a parabolic form. Pheme Perkins takes a similar tack as Jeremias, but she goes on to analyze the passage without its allegorical presentation. Therefore, her analysis is of little use for the present discussion (*Hearing the Parables of Jesus* [New York: Paulist Press, 1981], 181–94). Evans, on the other hand, does entertain the idea that the editor of *Gos. Thom.* redacted the story for his own purposes, de-allegorizing it in the process, as Luke does. In fact, he uses the Lucan version as an example of how the simpler form of the story is not necessarily the older form, and then argues that Mark's version preserves the oldest and most primitive form (*Mark 8:27–16:20*, 217–19).

[59] Donahue and Harrington say that the story is technically not an allegory, because not every element is given an interpretation (*The Gospel of Mark*, 341).

that clearly relates to the allegory. As I will argue below, Psalm 118 lends a Davidic emphasis to the presentation of Jesus as Son of God, which in part prepares the reader for the upcoming usage of the PssLam in the passion narrative.

The story is fairly straightforward in its presentation. It tells of a landowner planting a vineyard and building all the necessary components to it. Once the vineyard is built, he entrusts its care to tenant farmers (οἱ γεωργοί). Periodically, he sends a slave (δοῦλος) to collect his produce from the farmers, but each time the slave runs into trouble, either getting beaten or killed. Eventually, the landowner thinks that sending his son will have the desired effect of forcing the farmers to respect him through his son and hand over the produce. Instead, the farmers surmise that by killing the son and heir, they will gain his inheritance. After seizing the son, they kill him and cast him out of the vineyard. Jesus ends the story with a rhetorical question and answer, "What, then, will the lord of the vineyard do? He will come and destroy the farmers and give the vineyard to others" (τί [οὖν] ποιήσει ὁ κύριος τοῦ ἀμπελῶνος; ἐλεύσεται καὶ ἀπολέσαι τοὺς γεωργοὺς καὶ δώσει τὸν ἀμπελῶνα ἄλλοις, 12:9). Then he interprets the story with the quotation from LXX Ps 117:22–3: "Did you not read this scripture: 'A stone which the builders rejected, it has become the cornerstone; from the Lord this has happened and it is wonderful in our eyes'? (οὐδὲ τὴν γραφὴν ταύτην ἀνέγνωτε· λίθον ὃν ἀπεδοκίμασαν οἱ οἰκοδομοῦντες, οὗτος ἐγενήθη εἰς κεφαλὴν γωνίας· παρὰ κυρίου ἐγένετο αὕτη καὶ ἔστιν θαυμαστὴ ἐν ὀφθαλμοῖς ἡμῶν; 12:10–11). Once "they" (i.e., the chief priests, the scribes, and the elders) recognize that Jesus has spoken the parable against them, they want to arrest him, but they fear the crowd, let him go, and then go away themselves.

In the body of the story, the overtones of Jesus' beloved sonship are clear, especially with the allegorical presentation of the story.[60] Therefore,

---

[60] Matera (followed by Marcus, *The Way of the Lord*, 71) unnecessarily complicates the issue of beloved sonship in this story. He links it indirectly to the baptism and transfiguration of Jesus in Mark by way of Psalm 2 instead of staying at the level of Mark's narrative. See *Kingship*, 75–9. Both the baptism and transfiguration have already occurred in the story and are easily recalled by the construction of this parable by calling the son υἱὸς ἀγαπητός rather than simply υἱός. Kingsbury, on the other hand, sees in the parable Jesus "making obvious allusion to himself as God's 'Son'," *Christology*, 12; see Jeremias, *Parables*, 73, and Ched Myers, *Binding the Strong Man: A Political Reading of Mark's Story of Jesus* (Maryknoll, New York: Orbis, 1988), 308, for similar assessments. Roger D. Aus argues that "Jesus' choice of the term 'beloved' was not only influenced by the tradition behind the *Mekilta* on Exod 13:21 . . . with the term חבב. Rather, a Hebrew expression in Isa 5:1 also played a major role here" (*The Wicked Tenants and Gethsemane: Isaiah in the Wicked Tenants' Vineyard, and Moses and the High Priest in Gethsemane: Judaic Traditions in Mark 12:1–9 and 14:32–42* [Atlanta: Scholars Press, 1996], 57). The *Mekilta* interprets

they can be linked with the other places where Jesus' beloved sonship is explicit, namely at his baptism (1:11) and at the transfiguration (9:7). Later, the centurion at the cross declares Jesus to be Son of God, but it is not clear whether this is a positive, negative, or purposely ambiguous declaration. When Mark interprets the allegory through the character of Jesus, the nature of this sonship becomes more focused. Mark does this by a reference to LXX Ps 117:22–3, so it will help to have a better idea of what the passage means in its own context in order to understand the sense in which Mark may be using the text.

LXX Ps 117:22–3 falls at the end of an individual thanksgiving for deliverance from peril. Verse 22 ends the first person singular description of the peril and thanksgiving for deliverance, and verse 23 begins the more collective description of the thanksgiving and rejoicing in the salvation of the individual, which ends in verse 27. Starting in verse 5, the psalmist alternates between descriptions of a non-specific situation of danger and salvation from that danger, which he attributes to God. The effect is that the psalmist declares his exaltation by God from the midst of life-threatening danger at the hands of his enemies. This simultaneously communicates the power of God to save, the vulnerability of the psalmist, in relation to his enemies, the chosenness of the psalmist, in the sense that God chose to save him and not his enemies, and the power of the psalmist to overcome enemies with the help of God.

Verses 22–3 fit into this context, but nowhere else does the psalm talk about rejection, nor does it indicate who "the builders" (οἱ οἰκοδομοῦν-τες) are. Prior to this verse, the enemies of the psalmist require no deciphering. In verse 10, "all the nations surrounded me" (πάντα τὰ ἔθνη ἐκύκλωσάν με), and the subsequent verses show no indication that the identity of the enemies has changed. However, οἱ οἰκοδομοῦντες raises the question, "the builders of what?" One possibility is the leaders of the powerful nations who "build" their empires while rejecting the smaller, less powerful Israel. If read this way, then verse 22 again speaks about

Exod 13:21 by relating a narrative regarding Antoninus, who took a torch and lit the way for his sons. The passage reads: "It is merely to show you 'how dear my sons are to me' . . . 'so that you should treat them with respect'." The passage goes on to describe how dear Israel is to God by going before them "so that [the nations] should treat them [the sons of Israel] with respect." Aus then says, "Here God's sons are 'dear' (חבה) to Him, just as the owner of the vineyard in Jesus' parable has a 'dear' son" (ibid., 31). This seems like an unnecessary stretch by Aus to make sense historically of a fairly clear intratextual narrative device by Mark to identify Jesus with the son in the allegory. He does go on to say that Mark probably did not understand Jesus' reference to the prophet Isaiah in 12:6 (ibid., 61). Donahue and Harrington conclude, "At least at the Markan level of the parable's history the beloved son is Jesus" (*The Gospel of Mark*, 338).

the psalmist being chosen by God to be exalted and foundational for his people. A second possibility is that the psalm in general, and verse 22 in particular, is referring to David as king of Israel. Given the common understanding of David as the author of the Psalms, even those without a Davidic superscript, first-century Jewish readers most likely would have read Psalm 118 identifying David as the psalmist. In later Jewish writings this is certainly the case.[61] In this case, the stone would be David, and "the builders" could still be the nations rejecting the leader of Israel. But it could also have intra-national overtones, and therefore "the builders" could refer to leaders within Israel – those who "build" the nation. In the context of this psalm, then, those who reject the stone are those who reject or do not recognize David as king.[62]

There is clearly some uncertainty as to the identity of the builders, which can affect the meaning of the passage. Mark seems to exploit the flexibility of possible meanings with regard to the identity of the builders, in that he uses the imagery in tandem with the parable to interpret opposition to Jesus as stemming from the Jewish religious authorities.[63] If this is the case, Mark's use of LXX Psalm 117 aligns Jesus with David,

[61] Both the Targum to Ps 118:22 and the Midrash Tehillim referring to Ps 118:23 interpret the individual as David.

[62] At first, David is not brought before Samuel for consideration because he is the youngest and only a shepherd (1 Sam 16:11). In the battle with the Philistines, where Goliath challenges the warriors of Israel to defeat him, Saul discounts David's desire to fight, so David must convince Saul to give him an opportunity to fight Goliath (1 Sam 17:31–7). When he faces Goliath, he is laughed at by the much larger and more powerful warrior (17:43–4). Before David becomes king, Saul makes him a fugitive by pursuing him in order to kill him, which is not exactly a welcoming gesture for the newly anointed king. From these humble and endangered beginnings, he ascends to the throne of Israel, which can be interpreted as salvation from enemies and exaltation, similar to Psalm 118. Late in his life, David is rejected as king, in the sense that Absalom tries to co-opt his throne and take over as king (2 Samuel 15–19). Without going into detail, Evans simply says, "Although initially rejected by the religious establishment, including the prophet-priest Samuel, David comes to be recognized and blessed from the house of the Lord by the priests" (*Mark 8:27–16:20*, 238).

[63] As early as Mark 2:6, and definitely by 3:6, opposition to Jesus by the Jewish authorities mounts, which culminates in the demand by the Jewish Temple authorities to have Pilate crucify Jesus in 15:1–15. Without much argumentation, except by brief appeal to vineyard imagery from Jer 8:13; Hos 9:10; Mic 7:1; and Isa 5:1–7, Painter asserts that the tenant farmers represent the leaders of Israel in the allegory (*Mark's Gospel*, 162). Marcus takes a different tack by appealing to rabbinic sources where "the builders" is a common term for the leaders of Israel, who "build" Jerusalem by applying the Torah to contemporary issues and problems (*The Way of the Lord*, 124–5). Again, the problem with Marcus' argumentation is that he takes this late data and simply applies it to Mark's thinking as he constructed his Gospel. Evans also refers to rabbinic literature in discussing the custom of calling the leaders of Israel "builders," but he does it in a less determinative way, simply raising the issue to allow for comparison and determination of cultural/literary custom (*Mark 8:27–16:20*, 238).

in general, and with the aspect of the *persecuted and saved* David, in particular. By using LXX Psalm 117 in this particular way to interpret the parable allegorically with respect to Jesus and the Jewish authorities and combining it with the strong overtones of Jesus as the beloved son in the story, Mark also brings in the element of divine sonship that is assumed of David as king.[64]

With the themes of persecution, kingship, and divine sonship all inter-woven in the story, Mark again carefully emphasizes the non-militaristic aspects of David's earthly kingship when linking Jesus with David. He chooses a psalm that can be read as articulating the difficulties that David experienced as king, and from this psalm he chooses a verse that empha-sizes rejection and then interprets this rejection as intra-national rejec-tion. Much like his choice of Zech 9:9–10 in the story of Jesus' entry into Jerusalem, Mark chooses a place in the psalm that is not focused on the military triumph of the king, but rather articulates a quality of royalty that does not leap to mind immediately when thinking of a king. In the present case, the king is rejected by leaders and exalted by God to be the foundation of the building. Mark chooses a scriptural passage from the biblical tradition about David, appends it to a parable presented

---

[64] Psalms 2, 89 and 2 Samuel 7 are the clearest examples of the king being portrayed as a son of God. Kingsbury raises the possibility that LXX Ps 117:22 itself evokes "son"–"stone" imagery found in the Old Testament (1 Kgs 18:31; Isa 54:11–13; Lam 4:1–2). He argues that if this is so, "then the rejection-elevation of the 'stone' is an allusion to the crucifixion-vindication of God's 'son' Jesus" (*Christology*, 115). However, the three passages on which he bases this conclusion do not clearly use stone imagery to describe sons or children of Israel. It is accurate that stones and children are both mentioned in the three passages, but in 1 Kgs 18:31 stones are symbolic of the twelve tribes of Israel. In Isa 54:11–13, the poet uses metaphorical imagery of setting stones in order and rebuilding foundations, pinnacles, gates, and walls with precious stones as a way of promising the restoration of Israel. After this imagery, the promise comes that Israel's children will be taught by the Lord and that they shall prosper. So there is nothing to necessitate the connection between stones and children here. Lam 4:1–2 is the closest to bringing stone imagery together with children imagery, in that verse 1 describes the sacred stones being scattered in the streets and then verse 2 talks about the children of Zion being precious as gold but being treated as clay pots. But even here, the imagery is not clearly tied together, and therefore it is dubious to call the stone imagery in LXX Ps 117:22 an allusion to it and then apply it allegorically to its use in Mark 12:10. After this fairly weak argument, Kingsbury simply asserts that, as in the two previous passages in Mark where Jesus is called "beloved son" (the baptism and transfiguration), Jesus "again stands forth as royal Son of God" (*Christology*, 117). He makes this statement without grounding, and so its adequacy must be questioned. Evans focuses on the possible word-play between "son" (בן) and "stone" (אבן) to argue that there is not only a link between Ps 118:22–3 and Jesus' sonship, but that the quotation was original to the parable. He only briefly discusses the fact that the quotation is taken from the LXX, not the Hebrew version of Psalm 118 (*Mark 8:27–16:20*, 228–30). Gundry mentions this word-play, but raises no doubt that it is behind the Greek in the quotation. He mentions nothing further about it (*Mark*, 663).

as an allegory, and focuses the themes very carefully to present Jesus as Davidically royal and divinely affiliated as beloved son, and as rejected by leaders, yet exalted by God.[65] The first two themes are common enough in the tradition, but the third is unexpected for a royal messiah.

2.4   Jesus not the Son of David? (Mark 12:35–7)

Mark 12:35–7 is a short but important passage for our purposes. It quotes one of the most frequently used psalms in the New Testament, Psalm 110. Given the wide variety of texts that use this psalm to describe Jesus' post-resurrection enthronement in heaven at the right hand of God,[66] it is clear that this text became a locus of meaning for diverse groups of early followers of Jesus from a very early point in the reflection about the identity of Jesus. Generally, commentators look at its use in the Gospel of Mark – in 12:35–7 and 14:62 – as two separate passages that are independent, both from each other and from the rest of the narrative. As a result, the conclusions concern the historical Jesus and the historical development of the earliest Christological statements[67] or lead to an abstracted theological statement that downplays the relationship between Jesus and David.[68] If one looks at Mark 12:35–7 in its narrative context within

---

[65] Most commentators go the next step and see this depiction as a description of Jesus' crucifixion (thus the persecution) and resurrection (thus the exaltation or vindication). See Painter, *Mark's Gospel*, 162; Kingsbury, *Christology*, 115; Marcus, *The Way of the Lord*, 123. By focusing on the narrative flow of the Gospel, I choose instead to suspend statements about vindication of a character that has not been killed yet and to focus on the characterization that the Gospel is presenting for the reader.

[66] Ps 110:1 is quoted explicitly seven times, but the 27th edition of Nestle-Aland counts sixteen total references, because the editors also count the obvious allusions in Matt 22:44; 26:64; Mark 12:36; 14:62 (and 16:19); Luke 20:42–3; 22:69; Acts 2:34–5; Rom 8:34; 1 Cor 15:25; Eph 1:20; Col 3:1; Heb 1:3, 13; 8:1; 10:21–2. If, with Martin Hengel, one includes all the passages about the exaltation of Christ to the right hand of God, then Acts 2:33; 5:31; 7:55–6; Heb 12:2; 1 Pet 3:22 should be included. (See "'Sit at My Right Hand!' The Enthronement of Christ at the Right Hand of God and Psalm 110:1" in *Studies in Early Christology* [Edinburgh: T&T Clark, 1995], 133.) This list spans the synoptic Gospels, the Pauline corpus, Hebrews and 1 Peter. If one includes Ps 110:4, then the references include Rom 11:29 (possibly); Heb 5:6, 10; 6:20; 7:3, 11, 15, 17, 21. Nestle-Aland includes Rom 2:5 as a reference to Ps 110:5, but it is a doubtful reference at best, since the motif of God's wrath on the day of the Lord is common in the Jewish scriptures. Hengel also points out that Rev 3:21 develops the motif of "the commonality of throne between the Father and the exalted Son," in place of 'at the right hand' of Ps 110:1 (ibid., 134).

[67] See Hengel, "'Sit at My Right Hand!'," for a discussion of the role of Psalm 110 in early Christological speculation.

[68] Chilton, "Jesus *ben David*," tends toward this type of argumentation. Marcus, on the other hand, takes a path that upholds the relationship between David and Jesus, while at the same time heavily conditioning it (*The Way of the Lord*, 130–52). In general terms, I agree with Marcus' insight that there are several major things happening in this passage,

chapters 11–12, however, as well as with respect to chapters 14–15, then the relationship between Jesus and David is not completely negated, but it is conditioned strongly, as happens in the other three passages examined in this chapter. In other words, David remains an important figure for Mark's narrative presentation of Jesus' identity, but one must read Mark 12:35–7 within the overall context of the narrative in order to understand how.[69]

This short passage begins with Jesus in the temple, and while teaching he asks, "How do the scribes say that the Messiah is the son of David?" (πῶς λέγουσιν οἱ γραμματεῖς ὅτι ὁ χριστὸς υἱὸς Δαυίδ ἐστιν; Mark 12:35).[70] Jesus then goes on to quote Ps 110:1, but before he does so, he introduces the quotation by claiming that David spoke "in the Holy Spirit" (ἐν τῷ πνεύματι τῷ ἁγίῳ, 12:36). After the quoted material, he finishes his speech by offering the rhetorical question, "David himself calls him Lord, so how is he his son?" (αὐτὸς Δαυὶδ λέγει αὐτὸν κύριον, καὶ πόθεν αὐτοῦ ἐστιν υἱός; 12:37).[71] The passage ends with the crowd's reaction of delight at Jesus' teaching.

It is understandable that Jesus would go to a royal psalm to discuss the status of the Messiah, since the hope of a coming messiah in Second Temple Judaism was tied up in large part with Davidic kingship. However, the way Mark has Jesus use the psalm seems to undermine the link between David and the Messiah, at least in some sense.[72] At first glance, the only aspect of this relationship that Mark seems to be denying is the way that the scribes have construed the relationship. In other

but the conclusions we come to are quite different with regard to the role(s) of the Messiah. Gundry also tries to uphold the Davidic sonship of the Messiah and his lordship over David at the same time. He does this by stressing the fact that Jesus is not asking a question about superiority, "rather, about the scribes' *calling* the Christ 'Son of David' over against David's *calling* him 'my Lord'" (*Mark*, 721–2).

[69] See C. Burger, *Jesus als Davidssohn: Eine traditionsgeschichtliche Untersuchung* (FRLANT 98; Göttingen: Vandenhoeck & Ruprecht, 1970), 58–9, for a similar attempt to read this passage with the other David passages in chapters 10–12. However, he does not include the parable of the tenant farmers as part of his analysis.

[70] Schweizer thinks that, since the Davidic relationship with the Messiah was so deeply engrained in Jewish culture at the time of Jesus, πῶς should be translated not as "how" but as "to what extent" or "in what way" (*The Good News According to Mark*, 256).

[71] Gundry argues that πόθεν should be interpreted as asking for source. He takes the term literally and translates the verse, "where does the designation 'Son of David' come from?" He then argues that the contextually implied answer is, "Not from anyone speaking in the Holy Spirit!" So, his interpretation focuses less on Christological issues and more on the alleged attempt to discredit the scribes' non-inspired reading of scripture (*Mark*, 722–3).

[72] Kingsbury does not read this in deductive terms but as a discussion of antinomies of scripture passages whose solution resides in giving both parts of the antinomy their due. After consideration of many possibilities, he concludes that the antinomy in this case is "Son of David" versus "Son of God" (*Christology*, 109–13).

words, Mark wants to deny that the Messiah should be thought of as the Son of David.[73] Why is this important for Mark to do? Bruce Chilton argues that Jesus was trying "to deflect the growing suspicion that he claimed to be the messiah."[74] This simple teaching, however, hardly lays to rest the overwhelming presentation of Jesus as Messiah in the Gospel of Mark. It could also be an attempt to disavow Jesus' supposed Davidic lineage. But this seems unlikely from a narrative point of view, since just two chapters previously, the title "Son of David" was emphatically proclaimed by Bartimaeus and not muted at all by the character of Jesus in the story.[75] Why keep the title in that story and uphold it so strongly there, if there were a desire on Mark's part to deny the Davidic ancestry of Jesus? Mark could easily have chosen another title for Bartimaeus to use for Jesus as he passed by.

So, if Davidic ancestry is not at issue here, why uphold the title "Son of David" in 10:46–52 and then deny it in 12:35–7?[76] The answer must be found in Mark's careful characterization of Jesus and redefinition of what it means to be the Messiah. As we know, Jesus had already been identified as the Messiah back in 8:29 by Peter. So any subsequent narrative description of the Messiah must also contribute to the characterization of Jesus. I argued above that the first mention of Jesus as Son of David in 10:46–52 was carefully focused on the Solomonic aspect of this title. In 12:35–7, there is no such association with Solomon. There is no healing story and no mention of exorcism anywhere within two chapters of this passage. In fact, Bartimaeus is the last healing or exorcism that Jesus performs in the Gospel. Without clear connotations of healing or exorcism, the reader is left with the other image of the Son of David, which is that of a successor

[73] Painter disagrees with the claim that Mark is denying Davidic sonship. Instead, he argues that the Markan Jesus affirms that the Messiah is both the Son of David and the Son of God through his use of Ps 110:1 (*Mark's Gospel*, 168).

[74] Chilton, "Jesus *ben David*," 102. Chilton makes these comments from the perspective of historical reconstruction rather than the narrative of Mark.

[75] Evans appeals to the many places in the prophets where the lineage of the Messiah is linked to David to refute the disavowal of the relationship between the son of David and the Messiah (Isa 9:2–7; 11:1–9; Jer 23:5–6; 33:14–18; Ezek 34:23–4). See *Mark 8:27–16:20*, 274. Schweizer rightly points out that Davidic descent of the Messiah is not denied in other early Christian writings until the Epistle of Barnabas (12:10f), and therefore he thinks it unlikely that this passage is trying to deny Davidic descent of the Messiah (*The Good News According to Mark*, 256). Juel says, "there is nothing elsewhere in the Gospel to suggest Mark intends to prove that Jesus is not the 'son of David'" (*Messianic Exegesis*, 142).

[76] Marcus raises a similar question based both on previous sections of Mark and extensive documentation of the Davidic descent of the Messiah in the Old Testament and first-century Jewish texts (*The Way of the Lord*, 140). Gundry thinks that Mark is not denying the Davidic sonship of the Messiah, nor claiming that his lordship over David is superior to his Davidic sonship (*Mark*, 721–2).

to the earthly, royal, militaristic leader and judge of Israel, most clearly expressed in the *Ps. Sol.* 17:21–5, along with the similar characteristics of the Davidic messiah as described in the Dead Sea Scrolls. By denying the epithet "Son of David" for the Messiah, Mark denies the association of the Messiah with the earthly, bellicose characteristics most likely evoked by this title.[77]

At the same time that Mark denies that the Messiah is the Son of David in this passage in the sense of *Psalms of Solomon* 17, he defines the Messiah in reference to Ps 110:1.[78] To paraphrase, Mark 12:35–7 says, "the Messiah is not the Son of David, but David did speak of him as being enthroned at the right hand of God while God makes the Messiah's enemies subservient to him." So the linkage between David and the Messiah, and thus Jesus, is not completely severed. Instead, as he does in the other passages discussed above, Mark carefully defines the relationship between Jesus and David. In this case, the earthly, militaristic images evoked by the "Son of David" are downplayed and denied, but the royal imagery is still upheld by the quotation of Ps 110:1. God (κύριος) enthrones the Messiah (κυριός μου)[79] at his right hand. This fits well with the royal overtones of Jesus in Mark 11 and 12, and the royal overtones

---

[77] Schweizer argues that Mark uses Ps 110:1 as a way to express "the decision of the church which must finally separate itself from the leaders of the Jewish people, though not from the people themselves" (*The Good News According to Mark*, 255). Myers goes so far as to argue that the entire ideology of the restoration of the Davidic kingdom is repudiated (*Binding*, 319).

[78] Evans takes Jesus' (not Mark's) interpretation of Ps 110:1 not as a rejection of Davidic messianism, but a qualification of it. He appeals to Jesus' apparent definition of his messiahship in terms of the Son of Man from Daniel 7. See *Mark 8:27–16:20*, 274. However, this does not take into account the context into which Mark puts Jesus' interpretation of Ps 110:1, nor does it deal with how he is presented as Davidic even in the midst of this apparent denial of the title Son of David for the Messiah. Instead, it jumps to 14:62, where the link between Ps 110:1 and Daniel 7 is made explicit and then superimposes this correlation onto Mark 12:35–7.

[79] Many commentators make much of the implicit title "κύριος" for Jesus here, pointing to the other places in Mark where the title is used for Jesus. Some attempt to incorporate this title into the Christology of Mark, but in my opinion there are too few places where the title is used with enough narrative weight to necessitate its consideration as a major factor in interpreting this passage for the present purposes of this study. Matera goes so far as to say that κύριος is a "surrogate . . . for the kingly title" that will become explicit at Jesus' crucifixion (i.e., King of the Jews) (*Kingship*, 91). Evans thinks that, because there is explicit subordination of David to the Messiah in Mark 12:35–7 through the use of the title "κύριος" by David for the Messiah, this title points away from David and towards the "son of God" and "son of Man" understanding that Jesus (not the Markan Jesus) has of himself (*Mark 8:27–16:20*, 276). However, Marcus says, "If Mark's only purpose in quoting Ps. 110:1 had been to establish that David called the Messiah 'Lord,' he could have contented himself with citing the first words of the verse, 'The Lord said to my lord'" (*The Way of the Lord*, 134). Kelber argues that in this passage Mark not only disclaims the scribal notion of Davidic sonship, but also replaces it with the lordship of the Son of God (*Kingdom*, 95–6).

will also continue in the final two chapters of the Gospel, chapters 14 and 15 (especially 15). The fact that the Messiah (Jesus) is still given a royal character in 12:35–7 does not necessarily mean that it is a *Davidic* royal character. If this passage is read on its own without recourse to the rest of the Gospel, one might think that the Messiah is not the Son of David, but he is still a royal figure enthroned by God in heaven (i.e., at God's right hand). Although the most famous king in Israel is David, the Messiah in this passage seems to be closer to God as king[80] or to a heavenly king to whom God gives authority to rule[81] than to David as king.

Two important things happen in this passage simultaneously. Mark is delineating the aspects of the Messiah into earthly and heavenly categories. First, the earthly, militaristic aspects of the Messiah are being suppressed through the denial of the concept of the Messiah being the Son of David. When read in light of the three passages discussed above, this passage implies that the earthly role of the Messiah, namely Jesus, is not to gain political power through earthly, militaristic action. He is still a Davidic messiah, but he is not a Davidic messiah in the militaristic sense of the messiah hoped for in some Jewish circles in the Second Temple period. Second, the heavenly royalty of the Messiah is being upheld through the use of Ps 110:1 to describe the Messiah's association with God as enthroned at God's right hand.[82] In this passage and in Mark 14:62, where Mark combines the enthronement imagery of Psalm 110 with the Son of Man imagery in Daniel 7, Mark emphasizes the heavenly aspects in this messianic imagery. These aspects are held in narrative tension with the earthly aspects of the Messiah in Mark 14:62 because it is as a captive on trial on his way to the cross that Jesus makes these bold statements about the Son of Man's eventual fate. Both the heavenly and

---

[80] Although God is never explicitly called king in Ps 110:1, the insinuation is that there is some sort of joint kingship as the Lord enthrones "my Lord" at the right hand of God. Martin Hengel says, "He who is at the 'right hand of God' or whom God supports 'at his right hand', is the one that is elected by God in a unique fashion and who is closely allied with God" ("'Sit at My Right Hand!'," 136). Against this, Gundry says, "According to v. 37 . . . Jesus is using Ps 110:1 only for David calling the Christ 'my Lord,' not for the session at the Lord's right hand; and nothing here indicates that the Lord's right hand means a heavenly exaltation like Jesus's" (*Mark*, 721).

[81] The image of the Ancient of Days and one like a son of man in Daniel 7 comes to mind. The Ancient of Days sits on a throne and gives the one like a son of man kingship. So, the one like a son of man is not God, but he receives the authority to reign in the same way as God reigns.

[82] Donald Juel argues that the passage offers no distinction between an earthly and a heavenly deliverer, and "It is as the enthroned 'lord' that Jesus is son of David" (*Messianic Exegesis*, 144). I agree that there is continuity between the earthly and heavenly aspects of the Messiah, but to say there is no distinction between earthly and heavenly goes too far, in my opinion.

earthly aspects are important for Mark's overall Christology. But since we are concerned most with the relationship between David and Jesus, which involves the earthly aspects of Jesus' messiahship, it is enough to say that Mark 12:35–7 does not completely distance Jesus from David. It only distances Jesus from the earthly, militaristic aspects of a Davidic messiah.

3   Conclusion

We have argued that through four successive passages from the end of chapter 10 through chapter 12, Mark links Jesus with David in very carefully conditioned ways. First, Jesus is portrayed as linked to David through the title "Son of David" with respect to Jesus' ability to heal. Second, we saw that there is a continuation of Jesus as a Davidic royal figure in the narration of his triumphal entry into Jerusalem. However, at several key points, the expected militaristic actions are absent and undermined as the story unfolds. Third, in the story of the wicked tenant farmers, Mark allegorically connects images of royalty, rejection, and sonship in reference to Jesus through the use of Psalm 118, again downplaying the militaristic overtones that could be brought into the picture when using a royal psalm associated with David. Finally, Mark separates the earthly and heavenly aspects and roles of the Messiah through the use of Psalm 110 and by doing so downplays the militaristic overtones of the earthly role of the Messiah as Son of David.

The relationship between David and Jesus does not cease with Mark 12:35–7.[83] As the narrative progresses through these four passages the focus with regard to David moves away from the earthly qualities of the Messiah and away from the common notion that the Messiah would be a warrior king. In addition, chapters 8–10 prepare the reader for the suffering that Jesus will endure in Jerusalem through his three passion predictions (8:31; 9:31; 10:32–4) and his statement of purpose in 10:45, namely, to give his life as a ransom for many. His mission is focused on his self-sacrificial service to others. When these themes are brought together with the Davidic association so clearly and carefully presented in the four passages from chapters 10–12 discussed above, we begin to see how Jesus' suffering as Messiah can be understood. The link between Jesus and David is firmly established, and, as we look toward the passion narrative,

---

[83] Paul J. Achtemeier says Mark 12:35–7 "represents the final word Mark intends to say on the subject." He goes on to argue that association with David is not what Mark wants to stress: rather, Jesus as the Son of Man is Mark's most important title and Christological statement about Jesus (*Mark* [2nd edn; Philadelphia: Fortress, 1986], 58–9).

David's life continues to be an important model for understanding Jesus as the Messiah.

Much as in the four passages discussed in this chapter, the parallels between Jesus and David in chapters 14 and 15 do not picture Jesus as a royal figure who rules militaristically with divinely given power over a chosen people. Instead, the parallels focus on the trying times of David's life. Jesus ascends the Mount of Olives weeping and praying in Gethsemane (Mark 14:26–33), as does David in 2 Sam 15:30–1. Peter swears his loyalty to Jesus even if it means death (Mark 14:27–31), as Ittai does to David in 2 Sam 15:19–24. Jesus is betrayed by a trusted follower, Judas (Mark 14:43–50), as is David by Ahithophel in 2 Sam 17:23.[84] The redefinition of the relationship between Jesus and David continues to focus on David's betrayal and suffering, re-emphasizing the absence of the earthly, military aspects of the hoped-for Messiah embodied in the title "Son of David." Chapters 8–10 prepared us most explicitly to expect the Messiah, Jesus, to suffer, and the Davidic features that Mark gives Jesus in chapters 10–12 clearly link Jesus and David. Chapters 14–15 bring these two characterizations of Jesus together – one who suffers in a self-sacrificial way and one who does so as a Davidic royal figure. Therefore, we can understand the evocations of the PssLam in the passion narrative in this light, namely, as helping to define Jesus as the suffering Davidic Messiah.

[84] See John R. Donahue, "Temple, Trial, and Royal Christology (Mark 14:53–65)," in *The Passion in Mark* (ed. Werner H. Kelber; Philadelphia: Fortress, 1976), 75; Bassler, "A Man For All Seasons," 169; T. F. Glasson, "David Links with the Betrayal of Jesus," *ExpTim* 85 (1973–4): 118–19.

6

THE PASSION

1 Introduction

In Chapter 3, I argued that there are four PssLam evoked in a simple way[1] in six places in Mark 14–15. In this chapter, I will use the interpretations of the psalms that I proposed in Chapter 4 to guide my reading of the passion narrative. Although my analysis will be most detailed with respect to the passages that evoke these psalms, I will also consider their influence on Mark's passion narrative as a whole. This discussion will correspond to Ziva Ben-Porat's third and fourth stages of analysis of an alluding text. She proposes not only consideration of the local context of the alluding text, but openness to wider, more complex, and in-depth correspondences between the alluding and evoked texts.[2]

1.1 The main argument of this chapter

Theodore J. Weeden's work on Jesus' death scene in Mark typifies the way that scholars tend to address the issue of the allusions to the PssLam in the passion narrative. He says, "With regard to the presentation of the suffering Son of Man Christology in the scene, Mark has drawn upon motifs from certain Old Testament passages portraying the figure of the innocent Righteous One who suffers, yet is finally vindicated in his suffering."[3] In contrast to the monolithic portrait of Jesus that Weeden and

---

[1] In section 1 of Chapter 3, I took the position that a text is evoked in a simple way when one, and only one, text is evoked by the main text. There was one exception to this definition in Mark 15:29, because it is likely that other texts with similar imagery are being evoked. However, I argued that when 15:29 is read in its narrative context, Ps 21:8 becomes the dominant text evoked, given the clear and strong evocation of Ps 21:19 in Mark 15:24.

[2] See Ziva Ben-Porat, "The Poetics of Literary Allusion," 111, and the discussion of allusion in Chapter 1 of the present study.

[3] Theodore J. Weeden, "The Cross as Power in Weakness (Mark 15:20b–41)," in *The Passion in Mark: Studies on Mark 14–16* (ed. Werner H. Kelber; Philadelphia: Fortress Press, 1976), 117.

others paint, Edwin K. Broadhead argues, "Various patterns of repetition are employed in the death scene. Consequently the story of Jesus' death resounds with multiple voices and echoes which enrich its narrative effect."[4] Although Broadhead is talking about the death scene, I think his insight is valid for the entirety of Mark 14–16. One of these voices is that of the suffering David from the PssLam evoked in the passion narrative. It is this voice on which I will concentrate my attention in this chapter.

1.1.1 The scriptural justification for Jesus' death in light of the PssLam

As I perform my narrative analysis in light of Psalms 21, 40, 41–2, and 68, I will argue three main points that result from this analysis. First, I will argue that the scriptural justification for Jesus' suffering and death that occurs twice in Mark 14 (i.e., "the Son of Man must go as it is written of him" in 14:21 and "so that the scriptures may be fulfilled" in 14:49) becomes more problematic and complex than a simple appeal to scripture as an authorization of Jesus' death according to God's will. This two-fold scriptural justification does not refer to a specific text of scripture; rather, it is a general appeal to the scriptures in order to point the reader to the scriptures as the place where he or she must turn for an understanding of Jesus' suffering and death.[5] The evocations of scripture in chapters 14 and 15 are dense and varied, and the PssLam in question are part of this complex of scriptural allusions that Mark includes in his story. As will become evident below, a thorough consideration of these PssLam in concert with chapters 14 and 15 reveals a David who challenges God's role in his suffering, who searches for an understanding of his suffering in light of his past relationship with God, and who attempts to shame God to act on his behalf only because of his suffering. Mark alludes to these PssLam in reference to Jesus, and therefore David's concerns become woven into the depiction of Jesus. As a result, the very appeal to scripture

---

[4] Edwin K. Broadhead, *Prophet, Son, Messiah*, 198–9.

[5] Reinhold Liebers argues for references to many passages that might pre-figure the events of Mark's narrative in the Jewish scriptures. For the reference at Mark 14:21, he mainly appeals to the suffering of the righteous one and the textual background that Ruppert appeals to in his analysis. For Mark 14:48, he appeals to the LXX version of Jer 33:8, 43:26, and 44:13f, as well as the story of Elijah in 1 Kings, to talk about the treatment of prophetic figures as a possible parallel to Jesus' treatment. He also appeals to several psalms, 1, 2, and 4 Maccabees, and Isaiah 53 to try to understand the background of the reference. Clearly, Liebers does not point to only one passage that might be referred to in each of these scriptural justifications for the events in Jesus' being handed over. See *"Wie geschrieben steht": Studien zu einer besonderen Art frühchristlichen Schriftbezuges* (Berlin: Walter de Gruyter, 1993), 378–89.

to justify Jesus' suffering and death also includes a challenge to God's role in that suffering and death.

1.1.2   The role of Jesus the messiah in an apocalyptic framework of meaning

Given the strong overtones of apocalyptic eschatology used to tell the story of Jesus' death in Mark, I will argue my second major point in the chapter, namely, reading David's challenge to God as part of Jesus' going "as it is written of him" calls into question the supposed necessity for Jesus' death within an apocalyptic framework of meaning. Situating Jesus' death within a greater apocalyptic scenario raises the importance of his death to a cosmic level. However, the role of the Messiah within a general apocalyptic scenario is not uniformly defined in apocalyptic literature;[6] in Mark, Jesus is clearly God's agent who battles evil forces through his activities of exorcism, healing, and teaching. Most commentators think that Jesus' suffering and death are the most important part of the way in which Jesus exercises his divine agency in overcoming evil in Mark. In Mark 10:45, Jesus' death is foreshadowed through a possible evocation of the Servant's atoning suffering in Isaiah 53,[7] and so Jesus'

---

[6] See John J. Collins, *The Apocalyptic Imagination: An Introduction to Jewish Apocalyptic Literature* (2nd edn.; Grand Rapids, MI: Eerdmans, 1998) for a discussion of the various Jewish apocalyptic texts and their depictions of messianic figures. See Collins, *The Scepter and the Star* for a discussion of messianism in Second Temple Judaism.

[7] See Rikki E. Watts, "Jesus' Death, Isaiah 53, and Mark 10:45: A Crux Revisited," in *Jesus and the Suffering Servant: Isaiah 53 and Christian Origins* (ed. William H. Bellinger and William R. Farmer; Harrisburg, PA: Trinity Press International, 1998), 125–52. Watts argues against the doubts raised by Morna D. Hooker and C. K. Barrett that there is an allusion to Isaiah 53 in Mark 10:45 by assuming Mark's overall narrative framework is modeled after the New Exodus framework of Deutero-Isaiah. Within this narrative context, the lack of direct lexical parallels between Mark 10:45 and Isaiah 53 should not be the final determining factor in whether Mark meant to evoke Isaiah 53 or not. Instead, Mark's overall tendency in using scripture, especially his tendency to combine two unrelated passages in highly allusive ways, gives Watts the grounding for his claims to Mark 10:45 having its major, if not only, Old Testament reference in Isaiah 53. While I generally agree that Mark's narrative context should play a role in determining the nature or existence of a reference to scripture, I am not convinced by Watts' or Marcus' (on whom Watts relies for support of his claims) argumentation that the Isaian New Exodus paradigm should be determinative of how one reads Mark. Mark is a complex narrative, and if the New Exodus paradigm is present in Mark, it should be one among many voices to which a critic attends when trying to understand the narrative dynamics of the Gospel and its use of scripture. See Marcus, *The Way of the Lord*; and Joel Marcus, "Mark and Isaiah," in *Fortunate the Eyes That See: Essays in Honor of David Noel Freedman in Celebration of His Seventieth Birthday* (ed. A. B. Beck *et al.*; Grand Rapids, MI: Eerdmans, 1995), 449–66. See also C. K. Barrett, "The Background of Mark 10:45," in *New Testament Essays: Studies in Honour of T. W. Manson* (ed. A. J. B. Higgins; Manchester: Manchester University Press, 1959), 1–18, and Morna D.

death is imbued with an atoning element. However, by the time that Jesus' death is narrated in Mark 14 and 15, the voice of the lamenting David who challenges God's decision to allow his suffering becomes loud enough to question the need for Jesus' death within this constructed apocalyptic scenario.

1.1.3   The Suffering Servant or the suffering David?

Finally, and in light of my second major point, I will argue against the notion that the Servant of Isaiah 53 offers the best model for Jesus' suffering and death in Mark. Jesus is depicted as suffering mainly as a royal figure in chapters 14 and 15. Along with the plot elements within these chapters that parallel events in David's life, the suffering and lamenting David of the PssLam offers a model for Jesus' suffering that exists alongside that of the Servant from Isaiah. After Jesus' mocking and beatings, the only plausible evocation of Isaiah 53 in Mark 15 is found in 15:27, which refers to Jesus being crucified in between two criminals. Most commentators think that this is a reference to Isa 53:12, which states that the Servant is numbered among transgressors. However, the evocations of the PssLam in question are numerous in Mark 14–15, with three virtual quotations from three of these psalms and Jesus actually speaking the words of two of them. Given the strong royal overtones of the depiction of Jesus in these chapters, it makes better sense to turn to the suffering David of these psalms than to the Suffering Servant from Isaiah 53 when trying to understand Jesus' suffering and death.

1.2   Typological identification of David and Jesus

On this last point, Douglas J. Moo has argued for a "typological point of identification" between Jesus and the David of the PssLam:

> It should not be overlooked that David was universally considered to be the author of the psalms in the time of Christ, and that all the lament psalms appropriated in the passion sayings have in their titles "A Psalm of David." Further, the history of David's traitorous adviser, Ahithophel, has perhaps influenced the Judas

Hooker, *Jesus and the Servant* (London: SPCK, 1959). For an affirmation of the atoning significance of Jesus' death in Mark 10:45 without arguing for a strong evocation of Isaiah 53, see Adela Yarbro Collins, "The Significance of Mark 10:45 among Gentile Christians," *HTR* 90 (1997): 371–82.

tradition. Jesus was hailed as "Son of David" early in the Christological development, and Davidic motifs are found throughout
the gospels. For all these reasons it is probable that the typological point of identification in the lament psalms should be sought
in the Christological identification of Jesus with his ancestor,
the heir of the promises (II Sam. 7) . . . It is the underlying
typological identification of Jesus with David that legitimizes
the transfer of language from the record of the Israelite King's
experiences to the narratives of the sufferings of the "greater Son
of David."[8]

While I agree in part with Moo in linking Jesus with David, especially
when it comes to the suffering described in the PssLam, I do not agree
with his characterization of the literary relationship between the two as
typological. Robert Alter and Frank Kermode define a "type" as "an
Old Testament passage or character whose hidden sense is made plain
only when fulfilled by a New Testament antitype: e.g., the high priest
Melchizedek is a type of Christ."[9] John E. Alsup describes a similar
notion of typology in that this type of hermeneutical thinking "presupposes the unity of the OT and the NT. . . The meaning of the OT is finally
unclear without the NT as is that of the NT without the OT."[10] Robert
M. Grant puts it slightly differently: "The typological method is based
on the presupposition that the whole Old Testament looks beyond itself
for its interpretation."[11] There are several reasons why Moo's typological characterization of Jesus' literary relationship with David in Mark is
inadequate: (1) David is not being interpreted in light of Jesus by Mark,
at least overtly. Instead, as we will see, the evocations of the PssLam in
Mark's passion narrative do not find their final meaning in the death of
Jesus; they only express the suffering of Jesus in the familiar terms of an
important character from Israel's literary history; (2) Jesus is being characterized by Mark in such a way as to include David's life and actions
in the characterization, but this is not the same thing as calling David a
type to which Jesus is compared. The PssLam give Mark the ability to
imbue Jesus with certain characteristics that he thinks are key to understanding Jesus and his suffering; and (3) as Broadhead has stated from
the perspective of narrative repetition and I have expanded to include

---

[8] Douglas J. Moo, *The Old Testament in the Gospel Passion Narratives*, 299–300.

[9] Robert Alter and Frank Kermode, *The Literary Guide to the Bible* (Cambridge, MA: Harvard University Press, 1987), 672.

[10] John E. Alsup, "Typology," *ABD* 6: 682–3.

[11] Robert M. Grant, "The Old Testament in the New," in *A Short History of the Inter- pretation of the Bible*, Robert M. Grant and David Tracy (2nd edn.; Fortress, 1984), 37.

other voices, there are multiple ways that Jesus is portrayed in the passion narrative; David is not the only character from the Hebrew Bible with whom Jesus is associated,[12] and these associations are multifaceted and creatively construed by Mark. Never is Jesus simply the Suffering Servant, or the Danielic Son of Man, or King David. Mark takes certain aspects of each of these figures (and others) and creatively juxtaposes them to characterize Jesus. The result is a Jesus who is familiar because he is reminiscent of these traditional figures but who, upon closer examination, is also very unfamiliar because of Mark's creative collocation of the qualities of these figures. However, as we will see, the relationship between Jesus and David is expressed through the Psalms 21, 40, 41–2, and 68 in a way that allows Mark to portray Jesus partially as a suffering royal figure who struggles to understand the meaning of his suffering in light of his relationship with God.

2 Ambiguity, suffering and betrayal in the midst of faithful relationship: Psalm 40 in Mark 14:17–21

2.1 Reading Mark 14:17–21 in light of Psalm 40

In Chapter 3, I identified the phrase ὁ ἐσθίων μετ' ἐμοῦ as the marker that evokes Psalm 40:10. Therefore, the interpretation of the alluding text must be modified in light of the evoked text. In doing this, most commentators give only a brief statement of the evoked text's importance for understanding Mark 14:17–21. In his work on the exegesis of the Old Testament in Mark, Joel Marcus gives the evoked text more extensive treatment than most. He mentions the reference to Psalm 40 twice, and the first time he says that it is one of many references to the "Psalms of the Righteous Sufferer"[13] in Mark's Passion narrative. Marcus does this to contribute to his argument that these psalms are interpreted apocalyptically by Mark so that Jesus, as the Righteous Sufferer, is vindicated in the resurrection, which is a preview of the apocalyptic eschaton envisioned by

---

[12] One thinks of the Son of Man from Daniel and the Servant from Deutero-Isaiah.

[13] Marcus, *The Way of the Lord*, 172, uses the term "Psalms of the Righteous Sufferer" as "more descriptive of the actual content of the psalms" than H. Gunkel's "laments of the individual." There are serious problems with the title "Psalms of the Righteous Sufferer," and its use requires more explanation and argumentation than Marcus provides. The category clearly determines how he reads the way the psalms are used in Mark's passion narrative, thus giving him a pre-determined meaning for Mark's depiction of Jesus in the passion narrative. See section 1.2.2 of Chapter 1 above for an extended discussion of the category "Psalms of the Righteous Sufferer."

Mark.[14] John Donahue and Daniel Harrington briefly refer to the evoked text, saying that "Jesus continues to be presented as 'the suffering just one' of the psalms," giving psalms 41 and 55 (MT) as the primary psalms to examine for this usage in Mark.[15] Lothar Ruppert gives a similar treatment of Psalm 41 (MT), but Ben Witherington and Morna Hooker give even shorter treatments of the reference.[16]

The second time he treats Psalm 41 (MT), Marcus does so only after arguing that the references to Psalm 22 (MT) in Mark 15 include more than just the verses cited or evoked in Mark. He states that "the citation of Psalm 41:9 in Mark 14:18 is true to the wider context of the psalm since it not only speaks of betrayal but also situates this betrayal in the context of a *meal*. The continuation of the psalm, moreover, fits extremely well into the immediate Markan context and the larger flow of Mark's story." He goes on to discuss briefly the continuation of Psalm 41(MT) after verse 9 (10 in the LXX and MT) and reads it in terms of the psalmist being rescued and vindicated by God.[17] Although the context of Psalm 41:9 (MT) matters to Marcus, he offers no detailed analysis of Psalm 41 (MT), either in Hebrew or Greek, to understand fully how the context illuminates Mark 14.

As I argued in Chapter 4, Psalm 40 is a subtle but strong attempt by the psalmist to elicit a response from God to his suffering. The psalmist aligns himself with God's ways, describes to God his suffering at the hands of his trusted companions, and pledges his praise to God if God answers his call for deliverance. As we saw, the psalmist receives no direct answer from God.

By this point in Mark 14, Judas has already agreed to find a way to hand Jesus over to the chief priests (14:10–11), Jesus has accurately predicted the situation in the city as the disciples prepare the Passover (14:12–16), and the scene of Jesus' prediction of Judas' actions is at that meal. Jesus has chosen his twelve closest companions not only to share a meal, but also to share the Passover meal, a commemoration of the founding events of Israel's history. Jesus makes his prediction about Judas in the midst of this situation, and, as we have seen, he evokes Ps 40:10 in doing so. In the course of one verse, Mark narrates the closeness between the twelve and

---

[14] Marcus, *The Way of the Lord*, 172–86.

[15] Donahue and Harrington, *The Gospel of Mark*, 394, 399.

[16] Ruppert, *Jesus als der leidende Gerechte?*, 50; 51–2; Witherington, *The Gospel of Mark*, 372; Morna K. Hooker, *The Gospel According to Saint Mark* (Peabody, MA: Hendrickson, 1991), 336.

[17] Marcus, *The Way of the Lord*, 183. See also Ruppert, *Jesus als der leidende Gerechte?*, 50.

Jesus, reaffirms Jesus' connection with the divine world by his making an accurate prediction of the course of events, and aligns Jesus with the plight of the lamenter in Psalm 40. In this intimate moment, Mark juxtaposes two voices, that of the one who knows the divine world and that of Psalm 40, the one who suffers at the hand of his friend-turned-enemy. If we think of this second voice as the betrayed David, the parallels with David's life[18] and the royal overtones of the passion narrative begin to become apparent. I will discuss this in the next section.

When one considers the ambiguity that arises by the end of Psalm 40, Jesus' ambiguous relationship with God in Mark gains an added dimension. Without exploring this aspect of Mark's narrative extensively, let me point out several key elements that reveal this ambiguity before the passion narrative. Jesus is presented as a powerful healer, exorcist, and miracle worker. He is also presented as working with God's approval, as evidenced in the epiphany of his baptism (1:11) and the transfiguration (9:7). At the same time, elements of suffering begin to surface in the midst of Jesus' power and divine approval. The Jewish authorities continually oppose him, beginning in 3:6. His family accuses him of being out of his mind in 3:21, and then his family and members of his home town reject him in 6:3. This rebuff is understandable, especially when one thinks of the prophetic tradition in Israel, and thus far does not directly affect his relationship with God. However, when the theme of suffering begins to grow, Jesus' approval and authority, which he received from God, stand right alongside life-threatening suffering. Divine necessity is indicated in the first prediction of suffering and death (8:31) and implied in the other two predictions (9:31; 10:33–4). Mark 10:45 is a summary statement of Jesus' mission: "For the Son of Man did not come to be served but to serve and to give his life as a ransom for many." By juxtaposing Jesus' power and suffering, Mark tries to make sense of Jesus' death by placing it in the context of God's will and approval.

In chapter 14, Jesus' power becomes evident again, but the voice of the suffering lamenter comes to the fore in 14:18. Let us explore the perceived

---

[18] See Donahue, "Temple, Trial, and Royal Christology (Mark 14:53–65)," 76, for a discussion of the parallels between David's story and Jesus' story in Mark. In footnote 50, Donahue says, "The parallels with the David story suggest that, while in earlier stages of the formation of the Passion Narrative, the psalms and prophetic literature influenced the material, in the final narrative, the Old Testament narrative form provided a model." This seems to presume that the Psalms were used as a model for Jesus in a general way, while the Davidic parallels only come from narratives about David or royal figures in the Hebrew Bible. However, if we presume that Mark and his readers understood the author of the Psalms to be David, and the subject of many of the Psalms to be David, then the Davidic imagery and model for Jesus seem to be at the earliest stages of the development of the story of Jesus' death.

maltreatment of the psalmist in Psalm 40 a bit more deeply in conversation with Mark 14:17–21. The psalmist describes a situation where he is on his deathbed, at death's door. His associates do not come to his aid. In the psalmist's view, they speak evil things against him, wondering when he will die and his name be erased from memory (verse 6b); they gather lawlessness to themselves (verse 7b), whisper together against him (verse 8a), and devise evil things for him (verse 8b). Because of these actions, they cease being his countrymen and become his enemies[19] who abandon him during grave illness. They give up on him, as indicated by the strongly negative rhetorical question in verse 9, "The dead man will never rise again, will he?" (Μὴ ὁ κοιμώμενος οὐχὶ προσθήσει τοῦ ἀναστῆναι;). They consider him as good as dead. Certainly, the psalmist believes that his friends, especially his most intimate one, should support and accompany him in his darkest hour, even to the point of death. They all turn against him with their lawless and evil words, which culminate in the cunning of "the man of my peace." His associates and his friends have become his enemies; therefore, the psalmist is left to the mercy of his enemies and left to die in their hands. God is the only hope, but even in the midst of his cries there is no clear answer.

Jesus' situation seems similar in Mark. By this point in Mark's narrative, the Pharisees have begun to conspire with the Herodians in order to destroy him (3:6). And the chief priests and scribes were seeking how to take him ἐν δόλῳ, "with cunning," and kill him (14:1). The conspiracy of the Pharisees with the Herodians and the desire of the chief priests and scribes to take Jesus with cunning recalls the cunning (πτερνισμός) with which the psalmist was treated in Ps 40:10. Similarly, all of these people are Jesus' countrymen-turned-enemies, as in Psalm 40. Because of these plans to arrest and destroy Jesus and the fact that Jesus has predicted his suffering and death three times (Mark 8:31; 9:31; 10:32–3), Mark's audience plainly knows that death is coming. When the intimacy of the meal is depicted in 14:17, it is clear that Jesus is about to be handed over, something that the psalmist prays will never happen to him. When Jesus makes his prediction by evoking Psalm 40, the audience is encouraged to associate the injustice, the outrage, and the ambiguity of the psalmist's cries with Jesus' situation, the most serious aspects of which are the

---

[19] "The sick person was surrounded by enemies, by friends who had become enemies," Kraus, *Psalms 1–59*, 431. In Psalm 40, the antagonists are called ὁ ἐχθρός or οἱ ἐχθροί three times. It is clear that the psalmist is experiencing his fellow Israelites as enemies, since they are the ones who would be visiting him and supposedly would be caring for him during his sickness.

treachery of his most trusted companions and the question of God's presence in the midst of his suffering. When Jesus makes the statement that the Son of Man must go as it is written of him, this is no longer just a general statement of divine sanction through the appeal to scripture. Psalm 40 changes the coordinates with which one reads the rest of the story by bringing in the questions that are raised by the psalmist's cries – what kind of justice is God's justice? Where is God in the midst of this suffering? What is the purpose of this suffering, even if it is part of a greater plan to defeat evil ultimately? Does this have to happen? By evoking Psalm 40, Mark 14:17–21 begins the process of searching more deeply into the mystery of the relationship between Jesus and God in Mark.

2.2   Reading Mark 14:17–21 in light of David's Psalm 40

When thought of as the words of David, Psalm 40 adds another level of meaning to Mark 14:17–21. If David is viewed as the suffering, lamenting psalmist of Psalm 40, then he cries out in his suffering as faithful king chosen by God. The ambiguity, betrayal, lack of understanding of God's justice, and the demand for God's presence that David expresses through Psalm 40 become conditioned by the relationship that David has with God. The Son of Man must go "as it is written of him" but, because of the inclusion of Psalm 40 in the story of Jesus, the doors are open to allow the story of David to be plumbed as a way of understanding what "as it is written of him" might mean. Instead of an anonymous suffering psalmist who expresses the horrors of betrayal through Psalm 40, David as divinely chosen king expresses these horrors in the midst of his faithful relationship with God. The ambiguity and questions about the nature of the God–human relationship do not fade away because David's words are the ones evoked in Mark 14:18. But the relationship becomes more specific and understandable, because we can turn to a person whose place is very clearly defined as a heroic, ideal, royal figure in Israel's history.[20]

---

[20] The story of David as told in 1–2 Samuel shows a deeply flawed figure from a moral point of view. However, one thing makes David stand out as a figure that even the anti-monarchic Deuteronomist continues to hold up as the model for subsequent kings, and that is David's faithfulness to the God of Israel. In 1 Kgs 3:3, Solomon is described as loving God and following in the ways of his father, David. But Solomon's downfall comes when he marries foreign women. The result is, eventually, that Solomon's wives turn him to other gods, and "his heart was not true to the LORD his God, as was the heart of his father David" (1 Kgs 11:4, NRSV). See 1 Kgs 14:8; 15:3, 11, where David is held up as the model for faithful service to the God of Israel. In 14:8, Jeroboam's actions are contrasted with David's

As the story of Jesus' passion unfolds, this will become more and more important. Mark's very appeal to scripture includes elements that raise questions about David's suffering and, therefore, Jesus' suffering.

2.3   Wider effects of Psalm 40 in the sections leading up to Gethsemane

As the story continues in Mark 14:22, Jesus celebrates his last Passover meal with his disciples, during which he imbues the meal with additional significance by linking the bread with his body and the wine with the pouring out of his blood for many (14:22–4). In addition, he connects the cup, and therefore the pouring out of his blood for many, to the Kingdom of God, clearly giving the event of the meal and his death an eschatological significance. This will become important in the analysis of the evocation of Psalm 41–2 below, and I will discuss the eschatological imagery in more detail in that context.

After the end of the meal, Jesus takes the disciples out to the Mount of Olives, where he predicts his abandonment by them through a quotation of Zech 13:7. The theme of abandonment present in the evocation of Psalm 40 in Mark 14:18 lingers on into this portion of the story as well. As Peter and his companions all strongly deny that they will abandon Jesus in his darkest hour, the reader knows that this will certainly happen. Jesus' power and awareness of the imminent events have already proven to be reliable from earlier in chapter 14, so there is no reason to doubt him. And since we know that the Son of Man goes "as it is written," we know that Psalm 40's imagery of treachery and abandonment by those closest to the psalmist holds in this case as well. Peter's response to Jesus' prediction of triple denial, "Even if I must die together with you, I will certainly not deny you" (ἐὰν δέῃ με συναποθανεῖν σοι, οὐ μή σε ἀπαρνήσομαι), only heightens the sense of abandonment that Jesus will experience as the story progresses. As we come to the story of Gethsemane, Mark has presented two prominent images of Jesus side by side – one powerful and knowledgeable about the ensuing events, and one who faces the task in growing isolation as a result of abandonment and treachery by those closest to him, as in Psalm 40. Both of the images result from appeal to scripture. Power and weakness stand side by side in one figure, just as David, the powerful king of Israel's past, was weak in the face of abandonment and treachery.

faithfulness, and then, many times throughout the rest of 1–2 Kings, the sins of Jeroboam are used to describe the actions of the kings who are not faithful, thus implying the positive model of David as faithful king.

3   **Gethsemane: the embodiment of the lamenter**

3.1   Reading Mark 14:32–42 without Psalms 40 and 41–2

The scene in Gethsemane can be read without any recourse to Psalm 40[21] and without much recourse to Psalm 41–2.[22] In fact, most commentators pay no attention to Psalm 40's influence and only give a nodding glance to Psalm 41–2 in their treatment of the episode, instead preferring to focus on the possible source history,[23] exegetical issues,[24] or narrative structure[25] of the story without incorporating much about these psalms.[26] However,

---

[21] I have not found one commentator who considers the effects of Psalm 40 on the Gethsemane episode or on any part of the passion narrative in Mark other than 14: 17–21.

[22] Werner H. Kelber questions any connection between Mark and these Psalms. See "Mark 14:32–42: Gethsemane," *ZNW* 63 (1972): 178. Douglas J. Moo only points out the evocation of Psalm 41–2 in Mark 14:34, but offers no discussion of its function in the Gethsemane scene. His fewer than two pages on Gethsemane draw general parallels between the PssLam and Jesus' prayer to God. He concludes by saying, "The prayer to God for deliverance from distress is a common feature of the lament psalms, but Jesus' prayers are essentially different, being petitions for salvation from a tribulation that is imminent." See *The Old Testament in the Gospel Passion Narratives*, 246. Most other commentators simply mention it as Mark putting the words of the lamenting psalmist on the lips of Jesus (Myers, *Binding*, 366), borrowing the phraseology from Psalm 41–2 (Gundry, *Mark*, 867), or a simple mention of the origin of the implicit quotation (Schweizer, *The Good News According to Mark*, 314; Juel, *Mark*, 196). Donald Senior claims that it is unlikely that Mark relied directly on any specific psalm text in forming the Gethsemane passage, but instead he points out in a general way verbal echoes that exist between the Gethsemane passage and many PssLam. However, he does acknowledge that the language of Mark 14:34 repeats what is found in Psalm 41–2. His interpretation of Gethsemane takes into account Psalm 41–2, but only in a general sense as representative of many PssLam. See *The Passion of Jesus in the Gospel of Mark* (Wilmington, DE: Michael Glazier, 1984), 70–2.

[23] By "source history" I mean the attempt to delineate the possible sources that Mark used and the changes he made in the sources in constructing this story. See K. G. Kuhn, "Jesus in Gethsemane," *EvT* 12 (1952–3): 260–85; R. S. Barbour, "Gethsemane in the Tradition of the Passion," *NTS* 16 (1969–70): 231–51; Martin Dibelius, "Gethsemane," *Crozier Quarterly* 12 (1935): 254–65; Rudolf Bultmann, *The History of the Synoptic Tradition* (trans. John Marsh; Peabody, MA: Hendrickson, 1963), 267–8.

[24] See Brown, *Death of the Messiah*, I:146–236, for the best treatment of the exegetical issues of the Gethsemane scene in the Synoptics. See Taylor, *The Gospel According to St. Mark*, 551–7, for an excellent treatment of all the exegetical issues, as well as some discussion of Psalm 41 (MT) and its implications for the passage.

[25] See John Paul Heil, "Mark 14:1–52: Narrative Structure and Reader Response," *Bib* 71 (1990): 305–32. Heil does not mention the evocation of Psalms 40–1. Although Brown does not describe the narrative dynamics in the same way that Heil does, he argues that the literary artistry of the Gethsemane scene in Mark should not be undone by source criticism. See *Death of the Messiah*, I:166, 216–27.

[26] Mark Kiley argues that many of the events of Mark 14 can be seen as similar to the general experience of the psalmist in Psalm 116. Therefore, he argues that Psalm 116 was

unlike the evocation of Psalm 40 in Mark 14:18, the evocation of Psalm 41–2 is much more overt, spilling over the borders between allusion and quotation, as I have discussed in Chapter 3. Since the intentionality and influence of the author over the reader become more palpable the closer a biblical reference comes to a biblical quotation,[27] we must respect the way that the author directs the reader and consider the reference to Psalm 41–2 as important for understanding the story of Gethsemane. In addition, because the theme of abandonment and betrayal carries on throughout the rest of the passion narrative, I will continue to describe the ways in which Psalm 40 affects the story when appropriate, although the focus of my argument will be on the interplay between Psalm 41–2 and the Gethsemane story.

In what follows in this section, I will argue that several elements are drawn into the story of Jesus' Gethsemane experience in Mark as a result of reading Psalm 41–2 in tandem with Mark 14:32–42. First, I will argue that Jesus' distress is at least in part colored by the sense of abandonment and the inaction on God's part in the face of suffering that is communicated in Psalm 41–2. Second, Jesus' prayer to God can be viewed as a search for understanding with respect to God's will for Jesus to suffer and die, just as David's cry to God searches for understanding of God's inaction in the face of his suffering in Psalm 41–2. This results in a complex understanding of the scriptural basis for Jesus' suffering and death (i.e., "The Son of Man must go as it is written of him" [14:21]), one that upholds both an expression of God's will for Jesus to suffer and a challenge to the need for suffering to occur. Further, I will argue that this complex understanding of "as it is written" raises questions about the necessity of suffering within God's apocalyptic plan for salvation.

generative of Jesus' prayer and of the Gethsemane scene as a whole. See "'Lord, Save My Life' (Ps 116:4) as a Generative Text for Jesus' Gethsemane Prayer (Mark 14:36)," *CBQ* 48 (1986): 655–9. Evans rightly points out that the parallels that Kiley offers are too few and not detailed enough to hypothesize significant influence from Psalm 116 on the Gethsemane episode from the point of view of literary dependence. See *Mark 8:27–16:20*, 414. Roger David Aus also argues that the background of the Gethsemane story resides in Psalm 116. However, Aus tries to demonstrate that later rabbinic interpretations of Psalm 116, which deal with Moses' struggle in the face of his death, is what lies behind the Gethsemane story. So, in reality, Aus is not arguing for Psalm 116's influence on Gethsemane; he is arguing for the influence of later rabbinic interpretations of Psalm 116 on Gethsemane. The problems with his approach are obvious. See *The Wicked Tenants and Gethsemane*, 65–160. Donahue and Harrington devote some space to reflecting on the influence of Psalms 42–3 (MT) on the Gethsemane scene and on Jesus' suffering in general. Given the length of the commentary (fewer than 500 pages), these authors should be commended for their efforts. See *The Gospel of Mark*, 412–13.

[27] See section 2.5 of Chapter 1 of the present study, in which I refer to Gerd Häfner's spectrum of biblical references within the New Testament.

3.2 Mark 14:32–42 in light of Psalm 41–2: similarities between Jesus and the psalmist

3.2.1 Initial interaction between ἐκθαμβεῖσθαι and ἀδημονεῖν and the evocation of Psalm 41–2

After Jesus takes his disciples to the garden of Gethsemane, he progressively distances himself from them. First, he tells his disciples, "Sit here while I pray" (καθίσατε ὧδε ἕως προσεύξωμαι). Next, he leaves the rest of the disciples and takes Peter, James, and John with him. As he is walking ahead with these three, Mark says, "He began to be greatly distraught and troubled" (ἤρξατο ἐκθαμβεῖσθαι καὶ ἀδημονεῖν, Mark 14:33b). Then he tells his disciples, "My soul is very sorrowful unto death" (περίλυπός ἐστιν ἡ ψυχή μου ἕως θανάτου, 14:34a). As I have argued in Chapter 3, this is the reference to Psalm 41–2.[28]

The basic meanings of ἐκθαμβεῖσθαι and ἀδημονεῖν are "to be amazed or astonished" and "be in anguish" respectively. Raymond Brown nuances the meanings further by arguing that ἐκθαμβεῖσθαι "indicates a profound disarray, expressed physically before a terrifying event: a shuddering horror." He goes on to explain that ἀδημονεῖν "has a root connotation of being separated from others, a situation that results in anguish."[29] Although the words are difficult to render with two English equivalents, the depth of anguish they communicate is plain[30] and sets the stage for our engagement with Psalm 41–2 in Mark 14:34.[31]

Recall that in Psalm 41–2, one three-lined verse of the psalm occurs three times, which creates a rhythmic effect that shapes the lamenting in the psalm. Verse 6 of Psalm 41 is repeated in verse 12 and 42:5, and it reads:

> Why are you grieved, soul, and why do you trouble me?
> Hope in God, for I will confess concerning him:
> 'My God is the salvation of my face.'[32]

---

[28] As I also argued in footnote 23 of Chapter 3, ἕως θανάτου could be a reference to Jonah 4:9, but the first part of this phrase is almost a direct quotation from Psalm 41–2, and therefore it is most likely the one intended by Mark and the one most recognizable by his audience.

[29] Brown, *Death of the Messiah*, I:153.

[30] "Mark's language for Jesus' emotional state makes it clear that the suffering is real" (Sharon Echols Dowd, *Prayer, Power, and the Problem of Suffering* [SBLDS 105; Atlanta: Scholars Press, 1988], 155).

[31] "The verbs *ekthambeisthai* and *ademonein* (14:33) portray a Jesus who is overcome by anguish and horror in the face of death" (Werner H. Kelber, "The Hour of the Son of Man," in *The Passion in Mark* [ed. Kelber; Philadelphia: Fortress, 1976], 43).

[32] I use Albert Pietersma's translation of πρόσωπον as "face" (*The Psalms*, 40–1). However, πρόσωπον also connotes bodily presence indicating one's person.

ἵνα τί περίλυπος εἶ, ψυχή, καὶ ἵνα τί συνταράσσεις με;
ἔλπισον ἐπὶ τὸν θεόν, ὅτι ἐξομολογήσομαι αὐτῷ·
σωτήριον τοῦ προσώπου μου ὁ θεός μου.

Recall also that before each refrain, the psalmist describes (1) his longing for God's presence in the midst of affliction and ridicule by his enemy; this results in the psalmist pouring out his soul before God and promising praise in the house of God (Strophe 1); (2) the awesome power of God that overwhelms creation, and his desire to cry out to God day and night in prayer; in the prayer he asks why God, as protector, has forgotten him while he is insulted and ridiculed by those who afflict him (Strophe 2); and (3) his challenge to God to pass judgment on him and to answer why God has rejected him by letting him suffer; in addition, he asks God to send truth and light to guide him to God's holy place (Strophe 3). The main overtones of Psalm 41–2 include questions as to why the psalmist is suffering, why God has not responded by stopping the suffering, and why God has separated himself from the psalmist. God's absence and inaction in the face of suffering motivates the psalmist to pray the psalm. The psalm builds in its exhortation to God, so that by the time the third refrain comes the psalmist looks for an answer to the question, "Why did you reject me?" The self-encouragement expressed in the refrain is present throughout, but by the end of the psalm, because of the direct challenge to God and the conditional vow expressed in the third strophe, the refrain functions as a key part in the overall rhetoric of the psalm in attempting to persuade God to act on behalf of the psalmist. Therefore, ultimately, these two Psalms try to use rhythmic repetition as a persuasive device before God.

This sense of divine abandonment in the face of suffering conditions the meaning and usage of ἐκθαμβεῖσθαι and ἀδημονεῖν in Mark 14:33. The distress that these terms connote – the shuddering horror and anguish that results from separation – is intensified and qualified when read with Psalm 41–2. The distress that Jesus expresses through these terms should be understood as distress in light of his impending violent and humiliating death, which is certainly not a secret by this point in the story.[33] It is

---

[33] Besides the three predictions of suffering, rejection, and death in Mark 8:31, 9:31, and 10:33–4, chapter 14 conveys an overtone of betrayal and cunning (δόλος) on the part of Judas and the Jewish authorities. Gundry says that Jesus' distress is not about his death but about the fact that one of the Twelve will betray him, his disciples will forsake him, Peter will deny him three times, and that he will be given over into the hands of sinners. But then he goes on to say, "more than fear of death" contributed to Jesus' distress and that "Jesus becomes so grief-panicked over the prospect of his own death that he is about to die before being given over to his enemies . . . he does not want to die." See *Mark*, 867.

intensified and qualified through the use of Psalm 41–2, because God's action is now brought into the picture as a problem for Jesus, perhaps as *the* problem for Jesus to overcome in the upcoming verses.[34] I will say more about this at the end of this section, but first I will explore more carefully the relationship between Psalm 41–2 and Mark 14:32–42 in order to show how the problem of God's action with respect to Jesus is developed.

3.2.2 Structural and thematic similarities between Psalm 41–2 and Mark 14:32–42

The three-fold refrain and the prayer to God to act and be present in the midst of suffering are the major structural and thematic similarities between Psalm 41–2 and Mark 14:32–42. As Mark's story progresses, it narrates Jesus' three-fold prayer after he goes off each time a short distance from Peter, James, and John to pray to God in his distress. There is some debate about the third time, mainly because Mark does not explicitly describe Jesus going off a third time to pray. Verse 41a says, "And he came the third time and said to them" (καὶ ἔρχεται τὸ τρίτον καὶ λέγει αὐτοῖς); this clearly indicates a three-fold occurrence of Jesus' action of going ahead a short distance and praying.[35] The rhythm that is created with the threefold refrain in Psalm 41–2 is similar to that in Jesus repeatedly going off to pray in Gethsemane.

Also in a way similar to Psalm 41–2, Jesus prays to God for action in the midst of his impending suffering. Jesus' prayer is obvious, but its content with regard to suffering is indicated by the cup imagery he uses to describe what he wants God to do. In Mark 10:38, Jesus says to James and John, "Are you able to drink the cup which I drink" (δύνασθε πιεῖν τὸ ποτήριον ὃ ἐγὼ πίνω), in reference to the violent death which he will suffer. In addition, Jesus uses the cup at the Passover meal in 14:23–5 to imbue his violent death with meaning – more specifically, an eschatological meaning, because of the way in which Mark links Jesus' death with the Kingdom of God. There he says, "This is my blood of the covenant which is poured out for many" (τοῦτό ἐστιν τὸ αἷμά μου τῆς διαθήκης τὸ ἐκχυννόμενον ὑπὲρ πολλῶν), a sacrificial image that is

---

[34] "The central question that Mark's story of the death of Jesus poses, therefore, concerns God's role in relationship to suffering and to victory over it" (David J. Lull, "Interpreting Mark's Story of Jesus' Death: Toward a Theology of Suffering," *SBLSP* [Atlanta: Scholars Press, 1985], 3).

[35] See Dibelius, "Gethsemane," 254; Donahue and Harrington, *The Gospel of Mark*, 411.

reminiscent of his statement in 10:45.[36] Jesus goes on to say, "Amen I say to you that I will certainly no longer drink from the fruit of the vine until that day when I drink it anew in the Kingdom of God" (ἀμὴν λέγω ὑμῖν ὅτι οὐκέτι οὐ μὴ πίω ἐκ τοῦ γενήματος τῆς ἀμπέλου ἕως τῆς ἡμέρας ἐκείνης ὅταν αὐτὸ πίνω καινὸν ἐν τῇ βασιλείᾳ τοῦ θεοῦ, 14:25). So when Jesus uses the cup imagery again in 14:36, it has overtones of the suffering that he is about to experience,[37] and this suffering has deep connections to the Kingdom of God, and thus God's eschatological plans.[38]

3.2.3   The effects of the interaction of Psalm 41–2 and Mark 14:32–42

With the three-fold prayer and the suffering imagery linking Psalm 41–2 more closely with Mark 14:32–42 than an isolated evocation of one phrase, we can explore how Psalm 41–2 might deepen and inform our insight into the scene at Gethsemane. Like the psalmist, Jesus laments his situation of suffering with a prayer at night. He tries to convince God three times to take away his suffering by appealing to God's power and ability to do so:[39] "Abba, Father, all things are possible for you" (αββα ὁ πατήρ, πάντα δυνατά σοι, 14:36). Recall that the psalmist describes the power of God in Strophe 2 of Psalm 41. Here he recognizes the power of God even as he prays, saying that even the most powerful forces in creation respond to his might. Then the psalmist expresses his inundation by the power of God, as well (41:8). But the next verse juxtaposes the overshadowing power of God with the intimacy of prayer at night, "And by night, a song is with me, a prayer to the God of my life" (καὶ νυκτὸς ᾠδὴ παρ' ἐμοί, προσευχὴ τῷ θεῷ τῆς ζωῆς μου). In that prayer, the psalmist cries out to God about his suffering, "You are my protector; why did you forget me?" (Ἀντιλήμπτωρ μου εἶ· διὰ τί μου ἐπελάθου; 41:10). He goes on to tell God in his prayer that he walks around with the constant presence of his enemy who afflicts him and insults him. Daily they ask him, "Where is your God?" (Ποῦ ἐστιν ὁ θεός σου; 41:11).

---

[36] Mark 10:45 reads, καὶ γὰρ ὁ υἱὸς τοῦ ἀνθρώπου οὐκ ἦλθεν διακονηθῆναι ἀλλὰ διακονῆσαι καὶ δοῦναι τὴν ψυχὴν αὐτοῦ λύτρον ἀντὶ πολλῶν.

[37] Robbins, "Last Meal: Preparation, Betrayal, and Absence," 38; Brown, *Death of the Messiah*, I:153.

[38] Ibid., I:154, 170.

[39] "The use of the formula of omnipotence in Jesus' prayer suggests that the evangelist wants to say that God might still intervene, not that Jesus might still run away" (Dowd, *Prayer, Power, and the Problem of Suffering*, 156, n.25).

Jesus' prayer is not described in such detail. But with the inclusion of Psalm 41–2 at Mark 14:34, the reader is encouraged to imagine similar reasons why Jesus is so grieved based on Psalm 41–2. In Psalm 41–2, the psalmist repeats the refrain, "Why are you grieved, soul, and why do you trouble me?" right after every description of suffering. The suffering that the psalmist describes is not just suffering inflicted upon him by his enemy or those who afflict him, but he seems most troubled by the fact that God is absent and thus letting the suffering occur. At the beginning of the psalms, the psalmist expresses his deep, life-sustaining longing for God with the imagery of a deer longing for running water (41:2). This is not just an expression of general longing, because the psalmist goes on to ask, "When will I come and appear to the face of God?" (πότε ἥξω καὶ ὀφθήσομαι τῷ προσώπῳ τοῦ θεοῦ; 41:3). The psalmist expresses a distance from God, perhaps an exclusion from the presence of God. As the psalm moves on, we learn the reason is that God has "forgotten" (ἐπιλανθάνομαι, 41:10) and "rejected" (ἀπωθέομαι, 42:2) him. As I have argued above, the evocation of Psalm 40 in 14:18 brought to the fore the issue of the absence and silence of God in the midst of betrayal by trusted companions. If we take the imagery of Psalm 41–2 seriously, Jesus' great distress (ἐκθαμβεῖσθαι and ἀδημονεῖν) has clear overtones of abandonment and rejection by God.[40] Jesus cries out to God in Gethsemane, but just like the speakers of the two Psalms evoked in this chapter, he hears no answer.[41] Jesus' repeated appeals to God attempt to convince God to act, to deliver him from suffering and death, but Mark narrates no answer from God.

Each time Jesus returns to Peter, James, and John, his most trusted companions,[42] he finds them sleeping, failing to follow his instructions to stay alert (γρηγορεῖτε). Jesus isolates himself to pray, but as a result he finds himself more and more isolated and abandoned by his companions: as he physically moves away from his disciples and then from Peter,

---

[40] Evans argues that Jesus' greatest fear is abandonment by God, but he arrives at his conclusion by looking forward to Jesus' cry from the cross and then retrojecting this cry into Gethsemane. If Evans had argued for this point from the context of Gethsemane rather than from another place in the narrative, he would have been more convincing. See *Mark 8:27–16:20*, 411.

[41] "The narrator . . . has considered it very important to depict the agony of Jesus as it finds expression in lament and prayer. What he has not depicted is a strengthening and comforting of Jesus" (Dibelius, "Gethsemane," 254–5).

[42] Mark stresses their importance at several key parts of the narrative. They are the only three to whom Jesus gives nicknames (Mark 3:16–17), only these three are present during the raising of Jairus' daughter (5:37) and the transfiguration (9:2), and these three, along with Andrew, ask and are told privately about the time and signs for the accomplishment of "all these things" in Jesus' apocalyptic discourse (13:4).

James, and John, they become more distant from him, as they do not uphold his request for them to stay alert and pray (Mark 14:38).[43] By the end of the Gethsemane episode, Jesus' embodiment of the suffering, lamenting psalmist fully comes to the fore. In his three-fold cry to God, he embodies the lamenter who cries out to God for his saving presence in Psalm 41–2, and as his arresting party approaches, he embodies the psalmist who is handed over to his enemy in Psalm 40.

3.3   Davidic implications

3.3.1   *Scriptural justification for Jesus' death*

Like the Davidic figure from the psalms, Jesus does this all as a king who suffers and cries out to God for understanding. In light of Psalm 41–2, God's absence from and rejection of the psalmist become important elements of the story of Jesus. More specifically, God's absence from and rejection of *David* become important elements. Jesus' prayer in Mark 14:35–6 expresses Jesus' attempt at persuading God to act on his behalf, to remove his cup of suffering. It is clear that Jesus knows God's will,[44] but in a sense the prayer also expresses Jesus' search for an understanding of God's will – the necessity of suffering for Jesus' mission.[45] In Psalm 41–2 David expresses his suffering (41:4, 10–11; 42:2) and challenges God in Strophe 3, trying to convince God to act. But there is also a strong sense of asking why God has acted this way (Strophe 2), why God has rejected David when he has been faithful. When read together with the Gethsemane episode, this overtone gets carried into the prayer of Jesus, which results in his distress being present, in part, because of the inaction of God in the midst of his impending suffering. He prays to God for deliverance from suffering, but at the same time he prays for answers as to why he must suffer. "All things are possible for you" implies "So why does this have to happen?" He receives no answer – nor does David in Psalm 41–2 – other than that it is God's will that Jesus must drink the cup. The "must" of Jesus' suffering and death does not offer an explanation, only a command

---

[43] Brown, *Death of the Messiah*, I:164.

[44] This begins to be clearly presented at Mark 3:31–5, where Jesus redefines his family as those who do the will of God. The strong implication is that Jesus knows and does the will of God and therefore can judge who is part of his newly defined family.

[45] Werner Kelber argues that Jesus' prayer in Gethsemane "has every indication of a desire to bypass the cross." See "The Hour of the Son of Man," 43.

to which Jesus should submit.[46] Obedience demonstrates one traditional element of Jewish piety before God, but there is another dimension of this piety that is brought into play through the use of Psalm 41–2, where David demands an explanation of God's inaction and abandonment in the midst of suffering. The scriptural justification for Jesus' suffering – "The Son of Man must go as it is written of him" (Mark 14:21) – begins to be problematized by scripture itself – scripture written in the voice of David, one of the most influential figures from Israel's history.[47] Through David's voice, the "must" of Jesus' suffering becomes conditioned by the "why" asked of God's will for Jesus' suffering. Obedience to God's will gives way to a desire to understand God's will and even challenge it. "As it is written of him" is now more than a scriptural justification and expression of God's will for Jesus' suffering. It includes competing voices that offer a complex understanding of how humans should search for an understanding of God's ways in the midst of suffering.

3.3.2 Apocalyptic questions

Jesus' prayer includes an image of suffering with a deeper dimension than just normal suffering. He uses the image of the cup, as he did in the Passover meal in Mark 14:23–5. In section 3.2.2 above, I discussed the linking of the cup to suffering and Jesus' violent death, as well as the eschatological overtones that Mark gives to drinking from the cup, by linking it to the Kingdom of God. In this light, the use of Psalm 41–2 does not just begin to make the scriptural justification for Jesus' suffering more complex than a simple appeal to an authoritative text, it also raises questions about the necessity of suffering in God's apocalyptic plan – posited by some modern scholars – that has as its centerpiece Jesus' messianic activity on earth.[48] In other words, the question goes beyond

[46] "Even the knowledge that Jesus' suffering was God's 'will' does not prevent an outcry of protest against God's abandonment, of which Jesus' death on the cross seemed to be a sign (Mark 15:34)" (Lull, "Interpreting Mark's Story of Jesus' Death," 6). I agree with Lull here, but I think this outcry happens earlier than the cross. The cry from the cross is the culmination of the entirety of chapters 14 and 15 and even that of the whole Gospel. Evans acknowledges that Jesus' suffering is God's will, but this raises no question whatsoever for him, and so he posits no desire to understand what it might mean for God to will the suffering and death of his chosen Messiah. See *Mark 8:27–16:20*, 418.

[47] Frank J. Matera says, "Just as in 14:49, so in 14:21, the evangelist did not have a specific scripture in mind" (*Kingship*, 117). As I have moved through the narrative of Jesus' passion, this has become evident.

[48] Matera upholds the traditional view that suffering on the part of the Messiah is part of God's plan: "The mystery of the passion is more than the evil of men; it is grounded in

the specific, "Why must Jesus suffer?" and reaches a more general level, "Why must the Messiah suffer?" As we have seen, "as it is written," in the sense of "because it is God's will," is not a satisfactory answer, given the competing voice of the lamenting David who searches for and demands an answer to his perceived divine abandonment and inaction in the midst of his suffering. A clearer and more developed answer to the question of the necessity of messianic suffering is never given directly in Mark.

Howard Clark Kee has some insight into this: "But why is suffering necessary? Mark's only answer is to repeat the premise implicit in and at times asserted in the apocalyptic tradition: δεῖ γενέσθαι (Mark 13:7). The closest that Mark comes to a rationale for this apocalyptic dogma of suffering is to demonstrate that through it the scriptures are being fulfilled." He goes on to say, "No explanation is offered of the means by which suffering accomplishes redemption; all that is asserted is its divine necessity as recorded in the scriptures."[49] Adela Yarbro Collins goes deeper than Kee when she argues that Mark's answer to the question of theodicy is to narrate Jesus' deeds and death within an apocalyptic

---

God's plan of salvation . . . In the present age, Jesus exercises kingship in suffering and by enduring mockery" (*Kingship*, 119). Werner H. Kelber argues that in the Gethsemane scene, Jesus' desire to escape suffering questions the systematically presented theme of the suffering of Jesus (8:31; 9:31; 10:33–4) and related Kingdom theology in Mark. He also argues that Jesus in Gethsemane suffers as a model for Markan Christians: "[Jesus'] struggle at Gethsemane is thus designed to overcome vicariously a Christian objection to a suffering Messiah." See "The Hour of the Son of Man," 46, 59. This is a somewhat compelling historical argument in the sense that the Markan Jesus teaches disciples how to suffer. I agree with this, but from a different perspective: through the use of the PssLam, Mark gives his readers a legitimate way of interacting with God in the midst of suffering. Kelber's argument still leaves unexplored the deeper question of the need for suffering within God's apocalyptic plan of salvation. Dibelius argues vehemently that Gethsemane is told as part of the Messianic proof that Jesus had to suffer as Messiah according to God's will. The body of Messianic proof texts were those texts from the Hebrew Bible that depicted suffering, like the PssLam and Isaiah 53. "However strange this appears to us, that for the earliest Christians, for those who still read their passion narrative directly from the Old Testament, all this – fear, fright, and prayer – belonged to the Messianic proof texts; that all this showed that these things had taken place in accordance with God's will" ("Gethsemane," 258; see also 265). Howard Clark Kee concurs: "In keeping with his view of history as determined by God, and with the blueprint of the divine plan embodied in scripture, it was essential for Mark to show that the suffering and death of Jesus . . . were not to be regarded as occurring outside the divine plan, but that the suffering involved was an essential factor in the fulfillment of that plan . . . There is throughout Mark the unexplicated assertion that suffering is a necessary pre-condition for the coming of the Age of Deliverance (Mk 8:31; 9:11; 13:7; 14:31, etc.)" ("The Function of Scriptural Quotations," 174). Clearly, both Dibelius and Kee read Mark as an apologetic for the death of Jesus, and therefore they do not do justice to these texts from the scriptures, nor do they leave room for first-century readers to read these texts in ways other than as proof texts for Jesus' messiahship.

[49] Kee, "The Function of Scriptural Quotations," 175, 182.

framework of meaning. Within this framework, God not only allows evil to happen "but even wills it in order to accomplish a larger purpose – the redemption of all creation." The death of Jesus is "at the heart of this redemption."[50] I agree that the narration of Jesus' death within an apocalyptic framework of meaning does allow the reader to fill out a larger picture of God's actions than what happens in the earthly realm alone. But the logic by which Jesus' suffering effects the "redemption of all creation" is neither explained nor self-evident in such a scenario. Even within this framework, questions still arise regarding the place of suffering, especially the suffering of the chosen agent of God. The combat myth told within an apocalyptic framework as constructed by scholars like Joel Marcus may describe the events of the cosmic battle between Satan and God, and it may give hope that God will prevail in the end. But it does not explain the logic of the necessity of the suffering and death of the Messiah for God to accomplish ultimate victory. Marcus also argues for an apocalyptic framework of meaning, but he claims that the weaving of the "psalmic pattern" of suffering at the hands of one's enemies and then victory over them by the power of God together with the Isaian Servant gives the sense that "Jesus' death already is an apocalyptic victory over the oppressive cosmic power of sin."[51] We have already seen the problems with Marcus' methodology, in that he does not pay close enough attention to the details of each psalm that he considers and he commits the "trajectory fallacy," in that he bases much of his understanding of these psalms on later rabbinic interpretations of them. Therefore, his conclusions with regard to how Mark uses these texts from the Hebrew Bible are suspect. I will have a more extended discussion of Marcus' conclusions in the final chapter.

The members of Mark's audience are left to grapple with the questions of Jesus' suffering for themselves.[52] This conclusion, however, does not imply that the narrative of Mark does not offer some ways to enter into this search for understanding. A deeper appreciation of the way that David's experience poetically expressed in PssLam nuances the story of Jesus in Mark will aid in the struggle of Mark's audience to make sense of Jesus' suffering.

---

[50] Adela Yarbro Collins, "Suffering and Healing in the Gospel of Mark," in *The Beginning of the Gospel: Probings of Mark in Context* (Minneapolis: Fortress, 1992), especially 70–2.

[51] Marcus, *The Way of the Lord*, 194–5.

[52] Against Dibelius, who says with reference to Jesus' use of biblical language in Mark 14:34, "The choice of these biblical words furthermore proves that it is not a matter of Jesus' perplexity regarding his mission, for the man who utters biblical words in prayer knows himself in harmony with God." See "Gethsemane," 260.

3.3.3   The faithful, suffering king who searches for understanding

The biblical David does many unrighteous acts during his reign, but he never is rejected by God and remains in a faithful relationship with God from the moment he is anointed by Samuel as a young man until the moment he dies. He is the chosen and anointed king of Israel, but this does not make God's way transparent to David. The David of the Psalms suffers and cries out for understanding in the midst of his perceived abandonment by God even as he remains the chosen king. In other words, David's kingship and favor with God do not release him from the incomprehension of God's inaction in the face of suffering. For Jesus, this is no different. In Mark, Jesus is presented as someone greater and more powerful than David and one who knows that he was sent to give his life as a ransom for many. As God's chosen one, Jesus must suffer, according to Mark. But so far, the only reason this is the case is because "it is written of him" to do so; it is God's will. In the Gethsemane story, the evocation of David's struggle in Psalm 41–2 questions this reason for suffering, while at the same time remaining well within the scriptural rubric that constitutes the basis for Jesus' suffering.[53] In this case, "as it is written of him" proves itself to be a complex reason that holds in tension God's will, the chosenness of a powerful royal figure, incomprehension in the face of suffering, and a willingness to question that suffering by demanding God's intervention and presence. Sharon Dowd's insights are valuable here:

> It is important to recognize that in his prayer at the center of the Gethsemane pericope, the Markan Jesus does not reject miraculous rescue and choose to suffer. Rather, he rejects his own will, that is, he 'denies himself' as he advocated in 8:34, and chooses the will of God . . . The Markan Jesus prays for deliverance from suffering even in the face of overwhelming evidence that God wills *not* to intervene. Not only that, but the petition for rescue is repeated even after the initial submission to the will of God . . . The prayer of submission does not replace the prayer for divine intervention; it accompanies it.[54]

Dowd's arguments are solid, but she does not incorporate the added dimensions that arise when these important questions are considered in

---

[53] Donald Senior says, "The raw, honest and stunning humanness of such a prayer is totally within the great tradition of the Jewish lament. Prayer is not to be ideal, fully controlled, or strained with politeness. In a rush of emotion, complaint, and even recrimination, the believers pour out their hearts to God" (*The Passion of Jesus*, 76).

[54] Dowd, *Prayer, Power, and the Problem of Suffering*, 157.

light of Psalm 41–2.[55] Of course, in the end, Jesus chooses to deny his will and chooses God's will that he suffer and die, but this choice does not resolve the tension in the story. Jesus carries that tension with him to the cross.[56]

4   The arrest and trial: continued abandonment and fulfilling God's will to suffer

The episodes in Mark between Gethsemane and the cross contain some possible evocations of the PssLam, but as I discussed in Chapter 3, I am restricting this investigation to "simple evocations," that is evocations of only one PsLam at a particular point in Mark. Therefore, with regard to the episodes of the arrest and trial of Jesus before the Sanhedrin and Pilate, I will raise only the issues relevant to Psalms 40–2 as discussed above. Again, I raise these issues with the fourth stage of Ben-Porat's poetics of allusion in mind. As we will see, reading the arrest and trial of Jesus with Psalms 40–2 reinforces and intensifies three key points: (1) the scriptural justification for Jesus' suffering and death is complex in its reference and function; (2) alongside the images of the Suffering Servant from Isaiah 53, the suffering King David plays a key role in providing a model for Jesus' suffering; and (3) while the apocalyptic dimensions of Jesus' suffering and death become more pronounced, the image of the suffering King David from Psalms 40–2 continues to raise the question of the necessity of Jesus' suffering and death within this apocalyptic framework of meaning.

4.1   The scriptural justification for Jesus' suffering and death

Mark 14:18 points to a single person who hands Jesus over, but as the story continues, other characters abandon him as the narration of Jesus'

---

[55] Although Lull does not speculate about the effect of Psalm 41–2 on the Gethsemane scene, he does point out that only in Mark is the possibility that God could deliver Jesus from death emphasized. Matt 26:39 reads, πάτερ μου, εἰ δυνατόν ἐστιν, παρελθάτω ἀπ' ἐμοῦ τὸ ποτήριον τοῦτο, and Luke 22:42 reads, πάτερ, εἰ βούλει παρένεγκε τοῦτο τὸ ποτήριον ἀπ' ἐμοῦ, whereas Mark 14:36 reads, αββα ὁ πατήρ, πάντα δυνατά σοι· παρένεγκε τὸ ποτήριον τοῦτο ἀπ' ἐμοῦ. Mark's statement to God reminds God and the audience that it is well within God's abilities to deliver Jesus from death. Matthew's and Luke's conditional statements are more indirect than Mark's. See Lull, "Interpreting Mark's Story of Jesus' Death," 6.

[56] "The scene [at Gethsemane] is terrible, not because Jesus must suffer, but because his suffering is the will of the God who is powerful enough to prevent it, and who has eliminated so much suffering in the narrative prior to this scene . . . The God who wills to move the mountain does not always will to take away the cup" (Dowd, *Prayer, Power, and the Problem of Suffering*, 158).

death draws nearer. Even Peter, the leader of the chosen twelve, eventually denies Jesus and abandons him as false witnesses are slandering him at his trial.[57] Through the actions of one of his closest associates,[58] Jesus is handed over to his enemies. Notice the language of 14:41–2: "See, the Son of Man is handed over into the hands of sinners. Get up, let's go; see, the one who hands me over has come near" (ἰδοὺ παραδίδοται ὁ υἱὸς τοῦ ἀνθρώπου εἰς τὰς χεῖρας τῶν ἁμαρτωλῶν. ἐγείρεσθε ἄγωμεν· ἰδοὺ ὁ παραδιδούς με ἤγγικεν). What follows is the arrest of Jesus after the kiss by Judas, a sign of intimacy between the two, as well as an agreed-upon way to signal to those with him whom they should arrest. Judas becomes part of the chief priests, and the scribes' cunning (δόλος) by agreeing to hand Jesus over. In Psalm 40, those on whom David believes he should be able to rely turn into his enemies, they whisper and devise evil against him, and, by doing so, they abandon him as he comes close to death. Although the abandonment is not a physical flight as in Mark, it is clear that David views it as abandonment, and he expresses deep consternation at being treated with cunning by his closest friend, ὁ ἄνθρωπος τῆς εἰρήνης μου, and at being conspired against by his countrymen-turned-enemies.

In addition to the actions of Judas, notice the way in which Jesus submits to his arresters. He does not react violently to his arrest and impending suffering. Instead of resisting violently, he submits, "so that the scriptures may be fulfilled" (ἵνα πληρωθῶσιν αἱ γραφαί, Mark 14:49). Many commentators see this as a possible allusion to or echo of Isa 53:7, in that Jesus does not resist his arrest.[59] Indeed, Jesus does not

---

[57] The story of Peter's denial of Jesus frames the "trial" before the Sanhedrin, indicating that the two events happen almost simultaneously in Mark's narrative.

[58] The basic meaning of παραδίδωμι is "hand over," or in some contexts "arrest." Mark repeatedly uses this word, especially in the context of Jesus' suffering (9:31; 10:33 [twice]; 14:10, 11, 18, 21, 41, 42, 44; 15:1, 10, and 15). This could also be an evocation of Isaiah 53, which uses the word in verses 6 and 12 (twice) to indicate that the servant was handed over (by God in verse 6) for "our sins" (ταῖς ἁμαρτίαις ἡμῶν) or "because of their sins" (διὰ τὰς ἁμαρτίας αὐτῶν). As I will discuss later in this chapter, although there may be clear evocations of the servant in Isaiah 53 in Mark's passion narrative, I think David's suffering corresponds more closely to Jesus' suffering as described in Mark and so should garner more attention than has been given by critics in the past. The usage of παραδίδωμι with respect to Judas has the overtone of betrayal of Jesus. Judas betrays Jesus in that he knows where to find Jesus that particular night, he brings the arresting crowd to the place, and he reveals Jesus' identity so that the crowd can arrest him. Judas uses his relationship with Jesus and the others to expose him to the authorities so that they can arrest him. Mark's repeated description of Judas as ὁ παραδιδούς could be thought of here as "the betrayer."

[59] See Evans, *Mark 8:27–16:20*, 377; Moo, *The Old Testament in the Gospel Passion Narratives*, 109–10, suggests Isaiah 53 as one possibility, but argues for a broader context than this one passage; Francis J. Moloney agrees with Senior (*The Passion of Jesus*, 83–4), who argues that the general background of the suffering righteous one is enough to understand the fulfillment of scripture here. See *The Gospel of Mark*, 298. I have already demonstrated

physically resist his arrest, but he also does not go without protest, as Jesus challenges his arresters' actions by pointing out that they come to arrest him as if he were a dangerous criminal. He also points out their cowardice by highlighting the fact that they arrest him in private at night, even though they have had plenty of opportunity to do so in public in the temple (Mark 14:48–9a). These two challenges separate him from the silent and meek Servant of Isaiah 53 and put him more in line with the protesting David of Psalm 41–2. Mark 14:50 states that, once Jesus had submitted to his arrest, all of his followers fled. This is clearly a fulfillment of Jesus' prediction made earlier in 14:27–8, with reference to Zech 13:7, but it also has overtones of Psalm 40.

By the time Jesus is arrested and declares that scripture is being fulfilled, the justification refers to a multiplicity of scriptural references: an echo of Isa 53:7, a fulfillment of Zech 13:7, and David's abandonment and protest of Psalms 40–2. This multiplicity makes it difficult to say that Jesus' suffering and death are simply foretold in scripture, preordained by God, or a fulfillment of God's will, because the protest of David in Psalms 40–2 adds a voice that directly challenges these notions. As the trial and death of Jesus unfold, there are no more overt scriptural justifications like Mark 14:21 and 49, but the density of scriptural references increases, giving a clear indication of how important scripture is to the understanding of Jesus' suffering and death. Prominent among these scripture references is the increasingly loud voice of the suffering protest of David from the PssLam.

4.2 David as a model for Jesus' suffering

The royal portrayal of Jesus continues strongly throughout his trial in continuity with what has begun in chapters 11–12, as is argued by Frank J. Matera.[60] In short, Jesus is presented as a king, but as a king whose kingship is realized through suffering and death rather than through violent, military triumph.[61] As Jesus' condemnation comes down from the high priest and the whole assembly, his maltreatment is intensified. He is both physically abused and mocked when some of those present spit

---

in Chapter 1 the problems with Ruppert's abstraction of the Suffering Righteous One. Marcus asserts that there are references to the Suffering Servant of Isaiah 53 throughout the Markan passion account, so much so that Mark's Jesus is simply an amalgamation of the Righteous Sufferer (in abstracted form) and the Suffering Servant (in abstracted form). See *The Way of the Lord*, 186–95.

[60] Matera, *Kingship*.

[61] This conforms to the general pattern of Mark 11–12, in which Jesus is linked with David but distanced from his earthly, militaristic aspects. See Chapter 5 of the present study.

on him and call on him to prophesy while he is blindfolded and being beaten (περικαλύπτειν αὐτοῦ τὸ πρόσωπον καὶ κολαφίζειν αὐτόν . . . καὶ οἱ ὑπηρέται ῥαπίσμασιν αὐτὸν ἔλαβον, 14:65). A similar maltreatment happens in 15:16–20, only this time at the hands of the soldiers just after his condemnation is handed down from Pilate. After Jesus is flogged, the whole cohort comes together, and they dress him mockingly in a purple robe and a crown of thorns while hailing him as King of the Jews. They spit on him, strike him with a reed, and kneel before him in false homage.

The Servant passages of Isaiah 40–55 are often raised as the primary model for Jesus' suffering in the trial narrative, and indeed, one can legitimately argue that the silence of Jesus in the midst of accusations by false witnesses in Mark 14:55–61a and after the chief priests' accusations in 15:3–5 is reminiscent of the silence of the servant in Isa 53:7.[62] Pilate admits that Jesus did nothing wrong in Mark 15:14, which is close to Isa 53:9. And in Mark 14:65 and 15:19, Jesus is spat upon and insulted, which reminds the reader of Isa 50:6.[63] This is especially the case with the use of ῥάπισμα in Mark 14:65 and Isa 50:6. This word shows up only in the LXX in Isa 50:6, and it is used only three times in the NT – Mark 14:65 and John 18:22 and 19:3. These lexical and thematic links between Mark and Isaiah's Servant passages make a good case for Mark depicting Jesus as the Suffering Servant of God, at least in the trial scenes.

However, the imagery does not point monolithically to the Servant of Isaiah, because we must take into account the PssLam that have been referred to more overtly by Mark than the Servant passages of Isaiah. Although there are many other places in the Psalm where the psalmist is abused and ridiculed,[64] this certainly recalls the experience of the royal David of Psalm 41–2, as well.[65] In 41:10–11 David first cries out to God, "You are my protector; why did you forget me? (Ἀντιλήμπτωρ μου εἶ· διὰ τί μου ἐπελάθου;), and then "Why do I go around looking angry while my enemy afflicts me?"(ἵνα τί σκυθρωπάζων πορεύομαι ἐν τῷ

---

[62] Marcus, *The Way of the Lord*, 187.

[63] Most commentators raise these similarities; see Donahue and Harrington, *The Gospel of Mark*, 439. See also the introduction and relevant sections of Taylor, *The Gospel According to St. Mark*, where he consistently refers to Jesus as self-consciously acting as the Suffering Servant of Isaiah 53.

[64] Matera says that in Mark 15:1–20 "there is a noticeable absence of Old Testament allusions" (*Kingship*, 97). Although there are no formal evocations of particular texts, the PssLam evoked up to this point in Mark and the two references to events happening according to scripture lead the reader to consider Jesus' mockings in light of these texts.

[65] I point again to this psalm simply because up to this point in the passion narrative only Psalms 40 and 41–2 from the PssLam have been foregrounded in an exclusive way.

ἐκθλίβειν τὸν ἐχθρόν μου;). He goes on to say, "While crushing my bones, those who afflict me insult me" (ἐν τῷ καταθλάσαι τὰ ὀστᾶ μου ὠνείδισάν με οἱ θλίβοντές με). This is all poetic language for the suffering that David expresses in this psalm, but he combines physical mistreatment (crushing of bones and affliction) with verbal mistreatment (insults), in a way similar to that in which Mark depicts Jesus in 14:65 and 15:16–20. Therefore, the model of the suffering David fits well with the suffering Jesus in Mark.

There is also another interesting dimension that Psalm 41–2 adds to Mark's depiction of Jesus. What follows this description of suffering in Ps 41:11 is "while they say to me each day, 'Where is your God?'" (ἐν τῷ λέγειν αὐτούς μοι καθ᾽ ἑκάστην ἡμέραν Ποῦ ἐστιν ὁ θεός σου;). In other words, physical and verbal maltreatment is literarily surrounded by, and therefore linked with, two expressions of the absence of God – "Why did you forget me?" in 41:10a and "Where is your God?" in 41:11b. When these verses are read alongside Jesus' physical and verbal mistreatment in Mark 14:65 and 15:16–20, one cannot help but raise the question of God's absence in the suffering of Jesus, even if he does not express this question until 15:34.

The irony of Jesus' kingship is clear in Jesus' trials, and this point has been commented on extensively. The Jewish authorities condemn him as a blasphemer who claims divine kingship. Pilate condemns him to death as King of the Jews, and both the Jewish and Roman authorities mock and beat him as a royal pretender.[66] I only add here that foregrounding Psalms 40 and 41–2 adds to this irony by making Jesus' royalty more explicit, and it does so in a way that points to a suffering David from Israel's heritage. However, Jesus' silence is not absolute. His own testimony is what causes his condemnation in Mark 14:62–3,[67] and his reply to Pilate in 15:2 (σὺ λέγεις) sounds more defiant than the servant of Isaiah 53, who goes to his death without resistance. It seems to me that the suffering David who cries out to God for his saving action and challenges God to answer for

---

[66] The first beating and mocking is less overtly royal in its overtone, but at the time of Mark, David was considered a prophet as well as a king. Therefore, blindfolding Jesus, striking him, and then asking him to prophesy insinuates that a real Davidic king would have the ability to know his abusers, even blindfolded.

[67] See Hengel, *The Atonement: The Study of the Origins of the Doctrine in the New Testament* (trans. John Bowden; London: SCM Press, 1981), 40; Kingsbury, *Christology*, 151; and Donahue and Harrington, *The Gospel of Mark*, 424, for a similar assessment. Moloney calls Jesus "the innocent righteous sufferer" (*The Gospel of Mark*, 322, 323), but I do not think that this is a tenable statement, based on Jesus' self-incrimination and my reading of the PssLam as not expressing the suffering of a righteous person in the sense of a blameless person.

his absence in the midst of suffering is the model that lends itself readily to Jesus' situation in Mark.[68] The Davidic model carries the irony of the royal depiction of Jesus throughout the trial, but it also accounts for how Jesus suffers in Mark. The Davidic model also adds the dimensions of faithful dissent and the search for an understanding of God's will for the one who suffers.

4.3   Apocalyptic questions

While Jesus is being interrogated by the high priest in the midst of the assembly of Jewish leaders, his kingship is asserted in apocalyptic terms. In response to the high priest's question, "Are you the Christ, the son of the Blessed One?" (σὺ εἶ ὁ χριστός ὁ υἱὸς τοῦ εὐλογητοῦ; 14:61), Jesus answers affirmatively and then goes on to say, "And you will see the Son of Man seated at the right hand of the Power and coming with the clouds of heaven" (καὶ ὄψεσθε τὸν υἱὸν ἀνθρώπου ἐκ δεξιῶν καθήμενον τῆς δυνάμεως καὶ ἐρχόμενον μετὰ τῶν νεφελῶν τοῦ οὐρανοῦ, 14:62). Predictably, this results in Jesus' condemnation, thus negating any notion that Jesus goes to his death as an innocent sufferer, at least at the level of the narrative.[69] What is interesting is that Mark has emphasized the dichotomy between Jesus' present, earthly situation – facing death as a powerless captive of the powerful Jewish religious authorities – and the future, heavenly situation – visibly being enthroned at the right hand of God, in the image of Ps 110:1, and coming with the clouds of heaven, in the image of the Danielic Son of Man. Narratively, there is a tremendous discord between the earthly and the heavenly status of Jesus here.[70] Jesus is at his most powerless during this trial, and yet he claims for himself the most powerful future imaginable.[71]

As in Gethsemane, Mark leaves the relationship between Jesus' suffering and God's will for him unexplained in the trial of Jesus. In the latter

---

[68] Against Matera, who says, "The only Son, the King of the Jews, suffers in divinely appointed capacity as the Son of Man according to the scriptures" (*Kingship*, 97).

[69] See also Hengel, *The Atonement*, 41.

[70] Although Matera makes the royalty of Jesus the common thread between Jesus' earthly and heavenly status, he does not explain adequately why the earthly king must suffer, other than because it says so in scripture. He simply states, "In the present age, Jesus exercises kingship in suffering and by enduring mockery." See *Kingship*, 118–19.

[71] This is not the first time that Jesus is portrayed in this way from a narrative perspective. Throughout Mark 8:27–10:52, descriptions of Jesus' earthly weakness (his three passion predictions in 8:31, 9:31, and 10:33–4, and his insistence on self-denial in 8:34–7 and self-sacrificial service in 10:45) are juxtaposed with stories of Jesus' power (the Son of Man coming into his power and glory in 8:38–9:1, his transfiguration in 9:2–8, and the difficult healing of a possessed boy in 9:14–29).

scene, there is a positive future expressed with two scriptural references repeated from previous uses in Mark (Ps 110:1 was referred to in Mark 12:35–7 and Dan 7:13 was referred to in Mark 13:26), indicating a hope that Jesus' suffering and death will not be the end. However, Mark still does not justify Jesus' suffering in any specific way other than situating it in an apocalyptic reality that somehow relates to Jesus' suffering and death. It seems that Jesus' answering the chief priest as he does indicates an overtone of future vindication for Jesus, but vindication for something that happens to Jesus does not explain why it must happen or how it effects salvation. As I argued above, mere appeal to an apocalyptic reality does not necessarily resolve the issue of why Jesus must suffer as Messiah. As we move further on in the narrative, Jesus' suffering and death are coupled with more apocalyptic signs. At the same time, the voice of abandonment and protest from the David of the PssLam becomes louder and stronger, challenging God with regard to the necessity of Jesus' suffering and death.

5   The crucifixion and death of Jesus

As we move through the remaining scenes in Mark's story of Jesus' suffering and death, we can continue to see the same three main issues surface: (1) the way that the scriptural justification for Jesus' death becomes more problematic and complex, in this case with regard to Psalm 21 and 68; (2) the apocalyptic overtones of Jesus' suffering and death raise questions about the need for Jesus' suffering and death in a greater apocalyptic scenario; and (3) the fact that the suffering David of the PssLam, particularly from Psalm 21 and 68, shows himself to be a fitting model for Jesus' suffering.[72]

5.1   Reading Mark 15:22–39 without Psalms 21 and 68

As with regard to the reference to Psalm 41–2 in the Gethsemane episode, it is possible to read the crucifixion without much recourse to Psalms 21 and 68. However, to do so would be to ignore the blatant references to both

---

[72] Juel says, "The opening line [of Psalm 22] attributes the psalm to David, who is the king. The use of the psalm to speak about Jesus tells us only that the events that concluded his ministry were 'scriptural.' His identity is provided by the rest of the narrative. It seems likely that the use of the psalm is also bound to Jesus' identity as King of the Jews, though the derivation of this royal exegesis remains elusive" (*Messianic Exegesis*, 116). Hopefully, my analysis will continue to show that the evocation of Psalm 21 as a Davidic psalm helps to further both the royal and suffering dimensions of Jesus' character.

that have been included in the story by Mark. As I discussed in Chapter 3, there is a possible reference to Ps 68:22 in Mark 15:23, but the reference is opaque, at best, unlike the one to the same verse in 15:36. Therefore, I will hold any integration of Psalm 68 into the story of the crucifixion until the reference to it in Mark 15:36. The most influence over the story of Jesus' crucifixion and death comes from Psalm 21.[73] Both Mark 15:24 and 15:34 contain strong evocations of the lament portion of Psalm 21, each of which borders on quotations from the psalm, although they are not introduced by Mark in any formal way.

5.2   Reading Mark 15:22–39 in light of Psalms 21 and 68

5.2.1   Jesus is crucified

Mark's narration of Jesus' crucifixion is actually very stark[74] in comparison to the descriptions of his physical maltreatment that follows each of his condemnations (14:65 and 15:17–20). However, at the point at which Jesus is crucified, Mark highlights the evocation of Ps 21:19 (indicated

---

[73] Tertullian says, "the 21st psalm contain[s] the whole of Christ's passion" (*Adv. Marcion* 3.19.5 as cited in Brown, *Death of the Messiah*, II:1455). Donahue and Harrington (*The Gospel of Mark*, 445) and Juel (*Messianic Exegesis*, 114 and *Mark*, 219) characterize Psalm 21 as the "script" for Mark's depiction of Jesus' death, but Juel does not explore the script in much detail. This is understandable, since the purpose of his whole project in *Messianic Exegesis* is to show how biblical texts are strung together, as in rabbinic exegesis, in order to create a group of texts that biblically justify Jesus as Messiah. Schweizer, like Dibelius before him, says the church found "the description of the Passion" in the Old Testament, and thus attributed the words of Psalm 22 to Jesus. See *The Good News According to Mark*, 351, and Dibelius, "Gethsemane," 258. Brown, however, corrects this notion: "no psalm offers a parallel to the basic Gospel outline of Jesus' passion" (*Death of the Messiah*, II:1452). Many scholars who discuss Psalm 21 (usually Psalm 22 [MT]) become occupied by the issue of the pre-Markan traditions that gave rise to the passion narrative and never talk about the significance of the references to this psalm for Mark. They also tend to read the psalm eschatologically, pointing to other New Testament texts that seem to read the psalm this way (especially Heb 2:13; Rev 11:15; 19:5). Matera says, "The New Testament understood the psalm in terms of God's eschatological victory as well as Jesus' suffering" (*Kingship*, 131). However, Matera falls victim to the "trajectory" error I describe in Chapter 1. His is a problematic statement, in that the various books of the New Testament that refer to Psalm 22 all have their particular reasons for doing so. We have no way of determining the relationship between the communities for which these texts were written, and to claim a trajectory or a monolithic way that they read a psalm is fallacious. Each text must be examined on its own terms in conversation with Psalm 22 before a claim can be made regarding similarity or trajectory of interpretation.

[74] "So, in the simplest possible terms, the dread act is recorded! No attempt is made to describe the harrowing details familiar enough in the ancient world" (Taylor, *The Gospel According to St. Mark*, 589). See also, Juel, *Mark*, 219; Schweizer, *The Good News According to Mark*, 346; Moloney, *The Gospel of Mark*, 320; Donahue and Harrington, *The Gospel of Mark*, 444.

here by italics) by putting it in the middle of a short chiasm. Verses 24–5 read: "And they crucified him, and *they divided*[75] *his garments, casting lots for them* [to determine] who would take what. It was the third hour and they crucified him" (καὶ σταυροῦσιν αὐτὸν καὶ διαμερίζονται τὰ ἱμάτια αὐτοῦ βάλλοντες κλῆρον ἐπ' αὐτὰ τίς τί ἄρῃ. ἦν δὲ ὥρα τρίτη καὶ ἐσταύρωσαν αὐτόν). Given the framing of the reference, this is no casual evocation. Instead, Mark highlights it to incorporate Psalm 21 into the story of Jesus' crucifixion. This encourages the reader to center his or her efforts on Psalm 21 in order to understand the crucifixion.[76]

As I argued in Chapter 4, Psalm 21 consists of a long lament that ends at verse 22. Overall, the psalm is constructed to elicit a response from God to act on behalf of the suffering psalmist.[77] The description of suffering in the lament portion builds in its desperation and intensity until

---

[75] σταυροῦσιν and διαμερίζονται are examples of the historical present. Taylor says, "The use of the historic pres. is a striking feature of the Markan account of the crucifixion." He goes on to point out the different tenses in the narrative from verses 21–7 and concludes by saying, "The use of tenses gives great vividness to the scene; we see it before our eyes" (Taylor, *The Gospel According to St. Mark*, 588).

[76] Against Taylor, who says, "That they should have divided [the garments] by casting lots, using the dice by which they whiled away the time, is natural, and need not be regarded as a detail suggested by Ps. xxi. (xxii.) 19." However, he goes on to say that Mark's language shows that he has the passage in mind and says, "the question arises how far events have recalled OT passages, and to what extent these have coloured the accounts." He never addresses the question in this case. See Taylor, *The Gospel According to St. Mark*, 589, and Moloney, *The Gospel of Mark*, 320. Along the same lines, Gundry says, "We should resist the temptation to think that Mark means to show the fulfillment of OT prophecy by borrowing phraseology from Ps 22:19 (18) when he describes the division of Jesus' garments" (*Mark*, 945). Eugene LaVerdiere raises questions about Mark's intention to refer to all of Psalm 22 by questioning why he did not refer to parts of the Psalm more illustrative of Jesus' situation. See *The Beginning of the Gospel: Introducing the Gospel of Mark* (2 vols.; Collegeville, MN: Liturgical Press, 1999), II:292. Brown says, "The psalm parallels are to secondary details that fill in the story (mostly to incidents involving what other people do to Jesus)" (*Death of the Messiah*, II:1452). But the evocations of Psalm 22 (LXX 21) are more than secondary details. I agree with Juel, who says, "It is difficult to conceive the passion narratives without allusions to Psalm 22. It is as difficult to explain the allusions to the psalm as secondary" (*Messianic Exegesis*, 116). Moloney repeatedly says that Psalm 22 dominates the passion account in Mark, and thus correctly gives it pride of place in his discussion of the death of Jesus (*The Gospel of Mark*, 317–31).

[77] Against Matera, who says, "In the psalm, the scope of thanksgiving is such that it lends itself to a messianic and eschatological interpretation . . . Not only does it describe the suffering of the just one, it also portrays his victory in language that is susceptible to messianic and eschatological interpretation" (*Kingship*, 135). Brown also assumes an eschatological thrust to the psalm, as well as a depiction of "the just one." He also says that the use of Psalm 22 would have caused Christians "to highlight the reversal in an abandoned death and subsequent victory" (*Death of the Messiah*, II:1459, 1462). Donahue and Harrington say, "Psalm 22 is the prayer of a righteous person who has suffered greatly but has been vindicated, all the while retaining and being sustained by trust in God's power and care" (*The Gospel of Mark*, 445). I think by this time it is clear why I disagree with these arguments. Moo says, "From the point of view of the NT material, no evidence exists

the end, when the imagery describes extreme persecution and defeat. The lament ends with a series of four imperative phrases in verses 20–2 that express the desperate cry of the psalmist to God for help. Verse 19, the verse evoked in Mark 15:24, falls at the end of the last series of verses that describe the powerless situation of the psalmist before his powerful enemies. The verse lies right before the series of four imperative phrases, and its imagery communicates the psalmist's perception of persecution to the point of death.

In particular, the imagery evoked is that of the psalmist who is taken for dead after his enemies have mistreated and persecuted him. Ps 21:13–14 describes the psalmist's enemies as "young bulls" and "bulls" (μόσχοι and ταῦροι) surrounding and encircling him, and as a "lion" (λέων) ravishing and roaring, ready to pounce. Verses 15–16 continue this metaphorical language, but the imagery communicates the psalmist's perception that his situation is life-threatening. He is "poured out like water," his "bones are scattered," his "heart has become like wax melting" within him, his "strength has dried up like earthenware," and his "tongue has become stuck" to his throat. In the last line of verse 16, the psalmist directs the description to "you" (i.e., to God) and says, "and you sent me down into the dust of death" (καὶ εἰς χοῦν θανάτου κατήγαγές με). This implicates God directly in the suffering of the psalmist. Verse 17 continues the description of the psalmist being surrounded by his enemies, and verses 18 and 19 implicate the enemies directly in the actions that cause the psalmist express his nearness to death: "I counted all my bones, but they [his enemies] gazed and looked upon me. They divided my clothes among themselves, and for my clothing they cast lots" (ἐξηρίθμησα πάντα τὰ ὀστᾶ μου, αὐτοὶ δὲ κατενόησαν καὶ ἐπεῖδόν με. διεμερίσαντο τὰ ἱμάτιά μου ἑαυτοῖς καὶ ἐπὶ τὸν ἱματισμόν μου ἔλαβον κλῆρον). These two verses express the perception that the psalmist's enemies took him for dead, ready to take the spoils of the victim (his clothes).

This imagery is fitting for Jesus' situation in Mark 15:24 as well, because there is no reason to think that his situation will end in anything but death. Crucifixion was primarily a form of execution.[78] Following the expression of God's will for Jesus' suffering found in Gethsemane, the

for the interpretation of Jesus' Resurrection or exaltation in relation to the 'Thanksgiving' portion of the lament Psalm used to describe Jesus' suffering" (*The Old Testament in the Gospel Passion Narratives*, 294). Reading the PssLam, in this case Psalm 21, as I have in Chapter 4 would eliminate the need to consider the thanksgiving section as serving a different purpose from that of the lament portion.

[78] See Martin Hengel, *Crucifixion in the Ancient World and the Folly of the Message of the Cross* (trans. John Bowden; Philadelphia: Fortress, 1977), 22–38, for a detailed description of the practice of crucifixion as a form of torture and execution.

overtones of God's involvement in the psalmist's situation of suffering and persecution in Ps 21:17 serve to reinforce God's role in Jesus' crucifixion. If we read Ps 21:13–19 alongside the account of Jesus' crucifixion, it is difficult to look upon God's will for Jesus' suffering as a positive thing.[79]

In verses 13–19, there are three characters who are interwoven in the description of the suffering: the psalmist, whom we can think of as David, his enemies, and God. From David's point of view, it is clear that he is the victim and his enemies are the ones who inflict his suffering, but God's role is questionable, based on David's implication of God in his life-threatening situation described in verse 16c. Up to this point in the psalm, David continually attempts to elicit God's response by depicting the dissonance between God's past interaction with Israel and David, on the one hand, and God's current inaction in the face of his suffering, on the other hand. God's inaction and abandonment of David are certainly a cause for concern, but in verse 16c God actively sends him "into the dust of death." The language is hyperbolic, but it points to God's approving and causing David's persecution at the hands of his enemies, at least from his perspective. Furthermore, David does not see this as acceptable, and this section of the psalm is followed by a four-fold cry for deliverance from suffering. In light of God's will for Jesus to suffer as expressed in Gethsemane, and the problems with this raised by Psalm 41–2, it is easier to question Jesus' crucifixion in a similar way in light of Psalm 21.

5.2.2 Jesus is mocked

As we move through Mark's narrative, the focus of the story begins to shift to those who observe Jesus hanging on the cross. First, Mark overtly reminds the reader of Jesus' kingship by describing the ironic charge written above his head on the cross, "The King of the Jews" (ὁ βασιλεὺς τῶν Ἰουδαίων, 15:26). Mark goes on to say in 15:27 that Jesus is crucified between two rebels, which makes the charge of Jesus' kingship seem even more ironic. The actions of the Roman authorities seem to be mocking Jesus as much as the onlookers beginning in the next verse, which is another evocation of Psalm 21, this time of verse 8.[80]

---

[79] Against Moloney, who says, "The only ray of light comes from the allusion to Ps 22:19, and the first indication that this took place 'at the third hour.' These hints promise the reader that, in a mysterious way, God's design is being worked out in this brutal murder (cf. 10:45; 14:36)" (*The Gospel of Mark*, 321).

[80] As we saw in Chapter 3, there is some question as to whether this is a simple evocation of Ps 21:8 or a more complex use of Ps 108:25 (LXX), Lam 2:15 and even Wis 2:17–20. As

Mark 15:29–30 reads, "And the passers-by reviled him,[81] shaking their heads and saying, 'Ha, the one who tears down the Temple and builds it up in three days; save yourself by coming down from the cross'" (καὶ οἱ παραπορευόμενοι ἐβλασφήμουν αὐτὸν κινοῦντες τὰς κεφαλὰς αὐτῶν καὶ λέγοντες· οὐὰ ὁ καταλύων τὸν ναὸν καὶ οἰκοδομῶν ἐν τρισὶν ἡμέραις, σῶσον σεαυτὸν καταβὰς ἀπὸ τοῦ σταυροῦ). Similarly in Ps 21:8 the psalmist describes those who look at him (οἱ θεωροῦντές με) mocking him with bodily gestures (speaking with their mouths and shaking their heads). As we move to Mark 15:31–2, Mark tells of a similar mocking by the chief priests and the scribes: "Likewise, the chief priests mocked him among themselves with the scribes and said, 'He saved others, [yet] he cannot save himself; let the Christ, the King of Israel come down now from the cross so that we may see and believe.' Even those crucified with him insulted him" (ὁμοίως καὶ οἱ ἀρχιερεῖς ἐμπαίζοντες πρὸς ἀλλήλους μετὰ τῶν γραμματέων ἔλεγον· ἄλλους ἔσωσεν, ἑαυτὸν οὐ δύναται σῶσαι· ὁ χριστός ὁ βασιλεὺς Ἰσραὴλ καταβάτω νῦν ἀπὸ τοῦ σταυροῦ, ἵνα ἴδωμεν καὶ πιστεύσωμεν. καὶ οἱ συνεσταυρωμένοι σὺν αὐτῷ ὠνείδιζον αὐτόν).

Much like the evocation of verse 19 in Mark 15:24, 15:29–32 refers to a part of the psalm that is at the heart of a description about the suffering of David. In this case, the mocking comes after Ps 21:4–6, where he appeals to God's past saving actions with Israel, and before verses 10–11, where he appeals to the intimate relationship that he has shared with God from the beginning of his life. The mocking in verses 7–9 is the second wave of descriptions of David's suffering and reads, "But I am a worm and not a person, a disgrace of a man and a reproach of a people. All who look at me mock me, they speak with their lips, they shake their head[s], 'He hoped in the Lord, let him deliver him, let him save him for he wants him'" (ἐγὼ δέ εἰμι σκώληξ καὶ οὐκ ἄνθρωπος, ὄνειδος ἀνθρώπου καὶ ἐξουδένημα λαοῦ. πάντες οἱ θεωροῦντές με ἐξεμυκτήρισάν με, ἐλάλησαν ἐν χείλεσιν, ἐκίνησαν κεφαλήν. Ἤλπισεν ἐπὶ κύριον, ῥυσάσθω αὐτόν· σωσάτω αὐτόν, ὅτι θέλει αὐτόν). The similarities between Jesus' and the psalmist's mocking go beyond Ps 21:8.[82] Jesus has already been mocked and abused by those at his Sanhedrin trial (14:65) and by the soldiers serving Pilate after his trial with Pilate (15:16–20); he is now

---

I argued in that chapter, all of these are likely evoked texts, but given the narrative context of Mark at this point, with its clear evocation of Ps 21:19 just four short verses earlier, it is legitimate to consider it as the primary evoked text and subject it to the same sort of analysis as a simple evocation of Ps 21:8.

[81] "Revile" translates βλασφημέω here in agreement with the argument of Adela Yarbro Collins in "The Charge of Blasphemy in Mark 14:64," 379–401.

[82] Schweizer raises this possibility, but he does not explore it beyond the sentence that raises the possibility. See *The Good News According to Mark*, 349.

clearly insulted by all those who are present at his crucifixion, even the rebels who are crucified with him. Everyone from the most powerful (chief priests and scribes) to the lowliest (those crucified with him), from Roman to Jew, has joined in the mocking. This matches the hyperbolic language of Ps 21:7, where David calls himself the insult of humanity and the contempt of a people.

The content of the mocking in Mark 15:29b–30 provides another point of comparison with the mocking in Ps 21:7–9.[83] The passers-by taunt Jesus by referring to his claim to be able to tear down the Temple and rebuild it in three days. Then, in verses 31–2, the chief priests and scribes continue the derision by calling on Jesus to act on his status as the Messiah, King of Israel, and to come down so that they may see and believe. Underlying this double mocking is the idea that Jesus supposedly has superhuman power with the ability to tear down the Temple and raise it in three days. If he were the hoped-for Messiah, the King of Israel, then he would be the powerful agent of God, close to God in being the one to carry out God's will to deliver Israel. The mockers challenge Jesus to prove this by miraculously coming down from the cross as a demonstration of his power to overcome the authority of Roman justice. A similar mocking occurs in Ps 21:9: "He hoped in the Lord, let him deliver him, let him save him, for he wants him." They mock by saying that if David really were a delight to God, then God would deliver him from his desperate situation. In a sense, his mockers test God, or at least David's relationship with God, which can only be vindicated if God saves him. Similarly, in Mark 15:29–32, Jesus is the beloved son in whom God is well pleased (ὁ υἱός μου ὁ ἀγαπητός, ἐν σοὶ εὐδόκησα, 1:11), and the onlookers challenge him to save himself. By implication, they challenge his relationship with God as well. In other words, if Jesus really is God's chosen Messiah, the King of Israel, then why is God not giving him the ability to save himself?[84]

The relationship between God and Jesus finds an analogue in the relationship between God and David as expressed in Psalm 21. In verses 4–6 and 10–11 of Psalm 21, David expresses his understanding of the favored

---

[83] Moloney points this out, but goes in a slightly different direction based on his understanding of Psalm 22 as a Psalm of the Innocent Righteous Sufferer. See *The Gospel of Mark*, 322–3.

[84] Taylor argues that only the Matthean account of Jesus' mocking uses Ps 21:9 as its model, and he states that in Mark, "ἑαυτόν . . . σῶσαι is the only point of contact with the Psalm and is a reminiscence at most." See *The Gospel According to St. Mark*, 592. Brown argues that the use of Psalm 22 would have caused early Christians "to dramatize the mocking hostility shown to Jesus by those around the cross, challenging his claim to have God's help" (*Death of the Messiah*, II:1462).

relationship between him and God. In verses 4–6, David reflects on his heritage and God's interaction with his ancestors. He reminds God that God dwells "among holy ones" (ἐν ἁγίοις) and is "the praise of Israel" (ὁ ἔπαινος Ισραηλ). One of the reasons for this, David goes on, is that when his ancestors hoped in God, God delivered them, and they were not put to shame, "to you they cried out and they were saved" (πρὸς σὲ ἐκέκραξαν καὶ ἐσώθησαν). By his repeated use of "hope" (ἤλπισαν), David expresses the fidelity that God had shown to his ancestors, and in addition, he reflects on his place in this heritage as the chosen leader of God's people. As his ancestors did, he has hoped in God, but he has not received the deliverance that his ancestors received.

In verses 10–11, David's reconsideration of his relationship with God becomes more personal. He reminds God of the nearness and intimacy that they shared, even from birth. David essentially calls God his midwife in 10a and 11a: "For you are the one who drew me forth from the womb" (ὅτι σὺ εἶ ὁ ἐκσπάσας με ἐκ γαστρός) and "Upon you I was cast from the womb" (ἐπὶ σὲ ἐπερρίφην ἐκ μήτρας). And in 10b and 11b, he calls God his hope and his God, even from the point of his birth. The repeated use of womb imagery (γαστήρ, μήτρα, κοιλία) shows the foundational relationship that he has with God. David's rumination on his relationship with God not only reminds God of what they share, but it heightens the abhorrence of what David is experiencing in his suffering.

Although Mark does not express Jesus' relationship with God in ways exactly parallel to Psalm 21, Mark describes Jesus' relationship with God in loving, filial terms, similar in some ways to the intimate relationship with God that David describes in Psalm 21. God only speaks twice in Mark, both times to call Jesus, "my beloved son" (ὁ υἱός μου ὁ ἀγαπητός in 1:11 and 9:7). Jesus defines his community as a family who does the will of God, who is presumably the head of the family (3:31–5). There is an assumption here that Jesus is close enough to God to know the will of God and discern when people are acting on it. Furthermore, in the parable of the wicked tenants (Mark 12:1–12), Jesus indirectly presents himself as God's son. He also calls upon God in Gethsemane as "Abba" (14:36), certainly a term of endearment and closeness, and then he admits to being the "Son of the Blessed One" at his trial before the Sanhedrin (ὁ υἱὸς τοῦ εὐλογητοῦ, 14:61–2). Mark expresses an understanding from both God's side and Jesus' side that Jesus is God's chosen and beloved son. David's relationship with God as described in Psalm 21 heightens the vivid depiction of his suffering and causes the reader to question this relationship, even as David does. So also does Jesus' relationship with God as beloved son strongly contrast with the treatment that is described in the passion narrative. David questions God's abandonment which allows this suffering, and even God's active involvement in it (Ps 21:16). Perhaps Mark is doing the same by referring to this psalm in his depiction of Jesus' death.

The same voice of protest that was heard in Psalm 41–2, that of a faithful King David, is present again in these first two references to Psalm 21. Again, Mark adds an evocation of a PsLam to align Jesus' suffering with a scriptural passage, while at the same time using a passage that challenges the very suffering that it is justifying. By aligning Jesus' suffering with that of David in Psalm 21, Mark also shows that the suffering David of the PssLam proves to be an excellent model to which the reader can turn for understanding Jesus' suffering, perhaps even better than the Suffering Servant from Isaiah 53. Those who advocate the conclusion that the Servant is evoked at this point in the story usually point to Mark 15:27, which could refer to Isa 53:12, which numbers the Servant among transgressors. But this is a faint echo, at best, and the near quotation from Ps 21:19 and the similarities in Jesus' mocking to that of David in Ps 21:7–9 clearly align Jesus with the suffering David. In addition, the contexts of each of these evocations of Psalm 21 add a considerable amount of depth to the relationship between Jesus and God, when it is considered in conversation with David's relationship with God.

5.2.3   Jesus cries out

5.2.3.a   Psalm 21

After Jesus' mocking by the passers-by and the chief priests and scribes, Mark skips ahead to the sixth hour (approximately noon) and tells us that darkness has fallen "upon the whole land" (ἐφ᾿ ὅλην τὴν γῆν) until the ninth hour (Mark 15:33–4). This cosmic sign continues the apocalyptic depiction of Jesus' advent begun with the appearance of John the Baptist in the initial verses of the Gospel. It is often interpreted as a sign of God's judgment falling upon the earth.[85] But one could also view God as finally beginning to act after being silent in the narrative ever since the

---

[85] Witherington, *The Gospel of Mark*, 397; Myers, *Binding*, 389; Schweizer, *The Good News According to Mark*, 353. Brown points to the link between daytime darkness and the Day of the Lord in Zeph 1:15, Joel 2:2; 3:4 and Amos 8:9–10, and then he goes on to say, "Against this background one can interpret Mark to mean that while the mockers demanded of Jesus on the cross a sign . . . God is giving them a sign as part of a judgment on the world" (*Death of the Messiah*, II:1035). For an alternative view, see Whitney Taylor Shiner, "The Ambiguous Pronouncement of the Centurion and the Shrouding of Meaning in Mark," *JSNT* 78 (2000): 10. Shiner points to similar portents in the stories of Romulus (Plutarch, *Romulus* 27.6–28.6), Julius Caesar (Virgil, *Georgics* 1.463–8), Carneades (Diogenes Laertius 4.64), and Pelopidas (Plutarch, *Pelopidas* 295A). Evans makes a similar point (*Mark 8:27–16:20*, 506).

transfiguration in 9:2–8.[86] Ben Witherington points out that there are three moments in Mark that clearly "reveal the identity of Jesus at the beginning, middle and end of the story": at the baptism, the transfiguration, and the crucifixion. He correctly points out, however, that at the third moment, "there is no voice from heaven speaking to Jesus," as one would expect on the basis of the baptism and the transfiguration.[87] This heightens the sense of the absence of God in the midst of Jesus' suffering and calls into question the relationship between God and Jesus in Mark. There is a larger apocalyptic scenario happening that the reader/hearer, and maybe even Jesus as a character in Mark, might not fully appreciate. As supernatural signs swirl around, Jesus hangs on the cross approaching death. If darkness at high noon is possible, then surely saving the life of the Beloved Son is possible as well, is it not? But Mark portrays God as distant from Jesus,[88] which does not exactly encourage the reader to buy into the apocalyptic purposes of God. If Mark thinks that God does have a greater plan in which Jesus' suffering and death effect some sort of necessary and positive change in the configuration of the cosmos, then one might expect a narration of it by some positive interaction between Jesus and God at Jesus' most important moment. Instead, Jesus does not perceive God's presence or plan in the midst of his crucifixion in Mark, and this causes the reader to question whether or not Mark fully accepts this purported apocalyptic scenario. The cries of Jesus that follow seem to emphasize this assessment.

At the ninth hour, Jesus makes his now famous cry to God in the voice of David from Ps 21:2: "My God My God, why did you abandon me?" (ὁ θεός μου ὁ θεός μου, εἰς τί ἐγκατέλιπές με; Mark 15:34). Mark does not quote directly from the psalm; instead he transliterates Jesus' cry in David's words from Aramaic to Greek script and then translates it into the saying that we have in verse 34. In the previous evocations of the PssLam in the passion narrative – namely, in Mark 14:18 and 14:34 – Jesus used the words from Psalms 40 and 41–2, respectively, but only in his cry from the cross does Mark quote Jesus in his native tongue when referring to this PsLam. This does not affect the pattern of evocations to the LXX PssLam that has been consistent throughout the passion narrative, because, from a literary perspective, the Aramaic literarily sets up the misunderstanding

---

[86] Brown, *Death of the Messiah*, II:1036.   [87] Witherington, *The Gospel of Mark*, 398.

[88] Against Gundry, who says, "The supernatural character of the darkness . . . magnifies Mark's apologetic point: now that Jesus' prediction of mockery has reached complete fulfillment, God hides his Son from the blasphemers' leering" (*Mark*, 947). In response to Gundry's assessment, Evans says, "In view of the cry of abandonment in v 34, perhaps it is better to think that God has hidden his face from his son" (*Mark 8:27–16:20*, 506).

that ensues right after the cry, presupposing "that the whole scene is constructed in Greek, as the confusion involved in the play upon ἐλωΐ and Ἠλία would hardly take place in a Semitic context."[89] What follows the transliterated Aramaic is very close to a word-for-word quotation from Ps 21:2a.[90] Clearly, Mark assumes that the Greek-speaking audience will be more familiar with the LXX than with the MT or the Aramaic, but the literary device of using the Aramaic has the purpose of continuing Mark's major theme of misunderstanding of Jesus.

From a narrative point of view, the reference to Psalm 41–2 in the Gethsemane episode results in Jesus taking on the voice of the lamenting David, but he does not use the words as part of his prayer to God, as he does on the cross. There is no question that the crucifixion of Jesus is the center of Mark's story of Jesus, and when the climactic scene arrives, Mark is careful to use Psalm 21 to express Jesus' suffering in its most vivid terms. In addition, Jesus speaks these words in Aramaic. The reference does not just refer to a scripture passage to move the story along; rather, referring to the psalm in Aramaic gives the effect that Jesus takes on the character of the suffering David in a very personal way that can only be expressed in his native tongue.

The scholarly debate about Jesus' cry usually revolves around two interrelated issues: (1) Was Jesus' cry one of despair, hope, or something else?[91] and (2) Did he mean to refer to the first verse of the psalm or the

---

[89] Moloney, *The Gospel of Mark*, 326, n.264. See also Brown, *Death of the Messiah*, II:1061–3; Adela Yarbro Collins concurs: "It is given in Aramaic to prepare for the misunderstanding of some of the bystanders who conclude that Jesus is calling Elijah. Their misunderstanding appears to be deliberate, since the similarity between the two relevant words is not close. Thus, the reaction is presented as additional mockery" ("From Noble Death to Crucified Messiah," *NTS* 40 [1994]: 499).

[90] Ps 21:2a reads, "Ὁ θεὸς ὁ θεός μου, πρόσχες μοι· ἵνα τί ἐγκατέλιπές με" and Mark 15:34b reads, "Ὁ θεός μου ὁ θεός μου, εἰς τί ἐγκατέλιπές με."

[91] Here are some excerpts from the debate as I understand it: for hope or trust in God, see Matera, *Kingship*, 132; Jack Dean Kingsbury says: "Jesus' cry is to God . . . and it expresses continuing trust in God ('my God') in spite of abandonment into death. On balance, therefore, the scene of 15:33–36 is analogous to that of 15:29–32. In it, Jesus is pictured as going to his death as one who places his total trust in God" (*Christology*, 130). Taylor argues that reading the cry of Jesus as a cry of faith "is a reaction from the traditional view which fails to take the saying seriously. The depths of the saying are too deep to be plumbed, but the least inadequate interpretations are those which find in it a sense of desolation in which Jesus felt the horror of sin so deeply that for a time the closeness of His communion with the Father was obscured" (*The Gospel According to St. Mark*, 594). After pointing out that Luke changes Jesus' last words to an allusion to Ps 31:5 ("Father, into your hands I commit my spirit"; Luke 23:46) in order to portray Jesus' death as noble, Juel says, "It seems almost comical to argue that Jesus chose the opening line from Psalm 22 as his last cry to express his confidence in the God who vindicates the sufferer at the end of the psalm. Other texts would have been far more suitable for such purposes" (*Messianic*

entire psalm?[92] Raymond E. Brown says, "Perhaps the most frequently offered argument for softening the dour import of the Mark/Matt death cry is based on the general context of Ps 22." He goes on to rehearse the argument that if the whole psalm is taken into account, then the positive ending indicating the vindication of the psalmist wins the day. He disagrees with this interpretation of the cry, because he thinks that it expresses "almost the opposite meaning of what Jesus is portrayed as saying!"[93] If Ps 21:2 is not thought of as a cry of despair, and Psalm 21

Exegesis, 114). Schweizer insightfully holds in tension the abandonment expressed with Jesus' cry with the theological issue of his faith in God in the midst of his suffering: "The cry of Jesus summarizes in an extraordinarily meaningful way both aspects of what is happening here: it is a radical expression of the loneliness of Jesus' suffering. He has to bear not only the experience of being abandoned by men, but also of being forsaken by God. At the same time, however, it is a radical expression of a devotion to God which endures in every adverse experience – a devotion which continues to claim God as 'my God' and will not let him go although he can be experienced only as the absent One who has forsaken the petitioner" (*The Good News According to Mark*, 353). Brown argues for taking the cry as literally expressing the "pessimistic pathos" of Jesus and that Jesus is not questioning the existence of God or the power of God to do something, but he is questioning the silence of God (*Death of the Messiah*, II:1046, 1047). Moloney argues that the sense of abandonment expressed by Jesus in his cry should not be softened but maintained "to capture fully the Markan presentation of the crucified Christ" (*The Gospel of Mark*, 326). Gundry says that the narrative context points to the seriousness of Jesus' cry and concludes, "given these circumstances, not even a Jewish audience – much less Mark's Gentile audience – would hear the cry as pointing to a later salvific passage . . . It does not interpret that cry in the light of later verses in Psalm 22, for then phraseology would have been drawn from them" (*Mark*, 967). See Moloney, *The Gospel of Mark*, 326, and Brown, *Death of the Messiah*, II: 1047–51, for excellent discussions of the scholarship around this issue.

[92] Whole Psalm: Matera, *Kingship*, 133. Only first line: Cranfield, *The Gospel According to Saint Mark*, 458; Juel, *Messianic Exegesis*, 114; Taylor, *The Gospel According to St. Mark*, 594. Donahue and Harrington say, "A literary and theological investigation of Mark's account would rightly place more emphasis on Psalm 22 taken as a whole as the prayer of a suffering righteous person and an important element in Mark's christology" (*The Gospel of Mark*, 451). After briefly considering the function of the psalm in Mark, Daniel Guichard concludes, among other things, that when considered as a whole, the confession of the centurion in Mark 15:39 corresponds with the theme of universality at the end of Psalm 22. See "La Reprise du Psalm 22 dans le récit de la mort de Jésus (Marc 15, 21–41)," *FoiVie* 88 (1988): 64. I agree with the impulse to consider the whole of Psalm 21, but not with the characterization of the psalm by both of these works. Vernon K. Robbins says that those who consider the psalm as a whole, as he does, usually impose the rhetoric of the psalm onto the rhetoric of Markan discourse without considering how Mark's rhetoric differs from the psalm's rhetoric. Of the commentators I have read, Robbins combines better than anyone a careful analysis of Psalm 21 with close attention to Mark's use of it. His basic insight is that, because Mark uses the psalm in reverse order, he reverses the rhetoric of confidence, trust, and hope that is present in the psalm. See "The Reversed Contextualization of Psalm 22 in the Markan Crucifixion: A Socio-Rhetorical Analysis," in *The Four Gospels: Festschrift for Frans Neirynck* (ed. F. van Segbroeck; vol. II; Leuven: Leuven University Press, 1992), especially 1175–83. I disagree with Robbins' assessment of the rhetoric of the psalm, so I disagree with his conclusions about how Mark uses it.

[93] *Death of the Messiah*, II:1049–51. Marcus centers his whole interpretation of the passion narrative in Mark on this positive reading. See *The Way of the Lord*, 180–2.

is not thought of as ending with the eschatological vindication of the Suffering Righteous One, this opens up another possibility. As I argued in Chapter 2, each PsLam must be interpreted generally within the form-critical conventions of its category; but more importantly, each PsLam must be interpreted in terms of its own literary and rhetorical design. As I argued in Chapter 4, Psalm 21 is a carefully crafted attempt to elicit the saving response of God by (1) appealing to God's past relationship with Israel and with the psalmist, (2) vividly depicting the psalmist's sufferings, and (3) vowing praise that will bring untold glory to God. With this in mind, Mark 15:34 takes on a significance that does not fall into the either/or categories of despair or hope that have given rise to the polarization of scholarship on this verse.

By this time in the crucifixion scene, there have been two clear evocations of two different descriptions of David's suffering in Psalm 21 in Mark 15:24 and 15:29. Few verses in between these two do not have a relation to Psalm 21 in some sense.[94] When we see the clearest of all the references to the PssLam in Mark 15:34, it is highly unlikely that a biblically literate member of Mark's community would not have thought of the whole psalm when hearing this verse. As with the other two allusions, this verse comes from a description of David's suffering, this time from the first description. This is the first verse of the body of the psalm, which encapsulates the mood of the entire psalm – not despair, but outrage, anger, accusation, questioning, and pain at the thought that God has abandoned him in his time of greatest need. As we have seen, the sense of incomprehension and outrage is developed throughout the lament section of the psalm as David reflects on his relationship with God and describes his suffering in increasingly graphic and troubling terms. The psalm ends with a ten-verse promise of praise that is David's last attempt to elicit God's response. As is typical, Mark only briefly describes Jesus' mood with a reference to Psalm 21, but when read with the entire psalm, Jesus' cry can evoke overtones of outrage, abandonment, and incomprehension,[95] similar to David's in the psalm.

---

[94] This is against Christoph Burchard, who argues that nothing in Mark's narrative prepares the reader for Jesus' cry from the cross in the words of Psalm 21:2. See "Markus 15,34," *ZNW* 74 (1983): 1–11.

[95] Against Brown, who says, "It was not in rage but in prayer that Jesus screamed his loud cry, even as the martyrs in Rev 6:10 shouted with a loud cry their prayer for God to intervene" (*Death of the Messiah*, II:1044). But prayer does not necessarily exclude rage against God, especially in light of Psalm 21 and Psalm 68. Schweizer interprets Jesus' cry not as incomprehension or a search for understanding, but as a "search for faith which knows that God is real even in times when the believer feels forsaken and when the resources of thinking and experience have been exhausted" (*The Good News According to Mark*, 353).

We have seen already that reading Psalms 40–2 along with Mark's passion narrative has allowed us to integrate and foreground nuances of betrayal, abandonment, and the search for understanding in the face of suffering. It also has helped to recognize the complexities of the scriptural justification for Jesus' suffering, to raise questions about the need for Jesus' death in an apocalyptic scenario, and to show that the suffering David plays an important role in depicting Jesus and his relationship with God. With the addition of Psalm 21, all of these nuances are reinforced, and deeper questions about the nature of Jesus' relationship with God are evoked. Of the PssLam evoked thus far in Mark, Psalm 21 develops the relationship between David and God and expresses the outrage of David's suffering the most. With the cry of Jesus from the cross in the voice of David from Psalm 21, David's outrage becomes Jesus'. He is the one who cries day (on the cross) and night (at Gethsemane), only to hear silence from God (cf. Ps 21:3). He is the one who struggles to understand his suffering in light of God's past relationship with Israel and himself (cf. Ps 21:4–6 and 10–11). He is the one whose life has become a mockery (cf. Ps 21:8–9)[96] and whose enemies take him for dead (cf. Ps 21:13–19). In the story of Jesus' crucifixion, Jesus embodies the suffering David from Psalm 21 not to foreshadow Jesus' vindication at the resurrection, but to express the outrage of Jesus' suffering and God's abandonment in the midst of it.[97] David rages against his abandonment, but not in rebellion against God; rather, he does so in a way that tries both to understand how and why God would do such a thing and to get God's attention so that God will deliver him from the suffering. He gains neither understanding nor deliverance from suffering in the psalm, and when read with Jesus' crucifixion, the search for understanding and deliverance becomes Jesus' and the audience's.

5.2.3.b   Sour wine and Psalm 68

Instead of understanding and deliverance after Jesus cries out, he gets more mocking: "And after some of the bystanders heard [his cry], they said, 'Look, he is calling Elijah'" (καί τινες τῶν παρεστηκότων ἀκούσαντες ἔλεγον· ἴδε Ἠλίαν φωνεῖ, Mark 15:35).[98] Then one of them runs and

---

[96] Senior, *The Passion of Jesus*, 121.

[97] Brown also appeals to the relationship between the psalmist and God as a way of understanding Jesus' situation, although he does not develop the idea enough. See *Death of the Messiah* II:1050–1.

[98] See Robbins, "Reversed Contextualization," 1172; Matera, *Kingship*, 124; and Senior, *The Passion of Jesus*, 124. Juel does not categorize this as a mockery, but as a misunderstanding: "Part of the narrative function of Jesus' last words is to generate one

gets a sponge, soaks it in "vinegar" (ὄξος), puts it on a reed, and gives it to Jesus to drink (15:36). Here we come to the last of the evocations of the PssLam in Mark, the one to Ps 68:22, which reads, "And they gave gall for my food, and for my thirst, they gave me vinegar to drink" (καὶ ἔδωκαν εἰς τὸ βρῶμά μου χολὴν καὶ εἰς τὴν δίψαν μου ἐπότισάν με ὄξος).[99] Of Psalms 21, 40, 41–2, and 68, Psalm 68 is the most direct in implicating God in the suffering of the psalmist, David. As the discussion of Psalm 68 in Chapter 4 showed, the suffering that is described is certainly painful and humiliating, but what is most disturbing to the psalmist is that God is involved by not stopping it. It is not the suffering against which the psalmist rages, it is the fact that God does not respond to it. The evocation of Psalm 68 in Mark 15:36 brings to a dramatic culmination the questions about God's will for Jesus' suffering.[100]

From its start, Psalm 68 uses hyperbolic language to cry out to God for deliverance in the midst of suffering. The first three verses of the body of the psalm use images of drowning and being swamped by the suffering that the psalmist is experiencing. In the end, he is tired and weary of crying out to God so much and not being answered. He goes on to describe the unjust treatment he has received at the hands of his enemies (verse 5), but just after that he talks of the transgressions that do not remain hidden from God (verses 6–7).[101] These first six verses of the body of the psalm are typical of the hyperbolic language used to describe the psalmist's suffering in many PssLam. As the psalm continues, however, the psalmist

---

final misunderstanding in a career that has been consistently misunderstood: even his last, anguished cry is misheard by the crowd who believe he is calling for Elijah" (*Messianic Exegesis*, 114; see also *Mark*, 223). See Moloney, *The Gospel of Mark*, 327 for a similar reading. After considering the Aramaic of Jesus' cry from the cross, and the idea that his onlookers would misunderstand it, Schweizer concludes, "Then with vs. 35 [the Greek-speaking church] presented the traditional incident where Jesus was offered a drink from a sponge as an act which revealed absurd misunderstanding and ridicule" (*The Good News According to Mark*, 352).

[99] Witherington does not think this verse is anything but a description of a normal act of quenching the thirst of Jesus. He calls sour wine the "Gatorade of its day." Witherington offers no justification for this flippant remark, and I agree with those who think that there is more to this detail than simply giving Jesus a refreshing drink. See *The Gospel of Mark*, 399.

[100] In his brief comments on the reception of Psalm 69 (MT) in the New Testament, Erich Zenger correctly comments that it is not only the reference to verse 22 that should be considered when seeking out the psalm's influence on the death of Jesus. Instead, the whole psalm should be considered as fundamental for understanding the basis of comparison for the suffering, death, and resurrection of Jesus. See Frank-Lothar Hossfeld and Erich Zenger, *Psalmen 51–100* (Herders Theologischer Kommentar zum Alten Testament; Freiburg im Breisgau; Basel; Wien: Herder, 2000), 281.

[101] The language of the psalmist's wrongdoings before God is usually passed over in the characterization of this and other PssLam as "Psalms of the Suffering Righteous Person."

gradually implicates God in his suffering and blames God for the misery he is experiencing. Because of God, he has borne insults and humiliation (verse 8) and become alienated from his family (verse 9). His pious acts result in nothing but insult and ridicule (verses 9–13). After several verses of petition for deliverance from his suffering, the psalmist appeals to God in an interesting and important way. He abandons his attempt to influence God's action by describing his affliction. Instead, he appeals to the mercy and compassion of God several times: "according to the abundance of your compassion, look upon me" (κατὰ τὸ πλῆθος τῶν οἰκτιρμῶν σου ἐπίβλεψον ἐπ᾽ ἐμέ, verse 17), "because I am afflicted, without delay listen to me" (ὅτι θλίβομαι, ταχὺ ἐπάκουσόν μου, verse 18), "for you know my insult and my shame and my humiliation; before you are all those who afflict me" (σὺ γὰρ γινώσκεις τὸν ὀνειδισμόν μου καὶ τὴν αἰσχύνην μου καὶ τὴν ἐντροπήν μου· ἐναντίον σου πάντες οἱ θλίβοντές με, verse 20). The psalmist lays out his suffering before God and then calls on God to rescue him *only because he is afflicted and suffering*. As a result he seems even more appalled that God is allowing his suffering than he is by the suffering itself. As I argued in Chapter 4, these verses amount to the psalmist trying to shame God into acting. They also act as a challenge to the idea that God should allow this suffering to happen. When thought of in Davidic terms, it is a challenge to the idea that God should allow the chosen king to suffer and, more importantly, that God should cause this suffering to happen.

The verse evoked in Mark 15:36 comes right at the end of the section just discussed. These overtones of Psalm 68 add even more outrage to the cry of Jesus in Mark 15:34 and his death cry in verse 37. Like David in Psalm 68, God sees Jesus' suffering, and yet there is no response. God allows it to happen. The cry of Jesus from the cross is a cry of the search for understanding in the midst of suffering, and a cry for mercy from God. Psalm 68, the most effusive and accusatory of the PssLam Mark uses, heightens the effect of this cry by emphasizing the absence of God's mercy as Jesus' suffering reaches its peak. Mark's audience has observed all the mistreatment, the mocking, the beatings, the scourging, and finally the crucifixion of Jesus. Surely God sees this as well. David's cry to God for salvation is more than just for deliverance from suffering: it is a cry that questions God's mercy, challenges God's inaction, and seeks an answer to why this must happen to God's chosen king of Israel. Mark's use of Psalm 68 clearly brings to the fore these challenges to God as Jesus' suffering is viewed by the audience. Mark's use of scripture here goes far beyond simple authoritative justification, pre-ordination, or prophecy of Jesus' suffering. In fact, it encourages serious theological questions for the audience to ponder.

6   Conclusion

The evocation of Psalms 21, 40, 41–2, and 68 add a great deal of depth to the story of Jesus' death in Mark. As Frank J. Matera and Douglas J. Moo have pointed out, these psalms point to David as a model for understanding who Jesus is in Mark.[102] But considering their basic points in more detail and carefully reading the passion narrative in tandem with these psalms has yielded many interesting insights and raised many important questions to consider. As we have seen, the two references to scriptural justification in Mark 14:21 and 49 form a complex statement because of Mark's incorporation of Psalms 21, 40, 41–2, and 68. The references to scriptural fulfillment are not just appeals to the authority of scripture or an indication of the pre-ordination of Jesus' suffering and death. They hold in tension God's will, the chosenness of a powerful royal figure, incomprehension in the face of suffering, and a willingness to challenge that suffering by demanding God's intervention and presence.

As a result of this complex scriptural justification, the necessity of Jesus' death becomes questionable in a general way. Further, the need for Jesus' death within the apocalyptic framework in which Mark presents it raises questions about the need for the death of the Messiah in the context of an apocalyptic scenario. This is most clearly seen in Mark's narrative with the order in which he uses these particular PssLam. Psalm 40 – the first of the PssLam Mark evokes in the passion narrative – is the least developed in its description of suffering and the least overt in its challenge to God in light of his absence in the midst of suffering. Psalm 41–2 – the next PssLam evoked by Mark – offers more vivid descriptions of suffering, but more importantly, the voice of the suffering David becomes more overtly challenging to God. He openly questions why God has abandoned him as his chosen king. The next psalm that Mark evokes is Psalm 21, which contains very vivid descriptions of suffering, but it also contains heartfelt and developed reflections by David regarding his relationship with God. These reflections deepen the sense of abandonment and heighten the discord between David's understanding and experience of God and God's actions. This communicates the distance from God that

---

[102] See Moo, *The Old Testament in the Gospel Passion Narratives*, 299–300; and Matera, *Kingship*, 131.

David perceives in the midst of his suffering. Lastly, Mark evokes Psalm 68, which contains an effusive appeal to God's mercy qua mercy. There is no elaborate argument to convince God to act. There is only the plain challenge directed toward God to act because David is suffering and God knows it. In Mark, Jesus is suffering, and it is quite apparent to God. Yet nothing happens to show that God wants to save Jesus from this moment. What happens on the third day certainly changes things for Jesus and the audience, but the images of suffering, of challenging the suffering, and of searching for an understanding for its purpose evoked by Mark from the PssLam linger, drawing the audience back to the cross even in the midst of the glory of the resurrection.

7

CONCLUSION

I have foregrounded a small dimension of the complex story of Jesus' suffering and death in Mark's Gospel. And even the evocation of only four PssLam by Mark proved to be much more involved than a simple appeal to these psalms as a source for narrating this portion of Jesus' life or a justification for his suffering. I do not think that the portrayal of David in these four PssLam offers the hermeneutical key to unlocking the meaning of Jesus' suffering and death in Mark. They cannot bear the weight of such a claim. Mark has shown itself to be a rich document that incorporates many different strands of early tradition and belief in a creative way, the result of which is a unique portrayal of the founding events of the movement later called Christianity. No one key exists to the meaning of the story; rather, many doors exist through which one can enter and view the whole dwelling. I hope that I have demonstrated the fruit of using one such key, namely incorporating the concerns of the psalms in their entirety into Mark's story of Jesus' suffering and death. I also hope that I have provoked some thought about the implications of this reading for Mark's story of Jesus as a whole. What follows are some possible avenues one might venture down to unpack some of the questions raised by my reading of Mark's passion narrative through the lens of the PssLam evoked there.

1   Jesus the warrior king?

It is fairly obvious that Mark presents Jesus at the beginning of his Gospel as a divine agent sent, in part, to confront and defeat the forces of evil in his world. His exorcisms, his testing in the wilderness, and his power over chaotic waters witness to this in abundance. Clearly, Jesus is a man of great power who wields it against evil. But by the middle of Mark 8, this powerful picture of Jesus is complemented by a picture of a Jesus who suffers – more specifically, one who must suffer (8:31) – who serves others, and who gives his life as a ransom for many (10:45). Beginning in Mark 8, this image of a powerful Jesus is held in tension with the image of Jesus as one who is relatively weak, at least in political and militaristic terms. In Chapter 5, I argued that Jesus was linked with David but distanced from his militaristic tendencies. In Chapter 6, I argued that David is still important, but David's suffering is one of the key images that Mark uses to characterize Jesus as a suffering king. So the question arises as to how to understand the relationship between the powerful Jesus and the suffering Jesus that are both in Mark and both important to understanding who Jesus is and what the meaning of his death might be.

In the opening chapter of this study, I discussed Joel Marcus' influential study *The Way of the Lord* in terms of his method of studying Mark's use of scripture. In light of some of the conclusions reached by my analysis, we should revisit briefly some of Marcus' insights into the meaning of Jesus' death in this work. Marcus argues that Jesus' actions as told in Mark can best be understood as that of a warrior king in an apocalyptic battle. Marcus situates Mark's story of Jesus within the social and historical context of the Jewish War of 66–72 CE and claims that the Gospel of Mark was written as an alternative to the earthly, militaristic aspirations of groups like the Zealots, who wished to overthrow the Roman empire and take over rule of Jerusalem and, thus, Israel. Instead of these earthly, militaristic aspirations, Mark offers an apocalyptic drama that includes the earthly suffering of the Messiah (Jesus) as the way to overthrow the powers of evil definitively. The end goal is the same for both groups in the earthly realm, namely overthrowing evil, but the earthly realm becomes situated in a larger, heavenly context for Mark's community, and Jesus' death is the means by which Jesus exercises his warrior status.

Marcus' reading of the Gospel of Mark is based on an apocalyptic scenario of the heavenly holy war. As a result, he interprets Jesus as a royal figure and a holy warrior who fights to eliminate evil on a heavenly and cosmic level. According to Marcus, Mark both affirms and qualifies the Davidic image of the warrior, and to answer the question of what kind of holy warrior Jesus is, Mark stretches "the Davidic mold to the breaking point."[1] Marcus rightly points out that Jesus is only fully revealed as king in Mark as he is tortured and crucified, and so "a messianism that is not informed by the notion of Jesus' suffering is one that is woefully inadequate."[2] In the end, according to Marcus, Jesus' suffering is vindicated by his resurrection and glorification in heaven, the rightful place for the Messiah. Marcus' treatment of the passion narrative expresses this view

---

[1] Marcus, *The Way of the Lord*, 151.   [2] Ibid., 150.

insofar as he interprets virtually every reference to scripture there as witnessing to the eschatological victory that will come after the suffering is over.[3] For Marcus, Jesus is not a warrior messiah in the earthly, political way that was hoped for in Israel, especially by the Zealots, but he is still a warrior king in the greater apocalyptic drama whereby God conquers evil. Jesus' suffering is the means by which God conquers evil, and only after his suffering is Jesus crowned heavenly king. So, for Marcus, Jesus is the divine warrior king who conquers through suffering and not through political or military violence.

As we saw in the opening chapter, there are many problems with Marcus' basic method of studying the references to scripture within Mark's narrative, and within the passion narrative in particular. Among them are a mischaracterization of the PssLam as Psalms of the Righteous Sufferer, a lack of attention to the individuality of each psalm, and an assertion of an eschatological trajectory of interpretation of these psalms in post-biblical Judaism where there is not enough data to claim such a trajectory. In his treatment of the passion narrative, he argues that there were at least four elements that contributed to the Markan portrayal of Jesus' death: Zechariah 9–14, which "provides Old Testament background for the site of an important part of the drama, the Mount of Olives, and for the prophecy of the restoration of the disciples"; Daniel 7, which provides the image of Jesus as eschatological judge; the Psalms of the Righteous Sufferer, which supply some key graphic details of Jesus' death; and the Isaian Servant Songs, which "suggest that this suffering is not just the prelude to God's eschatological victory but already in a sense *is* that victory."[4] I agree with the first two elements and their contribution to Mark's story, although more could be said about each. But as we have seen, the PssLam offer much more than details of Jesus' suffering. They allow Mark to express Jesus' suffering as that of a suffering Davidic king who cries out to God for understanding and challenges God's complacency in his suffering. Marcus' understanding of "the Davidic mold" is not complete, because he does not make the connection between David's suffering in the PssLam and Jesus' suffering in Mark. Jesus as suffering king makes some sense if one sees the suffering David of the PssLam as a model for Jesus in Mark's Gospel. This hardly corresponds to the picture of Jesus as a sheep led silently to the slaughter in the image of the Isaian servant, as Marcus argues. In fact, the Markan Jesus as suffering king chosen by God matches much more closely to the suffering David than to the Suffering Servant. This is not to deny that some elements from the

---

[3] Ibid., chapter 8.   [4] Ibid., 196.

servant passages in Deutero-Isaiah contribute to the complex picture of Jesus in Mark, but I do not think they are as prominent an image of Jesus as a suffering king like David in the PssLam.[5]

Marcus' reading is certainly attractive, because it provides a clear scenario that helps explain the suffering of Jesus. But in spite of his insistence on the need to include suffering as an integral part of Jesus' messiahship, Marcus relegates it to an important but only fleeting element of Mark's apocalyptic scenario. If the only reason for this suffering is to play a role in an apocalyptic drama whose end could be accomplished in a myriad other ways, then the theme of suffering so prevalent in Mark's Gospel loses its effectiveness as the literary and theological center of the story of Jesus. In other words, if the suffering were simply the way to get to resurrection and victory, then the cross would be a temporary and somewhat meaningless stepping-stone along a path that has nothing to do with suffering in the end, only vindication and heavenly glory. If this were the case for Mark, the suffering of Jesus leading to his death would not take two chapters to narrate, the risen Jesus would not be described as Ἰησοῦν . . . τὸν Ναζαρηνὸν τὸν ἐσταυρωμένον[6] (Mark 16:6), and the resurrection scene would have been much more triumphant, perhaps with the inclusion of appearance stories.[7] As it is, even after he is raised, Jesus is still "the crucified one."

This is not to say that an apocalyptic context is not present, informing the story of Jesus in the Gospel of Mark. It is only to say that the story must be attended to in all its dimensions, including the earthly dimensions that describe and evoke suffering in such a fundamental and powerful way. The earthly dimensions should not be explained away by the heavenly, apocalyptic dimensions, but they should be held in creative tension so that the meaning of Jesus' death and resurrection as portrayed by Mark can be explored in all its depth and mystery. One needs to attend to the apocalyptic worldview clearly present in Mark's Gospel, but Mark's story also must be allowed to speak for itself as one story of Jesus that emerged from such a worldview. Perhaps the story attempts to refashion or even challenge some of the rubrics of this worldview, such as the necessity of the Messiah being brutally executed as a key part in God's cosmic battle against evil, if this even was part of the worldview.

---

[5] See Watts, "Jesus' Death, Isaiah 53, and Mark 10:45: A Crux Revisited," 125–52; and Rikki E. Watts, *Isaiah's New Exodus and Mark* (WUNT 2; Tübingen: Mohr Siebeck, 1997). See also Marcus, "Mark and Isaiah," 449–66.

[6] The use of the perfect tense here is telling, indicating either the ongoing effects of Jesus' crucifixion or his crucified state, even after resurrection.

[7] This assumes that Mark originally ended at 16:8, which I affirm.

Jesus is certainly a king in Mark. But Mark's Jesus is a king like the suffering David of the PssLam, one who experiences the realities of human rejection and suffering, expresses the horrors of his suffering, and cries out to God in the midst of that suffering, challenging God's perceived absence and complacency.

2   The veil and the centurion

At the end of his treatment of the death of Jesus, Francis J. Moloney says, "The Christology of the Gospel of Mark may be satisfactorily resolved as the veil of the temple tears asunder and a Roman centurion, gazing upon Jesus in his moment of death, confesses his faith in Jesus as the Son of God (15:38–39). Yet the narrative cries out for a more satisfactory dénouement: what of the disciples, and what of God?"[8]

I am not sure that it is the case that the Christology is resolved by the rending of the veil and the centurion's statement. Certainly, the veil is a supernatural sign that something important has happened at the death of Jesus, but it is not self-interpreting. One could read this both as positively revealing that the powers of the heavenly world are responding to Jesus' death by opening up new religious possibilities for Jews, breaking the barriers that separate the holiest of places, the place where God communes with Israel, from the world. Now, the world is God's dwelling-place. On the other hand, it could also be read as the powers of the heavenly world reacting to Jesus' death with wrath. The tearing of the temple veil could then be a sign of judgment upon the Jews for allowing God's agent, God's Messiah, to die such a horrible death. Either way, Jesus' death reveals something important.

In light of the presence of the PssLam I have discussed thus far, the question of Christology is not resolved by the rending of the veil. The question of Christology is not just one about Jesus' identity: it is also about Jesus' relationship with God. Supernatural signs that happen around Jesus that do not stop his suffering raise questions about the overall purpose of Jesus' suffering. If God can rend the veil in the temple, then certainly God could have thought of another way to effect salvation than to allow his Messiah to suffer on the cross. The presence of the PssLam, especially that of Psalm 21, within the story of Jesus' suffering encourages the reader to raise these questions and search for answers to them. They do not encourage skepticism or doubt but faithful questioning that drives one to search deeper for the answers to the questions that swirl around

---

[8] Moloney, *The Gospel of Mark*, 331.

the relationship between God and Jesus, and therefore between God and humans. Moloney does this at times:

> Although not explicit in the text, the reader is aware that it is as 'Son' that Jesus cries out 'my God.' This leads to a further important feature in the logic of the Markan narrative. Jesus' question leads the reader to wonder: if this is the way God deals with his Son, what kind of God is this? The answer to that question will not be found within the passion narrative . . . The question Jesus poses to God in 15:34 leads into the telling of the action of God in 16:1–8. There, although never explicitly mentioned, God is the main protagonist.[9]

It is correct for Moloney to raise the question about God's role in Jesus' suffering, as I have been arguing, but in contrast to Moloney I do not think the resurrection fully resolves it. The resurrection does not explain the deeper question of the need for the Son to suffer, even within an apocalyptic context. Again, the need for Jesus to suffer just to get to the resurrection does not make the suffering more palatable. We have seen the problems with characterizing Jesus as the Suffering Righteous One, as well as the problems with situating Jesus' suffering and death within a scenario of an apocalyptic holy war. Mark's references to Psalm 21 develop Jesus' relationship with God in a way that questions the purpose of his suffering, rather than providing a scriptural justification for it. The reference to Psalm 68 two verses later brings to a climax the perceived abandonment of Jesus by God.

In light of all this, one should think of the centurion's statement in Mark 15:39 as a continuation of the mocking that Jesus has experienced prior to this point in the narrative. Up to the point of the centurion's statement, Jesus has been disappointed by his three most important followers when they fell asleep in his deepest moment of need, handed over by a trusted member of his closest circle of companions, abandoned by the rest of those companions, mocked and physically maltreated by the Jewish authorities and Pilate's soldiers, crucified, and then mocked again on the cross by the chief priests and scribes, the passers-by, and those crucified with him. He cries out in anguish to God only to be left without an answer. Throughout this narrative, the PssLam have played an important role in narrating these events, and, in large part, they have functioned to call into question God's role in these events. In light of the narrative elements just described, it seems best to read the centurion's statement as adding to

---

[9] Ibid., 327.

the mocking and maltreatment of Jesus and furthering the questioning of God's relationship with Jesus.

At the very least, the statement should not be read as a confession of faith, because doing so would go against the pattern of the characters' actions from the beginning of chapter 14. There is no reason, narratively speaking, why the centurion should stand out as the one character since the beginning of chapter 14 who acts positively by faithfully confessing Jesus as Son of God. Certainly, one could read it as an ironic statement that reveals to the reader the true identity of Jesus. But one need not read it as a confession of faith by a Gentile in order to capture this irony. In fact, the irony is greater if the statement is read negatively – the head of those who led Jesus to crucifixion after they beat him and mocked him as a king declares in disbelief, "This man was truly a son of God?" (ἀληθῶς οὗτος ὁ ἄνθρωπος υἱὸς θεοῦ ἦν; with the addition of the question mark to capture the sarcasm perhaps evident in his voice). In other words, when the centurion saw how Jesus died – alone, abandoned, crying out to God with no answer – he questioned how a son of God, i.e., a king, could have died in such a way. The irony does not disappear because the reader knows from the beginning of the Gospel that Jesus is indeed the Son of God. But the way that Jesus is Son of God is revealed here by his death and the reaction to his death by the sarcastic centurion.

3   The rest of the story

Without the category of the vindication of the Suffering Righteous (or innocent) One from the PssLam in the forefront when these psalms are evoked in Mark's passion narrative, one begins to notice some features of Mark's overall narrative that are usually passed over. First, like David in at least two of these four psalms, Jesus is not innocent. He does not admit sin, as David does at the beginning of Psalms 21 and 40, but Jesus dies for that which he is accused, namely, being the Son of the Blessed One. In his trial before the high priest, the chief priests, the elders, and the scribes, Jesus is silent before his false accusers in Mark 15:55–61a. But then the high priest asks him, "Are you the Messiah, the Son of the Blessed One?" Jesus answers, "I am," and then he quotes Ps 110:1 and Dan 7:13: "And you will see the Son of Man sitting at the right hand of the Power and coming with the clouds of heaven." These are not the words of an innocent man before his accusers.[10] The innocence of Jesus does not

---

[10] This is against Moloney: "Jesus' response [at his arrest in Gethsemane] initiates another theme that will recur across the passion story: his innocence." He goes on to

seem to be the issue in Mark's passion narrative. Instead, Jesus dies for being the Son of the Blessed One, something that indicates his success in living God's will fully. If Jesus were innocent, then his punishment would be random and somewhat meaningless for Mark. Because Jesus died for being the Son of the Blessed One, Mark makes a strong statement about the powers of evil that hold sway in the society of his time and the need to confront them at every turn.

This takes us back to the three predictions of Jesus' suffering, death, and resurrection in 8:31, 9:31, and 10:33–4. All three predictions talk about Jesus' impending arrest, mistreatment, death, and resurrection. Only the prediction in 8:31 says that these things must happen (δεῖ), but it seems to be assumed in the other two. The fact that all this must happen is oftentimes interpreted as indicating divine design or plan.[11] Also implied in this interpretation is the idea that all this must happen so that Jesus may be vindicated at the resurrection. But there is nothing in these three predictions to necessitate a vindicatory relationship between Jesus' suffering and death, on the one hand, and Jesus' resurrection, on the other hand. In other words, without the overtone of vindication in these four PssLam, or the idea of Jesus' death as the death of an innocent person, then the predictions could be thought of as having some other kind of logic than that of prediction of wrongful suffering and vindicating resurrection. They could just describe the reasonable course of Jesus' life based upon Mark's presentation of him as God's agent who carries out the will of God in the face of the evil that he confronts.

In 14:21 and 14:49, Mark has Jesus talk about his death as "going as it is written of him" and "in order that scripture may be fulfilled." These two qualifications of Jesus' death are not directly preceded or followed by specific references to scripture, and so they do not function

argue that "the readers and listeners to the story know that Judas and his colleagues are the guilty characters in this encounter . . . The general background of the suffering of the righteous one is sufficient for Jesus' indications that his violent arrest is the fulfillment of scripture" (ibid., 298). Mark's presentation of Jesus' lack of innocence is different from the other Gospels. In the Gospel of Matthew, Jesus gives the more ambiguous answer, "You said" (σὺ εἶπας) (26:64), and he does not defend himself at the chief priest's accusations before Pilate. However, his lack of defense can be taken as acceptance of the charges, or at least an acceptance of his inevitable death as a result of his actions against the religious authorities. The Gospel of Luke clearly portrays Jesus as innocent, but Jesus does not cry out in the words of Psalm 21 in the Gospel. The Gospel of John also portrays Jesus as innocent, but he is fairly indifferent to the whole matter. Again, Jesus does not cry out in the words of Psalm 21 in this Gospel either. So, the portrayal of Jesus as an innocent victim is more determined by the narrative of each individual Gospel than it is by the evocation of Psalm 21.

[11] Ibid., 173; Donahue and Harrington, *The Gospel of Mark*, 261.

as formulaic quotations as they would in the Gospel of Matthew.[12] They are general statements regarding how one is to understand Jesus' death, namely, as according to scripture, and they are most frequently understood as describing Jesus' death as divinely planned, foretold by scripture, or pre-determined in some similar way.[13] The four PssLam are among the many scripture passages evoked in the passion narrative of Mark to which the reader/hearer is directed. By reading these PssLam as I proposed in this study, with David's variegated attempts at persuading God to act, including protest, outrage, anger, description of suffering, and conditional praise, the general appeal to scripture in Mark should be read to include an element of faithful challenge to God's perceived inaction in the face of suffering. So, instead of understanding the qualifications of Jesus' death as predicting it in some divinely pre-determined way, the PssLam make the situation more complex by adding an element of challenge to God's perceived inaction in the course of Jesus' suffering.[14] In Mark, it could be said that Jesus "goes as it is written of him," challenging his suffering and God's perceived part in it, thus encouraging the reader to challenge understandings of God that allow for divine plans of suffering and shameful death, no matter what lies at the other end of them.

The characterization of Jesus in relation to God, and ultimately the Christology and theology of Mark, could also be affected by this reading

---

[12] Although one could make a case that the reference in Mark 14:49 refers to the quotation from Zech 13:7 in Mark 14:27, given the events that occur at this point in the story. However, this is far from certain, and the uncertainty leaves open the possibility of it referring more generally to the fulfillment of scripture, including the PssLam evoked up to this point in the passion narrative.

[13] Moloney, *The Gospel of Mark*, 284. Donahue and Harrington say that in 14:21 "the divine necessity of suffering is stressed as in the Passion predictions" (*The Gospel of Mark*, 394). Vincent Taylor says that 14:21 suggests that the death of Jesus is "in accordance with the divine purpose" (*The Gospel According to St. Mark*, 541). Adela Yarbro Collins argues, "The fated nature of Jesus' death is expressed most clearly in the references to the scriptures, which foretell or determine it, but also in the way in which God has receded as a character in the narrative . . . The personal God recedes and the impersonal force of Scripture controls the events" ("From Noble Death to Crucified Messiah," 485).

[14] Sjef van Tilborg makes a similar observation about Matthew's use of Psalm 22: "The more intensive use of Psalm 22 in Matthew's text causes an intensification of the factual suffering. In a sense we can say that it has become even more absurd and repellent. The narrative is now about a 'son of God' who hangs on the cross in a burial place and who has been stripped by pagan dogs and is being ogled by them. The more extensive use of the psalms makes it even more difficult to 'explain' the suffering of the Messiah. If the use of Psalm 22 is intended as proof by prophecy, the least we can say is that the narrator of Matthew's gospel has not been very successful" ("Language, Meaning, Sense and Reference: Matthew's Passion Narrative and Psalm 22," *HvTSt* 44 [1998]: 906).

of the PssLam in Mark's passion narrative. If the story of Jesus' suffering and death is read or heard with the PssLam in mind, then the characterization of Jesus as the Suffering Righteous One might just have to give way to a Jesus who cries out for God to take notice of his suffering and answer his pleas. Instead of a Jesus who goes to his death willingly without a word, the PssLam bring up the possibility of a Jesus who goes to his death challenging God to answer his cries from the cross.

Again, I do not want to claim that the entire meaning of Jesus' death in Mark revolves around the proper understanding of the PssLam. There are certainly elements in the story that support the vindication of Jesus at the resurrection and the idea that Jesus voluntarily dies according to God's will. But reading these psalms as I have argued makes these issues a bit more complex, perhaps injecting a cautionary note to triumphalistic readings of the resurrection in Mark.[15] Instead, the reader is nudged to consider Jesus' death as resulting from his reluctance to compromise his attempts to embody God's will authentically, in contrast to an understanding of Jesus' suffering and death as something that God willed as part of a pre-ordained plan that cannot be changed. Jesus' successful attempt to do God's will is not about obeying the command to die on the cross without question. It is about embodying God's desires even to the point of death. It is about confronting evil without backing down, as Jesus does through his exorcisms, healings, and confrontations with those who would stand in the way of him doing God's will of living for others. If Jesus opted out of his suffering and death, then his efforts to confront evil would all be for naught, because he could not endure to the end (cf. Mark 13:13) as a witness to God's Kingdom at hand. His willingness to go through torture and execution is not about fulfilling God's plan to have the Messiah die; rather, it is about fulfilling God's will by witnessing to God's liberating reign all the way to the point of death. For Mark, this is what it truly means to be Son of God.

The question of Jesus' relationship with God is never fully resolved in Mark, even in the resurrection at the end of the story. Yes, Jesus is raised by God, but there are some curious elements to the scene that prevent me from fully accepting an understanding of the resurrection that claims that

---

[15] "Functional avoidance of Good Friday among many Christians is a heresy of long standing. Its tacit justification seems to be that Easter Sunday signals a victory so complete that God effectively annihilated Golgotha. Such confusion makes for a theology that is not merely bad, but heartless and even dangerous. In place of the Christian gospel of God's triumph, it substitutes the bad news of human triumphalism" (C. Clifton Black, "The Persistence of the Wounds," in *Lament: Reclaiming Practices in Pulpit, Pew, and Public Square* [ed. Sally A. Brown and Patrick D. Miller; Louisville, KY: WJK, 2005], 56).

Jesus was vindicated by God in the end. I will make a few points as a way of anticipating possible further lines of thought.

According to the Oxford English Dictionary, the idea of vindication presumes some sense of unjust condemnation that must be rectified or some sense that something went wrong that now has to be proven otherwise. An overtone of vengeance or triumph could also be implied. But the eight verses in chapter 16 that narrate the resurrection are far from triumphalistic, with a spare description of the resurrection, a lack of resurrection appearances, the fear of the women as the last word of the narrative, and the fact that even though Jesus has been raised he is still "the crucified one." This last epithet is most telling, because the Greek term used is ἐσταυρωμένον, a perfect passive participle, giving the nuance that Jesus' shameful death happened in the past but has ongoing effects, or even a stative quality, in the present. According to Mark, the resurrection does not undo the suffering and death that Jesus underwent, and his suffering and death have an enduring quality in and effect on the present.[16] The relationship between the crucifixion and resurrection of Jesus seems not to be one where the resurrection vindicates Jesus' crucifixion in the sense that it undoes it or proves that Jesus was really innocent of the crimes for which he was crucified. Instead, there seems to be a symbiotic relationship, where the crucifixion conditions the meaning of the resurrection as much as the resurrection conditions the crucifixion. This is not a linear story where resurrection solves the problem of suffering. It is a circular story where suffering and resurrection seem equally and inseparably important to Mark; therefore, we cannot think of the resurrection as the last word in Mark. The last word will come only in the last days when "you will see the Son of Man sitting at the right hand of the Power and coming with the clouds of heaven."

The cross is what makes the story of Jesus so compelling in Mark. Anything that sidesteps the horror or glorifies the suffering distorts Mark's presentation of Jesus' death. Mark's appeal to scripture was one way that he tried to make sense of Jesus' suffering – a common practice in early Christianity. But as we have seen, the use of PssLam evoked in the passion narrative does not explain away or sidestep the horror by claiming that it is okay because God willed it or by making it the first episode in a divine plan of eschatological vindication of the Righteous Sufferer. But

---

[16] Jack Dean Kingsbury notices the detail of the perfect tense, and claims something similar regarding the idea that the resurrection does not "undo" the cross. But he interprets the perfect tense as pointing to the cross as the "decisive event in Jesus' ministry" (*Christology*, 134).

inclusion of these psalms in the story of Jesus' suffering weaves into the story an ancient tradition of endurance, crying out to God in the midst of suffering, and faithful dissent. It seems that Mark's attempt at understanding Jesus' suffering and death is just as much about Mark's appreciation of the horror of human suffering as it is about the hope that belief in Jesus' resurrection can generate for Mark's readers.

WORKS CITED

Achtemeier, Paul J. *Mark*. 3rd edn. Philadelphia: Fortress, 1986.

Ackroyd, Peter R. "נצח – εἰς τέλος." *ExpTim* 80 (1968–9): 126.

Aejmelaeus, Anneli. "Translation Technique and the Intention of the Translator." Pp. 65–77 in *On the Trail of the Septuagint Translators*. Ed. A. Aejmelaeus. Kampen, The Netherlands: Kok Pharos Publishing House, 1993.

"What We Talk about When We Talk about Translation Technique." Pp. 531–52 in *X Congress of the International Organization for Septuagint and Cognate Studies: Oslo 1998*. Ed. Bernard A. Taylor. Atlanta: Society of Biblical Literature, 2001.

Ahearne-Kroll, Stephen P. "'Who Are My Mother and My Brothers?' Family Relations and Family Language in the Gospel of Mark." *JR* 81 (2001): 1–25.

Alexander, Philip S. "Incantations and Books of Magic." Pp. 342–79 in vol. III of *The History of the Jewish People in the Age of Jesus Christ*. Ed. Emil Schürer *et al*. 3 vols. Edinburgh: T & T Clark, 1995.

"Retelling the Old Testament." Pp. 101–21 in *It is Written: Scripture Citing Scripture. Essays in Honour of Barnabas Lindars*. Ed. D. A. Carson and H. G. M. Williamson. Cambridge: Cambridge University Press, 1988.

Alsup, John E. "Typology." Pp. 682–5 in vol. VI of *ABD*. Ed. David Noel Freedman. 6 vols. New York: Doubleday, 1992.

Alter, Robert. *The Pleasures of Reading in an Ideological Age*. New York: Norton, 1989.

and Frank Kermode. *The Literary Guide to the Bible*. Cambridge, MA: Harvard University Press, 1987.

Attridge, Harold W. *The Epistle to the Hebrews*. Hermeneia Series. Philadelphia: Fortress, 1989.

"The Psalms in Hebrews." Pp. 101–12 in *The Psalms in Community*. Ed. Harold W. Attridge and Margot Fassler. Atlanta and Leiden: Society of Biblical Literature and Brill, 2004.

Auffret, P. "'O bonheurs de l'homme attentif au faible!' Etude structurelle du Psaume 41." *Bijdragen* 50 (1989): 2–23.

Aune, David E. *Revelation 17–22*. WBC 52c. Nashville: Thomas Nelson, 1998.

Aus, Roger David. *The Wicked Tenants and Gethsemane: Isaiah in the Wicked Tenants' Vineyard, and Moses and the High Priest in Gethsemane: Judaic Traditions in Mark 12:1–9 and 14:32–42*. University of South Florida International Studies in Formative Christianity and Judaism 4. Atlanta: Scholars Press, 1996.

Baarda, T. "The Sentences of Syriac Menander." Pp. 583–606 in vol. II of *OTP*. Ed. James H. Charlesworth. 2 vols. New York: Doubleday, 1985.

Barbour R. S. "Gethsemane in the Tradition of the Passion." *NTS* 16 (1969–70): 231–51.

Barrett, C. K. "The Background of Mark 10:45." Pp. 1–18 in *Essays: Studies in Honour of T. W. Manson*. Ed. A. J. B. Higgins. Manchester: Manchester University Press, 1959.

Bassler, Jouette M. "A Man for All Seasons: David in Rabbinic and New Testament Literature." *Int* 40 (2, 1986): 156–69.

Begrich, J. "Das priesterliche Heilsorakel." *ZAW* 52 (1934): 81–92.

Ben-Porat, Ziva. "The Poetics of Literary Allusion." *PTL: A Journal for Descriptive Poetics and Theory of Literature* 1 (1976): 105–28.

Best, Ernest. "Mark's Readers: A Profile." Pp. 839–58 in *The Four Gospels*. Ed. F. Van Segbroeck *et al*. Leuven: Peeters, 1994.

    The Temptation and the Passion: The Markan Soteriology. 2nd edn. Cambridge: Cambridge University Press, 1990.

Betz, Hans Dieter. "The Early Christian Miracle Story: Some Observations on the Form Critical Problem." *Semeia* 11 (1978): 69–81.

Black, C. Clifton. "The Persistence of the Wounds." Pp. 47–58 in *Lament: Reclaiming Practices in Pulpit, Pew, and Public Square*. Ed. Sally A. Brown and Patrick D. Miller. Louisville, KY: WJK, 2005.

Bourdieu, Pierre and Loïc J. D. Wacquant. *An Invitation to Reflexive Sociology*. Chicago: University of Chicago Press, 1992.

Boyd-Taylor, Cameron, Peter C. Austin and Andrey Feuerverger. "The Assessment of Manuscript Affiliation with a Probabilistic Framework: A Study of Alfred Rahlfs's Core Manuscript Groupings for the Greek Psalter." Pp. 98–124 in *The Old Greek Psalter: Studies in Honor of Albert Pietersma*. Ed. Robert J. V. Hiebert, Claude E. Cox and Peter J. Gentry. JSOTSup 332. Sheffield: Sheffield Academic Press, 2001.

Bratcher, Robert G. and William D. Reyburn. *A Handbook on Psalms*. New York: United Bible Societies, 1991.

Brenton, L. C. L. *The Septuagint with Apocrypha: Greek and English*. Grand Rapids, MI: Zondervan, 1982; originally published in 1851.

Broadhead, Edwin K. *Prophet, Son, Messiah: Narrative Form and Function in Mark 14–16*. JSNTSup 97. Sheffield: Sheffield Academic Press, 1994.

Brown, Raymond E. *The Death of the Messiah: From Gethsemane to the Grave*. 2 vols. New York: Doubleday, 1994.

Brueggemann, Walter. "The Psalms as Prayer." Pp. 33–66 in *The Psalms in the Life of Faith*. Ed. Patrick D. Miller. Minneapolis: Fortress, 1995.

Bultmann, Rudolf. *The History of the Synoptic Tradition*. Trans. John Marsh. Peabody, MA: Hendrickson, 1963.

Burchard, Christoph. "Markus 15,34." *ZNW* 74 (1983): 1–11.

Burger C. *Jesus als Davidssohn: Eine traditionsgeschichtliche Untersuchung*. FRLANT 98. Göttingen: Vandenhoeck & Ruprecht, 1970.

Cartledge, Tony W. "Conditional Vows in the Psalms of Lament: A New Approach to an Old Problem." Pp. 77–94 in *The Listening Heart: Essays in Wisdom and the Psalms in Honor of Roland E. Murphy*. Ed. Kenneth G. Hoglund. JSOTSup 58. Sheffield: JSOT Press, 1987.

Catchpole, D. R. "The 'Triumphal' Entry." Pp. 319–35 in *Jesus and the Politics of His Day*. Ed. E. Bammel and C. F. D. Moule. Cambridge: Cambridge University Press, 1984.

Chandler, James K. "Romantic Allusiveness." *Critical Inquiry* 8 (3, 1982): 461–87.

Charlesworth, James H. and James A. Sanders. "More Psalms of David." Pp. 611–24 in vol. II of *OTP*. Ed. James H. Charlesworth. 2 vols. New York: Doubleday, 1985.

Chester, Andrew. "Citing the Old Testament." Pp. 141–69 in *It is Written: Scripture Citing Scripture. Essays in Honour of Barnabas Lindars*. Ed. D. A. Carson and H. G. M. Williamson. Cambridge: Cambridge University Press, 1988.

Childs, Brevard S. *Introduction to the Old Testament as Scripture*. Philadelphia: Fortress, 1979.

"Psalm Titles and Midrashic Exegesis." *JSS* 16 (2, 1971): 137–50.

Chilton, Bruce D. "Commenting on the Old Testament (with Particular Reference to the Pesharim, Philo, and the Mekilta)." Pp. 122–40 in *It is Written: Scripture Citing Scripture. Essays in Honour of Barnabas Lindars*. Ed. D. A. Carson and H. G. M. Williamson. Cambridge: Cambridge University Press, 1988.

"Jesus *ben David*: Reflections on the *Davidssohnfrage*." *JSNT* 14 (1982): 88–112.

The Temple of Jesus: His Sacrificial Program within a Cultural History of Sacrifice. University Park, PA: Pennsylvania State University Press, 1992.

Clayton, Jay and Eric Rothstein. "Figures in the Corpus: Theories of Influence and Intertextuality." Pp. 3–36 in *Influence and Intertextuality in Literary History*. Ed. Jay Clayton and Eric Rothstein. Madison: University of Wisconsin Press, 1991.

Collins, John J. *The Apocalyptic Imagination: An Introduction to Jewish Apocalyptic Literature*. 2nd edn. Grand Rapids, MI: Eerdmans, 1998.

Apocalypticism in the Dead Sea Scrolls. London: Routledge, 1997.

Daniel: A Commentary on the Book of Daniel. Hermeneia. Minneapolis: Fortress, 1993.

Jewish Wisdom in the Hellenistic Age. Louisville, KY: Westminster John Knox Press, 1997.

The Scepter and the Star: The Messiahs of the Dead Sea Scrolls and Other Ancient Literature. New York: Doubleday, 1995.

"The Son of Man in First Century Judaism." *NTS* 38 (1992): 448–66.

Cordes, Ariane. "Theologische Interpretation in der Septuaginta: Beobachtungen am Beispiel von Psalm 76 LXX." Pp. 105–24 in *Der Septuaginta-Psalter: Sprachliche und theologische Aspekte*. Ed. Erich Zenger. HBST 32. Freiburg: Herder, 2001.

Cox, Claude E. "Schaper's Eschatology Meets Kraus's Theology of the Psalms." Pp. 289–311 in *The Old Greek Psalter: Studies in Honour of Albert Pietersma*. Ed. Robert J. V. Hiebert, Claude E. Cox, and Peter J. Gentry. JSOTSS 332. Sheffield: Sheffield Academic Press, 2001.

Craigie, Peter C. *Psalms 1–50*. WBC 19. Waco, TX: Word Books, 1983.

Cranfield, C. E. B. *The Gospel According to Saint Mark*. Reprinted with supplementary notes. Cambridge: Cambridge University Press, 1966.

Culpepper, R. Alan. "Mark 10:50: Why Mention the Garment?" *JBL* 101 (March 1982): 131–2.

Daly-Denton, Margaret. *David in the Fourth Gospel: The Johannine Reception of the Psalms*. AGJU 47. Leiden: Brill, 2000.

Dibelius, Martin. "Gethsemane." *Crozier Quarterly* 12 (1935): 254–65.

Dio Cassius. *History of Rome*. Trans. and ed. Earnest Cary. LCL. Cambridge, MA: Harvard University Press, 1914–27.

Dodd, C. H. *According to the Scriptures: The Sub-structure of New Testament Theology*. London: Nesbet & Co., 1952.

Donahue, John R. "Temple, Trial, and Royal Christology (Mark 14:53–65)." Pp. 61–79 in *The Passion in Mark*. Ed. Werner H. Kelber. Philadelphia: Fortress, 1976.

—— and Daniel J. Harrington. *The Gospel of Mark*. Sacra Pagina 2. Collegeville, MN: Liturgical Press, 2002.

Douglas, Michael C. "Power and Praise in the Hodayot: A Literary Critical Study of 1QH 9:1–18:14." Ph.D. diss., The University of Chicago, 1998.

Dowd, Sharon Echols. *Prayer, Power, and the Problem of Suffering*. SBLDS 105. Atlanta: Scholars Press, 1988.

Duff, Paul Brooks. "The March of the Divine Warrior and the Advent of the Greco-Roman King: Mark's Account of Jesus' Entry into Jerusalem." *JBL* 111/1 (1992): 55–71.

Duling, D. C. "Solomon, Exorcism, and the Son of David." *Harvard Theological Review* 68 (1975): 235–52.

—— "Testament of Solomon: A New Translation and Introduction." Pp. 935–87 in vol. I of *OTP*. Ed. James H. Charlesworth. 2 vols. New York: Doubleday, 1985.

Evans, Craig A. *Mark 8:27–16:20*. WBC 34B. Nashville: Thomas Nelson Publishers, 2001.

Feldman, Louis H. "Josephus' Portrait of David." *HUCA* 60 (2001): 129–50.

Firmage, Edwin. "Zoology." Pp. 1109–67 in vol. VI of *ABD*. Ed. David Noel Freedman. 6 vols. New York: Doubleday, 1992.

Fisher, Loren R. "Betrayed by Friends: An Expository Study of Psalm 22." *Int* 18 (1, 1964): 20–38.

Fitzmyer, Joseph A. *The Gospel According to Luke I–IX*. AB 28. New York: Doubleday, 1981.

Garcia Martinez, Florentino and Eiber J. C. Tigchelaar, eds. *The Dead Sea Scrolls Study Edition*. 2 vols. Leiden, Grand Rapids, MI: Brill and Eerdmans, 1997, 1998.

Garner, Richard. *From Homer to Tragedy: The Art of Allusion in Greek Poetry*. London: Routledge, 1990.

Gerstenberger, E. S. *Psalms; Part 1: With an Introduction to Cultic Poetry*. FOTL 14. Grand Rapids, MI: Eerdmans, 1988.

Glasson, T. F. "David Links with the Betrayal of Jesus." *ExpTim* 85 (1973–4): 118–19.

Gnilka, Joachim. *Das Evangelium nach Markus*. EKKNT 2. 2 vols. Zurich: Benziger Verlag, 1978, 1979.

Good, Deirdre J. *Jesus the Meek King*. Harrisburg, PA: Trinity Press International, 1999.

Grant, Robert M. and David Tracy. *A Short History of the Interpretation of the Bible.* 2nd edn. Fortress, 1984.

Guichard, Daniel. "La Reprise du Psalm 22 dans le récit de la mort de Jésus (Marc 15, 21–41)." *FoiVie* 88 (1988): 59–64.

Gundry, Robert H. *Mark: A Commentary on His Apology for the Cross.* Grand Rapids, MI: Eerdmans, 1993.

Gunkel, Hermann. *Introduction to the Psalms: The Genres of the Religious Lyric of Israel.* Completed by Joachim Begrich. Trans. James D. Nogalski. Macon, GA: Mercer University Press, 1998.

Häfner, Gerd. *"Nützlich zur Belehrung" (2 Tim 3, 16): Die Rolle der Schrift in den Pastoralbriefen im Rahmen der Paulusrezeption.* HBSt. Freiburg: Herder, 2000.

Hatina, Thomas R. *In Search of a Context: The Function of Scripture in Mark's Narrative.* JSNTSup 232. Sheffield: Sheffield Academic Press, 2002.

Hays, Richard B. *Echoes of Scripture in the Letters of Paul.* New Haven: Yale University Press, 1989.

and Joel B. Green. "The Use of the Old Testament by New Testament Writers." Pp. 222–38 in *Hearing the New Testament: Strategies for Interpretation.* Ed. Joel B. Green. Grand Rapids, MI: Eerdmans, 1995.

Hebel, Udo J. "Towards a Descriptive Poetics of Allusion." Pp. 135–64 in *Intertextuality.* Ed. Heinrich F. Plett. Berlin: Walter de Gruyter, 1991.

Heidler, Johannes. "Die Verwendung von Psalm 22 in Kreuzigungsbericht des Markus: Ein Beitrag zur Frage nach der Christologie des Markus." Pp. 26–34 in *Christi Leidenspsalm: Arbeiten zum 22. Psalm.* Ed. Hartmut Genest. Neukirchener-Vluyn: Neukirchener, 1996.

Heil, John Paul. "Mark 14:1–52: Narrative Structure and Reader Response." *Bib* 71 (1990): 305–32.

Hengel, Martin. *The Atonement: The Study of the Origins of the Doctrine in the New Testament.* Trans. John Bowden. London: SCM Press, 1981.

Crucifixion in the Ancient World and the Folly of the Message of the Cross. Trans. John Bowden. Philadelphia: Fortress, 1977.

"'Sit at My Right Hand!' The Enthronement of Christ at the Right Hand of God and Psalm 110:1." Pp. 119–225 in *Studies in Early Christology.* Edinburgh: T&T Clark, 1995.

Herodotus. *History, Books 1 and 2.* Trans. A. D. Godley. LCL. Cambridge, MA: Harvard University Press, 1920.

Hirth, Volkmar. "Psalm 22 als zeitumspannendes Gebet." Pp. 13–25 in *Christi Leidenspsalm: Arbeiten zum 22. Psalm.* Ed. Hartmut Genest. Vluyn: Neukirchener, 1996.

Hooker, Morna D. *The Gospel According to Saint Mark.* Peabody, MA: Hendrickson, 1991.

Jesus and the Servant. London: SPCK, 1959.

Hossfeld, Frank-Lothar and Erich Zenger. *Die Psalmen I.* Würzburg: Echter, 1993.

Psalmen 51–100. Herders Theologischer Kommentar zum Alten Testament. Freiburg im Breisgau; Basel; Wien: Herder, 2000.

Houlden, Leslie. "Why Were the Disciples Ever Called Disciples?" *Theology* 105 (Nov./Dec., 2002): 411–17.

Hutton, Rodney R. "Korah, 2." Pp. 100–1 in vol. IV of *ABD.* Ed. D. N. Freedman. 6 vols. New York: Doubleday, 1992.

Irsigler, Hubert. "Psalm 22: Endgestalt, Bedeuten und Function." Pp. 193–239 in *Beiträge zur Psalmenforschung: Psalm 2 und 22*. Ed. Josef Schreiner. Würzburg: Echter Verlag, 1988.

Jeremias, Gert. *Der Lehrer der Gerechtigkeit*. SUNT 2. Göttingen: Vandenhoeck & Ruprecht, 1963.

Jeremias, Joachim. *The Parables of Jesus*. 2nd rev. edn. Trans. S. H. Hooke. New York: Charles Scribner's Son, 1972.

Jobes, Karen H. and Moises Silva. *Invitation to the Septuagint*. Grand Rapids, MI and Carlisle: Baker Academic and Paternoster, 2000.

Josephus. *Jewish Antiquities*. Trans. H. St. J. Thackery and Ralph Marcus. LCL. Cambridge, MA: Harvard University Press, 1934.

Juel, Donald H. *Mark*. Augsburg Commentary on the New Testament. Minneapolis: Augsburg Fortress, 1990.

A Master of Surprise: Mark Interpreted. Minneapolis, MN: Fortress, 1994.

Messianic Exegesis: Christological Interpretation of the Old Testament in Early Christianity. Philadelphia: Fortress, 1988.

Kaltner, John. "Psalm 22:17b: Second Guessing 'The Old Guess'." *JBL* 117 (1998): 503–6.

Kee, Howard Clark. "The Function of Scriptural Quotations in Mark 11–16." Pp. 165–88 in *Jesus und Paulus: Festschrift für Werner Georg Kümmel zum 70. Geburtstag*. Ed. E. Earle Ellis and Erich Gräßer. Göttingen: Vandenhoeck & Ruprecht, 1975.

Kelber, Werner, H. "The Hour of the Son of Man." Pp. 41–60 in *The Passion in Mark*. Ed. Werner H. Kelber. Philadelphia: Fortress, 1976.

The Kingdom in Mark. Philadelphia: Fortress, 1974.

"Mark 14:32–42: Gethsemane." *ZNW* 63 (1972): 166–87.

Kennedy, George A. "Historical Survey of Rhetoric." Pp. 3–42 in *Handbook of Classical Rhetoric in the Hellenistic Period 330 B.C.–A.D. 400*. Ed. Stanley E. Porter. Boston, Leiden: Brill, 2001.

Kiley, Mark. "'Lord, Save My Life' (Ps 116:4) as a Generative Text for Jesus' Gethsemane Prayer (Mark 14:36)." *CBQ* 48 (1986): 655–9.

Kingsbury, Jack Dean. *The Christology of Mark's Gospel*. Philadelphia: Fortress, 1983.

Klausner, Joseph. *The Messianic Idea in Israel*. London: Allen and Unwin, 1956.

Kuhn, K. G. "Jesus in Gethsemane." *EvT* 12 (1952–3): 260–85.

Kraus, Hans-Joachim. *Psalms 1–59*. Trans. Hilton C. Oswald. Minneapolis, MN: Augsburg, 1988.

LaVerdiere, Eugene. *The Beginning of the Gospel: Introducing the Gospel of Mark*. 2 vols. Collegeville, MN: Liturgical Press, 1999.

Liebers, Reinhold. *"Wie geschrieben steht": Studien zu einer besonderen Art frühchristlichen Schriftbezuges*. Berlin: Walter de Gruyter, 1993.

Linafelt, Tod. *Surviving Lamentations: Catastrophe, Lament, and Protest in the Afterlife of a Biblical Book*. Chicago: University of Chicago Press, 2000.

Lindars, Barnabas. *New Testament Apologetic: The Doctrinal Significance of the Old Testament Quotations*. London: SCM Press, 1961.

Longenecker, Richard N. *Biblical Exegesis in the Apostolic Period*. 2nd edn. Grand Rapids, MI: Eerdmans Publishing, 1999.

Lull, David J. "Interpreting Mark's Story of Jesus' Death: Toward a Theology of Suffering." Pp. 1–12 in *SBLSP*. Society of Biblical Literature Seminar Papers 22. Atlanta: Scholars Press, 1985.

Lust J., E. Eynikel and K. Hauspie. *A Greek–English Lexicon of the Septuagint: Parts I and II*. Stuttgart: Deutsche Bibelgesellschaft, 1992, 1996.

Malbon, Elizabeth Struthers. *In the Company of Jesus: Characters in Mark's Gospel*. Louisville, KY: Westminster John Knox Press, 2000.

Marcus, Joel. "Mark and Isaiah." Pp. 449–66 in *Fortunate the Eyes That See: Essays in Honor of David Noel Freedman in Celebration of His Seventieth Birthday*. Ed. A. B. Beck *et al*. Grand Rapids, MI: Eerdmans, 1995.

The Way of the Lord: Christological Exegesis of the Old Testament in the Gospel of Mark. Louisville, KY: Westminster/John Knox, 1992.

Matera, Frank J. *The Kingship of Jesus: Composition and Theology in Mark 15*. SBLDS 66. Chico, CA: Scholars Press, 1982.

Mauser, U. *Christ in the Wilderness: The Wilderness Theme in the Second Gospel and Its Basis in the Biblical Tradition*. SBT 39. Naperville, IL: Alec R. Allenson, 1963.

Menken, M. J. J. "The Translation of Psalm 41:10 in John 13:18." *JSNT* 40 (1990): 61–79.

Meyers, Carol L. and Eric M. *Zechariah 9–14*. AB 25C. New York: Doubleday, 1993.

Moloney, Francis J. *The Gospel of Mark: A Commentary*. Peabody, MA: Hendrickson, 2002.

Moo, Douglas J. *The Old Testament in the Gospel Passion Narratives*. Sheffield: The Almond Press, 1983.

Mowinckel, Sigmund. *The Psalms in Israel's Worship*. Trans. D. R. Ap-Thomas. Nashville: Abington Press, 1962.

Myers, Ched. *Binding the Strong Man: A Political Reading of Mark's Story of Jesus*. Maryknoll, NY: Orbis, 1988.

Nickelsburg, George W. E. "The Qumranic Transformation of a Cosmological and Eschatological Tradition (1QH 4:29–40)." Pp. 649–60 in *Madrid Qumran Congress*. Leiden: E J Brill, 1992.

Oeming, Manfred. *Das Buch der Psalmen: Psalm 1–41*. Neuer Stuttgarter Kommentar: Altes Testament 13/1. Stuttgart: Verlag Katholisches Bibelwerk GmbH, 2000.

Olofsson, Staffan. *God Is My Rock: A Study of Translation Technique and Theological Exegesis in the Septuagint*. Stockholm: Almquist & Wiksell, 1990.

Painter, John. *Mark's Gospel: Worlds in Conflict*. London: Routledge, 1997.

Perkins, Pheme. *Hearing the Parables of Jesus*. New York: Paulist Press, 1981.

Perri, Carmella. "On Alluding." *Poetics* 7 (1978): 289–307.

Peters, Melvin K. Review of Joachim Shaper, *Eschatology in the Greek Psalter*. *JBL* 116 (2, 1997): 350–2.

Petersen, David L. *Zechariah 9–14 and Malachi, A Commentary*. OTL. Louisville, KY: Westminster John Knox Press, 1995.

Pietersma, Albert. "David in the Greek Psalms." *VT* 30 (1980): 213–26.

A New English Translation of the Septuagint: The Psalms. New York: Oxford University Press, 2000.

"The Present State of the Critical Text of the Greek Psalter." Pp. 12–32 in *Der Septuaginta-Psalter und seine Töchterübersetzungen*. Ed. A. Aejmelaeus and U. Quast. Göttingen: Vandenhoeck & Ruprecht, 2000.

Pliny. *Natura History*. LCL 370; trans. H. Rackham. Cambridge, MA: Harvard University Press, 1968.

Preuss, H. D. "Die Psalmenüberschriften in Targum und Midrasch," *ZAW* 71 (1959): 44–54.

Rahlfs, Alfred. *Psalmi cum Odis*. Göttingen: Vandenhoeck & Ruprecht, 1931.

Rhoads, David, Joanna Dewey, and Donald Michie. *Mark as Story: An Introduction to the Narrative of a Gospel*. 2nd edn. Minneapolis: Fortress, 1999.

Ricoeur, Paul. *Time and Narrative*. Trans. Kathleen McLaughlin and David Pellauer. 3 vols. Chicago: University of Chicago Press, 1984–8.

"Toward a Hermeneutic of the Idea of Revelation." Pp. 73–118 in *Essays on Biblical Interpretation*. Ed. Lewis S. Mudge. Philadelphia: Fortress, 1980.

Robbins, Vernon K. "The Healing of the Blind Bartimaeus in Markan Theology." *JBL* 92 (1973): 224–43.

"The Reversed Contextualization of Psalm 22 in the Markan Crucifixion: A Socio-Rhetorical Analysis." Pp. 1161–83 in vol. II of *The Four Gospels: Festschrift for Hans Neirynek*. 2 vols. Ed. F. van Segbroeck. Leuven: Leuven University Press, 1992.

"Last Meal: Preparation, Betrayal, and Absence." Pp. 21–40 in *The Passion Narrative*. Ed. Werner H. Kelber. Philadelphia: Fortress, 1976.

Roberts, J. J. M. "A New Root for an Old Crux, Ps. XXII 17c." *VT* 23 (1973): 247–52.

Ruppert, L. *Jesus als der leidende Gerechte? Der Weg Jesu im Lichte eines alt- und zwischentestamentlichen Motivs*. Stuttgart: KBW Verlag, 1972.

Der leidende Gerechte. Eine motivgeschichtliche Untersuchung zum Alten Testament und zwischentestamentlichen Judentum. FzB 5. Würzburg, 1972.

Schaefer, Konrad. *Psalms. Berit Olam* Studies in Hebrew Narrative and Poetry. Collegeville, MN: The Liturgical Press, 2001.

Schneiders, Sandra M. *The Revelatory Text: Interpreting the New Testament as Sacred Scripture*. New York: HarperCollins, 1991.

Schürer, Emil. *The History of the Jewish People in the Age of Jesus Christ*. 3 vols. Edinburgh: T&T Clark, 1973–87.

Schweizer, E. *The Good News According to Mark*. Trans. Donald H. Madvig. Atlanta: John Knox, 1970.

Semler, J. S. *Epistola ad Griesbachium de emendandis graecis V. T. interpretatibus* (1770).

Senior, Donald. *The Passion of Jesus in the Gospel of Mark*. Wilmington, DE: Michael Glazier, 1984.

Shaper, Joachim. *Eschatology in the Greek Psalter*. Tübingen: Mohr (Siebeck), 1995.

Shiner, Whitney Taylor. "The Ambiguous Pronouncement of the Centurion and the Shrouding of Meaning in Mark." *JSNT* 78 (2000): 3–22.

Follow Me! Discipleship in Markan Rhetoric. SBLDS 145. Atlanta: Scholars Press, 1995.

Smith, Stephen H. "The Literary Structure of Mark 11:1–12:40." *NovT* 31 (April 1989): 104–24.

Smyth, Herbert Weir. *Greek Grammar*. Cambridge, MA: Harvard University Press, 1984.

Sommer, Benjamin D. *A Prophet Reads Scripture: Allusion in Isaiah 40–66*. Stanford: Stanford University Press, 1998.

Sophocles. *Ajax, Electra, Oedipus Tyrannus*. Ed. and trans. Hugh Lloyd-Jones. LCL. Cambridge, MA: Harvard University Press, 1997.

  Antigone, The Women of Trachis, Philoctetes, Oedipus at Colonus. Ed. and trans. Hugh Lloyd-Jones. LCL. Cambridge, MA: Harvard University Press, 1998.

Strack, H. L. and G. Stemberger. *Introduction to the Talmud and Midrash*. Minneapolis: Fortress, 1992.

Strawn, Brent A. "Psalm 22:17b: More Guessing." *JBL* 119 (3, 2000), 439–51.

Tanner, Beth LaNeel. *The Book of Psalms Through the Lens of Intertextuality*. Studies in Biblical Literature 26. New York: Peter Lang, 2001.

Taylor, Vincent. *The Gospel According to St. Mark*. Repr. 2nd edn. Grand Rapids, MI: Baker Books, 1981.

Telford, William R. *The Barren Temple and the Withered Tree: A Redaction-Critical Analysis of the Cursing of the Fig-Tree Pericope in Mark's Gospel and Its Relation to the Cleansing of the Temple Tradition*. JSNTSup 1. Sheffield: Sheffield Academic Press, 1980.

Thackeray, H. St. J. "Josephus," *LCL* 281 (Cambridge, MA: Harvard University Press) 1950.

van Tilborg, Sjef. "Language, Meaning, Sense and Reference: Matthew's Passion Narrative and Psalm 22." *HvTSt* 44 (1998): 883–908.

Torijano, Pablo A. *Solomon the Esoteric King*. Leiden: Brill, 2002.

Tov, Emanuel. *The Text Critical Use of the Septuagint in Biblical Research*. 2nd edn. Jerusalem: Simor Ltd, 1997.

  "Theologically Motivated Exegesis Embedded in the Septuagint." Pp. 215–33 in *Proceedings of a Conference at the Annenberg Research Institute May 15–16, 1989*. JQR Supplement: Philadelphia, 1990.

Trocmé, Etienne. *L'Evangile selon Saint Marc*. Commentaire du Nouveau Testament 2. Genève: Labor et Fides, 2000.

Vall, Gregory. "Psalm 22:17b: 'The Old Guess'." *JBL* 116 (1997): 45–56.

Waanders, F. M. J. *The History of ΤΕΛΟΣ and ΤΕΛΕΩ in Ancient Greek*. Amsterdam, B. R. Grüner, 1983.

Waltke, Bruce K. "Superscripts, Postscripts, or Both." *JBL* 110 (4, 1991): 583–96.

  and Michael O'Connor. *An Introduction to Biblical Hebrew Syntax*. Winona Lake, IN: Eisenbrauns, 1990.

Watts, Rikki E. *Isaiah's New Exodus and Mark*. WUNT 2; Tübingen: Mohr Siebeck, 1997.

  "Jesus' Death, Isaiah 53, and Mark 10:45: A Crux Revisited." Pp. 125–52 in *Jesus and the Suffering Servant: Isaiah 53 and Christian Origins*. Ed. William H. Bellinger and William R. Farmer. Harrisburg, PA: Trinity Press International, 1998.

Weeden, Theodore J. "The Cross as Power in Weakness (Mark 15:20b–41)." Pp. 115–34 in *The Passion in Mark: Studies on Mark 14–16*. Ed. Werner H. Kelber. Philadelphia: Fortress, 1976.

Weiser A. *The Psalms*. OTL. Philadelphia: Westminster, 1962.

Westermann, Claus. *Praise and Lament in the Psalms*. Atlanta: John Knox Press, 1981.

    The Praise of God in the Psalms. Trans. Keith Crim. Richmond: John Knox Press, 1965.

    "The Role of Lament in the Theology of the Old Testament." Trans. Richard N. Soulen. *Int* 28 (1974): 20–38.

Wilder, Amos N. *Early Christian Rhetoric: The Language of the Gospel*. Cambridge, MA: Harvard University Press, 1964.

Witherington III, Ben. *The Gospel of Mark: A Socio-Rhetorical Commentary*. Grand Rapids, MI: Eerdmans, 2001.

Yarbro Collins, Adela. "The Appropriation of the Psalms of Individual Lament by Mark." Pp. 223–41 in *The Scriptures in the Gospels*. Ed. C. M. Tuckett. Leuven: Leuven University Press, 1997.

    "The Charge of Blasphemy in Mark 14:64." *JSNT* 26 (2004): 379–401.

    "From Noble Death to Crucified Messiah." *NTS* 40 (1994): 481–503.

    "The Significance of Mark 10:45 among Gentile Christians." *HTR* 90 (1997): 371–82.

    "Suffering and Healing in the Gospel of Mark." Pp. 29–72 in *The Beginning of the Gospel: Probings of Mark in Context*. Minneapolis: Fortress, 1992.

INDEX